The Cambridge Companion to '

This *Companion* offers a comprehensive introdu
of the highly influential twentieth-century critic and theorist walter Denjamin.
The volume provides examinations of the different aspects of Benjamin's
work that have had a significant effect on contemporary critical and historical
thought. Topics discussed by experts in the field include Benjamin's relation
to the avant-garde movements of his time, the form of the work of art, his
theories on language and mimesis, modernity, his relation to Brecht and the
Frankfurt School, his significance and relevance to modern cultural studies, his
formative interpretation of Romanticism, and his autobiographical writings.
The volume is aimed at readers who may be coming to Benjamin for the first
time or who have some knowledge of Benjamin but would like to know more
about the issues and concepts central to his work. Additional material includes
a guide to further reading and a chronology.

THE CAMBRIDGE
COMPANION TO
WALTER BENJAMIN

EDITED BY

DAVID S. FERRIS

CAMBRIDGE
UNIVERSITY PRESS

PUBLISHED BY THE PRESS SYNDICATE OF THE UNIVERSITY OF CAMBRIDGE
The Pitt Building, Trumpington Street, Cambridge, United Kingdom

CAMBRIDGE UNIVERSITY PRESS
The Edinburgh Building, Cambridge, CB2 2RU, UK
40 West 20th Street, New York, NY 10011-4211, USA
477 Williamstown Road, Port Melbourne, VIC 3207, Australia
Ruiz de Alarcón 13, 28014 Madrid, Spain
Dock House, The Waterfront, Cape Town 8001, South Africa

http://www.cambridge.org

First published 2004

Printed in the United Kingdom at the University Press, Cambridge

Typeface Sabon 10/13 pt   *System* LATEX 2$_\varepsilon$ [TB]

A catalogue record for this book is available from the British Library

Library of Congress Cataloguing in Publication data

The Cambridge Companion to Walter Benjamin / edited by David S. Ferris.
p.   cm. – (Cambridge Companions to Literature)
Includes bibliographical references and index.
ISBN 0 521 79329 7 (hardback) ISBN 0 521 79724 1 (paperback)
1. Benjamin, Walter, 1892–1940 – Criticism and interpretation.   1. Ferris, David S., 1954–
II. Series.
PT2603.E455Z5912   2004
838'.91209 – dc21   2003053297

ISBN 0 521 79329 7 hardback
ISBN 0 521 79724 1 paperback

CONTENTS

List of contributors   *page* vii
List of abbreviations and short titles   ix
Chronology   xi

Introduction: Reading Benjamin   1
DAVID S. FERRIS

1 Walter Benjamin and the European avant-garde   18
MICHAEL JENNINGS

2 Art forms   35
JAN MIESZKOWSKI

3 Language and mimesis in Walter Benjamin's work   54
BEATRICE HANSSEN

4 Walter Benjamin's concept of cultural history   73
HOWARD CAYGILL

5 Benjamin's modernity   97
ANDREW BENJAMIN

6 Benjamin and psychoanalysis   115
SARAH LEY ROFF

7 Benjamin and the ambiguities of Romanticism   134
REBECCA COMAY

Contents

8 Body politics: Benjamin's dialectical materialism between
   Brecht and the Frankfurt School   152
   RAINER NÄGELE

9 Method and time: Benjamin's dialectical images   177
   MAX PENSKY

10 Benjamin's phantasmagoria: the *Arcades Project*   199
   MARGARET COHEN

11 Acts of self-portraiture: Benjamin's confessional and
   literary writings   221
   GERHARD RICHTER

   Guide to further reading   238
   Index   242

CONTRIBUTORS

ANDREW BENJAMIN has taught in universities in the United Kingdom and the United States. He is currently Professor of Critical Theory at Monash University, Australia. His publications include: *Present Hope* (1997); *Architectural Philosophy* (2000); and *Philosophy's Literature* (2001). He is joint editor of the series *Walter Benjamin Studies* published by Continuum Press.

HOWARD CAYGILL is Professor of Cultural Studies at Goldsmiths College, University of London, where he teaches philosophy, aesthetics, and cultural history. His publications include: *Art of Judgment* (1989); *A Kant Dictionary* (1995); *Walter Benjamin: The Colour of Experience* (1998); and *Levinas and the Political* (2002).

MARGARET COHEN is Professor of French and Italian at Stanford University. She is the author of *Profane Illumination: Walter Benjamin and the Paris of the Surrealist Revolution* (1993) and *The Sentimental Education of the Novel* (1999). She is also co-editor of *Spectacle of Realism – Body, Gender, Genre* and *The Literary Channel – The International Invention of the Novel* (2002).

REBECCA COMAY teaches Philosophy and Literary Studies at the University of Toronto. She is currently working on a book on Hegel and melancholia and completing a collection of essays on Benjamin.

DAVID FERRIS is Professor of Comparative Literature and Humanities at the University of Colorado at Boulder. He is the author of *Theory and the Evasion of History* (1993) and *Silent Urns: Romanticism, Hellenism, Modernity* (2000); and the editor of *Walter Benjamin: Theoretical Questions* (1996). He is currently completing a book on Walter Benjamin entitled *Torsos of Modernity: Walter Benjamin and the Moment of Criticism.*

BEATRICE HANSSEN is Professor of German at the University of Georgia, Athens. She is the author of *Walter Benjamin's Other History: Of Stones,*

Animals, Human Beings, and Angels (1998) and *Critique of Violence: Between Poststructuralism and Critical Theory* (2000) and co-editor of *The Turn to Ethics* (2000). She is also co-editor of Walter Benjamin Studies, which includes the volume *Walter Benjamin and Romanticism* (2002), and editor of *Walter Benjamin and the Arcades Project* (2004).

MICHAEL JENNINGS is Professor of German at Princeton University. He is the author of *Dialectical Images: Walter Benjamin's Theory of Literary Criticism* (1987). He also serves as the General Editor of the *Selected Writings* of Walter Benjamin (Harvard University Press).

JAN MIESZKOWSKI is Assistant Professor of German and Humanities at Reed College. His publications include essays on Kleist, syntactic revolutions after Fichte, and the theory of performance in Kafka. He has recently completed a book on the conception of historical experience that emerges at the intersections of German Romanticism and classical political economy, tentatively titled *Ideology and Interest*.

RAINER NÄGELE is Professor of German at the Johns Hopkins University. He has published widely on German literature and thought. His publications include: *Reading After Freud* (1987); *Theater, Theory, Speculation: Walter Benjamin and the Scenes of Modernity* (1991); *Echoes of Translation: Reading Between Texts* (1997); and *Literarische Vexierbilder. Drei Versuche zu einer Figur* (2001).

MAX PENSKY is Professor of Philosophy at the State University of New York at Binghamton. He is the author of *Melancholy Dialectics: Walter Benjamin and the Play of Mourning* (1993). He is also the editor of *The Actuality of Adorno: Critical Essays on Adorno and the Postmodern* (1995) and *Jurgen Habermas: The Postnational Constellation* (2000). His forthcoming book is entitled, *The Ends of Solidarity: Studies in Critical Theory*.

GERHARD RICHTER is Associate Professor of German and an Affiliate Professor in Comparative Literature at the University of Wisconsin-Madison. He is the author of *Walter Benjamin and the Corpus of Autobiography* (2000) as well as the editor of *Benjamin's Ghosts: Interventions in Contemporary Literary and Cultural Theory* (2002) and *Literary Paternity, Literary Friendship: Essays in Honor of Stanley Corngold* (2002).

SARAH HEY ROFF has taught as Assistant Professor of German at Princeton University. She currently works for the Democratic Party of Oregon. She has recently published articles on psychoanalysis and cultural history, Benjamin's *Arcades Project*, and Ernst Jünger. She is at work on a book called *Hitler Cracking Up*.

ABBREVIATIONS AND SHORT TITLES

Generally, references to Benjamin's works are given parenthetically in the text (by short title where needed, followed by volume and page reference). A list of the abbreviations used as well as short titles for the most frequently cited of Benjamin's essays follows. For the titles of Benjamin's works, this volume has followed those used in the *Selected Writings*. In the case of Benjamin's "On the Concept of History," it should be noted that, although this text is referred to by this title alone, reference has also been made to the earlier translation of this text in *Illuminations* (where it appeared as "Theses on the Philosophy of History"). A special note is required for references to the *Arcades Project*. The materials contained in this volume are referred to by page reference except where there is also a convolute numbering system; in this case, references are to the page number first, then the convolute number (for example, "*Arcades*, 460; N1a, 8").

Abbreviations

BA/B *Adorno/Benjamin Briefwechsel 1928–1940*. Ed. Henri Lonitz. Frankfurt am Main: Suhrkamp, 1994.

C *The Correspondence of Walter Benjamin*. Trans. Manfred R. Jacobson and Evelyn M. Jacobson. University of Chicago Press, 1994.

CA/B Theodor W. Adorno and Walter Benjamin, *The Complete Correspondence 1928–1940*. Cambridge, MA: Harvard University Press, 1999.

GBr *Gesammelte Briefe*. 6 vols. Ed. Christoph Gödde and Henri Lonitz. Frankfurt am Main: Suhrkamp, 1995–2000.

GS *Gesammelte Schriften*. 7 vols. Ed. Rolf Tiedemann and Herman Schweppenhäuser. Frankfurt am Main: Suhrkamp, 1972–89.

Ill *Illuminations*. Ed. Hannah Arendt. New York: Schocken, 1968.

R   *Reflections*. Ed. Peter Demetz. New York: HBJ, 1978.
SW   *Selected Writings* [followed by volume number]. Ed. Michael
       Jennings et al., 4 vols. Cambridge, MA: Harvard University Press,
       1996–2003)

Short titles

Arcades	*The Arcades Project*. Trans. Howard Eiland and Kevin McLaughlin. Cambridge, MA: Belknap Press of Harvard University Press, 1999.
Concept of Criticism	*Concept of Criticism in Early German Romanticism*. In *SW* I, 116–200.
"Doctrine"	"Doctrine of the Similar." In *SW* II, 694–98.
Friendship	Gerschom Scholem, *Walter Benjamin: The Story of a Friendship*. New York: Schocken, 1981.
"Goethe"	"Goethe's *Elective Affinities*." In *SW* I, 297–360.
"Motifs"	"On Some Motifs in Baudelaire." In *SW* IV, 313–55.
"On Language"	"On Language as Such and on the Language of Man." In *SW* I, 62–74.
Origin	*The Origin of the German Tragic Drama*. Trans. John Osborne. London: NLB, 1977.
"Proust"	"On the Image of Proust." In *SW* II, 237–47.
"Task"	"The Task of the Translator." In *SW* I, 253–63.

CHRONOLOGY

For fuller details, the reader is referred to the works listed in the "Biographical" section of the Guide to Further Reading at the end of this volume as well as to the full chronology presented at the end of each volume of the Harvard *Selected Writings*.

1892   Walter Benjamin born July 15, in Berlin. He is the first of
           three children.

1902–1905 Attends Kaiser Friedrich Gymnasium, a well-regarded
           secondary school in Berlin.

1905–1907 Attends Landerziehungsheim Haubinda, a progressive, rural
           boarding school in Thuringia. Benjamin is greatly influenced
           by one of the directors of this school, Gustav Wyneken, an
           education reformer.

1907–1909 Returns to Berlin and attends high school at the Kaiser-
           Friedrich-Gymnasium.

1910–11   First writings published in a student journal, *Der Anfang*
           [*The Beginning*] founded in 1908 by a disciple of Wyneken.

1912   Begins university studies at Albert-Ludwigs-Universität in
           Freiburg im Breisgau with the intent to study philosophy.
           Begins friendship with the poet Fritz Heinle. Returns to
           Berlin in August and enrolls at the Friedrich-Wilhelms-
           Universität.

1913   Returns to Freiburg and continues his studies there. Attends
           lectures by the prominent neo-Kantian, Heinrich Rickert with
           whom Martin Heidegger had also studied. Benjamin makes
           his first visit to Paris in May.

1914   Outbreak of First World War. Benjamin attempts to enlist but
           is rejected. Fritz Heinle and his fiancée commit suicide.
           Elected President of the Berlin "Free Student Group." Meets
           Dora Sophie Pollak. Begins acquaintanceship with Martin

Buber and Ludwig Klages. Later this year, Benjamin is conscripted but feigns palsy and is granted a one year deferment. Writes "The Life of Students," and "Friedrich Hölderlin: Two Poems."

1915   Breaks with Wyneken. Begins his lifelong friendship with Gershom Scholem. Obtains another one year deferment. Leaves Berlin to continue his studies at Ludwig-Maximillians-Universität in Munich.

1916   Meets the German lyric poet Rainer Maria Rilke. Writes "On Language as such and on the Language of Man."

1917   Draft review rules that Benjamin is capable of light field duties but an attack of sciatica prevents his enlistment. Benjamin marries Dora Pollak and moves to Bern, Switzerland where he continues his studies and begins contemplation of an academic career. Begins work on his doctoral project.

1918   Birth of his son, Stefan Rafael.

1919   Receives doctorate for his dissertation, "The Concept of Criticism in German Romanticism," completed under the direction of Richard Herbertz. Meets Ernst Bloch.

1920   Returns to Berlin. Envisages an academic career.

1921   Begins friendship with Florens Christian Rang, a conservative intellectual. "Critique of Violence," "The Task of the Translator" written. Starts writing his essay "Goethe's *Elective Affinities*." Marriage to Dora falls apart. Project to found a journal to be titled, *Angelus Novus* [named after Klee drawing purchased this year by Benjamin] but does not come to fruition. Begins affair with Julia Cohn.

1922   Period of closeness to Rang.

1923   Meets Theodor W. Adorno and Siegfried Kracauer. Scholem emigrates to Palestine. Translates Baudelaire's *Tableaux parisiens*. "The Task of the Translator" appears. Hugo von Hofmannsthal accepts Goethe essay for publication in his journal.

1924   Meets Asja Lacis for the first time while on vacation on Capri. Death of Florens Christian Rang. First part of "Goethe's *Elective Affinities*" (second appears in January 1925).

1925   Finishes his Habilitation dissertation on the *Trauerspiel* [Origin of the German Tragic Drama]. In July, Benjamin's dissertation is rejected. In August, he withdraws his application for an academic position at the University of Frankfurt. Completes *One-Way Street*. Travels to Riga,

	Russia, to see Asja Lacis who expresses no interest in continuing their affair.
1926	Death of Benjamin's father. Travels to Paris in the spring and to Moscow in December upon hearing of Asja Lacis' breakdown, stays until February, 1927.
1927	Returns to Berlin. Interviews André Gide. Visits Paris from April to November. Last meeting with Scholem until 1938. Begins to work on the *Arcades Project*. First experimentation with hashish. First volume of the Proust translation appears. Gives first radio talk.
1928	Publication of *The Origin of the German Tragic Drama* and *One-Way Street*. Asja Lacis in Berlin, they live together for two months.
1929	Publication of the essays, "Surrealism: the Last Snapshot of the European Intelligentsia," and "The Image of Proust." Begins series of regular broadcasts for radio stations in Frankfurt and Berlin. Introduced to Bertolt Brecht by Asja Lacis. Travels to Paris at end of year.
1930	Deepening of friendship with Brecht. Divorced from Dora. Travels to Norway. Second volume of Proust translation appears. Plans journal, to be called *Krisis und Kritik*, with Brecht. Death of Benjamin's mother.
1931	Benjamin withdraws from *Krisis und Kritik* project. Essay on Karl Kraus and "Little History of Photography" are published.
1932	First stay on Ibiza (April to July). Prepares to commit suicide in Nice but has change of mind. Gives last radio talk in Berlin. Adorno gives seminar on Benjamin's *Origin of the German Tragic Drama* at the University of Frankfurt. Begins writing the *Berlin Chronicle*.
1933	Burning of the Reichstag in Berlin. In March Benjamin goes into exile in Paris. Second visit to Ibiza from April to September. Writes "The Doctrine of the Similar" and "On the Mimetic Faculty." Arrest of his brother in Germany.
1934	Kafka essay published. Visits Brecht in Denmark. Horkheimer invites Benjamin to New York.
1935	Attends First International Writers Conference in Paris. Completes first version of "The Work of Art in the Age of its Technological Reproducibility."
1936	Second visit to Brecht in Denmark. "The Work of Art in the Age of its Technological Reproducibility" appears in a French

translation. "The Storyteller," and *Deutsche Menschen* [German People] published.

1937   "Edward Fuchs, the Historian and Collector" appears.

1938   Makes last visit to Brecht in Denmark. Completes version of *Berlin Childhood around 1900*. Writes "Paris of the Second Empire in Baudelaire."

1939   Outbreak of Second World War. Interned in France from September to November. "Some Motifs in Baudelaire," and "What is Epic Theater" published.

1940   Writes theses "On the Concept of History." With the help of Max Horkheimer, Benjamin receives visa for the United States. Leaves Paris in June and travels to Lourdes. Benjamin dies at Port Bou, Spain, after taking a lethal dose of morphine.

1955   Two-volume selection of Benjamin's writings, edited by Theodor W. Adorno and Gretel Adorno, is published by Suhrkamp in Germany.

1968   *Illuminations*, edited by Hannah Arendt, marks the appearance of the first volume of Benjamin's writings in English translation.

1972   Suhrkamp begins publication of Benjamin's collected writings in 7 volumes; completed in 1989.

DAVID S. FERRIS

Introduction: Reading Benjamin

With the appearance of Harvard University Press's edition of Walter Benjamin's *Selected Writings*, the great range of this thinker, critic, social commentator, and theorist has become even more apparent in the English-speaking world. Making this range more readily available will undoubtedly prompt the discussion and understanding of Benjamin to move beyond the limited number of essays that have achieved canonical status wherever the name of Benjamin is evoked, particularly in Anglo-American criticism. Admittedly this access to a wider range of material in English will complicate the received picture of Benjamin even as it offers greater scope to track the development of his thought and the concepts through which it was expressed. In many ways, this Cambridge Companion has been edited with a view to providing a guide to the concepts and issues that will come under scrutiny as this fuller evaluation of Benjamin's thought gets under way within the English-language interpretation of his writings.

The organization of the volume has been guided by two concerns. First, to achieve an adequate account of key elements in Benjamin's thought and, second, to place these elements in relation to each other so that the shifting emphases and material through which Benjamin developed his thinking can be discerned. The organization is then thematic, taking up issues that traverse Benjamin's writing. While every attempt has been made to be comprehensive, the essays commissioned for this volume do not exhaust the wealth of interest in philosophical, cultural, theological, or historical materials exhibited by this critic. With such a multifaceted thinker as Benjamin, choices have to be made if the intentions of a series such as this one are to be fulfilled. In some cases, subjects that could, in a different context, receive the attention of individual scrutiny have been treated across several of the essays published here. What should be focused on in Benjamin's voluminous œuvre has also been guided by what is most useful for someone coming to Benjamin for the first time. To this end, the volume attempts to give a strong sense of the philosophical and historical context within which he writes and with which he so frequently takes issue.

Given the breadth of Benjamin's intellectual interest, introducing him in single essay is a task that threatens to overwhelm even the most focused of intentions. Rather than provide an overview, or synopsis of the contents of this volume, this introduction will be concerned with the task that confronts even the most elemental encounter with Benjamin: the task of reading a prose that varies from the curtly aphoristic to the strenuously discursive. This is, of course, a task that Benjamin, as a writer, was well aware of and also addressed in his writing. The task of this introduction, then, will be to engage the question of reading Benjamin which is, perhaps, just another way of saying that it will engage with the difficulty of reading Benjamin. But, first, some signposts crucial to an understanding of Benjamin's career and the singular nature of his writing.

The period from the 1910s to the late 1930s witnessed historical and intellectual changes whose effects are in many ways still being played out in the postmodern. For Benjamin, in particular, this meant not only the political effects of nineteenth-century capitalism and the social transformations they fostered but also an intellectual journey that begins under the influence of neo-Kantianism and progresses through German idealism, Freud, Surrealism, the kabbalah, Marx, and Brecht. The different stages of this career mark the extent to which Benjamin also offers an index to some of the dominant influences on the social, political, and intellectual history of the twentieth century as it forged its modernity. Yet, this index is rather a singular refraction. What Benjamin took up in his thought was rarely, if ever, returned to its source intact. This characteristic already indicates that what was almost never at stake in Benjamin's understanding was an accurate historical account of say, works by Proust, Goethe, Kafka, and so on. Benjamin was not a critic in that sense. His tendency is to read how the work of others grappled with issues that were essential to his own time and intellectual formation. Although his reading and the work it produced reflects the attempt to understand a modernity no longer capable of the philosophical and political accounts the past has bequeathed to it, it was to this past that Benjamin would insistently turn in order to confront central questions in his work: in what philosophy, in what politics, and in what language is modernity to articulate its present, its future? That this articulation frequently took the form of an examination of the past – and of history itself – should not be seen as contradictory, since it is in the way the present reads the past that its modernity is expressed. For this reason, Benjamin deserves to be read first and foremost as an acute reader of the means through which the past is known to us – and this past takes many forms in Benjamin: literature, art, culture, philosophy. For the same reason, Benjamin also demands to be read with much care. His emphasis on the means through which the past becomes known (which translates more generally into a concern with how knowledge is produced and passed on in both high and mass culture) underlines the extent to which Benjamin's writing will also be concerned with how it will be read and understood. Such a concern also indicates the way in which Benjamin's writing is intimately linked to his thought rather than, in the classical sense, serving as a mere medium for that thought.

Early in his introduction to *The Origin of the German Tragic Drama*, Walter Benjamin describes the method of a treatise as digression. Clarifying this idea of digression, he then goes on to say that its "primary characteristic is the renunciation of the uninterrupted progress of an intention" (*Origin*, 28). With such a remark Benjamin signals the difficulty that his own work will pose. Benjamin's writing is one in which this kind of interruption figures prominently. Although this characteristic can easily be seen to be repeated in the experiments with literary form that abound during the Modernist period in which he wrote, the use of interruption in Benjamin's writing is more complex than this parallel suggests. Rather than reflect an external historical and social situation, this aspect of Benjamin's writing is closely tied to the significance he attached to the means by which knowledge, history, and even their interpretation are all given to us.

Even in the phrase cited above, an indicator of this complexity is present – and one that gives a strong sense of how important Benjamin's style of writing is to his thought. Benjamin does not simply say in this phrase that the primary characteristic of the digression is to interrupt what he describes as the intention of a written work. If this is what had been said, his remark on method would suggest that interruption is to be valued above all else and that any other intention is to be superseded by a characteristic more in keeping with a modern world. But, Benjamin does not quite say this. Here, the wording of his thought takes on a prominence that cannot be ignored. Benjamin speaks of method as possessing an intention that is also interrupted. Benjamin does not oppose interruption to intention here. To take only this from his words would be to avoid much of the complexity of his thought. It would also be to assume that any writing in which intention dominates simply belongs to a past we should leave behind, preferring instead to favor interruption as the distinguishing mark of a writing that is genuinely modern. The issue is never that simple in Benjamin, and reading his work demands that we question the habit of thought that would simply oppose intention to interruption and see them as two separate models of writing.

To question this habit of thought is to question the kind of seamless progression toward meaning that makes reading an exercise whose purpose is to affirm an essay's intention as if it were also its conclusion. To do so not only is to avoid engaging with the nature of writing as Benjamin understands it, it is also to refuse the particular relation between writing and thought that is central to so much of Benjamin's writing. Through this relation between intention and the interruption occasioned by a digressive method, Benjamin pursues a method that demands the thoughtful response of his readers, demands what Benjamin will describe as the "process of contemplation" (*Origin*, 28).

Although one contribution to this volume will discuss interruption in greater detail and with greater reference to Benjamin's other work, its significance as an essential starting point for reading Benjamin cannot be avoided.[1] This is especially important since the interruption referred to here is not presented in Benjamin's work as a subject or a theme in the same way that the artwork, translation, language, or even works such as Goethe's *Elective Affinities* are the subjects of individual essays.

Following his remarks on the treatise in the Introduction to *The Origin of the German Tragic Drama*, Benjamin develops further the effect of a writing characterized by interruption. This mode of writing is compared to the movement of thought. Benjamin writes: "Tirelessly thought begins continually from new things, laboriously returning to the same object. This continual pausing for breath is the mode most proper to the process of contemplation" (*Origin*, 28). The end effect is to induce a contemplation, but not simply the contemplation of a single object as would be the case when we understand contemplation to describe the way in which our thought can be wholly preoccupied by whatever we direct our attention toward. Rather, contemplation is here understood as a process in which the different levels of meaning that can be attached to the original object are recognized and experienced. This signals an important aspect of Benjamin's investigations, in particular, it draws attention to the way in which they are given to us. First, these investigations are as much concerned with their chosen subjects (for instance, film, photography, aura, storytelling, translation) as they are with the means by which these subjects are made and have been made significant. For Benjamin, cultural and historical artifacts reveal a sedimentation of meaning. Benjamin, however, is less interested in adjudicating between the competing claims of these layers of meaning. The issue for Benjamin is to grasp what the factual existence of such layers means. To do this requires not only a mode of inquiry that is sympathetic to this approach, but also a style of presentation in which the understanding Benjamin wishes to grasp can be made known to the reader. This is why the pausing for breath is favored by

Benjamin; the pausing marks the moment at which the beginning of another level of meaning is indicated.

This style of presentation demands much of the reader. It is perhaps easiest to grasp it by recalling Benjamin's own metaphor for the effect it produces: a mosaic. Having lost any sense of a continuous unbroken development, such a writing takes on the character of discrete moments punctuated by pauses. To borrow Benjamin's metaphor, the task of reading such a writing is comparable to being confronted with the individual pieces of ceramic tile from which a mosaic is formed. Each of these pieces can be understood as one level of meaning. However, it is not Benjamin's intention to produce a work or a text that is merely a collection of fragments – despite the condition in which his major work, *The Arcades Project*, was left at the time of his death.

Benjamin describes the effect of the mosaic and its relation to contemplation in the following words: "Just as the majesty of mosaics remains despite their fragmentation into capricious particles, so philosophical reflection need not be concerned about its vitality" (*Origin*, 28). With the example of the mosaic and the visual image produced from its fragmentary parts, another understanding emerges from the continually interrupted process of contemplation. According to what Benjamin has already said, this understanding cannot be seen as simply what the mosaic intended to represent. But how is such an understanding to be conveyed? In the example of the mosaic it is easy to see because of the material it is composed from. In the case of writing it is much more difficult, especially since the metaphors we frequently use to describe writing have established a standard for judgment, and this standard is at considerable odds with what Benjamin will explore both in the practice of his writing and in his thought.

Characteristically, for Benjamin, the difficulty of arriving through thought or contemplation at the image so readily made available, or intended, by the mosaic brings us closer to the understanding he wishes to convey. Where thought is concerned, the relation between the pieces of the mosaic and the overall image it presents is nowhere seen as a direct one for Benjamin. In the case of the mosaic, this difficulty is noted by Benjamin when he draws attention to the difference between an artistic medium made up of "individual and disparate" (*Origin*, 28) pieces and the sacred image this form was so frequently employed to portray in the Middle Ages. In the case of thought and contemplation, the importance of the individual pieces or levels of meaning increases as their difference from this image becomes more pronounced. Benjamin describes this relation in the following words: "The value of fragments of thought is all the more decisive the less they are able to gauge their unmediated relation to the underlying idea, and the brilliance of the presentation depends as much on this measure as the brilliance of the mosaic does on the quality of the glass paste" (*Origin*, 29). Simply put, the value of individual thoughts is derived from how strongly individual they are, from how indirectly they relate to the underlying idea – just as the mosaic owes its brilliance not to the overall image it presents but to the brilliance of each individual piece of glass; and how more different could an overall picture be from one piece of glass? The significance of this manner of thinking (and which contributes greatly to its difficulty) can be traced to a refusal to accept the kind of understanding that would judge, for example, the brilliance of the mosaic according to the subject it represents. Benjamin focuses on the means by which such images are made possible, he focuses on the individual pieces, the details and discovers brilliance on this level. Contrary to traditional expectations, the significance of these details is derived not from the overall picture or underlying idea (which would be a direct relation) but from the stark contrast between such a picture or idea and the fragmentary, discontinuous material it is composed from.

As a result of refusing this traditional understanding, the significance of the parts is no longer dependent on the whole. But, as Benjamin insists, this does not mean that the parts have no relation to the overall picture or underlying idea. Rather, it means that the relation between them is no longer imposed from the top down, instead, it has to be thought from the bottom up, from what Benjamin terms "immersion in the most minute details of the material content" (*Origin*, 29). By privileging the detail, Benjamin undertakes a significant shift that has both historical and philosophical effects. For example, history is no longer conceived of as a master narrative within which every detail can be given its place. Instead, history is understood to reside in a mass of material detail whose existence works against any linear, continuous model of historical development. Nowhere is this understanding more in evidence than in the project that remained incomplete at the time of Benjamin's death, the *Arcades Project*; but, its effect can also be seen on a less extended scale, and it is here that the philosophical import of this emphasis on the detail finds its expression.

After describing how the process of contemplation resembles the mosaic, Benjamin turns to the form of writing, in particular, to its unavoidable and most essential unit, the sentence. Although Benjamin will distinguish speech from writing, when he does, the distinction is made in order to indicate how writing lacks an effect that will always try to realize the underlying idea or overall picture of the mosaic. Benjamin writes:

> While the speaker uses voice and the gesture of mime to support individual
> sentences, even where they cannot stand up on their own, constructing out of

them – often vaguely and precariously – a sequence of ideas, as if producing a bold sketch in a single attempt, the writer must stop and restart with every sentence. (*Origin*, 29)

Lacking the secondary help of mimic gestures (the word Benjamin uses here evokes pantomime) or even tone of voice, writing is like a mosaic unable to present its overall picture. Some further precision is necessary here – as it is almost everywhere in Benjamin. This does not mean that there is no overall picture. Rather, it is a question of how such a picture is produced. For Benjamin the picture is the result of how we put together the different pieces of the mosaic given to us in writing. Unfortunately, writing, unlike the mosaic, does not yield its overall picture if we simply step back and open our eyes. In the case of writing, such a picture is always produced through the employment of our understanding. Benjamin indicates that, in writing, this understanding is constantly spurned into action by the stopping and restarting of every sentence. In this respect, Benjamin sees the strongest possible affinity between the contemplation of an object and an essential element of all writing. Benjamin describes this affinity in the following words but also attaches a warning to this description – as if to preempt any misreading. After describing the form of writing, Benjamin states: "this applies to the contemplative mode of presentation more than any other. Its aim is not to sweep the reader along and inspire him with enthusiasm" (*Origin*, 29). The form of writing is not some rhapsodic sequence of waves breaking over the barriers of our understanding and carrying us away goodness knows where. Benjamin is much more precise than this and such precision points directly to how his writing is to be read. Rather than be swept away by an endless wave of sentences, the stopping and restarting are understood as moments in which the reader is forced to pause and reflect. This is explicitly stated by Benjamin as he describes the form of writing: "this form can be counted successful only when it forces the reader to stop" (*Origin*, 29). If this were not enough, Benjamin adds, "the more significant its object, the more interrupted the contemplation must be" (*Origin*, 29). Not only are we required to pause and reflect by a prose style in which a sentence causes us to halt before proceeding to the next but we are also required to recognize that the contemplation this interruption gives rise to must also be similarly detached from its object, especially, in cases where what is being contemplated is of great significance.

Benjamin's insistence on this detachment prompts the question of why he should take such pains to draw our attention to the means by which his thought can be presented. A remark following the sentence last cited indicates why Benjamin is so insistent. Benjamin describes this interrupted writing as "sober prose" and then goes on to state that it is "the only style suited to philosophical investigation" (*Origin*, 29). This squarely relocates thought in the means of expression rather than seeing it as something that an expression represents. Indeed, one of the crucial shifts to register while reading Benjamin is this shift away from a prose that strives to represent thought. In its place Benjamin offers a prose that strives to present thought. The difference made by this particle "re" is crucial here – unfortunately it is not always well registered in the translation of Benjamin's writings. The determining characteristic of this prose is its pausing for breath, its avoidance of a seamless continuity. This is the style of writing Benjamin refers to as "sober prose." This description may appear odd if it is considered from the perspective from which we are taught to judge prose. Nothing would appear to be more sober than a prose clearly in the grasp of an intention that it successfuly expresses. With Benjamin it is precisely the reverse. Only an interrupted writing is sober and only a sober writing can give access to genuine thought. All else fails to register that thought can only be discovered in the means by which it is expressed. Accordingly, to read Benjamin is to face the form, the style of his writing as much as it is to register what he says about a given subject.

A sense of this style of writing can be conveyed if the phrases from the introduction to Benjamin's *The Origin of German Tragic Drama* cited individually above are assembled as they are written (in what follows, the order of ideas now adheres more closely to the order of Benjamin's words):

> In the canonical form of the treatise, the single persisting sign of an intention that is more closely educative than didactic appears in the authoritative citation. Presentation is the essential of its method. Method is digression. Presentation as digression – that is the methodical character of the treatise. Renunciation of the uninterrupted progress of an intention is its primary characteristic. Tirelessly thought begins continually from new things, laboriously returning to the same object. This incessant pausing for breath is the most authentic form of existence of contemplation. For, while it [thought] follows the different levels of meaning in the contemplation of one and the same object, it receives the impetus of its continually renewed beginning and the justification of its intermittent rhythm. Just as the majesty of mosaics remains despite their fragmentation into capricious particles, so philosophical reflection need not be concerned about its vitality.   (*Origin*, 28)

The almost telegraphic character of each sentence in this group already indicates the extent to which Benjamin's thought is focused at the level of the individual sentence. Each sentence has its idea. At the same time, each sentence remains emphatically fixed on that idea as if we were indeed being presented with one brilliant piece of mosaic glass at a time. The sentence in which the mosaic is first introduced is a particularly good example of this. The mosaic does not necessarily follow from what has gone before; its appearance causes one to pause by the end of the sentence and consider why it has in fact materialized. One cannot simply move on to the next sentence, one is forced to pause and consider its origin. This pattern whereby a sentence introduces something unforeseen (as a result of which the new element appears to stand alone) and then forces us to contemplate its relation to what has gone before is the way in which Benjamin's "sober prose" challenges its reader, challenges the expectation that the content of what Benjamin has to say can be uncovered once its medium has been penetrated. For Benjamin, the medium and its form are essentially related to his thought. To fail to take this relation into account is to fail to recognize the extent to which his writing demonstrates that our knowledge of a subject is not directly attributable to that subject nor does it allow us to possess that subject. Rather, our knowledge of a subject is the means by which we relate to what we do not possess. Sobering indeed.

The sobriety Benjamin describes as the essential characteristic of a thoughtful prose is not without precedent. It occurs first within German Romanticism about which Benjamin wrote in his first published book, *The Concept of the Criticism of Art in the Early German Romantics* (1920). Although this book displays less of the "sober prose" that would become characteristic of Benjamin's writing, it does display the elements that would combine in his writing. Sobriety as it is presented by the German Romantics, in particular the foremost theoretician of this movement, Friedrich Schlegel, refers to their attempt to render all sacred, infinite, absolute, and transcendental matters profane. No longer intoxicated by the thought of the transcendent we are rendered sober. The shift in understanding the Romantics sought may be best typified if sobriety is thought of as an antidote to mysticism. Yet, as Rodolphe Gasché has shown in an essay on this work, Benjamin does not quite take up this meaning of sobriety. Indeed, Benjamin is critical of the way in which the Romantics sought to make everything finite, even the infinite, by means of their sobering intentions. Gasché, after citing several sentences from the end of Benjamin's study of the Romantic concept of criticism makes the following remarks on this tendency and Benjamin's relation to it:

"This can be illustrated in an image as the production of the blinding brilliancy in the work. This brilliancy – the sober light – extinguishes the plurality of the works. It is the Idea" (119). These final lines of Benjamin's dissertation speak a final critical word about Romantic criticism. The sober light of the prosaic Absolute that criticism exhibits in all works is a blinding light. It is so dazzling that it becomes deceptive. In its brilliancy, all differences fade absolutely. Its spell, the fascination it exerts, is that of the fact – of the Absolute become secular.[2]

In comparison to the sober prose Benjamin describes in the introduction to *The Origin of the German Tragic Drama*, the Romantics are perhaps a little too sober, a little too inebriated by their own sobriety. Yet, it is clearly from them that Benjamin has picked up the notion of a sober prose. The distinction between the sobriety of Benjamin and that of the Romantics is alluded to by Gasché in the passage just cited when he observes that the sobriety of the Romantics causes "all differences [to] fade absolutely." If this is the task of criticism in the German Romantics then it runs to what Benjamin understands as the task of criticism. Gasché again remarks: "[Benjamin] shows that, for the Romantics, criticism has no pedagogical aim. Its function is not to assess or judge the work."[3] Benjamin, by differentiating himself from the Romantics on this point, indicates what his sober prose aims at: it seeks to preserve a criticism in which the understanding still has a crucial role to play. This does not mean that criticism in Benjamin's hands is to be understood as a synonym for the interpretation of another work. The Romantics had in any case pushed the concept of criticism far beyond such a role when they defined the task of criticism as an exercise in exposing the "prosaic kernel" at the center of every work of art – a task that sought to demonstrate that every artwork exposes the absolute as finite, as something prosaic, secular and therefore not transcendent. So defined, every artwork produces the same result. This result is the price the Romantics had to pay for the sober understanding they brought to the work of art. In contrast, the understanding of sobriety exhibited by Benjamin points rather to a desire to preserve the differences the Romantics sought to dissolve.

Why Benjamin took this path can be understood if the full consequences of the Romantics' definition of criticism is recognized. Since the Romantics separated the task of understanding from the task of criticism, Benjamin's rejection of their position indicates the attempt to return the task of understanding to criticism (in effect, Benjamin returns criticism to a field dominated by questions about the status of knowledge and how we arrive at it).

Crucially, Benjamin sought to preserve a difference that would legitimize criticism after the Romantics. Benjamin sought, in effect, to preserve the difference between a necessarily limited and finite activity such as criticism and something infinite such as the absolute. In this respect, Benjamin, unlike the Romantics, demands that whatever is absolute should not participate or be discovered in whatever is finite or limited. Already in 1916, this thinking is particularly evident in his reflections on language. In a letter to Martin Buber from this year, Benjamin writes:

> My concept of an objective and, at the same time, highly political style and writing is this: to awaken interest in what was denied to the word; only where this sphere of speechlessness reveals itself in unutterably pure power can the magic spark leap between the word and the motivating deed. (C, 80)

This interest in what is denied, what is inexpressible, what is speechless, unutterable, is not only reiterated in an essay written at the same time, "On Language as Such and on the Language of Man," but also figures prominently in a later essay written between 1919 and 1922, "Goethe's Elective Affinities." This insistence on what is inexpressible does not mean, however, that Benjamin wants to return to the kind of understanding the Romantics could no longer accept, namely an absolute that governs and determines all our experience from without, that is, from the top down. Benjamin's thought on this matter is more nuanced. Essentially, it is an attempt to rescue the possibility of criticism after the Romantic, that is, to rescue the critical distinction of the absolute from the Romantics.

The difficulty facing Benjamin's attempt to recover criticism from the Romantics can be easily appreciated as long as the situation into which he placed himself is firmly grasped: not only does he refuse the Romantics' understanding of criticism, but he also refuses what the Romantics had themselves rejected. Negotiating this difficulty poses several problems, the most notable of which involves a far-reaching diagnosis of the situation in which modern criticism finds itself. In Benjamin's analysis, the Romantics transformed the task of criticism to such an extent that critical writing was indistinguishable from the artistic work. To lose the difference between criticism and art work is then, according to Benjamin, to have renounced any pretence to understanding. To state this in closer relation to what Benjamin says about writing in the introduction to *The Origin of the German Tragic Drama*, the Romantics renounced any attempt to reflect on criticism as a form of thought, as a form in which thought and understanding can be presented. The emphasis Benjamin places on presentation in that introduction is crucial to this attempt (and contradicts the current translation of the word Benjamin uses, *Darstellung*, as representation: representation suggests too strongly that the medium in which Benjamin's thought is given, that is, language, merely describes something already existing, whereas Benjamin, by emphasizing presentation, indicates that thought and understanding are the effect of that medium and not its master).

A first attempt to realize this shift can be recognized in the Afterword to Benjamn's 1920 study of the Romantics. The prose produced by this shift is not called "sober" (to do so would have been confusing in a work that the rejects the sobriety of the Romantics). Instead of "sober prose" Benjamin refers to this Afterword as an example of "esoteric writing." In a letter written while Benjamin was working on his study of the Romantics, Benjamin writes: "I have written an esoteric Afterword for the dissertation, it is for those to whom I would have to present it as *my* work" (C, 141). The distinction Benjamin makes between what he writes in the Afterword and what he writes in the rest of the dissertation underscores the extent to which his thought was unable to remain within the expectations of academic commentary – and precisely because the writing Benjamin describes here as esoteric but later as sober prose is a writing that seeks to expose the presuppositions of not just academic commentary but also the practice of criticism.[4] Yet, with this aim in mind, Benjamin's writing finds itself in a difficult position. If the truth of art is to be revealed, it cannot be revealed as the representation of some preceding idea or historical moment. How then to articulate such a truth? It is in large part the result of Benjamin's attempt to explore this position that makes reading his work very different from reading the style of social, aesthetic, or philosophical commentary that precedes his writing. The announcement for a journal, to be entitled *Angelus Novus* (after the Paul Klee drawing Benjamin owned), clearly states Benjamin's intentions in this respect:

> If in its infancy criticism was forced to combat commonplace viciousness, the situation nowadays is different. Formerly, the stage was dominated by products that were backward-looking and tasteless and by producers who were naive bunglers. Now it is confronted at every point by talented fakes. Furthermore, for over a century every grubby literary rag in Germany has advertised itself as an organ of criticism so that redoubled efforts are needed to restore criticism to its former strength. (*SW* I, 293)

To restore or rescue criticism will require Benjamin to preserve the sense of an absolute that the Romantics rendered worldly, prosaic. For Benjamin, this sense alone could guarantee the activity of criticism since only an absolute that remains truly absolute can guarantee that criticism is a finite, limited activity (thereby avoiding the confusion of the Romantics who transformed criticism in to an infinite activity). Only if these two are kept rigorously separate can the task of criticism and its limits be known for Benjamin. By the same token, only by refusing to allow itself to be subject to criticism can such an absolute retain not only its legitimacy but also its power to legitimize the limited activity of criticism (whose limitation can only be known by being contrasted with an absolute).[5] What Benjamin achieves by returning the absolute to its literal role is, however, double-edged. Only by being absolute can it affirm the the limited practice of criticism, but by being absolute it can never confirm this limitation since to do so would be to reveal itself as less than absolute. As a result, criticism, as Benjamin understands it, must recognize the position the absolute puts it in: it is tied to an absolute without which it cannot be recognized, but that absolute cannot confirm such a recognition and remain absolute.

The consequences of this position make themselves felt first in the style of exposition Benjamin adopts for his thought. Whether esoteric (in the sense of withholding the understanding that justifies a certain writing) or the sober prose that continually pauses for breath, the effect sought is an awareness of the medium in which knowledge is given. This awareness turns Benjamin's language from a means of communication into a means of reflection. Such a turn gives a crucial role to language as the means by which thought secures itself, however momentary, in a world where an absolute is needed to assure communication but cannot communicate that assurance. Faced with this situation, Benjamin's writing emerges as a continual attempt to wrestle its subject away from a past whose traditions have ossified into formulae and clichés while he remains unyieldingly aware that his language is itself unable to guarantee enduring meaning. A passage from Benjamin's autobiographical work, *A Berlin Chronicle*, spells out this situation and its consequences:

> The matter itself is merely a deposit, a stratum which yields only to the most meticulous examination what constitutes the real treasure hidden within the earth: the images, severed from all previous associations that stand – like ruins or torsos in the collector's gallery – in the sober rooms of our later insights.
>
> (*SW* II, 611)

Beneath the subject to be inquired into, there rests what Benjamin calls the "real treasure." This treasure is to be revealed through the kind of meticulous examination already drawn attention to in the introduction to *The Origin of the German Tragic Drama* cited above: the "immersion in the most minute details of the material content" (*Origin*, 29). From immersion in these most minute details, Benjamin anticipates the appearance of an image no longer seen as it has been previously seen – as if the most meticulous examination of a mosaic were to yield an image obscured by the subject matter it is traditionally understood to represent. What is characteristic about these images is that they are severed from their past, they all emerge, to use a phrase from Benjamin's later reflections on history, blasted out of the continuum of history (*SW* IV, 396). Only in this separation does understanding appear to take place. Understanding is in effect the blasting of the image out of its past so that it can be recognized in the present. It goes without saying (or at least it should) that historical understanding in Benjamin has little to do with the recovery of the historical context or conditions of an event or even an artwork. Such a view would see history as a fixed source of meaning, as if the moment in which an event or events took place had already an unchanging meaning that later generations only had to uncover. For Benjamin, historical meaning is what survives the moment or time in which it occurs, and it is only in the terms of later understandings that its significance can be recognized. Yet, this recognition, as the metaphors Benjamin uses to indicate its occurrence confirm, is fleeting; it is seen as a "flash of lightning" or as something that "flits by."

As if this shift in our understanding of where historical knowledge comes from were not enough to contend with, Benjamin goes one step further. Even the moment in which this recognition occurs is understood to be unsustainable from one moment to the next: whatever is rescued from the past in this way, Benjamin states, is "in the next moment already irretrievably lost" (*Arcades* 473; N9, 7). This loss will, of course, confirm the limited, finite nature of this knowledge, but it also reflects the understanding of history at the core of Benjamin's writing: to paraphrase an entry from the *Arcades Project*, history is no longer what casts light on the present, nor is it the present casting light on the past. The problem with both of these alternatives is that they assume a stable past that can either be used to interpret the present (and therefore deny the present any significance of its own) or can be interpreted by the present (and therefore become a mere projection of a present that stabilizes its world view in an unchangeable past). Either way, historical knowledge is understood to be based on a stable, fixed moment – as if it stood outside of time like some absolute. The position Benjamin criticized the Romantics for can be seen here. The point from which history is understood is essentially ahistorical if it is located *only* in the past or the present. In contrast, Benjamin sought to shift the understanding of history away from the representation of either the past or the present. Instead, history, for Benjamin, is to be understood as an image in which the past comes together in the present.[6] Since this occurs as an image in the present – what Benjamin calls "the now of recognizability" – history is no longer defined by its usual temporal terms (as what is past or what survives from the past). Rather, it is an image in which our understanding experiences the past in the full awareness of the temporary, fleeting source of all experience: the present. For Benjamin, the image is the fitting form for such knowledge.

To the extent that Benjamin sought to produce such images as the form most appropriate to how he viewed not only history but also knowledge, it can be expected that reading his work creates unusual demands. This is particularly so in a writer who remains constantly aware of how the image operates as a mode of understanding: what it preserves in one moment is

"irretrievably lost" in the next. To write from within the perspective of this
understanding is to produce a writing that is continually in conflict with
itself since it is continually struggling against a tendency it knows to be false
(render an absolute understanding in a finite form). At the same time, such
a writing recognizes that the limited nature of its understanding can only
confirm an absolute that can provide no help or guidance if it is to remain
absolute. Benjamin's understanding of the image seeks to reflect this situation
in a continually momentary rescue of knowledge. To read this rescue is
to experience not only Benjamin's thought but also to experience how the
form in which that thought is given has a critical effect upon its readers.
While this critical effect can be traced to the pausing for breath Benjamin's
prose stives for, the critical experience is realized in the reader's increased
awareness of how this prose resists the tendency toward conformity or easy
understanding that lurks dangerously in all reading. This is why reading
Benjamin is best described as a task, since his writing is a site in which
the past has to be continually rescued from a conformity in which neither
history not knowledge can take place. Although this rescue is continual, it
is not continual in the sense of an unbroken line but rather in the sense of
what has to be repeated over and over again, what in fact has to be begun
over and over again.

Perhaps nowhere is this task of reading Benjamin more pronounced than
in the project that consumed the last part of his career and which remained
incomplete at the time of his death in 1940. The direct link between this
project and the style of presentation Benjamin described in the introduction to *The Origin of the German Tragic Drama* is expressed by Benjamin
in this last project in the following words: "The book on the baroque exposed the seventeenth century to the light of the present day. Here, something
analogous must be done for the nineteenth century, but with greater distinctness" (*Arcades*, 459; N1a, 2). A greater distinctness is made apparent by the
fragmentary state of this work. More than any of Benjamin's other works,
the *Arcades Project* poses the question of how to read Benjamin. Indeed,
what does one do when faced with a mass of quotations interspersed with
a commentary presented in a fragmentary form identical to the quotations
that make up so many of the entries Benjamin recorded in this unfinished
work?[7] The difficulty posed by this work is no doubt the reason why one
of its sections (named "Convolutes" by Benjamin) is cited the most. This
section, known as Convolute N, provides a reflection on the epistemological
consequences of this project. In this convolute, Benjamin offers some insight
into the rationale for this kind of presentation when he writes about "the
properly problematic component" of this project. He locates this problematic component in a "refusal to renounce anything that would demonstrate

the materialist presentation of history as imagistic in a higher sense than in traditional presentation" (*Arcades*, 463; N3, 3). To apply the standards and expectations of traditional presentation (continuity of discourse, etc.) to this project is seen by Benjamin as a refusal to renounce what is most deeply problematic. To read Benjamin, this refusal to renounce such continuity must itself be rejected, but, at the same time, and Benjamin is acutely aware of this, no reading can take place if traditional presentation is rejected in a wholesale manner. Only its refusal to renounce is to be rejected. Only through this rejection can recognition of the problematic nature of continuity in both writing and history be obtained.

For Benjamin, the consequences of this rejection are discovered in a writing that favors the imagistic – as the concept of the "dialectical image" that dominates his later work amply shows. Although the critical force of this concept no longer appeals so openly to what is inexpressible for its significance, it does depend on the continued operation of a moment which allows understanding to occur but which plays no decisive role in determining what that understanding is. It is, in this respect, a condition of knowledge, it allows the image to appear but does not define the character of that image – just as the flash of lightning (one of Benjamin's favourite metaphors for how such images appear) illuminates but does not define what falls within its illumination. Such a condition admits another element into criticism. This element became essential to the study of culture and art that became increasingly important for him in the 1920s. This element is the historical. But, like the prose style of the treatise that Benjamin dismisses for its pretension to continuity, the historical has nothing to do with continuity either. For Benjamin, history happens at the moment when continuity is arrested and such an arrest only occurs in a dialectical juxtaposition of past and present. Since the medium of this arrest is the image, the form of its expression became a broken prose in whose sobering effect Benjamin sought not only a criticism of historicism and its continuity but also refuge from the constant danger of its return.

To read Benjamin at his fullest is to take stock of an understanding no longer able to rely upon the extraction of a content. The hidden riches of the earth, which Benjamin refers to in the passage from *Berlin Chronicle* cited above, only yield their significance in a collector's gallery where they are exposed for what they are: ruins, torsos. Only in such a setting can they appear in this way. Only in the gallery, the place in which one expects to find the continuity of past presented, can the critique of that continuity appear in its most forceful way. But, it is important to remember here that the setting in which such continuity is expected plays a crucial role in recognizing that the materials to be connected are originally ruins and torsos. While the spatial arrangements of a gallery allow this distinction to be seen, the same cannot be said so easily about writing. In writing, the gallery and torso are indistinguishable from one another, they use the same words, the same syntax. What makes the task of reading Benjamin so challenging is the ongoing struggle of his writing, a writing that struggles against its own collective power in order to rescue criticism from becoming yet another ruin in a gallery of its own making.

NOTES

1. See Andrew Benjamin's chapter below.
2. Rodolphe Gasché, "The Sober Absolute: On Benjamin and the Early Romantics," in *Walter Benjamin: Theoretical Questions*, ed. David S. Ferris (Stanford University Press, 1996), 72.
3. Ibid., 71.
4. On this relation between commentary and esoteric writing in Benjamin's dissertation, see my "Benjamin's Esoteric History of Romanticism" *Studies in Romanticism* 31:4 (Winter 1992), 455–80.
5. On this power as it is expressed in Benjamin's examination of the Romantics, see Gasché, "The Sober Absolute," 72–74.
6. See, *Arcades*, 463; N3, 1.
7. The German edition of this work ignored this aspect by using two different sized typefaces to distinguish Benjamin's citations from Benjamin's reflections. To a lesser degree this precedent is repeated in the English translation by its use of two different styles of typeface. Benjamin's manuscript gives no authority for this presentation.

I

MICHAEL JENNINGS

Walter Benjamin and the European avant-garde

The year 1924 produced a series of crucial turns in Walter Benjamin's career. The years leading up to 1924, to which he later referred as his "apprenticeship in German literature," saw Benjamin intent on a reevaluation of German Romanticism, and the development of a theory of criticism with deep roots in that very Romanticism. His major published works of the period included studies of Goethe's novel *Elective Affinities*, a dissertation on Friedrich Schlegel's theory of criticism, and, in 1924, a major study of German baroque mourning plays, *The Origin of the German Tragic Drama*; in each of these texts, Benjamin develops his own literary theory from concepts and procedures evident in the works themselves, only to turn the new theory back on the text from which it in some sense sprang. The rhythms of Benjamin's practice and theory of criticism in these years contain two intertwined movements. On the one hand, his criticism entails the demolition or demystification of the unified work of art – what we today call its disenchantment. Benjaminian criticism reduces the apparently coherent, integrally meaningful work to the status, to name but a few of Benjamin's figures, of ruin, of torso, of mask. In the study of *The Origin of the German Tragic Drama* he writes that "criticism is the mortification of works" (*Origin*, 182; trans. modified). On the other hand, his theory also entails a positive moment: the isolation and redemption of charged shards of an "immanent state of perfection" that had been shattered and denatured – made meaningless – in the course of history ("Life of Students," *SW* I, 37). In the essay on Goethe's novel *Elective Affinities*, Benjamin defines the object of criticism as the discovery of the "truth content" of art. These essays and books produced between 1912 and 1924, some of them published only after Benjamin's death, constitute a major body of work; the dense interweaving of immanent interpretation and broad-gauged cultural theory has ensured a special status for these texts in the history of criticism.

In the decade between 1924 and 1934, however, Benjamin's writings changed radically: it is as if he woke up sometime in 1924 as a different writer. Before 1924, Benjamin had written precisely one piece on contemporary literature, an unpublished essay on the German author of a series of gently utopian science fictions, Paul Scheerbart. Before 1924, Benjamin's understanding of politics and his political engagement are a matter of intense debate; he is described variously as apolitical, an anarchist, or a right-wing radical, and, up until 1924, Benjamin had planned, albeit with considerable ambivalence, a career in the university. Beginning in 1924, he turned his attention and his energies in precipitously new directions: to contemporary European culture, to Marxist politics, and to a career as a journalist and wide-ranging cultural critic. These three central aspects of Benjamin's turn in 1924 have received varying attention: the turn to Marxism is very well documented and plays a role in nearly every reading of the life and work; the failed academic career and the decision to pursue a career as a freelance cultural critic has, surprisingly, remained undervalued; but the shift from German Romanticism and its predecessors to contemporary European culture, which is in many ways the most momentous decision for Benjamin in the 1920s, remains a black hole in Benjamin scholarship.

At first haltingly, and then, beginning in 1926, with a vengeance, Walter Benjamin turned his thought and writing to Europe, and especially to the modernist and avant-garde culture being produced in France and the Soviet Union. His range in the period is astonishing: between 1926 and 1931, Benjamin produced essays on children's literature; toys; pedagogy; gambling; graphology; pornography; folk art; the art of excluded groups such as the mentally ill; food; and a wide variety of media including film, radio, photography, and the illustrated press. Partly as a professional strategy, but mainly driven by new political and aesthetic commitments, Benjamin sought to establish himself as the principal mediator between Germany and the new cultural forms emerging in France and the Soviet Union. His frequent visits to Paris inspired essays on high modernism in France (Paul Valéry; André Gide; Marcel Proust), as well as extraordinarily influential presentations and analyses of the French historical avant-garde and especially Surrealism.[1] Although Benjamin visited the Soviet Union only once, in 1927, he developed an extensive knowledge of Russian culture, and produced a number of synoptic essays on Russian literature and film, as well as individual pieces on Lenin, Maxim Gorki, Sergei Eisenstein, and Vladimir Mayakovsky.

The common view of Benjamin as a distanced, ineffectual loner laboring in the ivory tower may conform to the self-understanding of some of Benjamin's critics, but it has little to do with his life. Writing for some of the most prominent weeklies and monthlies in Germany, Walter Benjamin established himself in the late 1920s as a visible and influential commentator on cultural matters. Yet this period, like each one in his life, has other peculiarities. His *theoretical* writing, for all its brilliance and occasional jabbing, unforgettable insight, had lost some of the force and all of the systematic complexity of his pre-1924 work; it gave way in part to a new interest in the creation of new literary forms. Only somewhat tentatively in 1929, with major essays on Surrealism and Proust, and then with full force in 1931 with a great essay on Karl Kraus and a magisterial essay on photography, would Benjamin return to the admixture of interpretation and theory that had marked his early work and would again mark his major work of the later 1930s. It is as if Benjamin felt that his own theoretical model, constructed on the basis of a reading of pre-modern literature, would fail to open up the new material with which he was dealing. In the major works of the period after the Kraus essay – I am thinking here of "Experience and Poverty" of 1933, "The Author as Producer" and "Franz Kafka" of 1934, and, beginning in 1935 and continuing to the end of his life, the intensive absorption into the world of the Parisian arcades and Charles Baudelaire, an absorption that would produce central essays on Baudelaire, on "The Work of Art in the Age of its Technological Reproducibility," on the philosophy of history, and the great torso of the *Arcades Project* – Benjamin "returned" to his earlier practice, developing an extensive methodological superstructure based not only on his early theory but also on his reading of contemporary cultural material. It is clear that some of Benjamin's theoretical energies were diverted in the 1920s from the practice of criticism into the creation of a new literary form. The years between 1924 and 1931 saw the emergence of Benjamin as a creative writer. Certainly his central achievement in this period is *One-Way Street*, a carefully structured collection of short prose pieces published by Rowohlt Verlag in 1928. In what follows, I will look at *One-Way Street* as a summa of Benjamin's work in the decade after 1924.

A number of important questions arise, then, when the trajectory of Benjamin's career is viewed in this way, questions that have seldom been broached and certainly never answered satisfactorily. What precipitated the turn from Romantic to contemporary culture? From Germany to Europe? And from pure criticism to a career that mixed criticism with the creation of new literary forms? A certain number of answers have been put forward to the question as to Benjamin's precipitous turn to contemporaneity. The most prevalent of these reads: "Marxism." In 1924, under the personal influence of the Latvian communist theater director Asja Lacis and – no turn without a book to ground it in – after a reading of Georg Lukács's *History and Class Consciousness*, Benjamin incorporated central aspects of historical materialist thought into his own work. This often-discussed turn, as central as it is for Benjamin, and, as we will see, for *One-Way Street*, would not seem in and of itself to explain a sudden interest in contemporary culture.

Benjamin's model here, after all, was Lukács, and Lukács had already in 1924 begun to define himself as the great enemy of avant-garde culture that he would become only later, in the debates on expressionism in the 1930s. It has also been proposed that the rejection of *The Origin of the German Tragic Drama* as Benjamin's *Habilitationsschrift* (the second dissertation required of all German academics who aspire to a professorship) set him free for a career as a journalist, a career that would necessarily center on the criticism of contemporary culture; and, of course, there is some truth in this. But any such purely professional, indeed venal turn would hardly have led Benjamin to look beyond Germany, and certainly not to the work of the European avant-garde, whose cultural production was hardly the stuff of the weekly and monthly magazines on which Benjamin would be dependent for publication venues. Instead, I propose, a barely traced constellation in Benjamin's life explains fully and satisfactorily not just the questions posed here, but also a number of the most puzzling aspects of *One-Way Street*.

Walter Benjamin was a Berliner to his core. Yet in the years just before and during the war, he had moved only on the furthest margins of the Berlin artistic culture that defined German modernism. His letters and essays contain occasional references to sightings of Elsa Lasker-Schüler, Herwarth Walden, and other members of the circle around the journal *Der Sturm* – the most important modernist cenacle in Berlin during the war – but neither Benjamin's age nor his then-current predisposition to older literature would have propelled him closer than his role as voyeur. Beginning in 1923, however, a very different picture of Benjamin emerges, though this is a picture that can be read only in the mirror of other people's letters and recollections. Sometime in that year, Benjamin's circle of friends and intellectual partners began to intermingle with a very different group of Berlin intellectuals, a group now referred to as the "G-Group." In 1923, long before Walter Benjamin seemed to move beyond his German literary homeland and toward Europe, Europe came to Benjamin in Berlin.

In late 1922 and early 1923 a new avant-garde began to form in Berlin, where refugees from a number of nations and earlier aesthetic directions began to gather. The group met in the ateliers of a number of artists and architects, among them Laszlo Moholy-Nagy, the Hungarian artist later to become a central figure at the Bauhaus and indeed in European photography, Mies van der Rohe, who would become one of the two or three most influential architects of the twentieth century, and El Lissitsky, the Russian constructivist who played a decisive role in the shaping of the new, "objective" culture of Weimar Germany.[2] A small inner circle soon formed, a circle intent on propagating a new direction for European culture. The dominant personality in the group – and indeed the group met most frequently at his studio – was Hans Richter, a German artist and filmmaker who had been active on the fringes of Zürich Dada. The group soon came to include representatives of four important avant-garde movements. The former Dadaists Richter and Raoul Hausmann were core members; their friends and colleagues from the Dada circles in Zürich and Berlin, Kurt Schwitters, Hans Arp, George Grosz, John Heartfield, and Hannah Höch were all intermittent contributors. A strong Russian constructivist influence emanated from El Lissitsky, who was supported by Moholy-Nagy, Naum Gabo, Antoine Pevsner, and Nathan Altmann. Mies and Ludwig Hilberseimer brought to the discussions a kind of proto-international style that looked primarily to an "American" technological modernism for its inspiration. And Tzara, together with Man Ray and Max Burcharz, introduced elements of an early Surrealism. The G-Group was not limited, though, to artists: a group of friends, all of them Berlin intellectuals, soon found their way into the intensive discussions. This was a group of friends centered around Walter Benjamin. They included his wife, Dora, a prominent journalist, and his close friend Ernst Schoen, a musician and music theorist who would go on to become the cultural director of one of the national radio stations.

When Richter, Lissitsky, and Mies decided to publish a journal to propagate the new direction, they named it G. *Zeitschrift für elementare Gestaltung* (G. Journal for Elementary Form Production).[3] As Richter remembers, the Dutch architect and theorist Theodor van Doesburg, an occasional participant whose ideas ran parallel to those of the group, suggested the name as a reference to the term "Gestaltung," shaping or forming, a frank reference to the group's movement away from the notion of individual creation and toward a more sober, industrially oriented cultural production with strong roots in constructivism and Berlin Dada. While the journal itself had little *direct* importance for the development of Weimar culture, it would be hard to *overestimate* the importance of the discussions which led to its production for that culture and for twentieth-century culture more generally. Artists and writers such as Moholy, Mies, Richter, and Benjamin had their careers ahead of them, and decisive elements of those careers were forged in the ateliers of the G-Group. The importance of that influence cannot be ascribed to one person or direction: the particular confluence in G of constructivism, late Dadaism, the new Americanism, and an awakening surrealism is crucial.

Although I will turn to the specific role of "G"-thinking in *One-Way Street* in a moment, it is important that we gain here some sense of the importance for Benjamin of his participation in the group. It is only after the discussions with his colleagues that Benjamin will "discover" his new thematic focuses: industrial art; architecture; photography; mass culture; and, above all, the emergence of startlingly new cultural forms in France and Russia.[4] And it is not merely the discovery of a new cultural sphere that emanates from Benjamin's participation in the group. From it he will derive a new conception of the work of art and its place in the culture. Both Benjamin's technological utopianism, evident in later essays such as "Little History of Photography," "The Author as Producer," and especially "The Work of Art in the Age of its Technological Reproducibility," and his analysis of the de-mystification of the artwork – the destruction of its "aura" – must be traced to the discussions in the G-Group. The "Copernican turn" in Benjamin's thinking in 1924 is grounded, then, not just in his newly discovered Marxism. As nearly everything he wrote in the seven years after *One-Way Street* indicates, the dense intermingling of an idiosyncratic historical materialism and a less idiosyncratic but so far unremarked "G-ism" is determinative for his writing. In what follows I will analyze three key figures in the rich textural carpet of *One-Way Street*, using as an organizational strategy the three avantgardist techniques upon which Benjamin draws in order to fashion a new kind of text.

One-Way Street and the new avant-garde fusion

At the most basic formal level, *One-Way Street* attempts to establish, if not a new genre, then a new avantgardist form. If it is all but impossible to discern today the heritage and import of Benjamin's text, then much of this difficulty stems from its hybrid quality. Benjamin attempts to achieve in one text a new avant-garde fusion, a synthesis of Dada, constructivism, and Surrealism that will open the way for new directions in German cultural production and, ideally, in cognition and a consequent political action. *One-Way Street* consists of sixty short prose pieces; these differ wildly in terms of genre, style, and intent. There are aphorisms among the texts, and jokes and dream protocols; there are also descriptive set pieces, cityscapes, landscapes, mindscapes; pieces of writing manuals; trenchant contemporary political analysis; prescient appreciations of children's games, behavioral patterns, and moods; decodings of bourgeois fashion, living arrangements, and courting patterns that anticipate the Barthes of *Mythologies*; and, time and again, remarkable penetrations into the heart of everyday things, what Benjamin would later call the "exploration of the soul of the commodity." Two features of the text call here for our particular attention, because they have thus far hindered sustained attention to the architectonics and thematic coherence of the text as a whole: first, the specific gravity of Benjamin's prose in each individual piece, and, second, the thematic diversity of the collection.

It is only in *One-Way Street* that Walter Benjamin finds his way to the prose that has earned him the reputation as one of the foremost stylists of the century. As a producer of memorable sentences, his only real competitors are Franz Kafka and Robert Musil, two writers of fiction long since elevated to the stylistic pantheon. The similarity of Kafka's prose and that of Benjamin has long been noted: they share not just a lapidary quality, a beauty and trenchancy of expression, but especially the ability to generate multivalence from an extreme economy of means. "These are the days," Benjamin writes in the section called "Chinese Curios," "in which no one should rely unduly on his 'competence.' Strength lies in improvisation. All the decisive blows are struck left-handed" (*SW* I, 447). Or, in the section "To the Public: Please Protect and Preserve These New Plantings": "Commentary and translation stand in the same relation to the text as style and mimesis to nature: the same phenomenon considered from different aspects. On the tree of the sacred text, both are only the eternally rustling leaves; on that of the profane, the seasonally falling fruit" (*SW* I, 449). These are examples of what Benjamin would later call the "thought figure" [*Denkbild*]. This short prose form, which combines features of the aphorism with description of the material world, describes, as Gershom Scholem once said of Benjamin's work as a whole, a "philosophy of its object." Although Benjamin published many individual thought figures as well as collections in Weimar journals,[5] the most important example of the form is *One-Way Street*.

My second point is related to this: the trenchancy and seeming autonomy of the individual sections, together with the diversity of Benjamin's thematics have created a tendency to read the text as a series of only loosely connected aphorisms and short prose pieces. Any such reading, though, soon becomes unsatisfactory: there is simply too much cross-talk between the pieces, too much internal resonance and perplexing contradiction. Benjamin's own comments make it clear that he, too, at first thought of the text as a loose framework within which to mount autonomous prose pieces. The first mention of the project in 1924 refers to a collection of "aphorisms, jokes, dreams" (*GBr* II, 510); in 1925, the text had become a "small aphorism manuscript" (*GBr* III, 50); and in 1925 and early 1926 simply "the aphorism book" (*GBr* III, 122). Toward the end of 1926, though, Benjamin himself came to see his text differently: "I am working on the book of jottings, which I don't like to call an aphorism book" (*GBr* III, 161). It had become clear to him that the book, in its complexity and especially in its structure, no longer resembled a series of autonomous pieces: it had become a record of its age and, coincidentally, that of its author, a multiple exposure of his "younger and older physiognomy" (*GBr* III, 133). And Benjamin is intensely aware of the contradictions that shape his text, endowing it with a terrible difficulty.

"It represents something heterogeneous or rather polar; certain flashes emanate from its tensions too harshly, certain discharges too hauntingly" (*GBr* III, 208).

The earliest section of *One-Way Street*, "Imperial Panorama: A Journey through the German Inflation," had its inception in 1923, at the height of the German hyperinflation. "These last days of travel through Germany," Benjamin wrote at that time, "have again led me to an edge of hopelessness and have allowed me to look into the abyss" (*GBr* II, 317). Benjamin continued to write, and occasionally to publish, the small prose texts that would eventually make up his montage-book. The first excerpt appeared in the *Berliner Tageblatt* in 1925; from this point on it appeared in a steady trickle right up through the publication in book form in 1928. Reading the book as a coherent, though anti-narrative ensemble, it becomes clear that the avant-garde strategies are dictated not by aesthetic, but by political concerns.

Although direct topical references to inflation abound in Benjamin's text, his main critique of the conditions that prevent recognition of the actual character of life in Weimar Germany takes place at a theoretical level and centers on the categories of commodity and phantasmagoria. It is, in fact, in *One-Way Street* that Benjamin initiates his sustained attempt to theorize the commodity, building on Marx and Lukács, even if the full force of that theory and its critique of capitalism will emerge only in the essays of the 1930s associated with Benjamin's "*Arcades Project.*" In the section "Imperial Panorama," the pervasive note is the absolute misery of the underclass. "What completes the isolation of Germany in the eyes of other Europeans, what really engenders the attitude that they are dealing with Hottentots in the Germans (as it has been aptly put), is the violence, incomprehensible to outsiders and wholly imperceptible to those imprisoned by it, with which circumstances, squalor, and stupidity here subjugate people entirely to collective forces, as the lives of savages alone are subjected to tribal laws." It is utterly characteristic of Walter Benjamin that the attestation of the condition of "naked misery" (*SW* I, 452–53) is constantly accompanied by an analysis not of the objective economic conditions that cause that misery, but rather of those conditions that prevent its recognition, analysis, and eventual eradication. In the middle years of the Weimar Republic, first inflation and then the illusory sense of stability have combined to bring about the progressive decay of the perceptual and cognitive apparatus in Germany: "The people cooped up in this country no longer discern the contours of human personality" (*SW* I, 453); "mass instincts have become confused and estranged from life . . . society's attachment to its familiar and long-since forfeited life is so rigid as to nullify the genuinely human application of intellect, forethought, even in dire peril" (*SW* I, 451). These human faculties have fallen prey, first of all, to the confusions of the inflation, but also more generally to the influence of commodities, to the "boundless resistance of the outside world" (*SW* I, 454):

> Warmth is ebbing from things. The objects of daily use gently but insistently repel us. Day by day, in overcoming the sum of secret resistances – not only the overt ones – that they put in our way, we have an immense labor to perform. We must compensate for their coldness with our warmth if they are not to freeze us to death, and handle their spines with infinite dexterity, if we are not to perish by bleeding. (*SW* I, 453–54).

Benjamin's analysis of this power, what he later called the "sex-appeal of the anorganic," relies on his particular inflection of the concept of reification that he derives from Marx and Lukács. Marx, in *Capital*, had attributed to the commodity – an apparently "easily understood, trivial thing" – "sensuous, yet extrasensory [sinnlich übersinnlich]" properties. Commodities appear "granted a life of their own, they become independent entities which stand in relationship to one another and to men."[6] Marx attempted to explain this phenomenon metaphorically; he referred to the propensity of commodities to form networks of significance and influence as their "fetishism." Benjamin had signaled his use of this concept early in *One-Way Street* in the section "Mexican Embassy": He there first quotes Baudelaire on the power of fetishes and then relates an anecdote of a missionary station in Mexico. "Toward a wooden bust of God the Father fixed high on a wall of the cave, a priest raised a Mexican fetish. At this, the divine head turned thrice in denial from right to left" (*SW* I, 448–49). He is also quite specific as to the direct effect of this fetishism on human perception and intellect. The primary characteristic of commodity fetishism is ambiguity: "all things, in a perpetual process of mingling and contamination, are losing their intrinsic character while ambiguity displaces authenticity" (*SW* I, 454). Ambiguity is for Benjamin at once an epistemological and a moral category. The cognitive disorientation that results from encounters with the deeply ambiguous world of things prevents the human subject from an adequate moral agency and above all denies her a capacity for resistance and social change.

In *One-Way Street*, the effects of this disorientation are rendered brilliantly: as space. The spatial dimension is, of course, already present in the title; the book is a figure for a street, down which the reader strolls, encountering street signs, shop windows, and the material culture of modern capitalism. Looking down this street should be like looking over the edge of a chasm. This is indeed the effect described in "Manorially Furnished Ten-Room Apartment." Benjamin asserts only partially scurrilously that the detective novel – of which he was an avid reader – arose out of the necessity of making clear the layout of the bourgeois apartment. This thought figure performs, like a detective, the necessary rational, cognitive mapping of an essentially irrational space. The apartment of the nineteenth century, which "fittingly houses only the corpse," is replete with "gigantic sideboards distended with carving, the sunless corners where palms stand," in short "that rank Orient inhabiting their interiors: the Persian carpet and the ottoman, the hanging lamp and the genuine Caucasian dagger" (SW I, 447). This space is marked by an insurmountable ambiguity. On the one hand, hermetically sealed and safe from all assaults from revolution in the streets – the balcony is "embattled behind its balustrude" – the apartment is a fortress and a coffin. On the other hand, it is always also elsewhere, conjuring a metaphorical orient whose exoticism blurs and conceals the mundaneness of the real surroundings. The inhabitant is at once trapped and eternally escaping, subject to a spatial disorientation which robs his existence of solidity and authenticity. This ambiguity can prove fatal: "Behind the heavy, gathered Khilim tapestries the master of the house has orgies with his share certificates, feels himself the Eastern merchant, the indolent pasha in the caravanserai of otiose enchantment, until that dagger in its silver sling above the divan puts an end, one fine afternoon, to his siesta and himself" (SW I, 447). Spatial disorientation is not merely a political category: it is a mortal one.

Perhaps the most brilliant evocation of this form of spatial displacement occurs toward the end of the volume, in "Stand-Up Beer Hall." There, sailors are suggested as the most telling examples of the influence of commodities on human cognition as they and their power are organized and deployed by international capital. "The international norm of industry is present for them right in the bones; they aren't the dupes of palms and icebergs" (SW I, 485). The bourgeoisie experience the disorienting power of commodities in a mediated manner: the forced exoticism of the bourgeois interior deploys commodities within allegorical frameworks. For the sailor, however, whose work "in the rump of the ship maintains contact with the commodity," the world actually travelled and lived in ceases to have any local character. "The city isn't visited but rather bought. In the trunk of the sailor lies the leather belt from Hong Kong next to the panorama of Palermo and a photo of a girl from Stettin…He lives on the open sea in a city where a bar in Port Said stands across from a Hamburg bordello on the Cannebière in Marseilles" (SW I, 485). "And listening to them, one realizes what mendacity resides in voyaging" (SW I, 486).

In the section called "Toys," Benjamin extends this analysis of spatial displacement and the effacement of boundaries to an enclosed atmosphere. This section is the most powerful of all literary evocations of the phantasmagoric quality of modern life in the city. The shifting, wholly anti-perspectival quality of the street is caught in the second subsection, "Shooting Booths," in which the visitor to the fair moves with his rifle from one interior to the next. Even more powerfully, "Not for Sale," an anticipation of the more famous, if less complex metaphor of the Turkish puppet in Benjamin's late meditation "On the Concept of History" evokes a particular vision of history as it is perceived through the phantasmagoric veil of modern life. This piece shares with the later tale of the Turkish puppet the idea that history is driven by unseen forces working below the surface. Unlike the later meditation, though, those forces are here not named. Instead, we see only the *results* of historical change. Even the configuration of the tables in the booth – set at an angle, their inner edges converge precipitously – stands as a metaphor for history; like the one-way street, history moves inevitably toward constriction, toward a reduction of human liberty. Yet that process is visible only through distorted mirrors and in the guise of pleasure. At the center of the piece, then, is Benjamin's reading of the experience of contemporary history. The description of a series of vivid tableaux evokes the fragmented, discontinuous experience of a distorted history; the puppets in the tableaux, in their gruesome combination of verisimilitude and ostentatious machine action, comment on the character of human response – on the sort of reception and action available to agents in a historical process – as conditioned, incomplete, above all endlessly repetitious, without the possibility of change. At a deeper level, the tableaux are thematically related. The rulers give way to biblical figures who are either tyrants or victims of tyranny. In the genre scenes, the results of this historical condition are depicted. Humans become not so much thing-like as bestial – throughout Benjamin's career, human bestiality functions as a code word for a complex of ideas related to the encroachment of the inhuman into properly human spheres such as rationality, morality, and relations between persons. He expands on this in "Gloves": "In horror of animals the dominant sensation is the fear of being recognized by them when we touch. What is most horrifying to humans is the dark consciousness that there is something in humans that is so little foreign to these repulsive animals that they can recognize it in us" (*SW* I, 448). It is thus no surprise that the final tableaux in "Not for Sale" concern the artificiality and even impossibility of genuine relations with other persons.

In Benjamin's view of life under capitalism, "everyone is committed to the optical illusions of his isolated standpoint" (*SW* I, 453); the creation of a *new* standpoint is in fact at the heart of Benjamin's attack here. The word was not chosen at random, since its position in an optical and a political rhetoric is crucial to both layers of the text. Clearly enough, Benjamin's strategy involved the creation of a form which was unstable, a form which could, through a certain lability, penetrate the "air so full of phantoms, mirages of a glorious cultural future" and bring to consciousness the "true history" which lay embedded in cracks and fissures. His deployment of the strategies of the historical avant-garde in a new fusion is thus not aesthetic, but political, an attempt at the demystification of a world shrouded in myth and unreason.

Constructivism

We need to understand the "concrete" character of Benjamin's text through two complementary lenses: the technological optimism to which Benjamin was first exposed through contact with Moholy-Nagy in the G-Group and Benjamin's own enthusiasm for an indigenous German constructivism represented by Lissitsky and his followers.[7] Benjamin's text attempts to find a prose form equivalent to the constructivist practice of incorporating the materials of concrete industrial objects into cultural objects. Hegel's rejection of facticity in favor of theory – "so much the worse for the facts" – has little to do with Benjamin's text. *One-Way Street* thus juxtaposes theoretical fragments with titles that refer to seemingly unrelated aspects of the material culture: gas stations, stamp collections, war memorials, fire alarms. Interestingly enough, most citations of these shards of life in Weimar make no attempt to describe or evoke the objects in question. The entire "real weight" of each section rests on the title alone. Unlike the practice of most constructivists, Benjamin thus attempts to *theorize* the material cited, both through the text that follows and comments on each title, and through the position of the material in the larger montage that is *One-Way Street*. It is thus no accident that Benjamin evokes the power of the industrial machine as he calls for the creation of a new "prompt language" in the first section of the book, "Filling Station": "Opinions are to the vast apparatus of social existence what oil is to machines: one does not go up to a turbine and pour machine oil over it; one applies a little to hidden spindles and joints that one has to know" (*SW* I, 444). The most important articulation of this new, "constructivist" language occurs in the section "Attested Auditor of Books." Contemplating an age in which the supremacy of the book is nearing its end, Benjamin imagines a new communicative form based on "constructive principles" that can "incorporate the graphic tensions of the advertisement" (*SW* I, 456). "Script," that is, language in its printed, pictorial form, will advance "ever more deeply into the graphic regions of its new eccentric figurativeness, will suddenly take possession of an adequate material content." And this will happen when it masters "the fields in which...it is being constructed: statistical and technical diagrams" (*SW* I, 456–67). In "This Space for Rent," Benjamin envisions the advertisement even more specifically as a replacement for criticism: "Today the most real, the mercantile gaze into the heart of things is the advertisement. It abolishes the space where contemplation moved and all but hits us between the eyes with things as a car, growing to gigantic proportions, careens at us out of a film screen" (*SW* I, 476). Benjamin's theory of experience, with its championing of the violent shock as a liberating moment, is at play here. We are granted, through shock, in a state of distraction brought on by the ubiquity and sameness of advertising, a privileged glance into "the heart of things," that is, into the conditions that structure and obscure our ability to understand our world. Benjamin's constructivist contribution to the "New Seeing" that took shape in photography and film in Germany in the mid-1920s was thus a literary form. His text, in the sparse trenchancy of its language, in its refractory, diagrammatic character, and in its understanding of script as a necessary human prosthesis aims to instantiate – rather than merely describe – the role claimed by Moholy-Nagy for new technological media: the ability to alter the human sensorium through exposure to new, "productive" relationships among the complex multiplicity of the objects of human sensation under modernity.[8]

Dada photomontage and the politics of montage form

Alongside its preference for the concrete, *One-Way Street* shows a decided preference for the unfinished, the fragmentary, the marginal. "To great writers, finished works weigh lighter than those fragments on which they work throughout their lives" (*SW* I, 446). These fragments are the same linguistic and visual forms that had found their way into the photomontage practices of the Berlin Dadaists: "inconspicuous forms" that eschew "the pretentious, universal gesture of the book" such as "leaflets, brochures, articles, and placards" (*SW* I, 444).[9] Benjamin's practice stems from the Dadaist conviction that it is only that which lies unused or already discarded that is free of the ideological contamination of the ruling formation. In the section with the suggestive title "Construction Site" Benjamin says the following:

> For children are particularly fond of haunting any site where things are being visibly worked on. They are irresistibly drawn by the detritus generated by building, gardening, housework, tailoring, or carpentry. In waste products they recognize the face that the world of things turns directly and solely to them.

In using these things they do not so much imitate the works of adults as bring together, in the artifact produced in play, materials of widely differing kinds in a new, intuitive relationship. Children thus produce their own small world of things within the greater one. (*SW* I, 449–50)

This small text holds an important key to the puzzle of Benjamin's methodology. It is at once a comment on the constructive principles of the text and a powerful political allegory. Benjamin's text is built up of a kind of detritus, that which has been overlooked or misused. It thus allegorizes the German Revolution of 1918–19, which was proof of nothing so much as the necessity of finding new blocks with which to build an edifice; a mere reconfiguration of the old materials of the German Empire simply would not do. Children play a central role here and in much of Benjamin's work. As late as the final drafts for a book on Charles Baudelaire, which date from the last year of Benjamin's life, he reflected on Charles Fourier and the role of children in a utopian socialist society. Here, he attributes to children the power to circumvent the entrenched structures of society. Children have not yet fallen prey to the European malaise of cultural exhaustion and ideological strangulation. Their possession of a new intuition again suggests the necessity for society to discover new constructive principles. These are, *in nuce*, the properties ascribed by the Dadaists to photomontage.

Benjamin's montage – *One-Way Street* itself – thus requires a new kind of reading adequate to a new, montaged, and non-narrative form. Benjamin's text exhibits what Joseph Frank long ago called "spatial form": a form that places unusual demands on the reader. If "new aspects of his inner self" are to be opened within the reader by the process of reading, the reader must follow "the movement of his mind" as the text "calls forth distances, belvederes, clearings, prospects at each of its turns like a commander deploying soliders at a front" (*SW* I, 448). Each individual section of the text, as one element in a montage, forms, in a favorite Benjaminian metaphor, one star in a constellation: from that star, prospects and "eccentric figurativeness" open out onto other sections of the text, often at a considerable remove. The rational decipherment of such relationality is not, however, the only constructive principle operative in *One-Way Street*.

Textual erotics: Surrealism, the body, and the dream

Although Benjamin encountered a kind of "proto-surrealism" in the G-Group, a contact with ideas from a Paris Dada then in transition, his visits to Paris in the years after 1924 swept him into the maelstrom of the surrealist movement.[10] If his great essay of 1929, "Surrealism: The Last Snapshot of the European Intelligentsia" offers his most penetrating analysis of the movement, and the *Arcades Project* his most moving tribute to its creative potential, *One-Way Street* documents his first encounters with Surrealist ideas and, as was the case with constructivism and Dada, represents an attempt to bend those ideas to the creation of his own hybrid form. Just as the concreteness of the new forms and their integration into a montage aimed to penetrate behind the commodity-induced illusions of the lived world, so, too, could the dream as deployed in Surrealism offer ways to change life and transform the world, the two Surrealist watchwords derived, respectively, from Rimbaud and Marx. We thus find operative in *One-Way Street*, alongside the rational attempt to decode irrationality, a faith in the power of dream to liberate the unconscious and allow it to take its place in an integrated human psychic economy which is now characterized by fragmentation and delusion. The Surrealists called for the remaking of all existence through the unleashing of the creative energy now hidden in the unconscious. The dream thus represents a troubling or disturbing of an apparently unified and coherent reality; when troubled, the natural order may give access to what Breton calls "the marvelous," and thus to a new conception of human being. The Surrealists tended to equate the resulting decentering of the human subject with political liberation.

In "No. 113," the second section of *One-Way Street*, Benjamin recalls a dream that lays bare the "ritual by which the house of one's life was erected" (*SW* I, 445) The dream lays bare the past: here it is the familial past, the individual past, but elsewhere it is the dreamed remembrance of an ideal history of Germany. In the final pages of *One-Way Street* a theme that had been touched on occasionally suddenly becomes dominant, the theme of love and eroticism. Most obviously, love is portrayed as the most basic unit of societal bonding, the initial unit of two persons being the form upon which a society must be built. In "Betting Office," Benjamin addresses the increasing privatization of courtship, and contrasts its private, bourgeois form with feudal and proletarian wooing, which emphasizes not the private subjugation of the partner, but rather the overcoming of one's competitors as an action which inaugurates the partner's freedom. This "shift to the public sphere" (*SW* I, 485) introduces a series of thematically related meditations on birth. In "Doctor's Night Bell," a new life is the product of sexual fulfillment; in "Torso," of past travail. In both cases, Benjamin allies the most personal vision of *One-Way Street* with the most political: the vision of the birth of a new society. Human body and body politic, human coupling and the slow construction of a new nation, both are related rhythmically and with subtle suggestiveness. Although this union remains implicit through most of the text, the two discourses of erotics and politics are conjoined so powerfully in the final section, "To the Planetarium," that a retrospective light is shed on the entire collection:

> In the nights of annihilation of the last war the human frame was shaken by a feeling that resembled the bliss of the epileptic. And the revolts that followed it were the first attempt by mankind to bring the new body under its control. The power of the proletariat is the measure of its convalescence. If it is not gripped to the very marrow by the discipline of this power, no pacifist polemics will save it. Living substance conquers the frenzy of destruction only in the ecstasy of procreation. (*SW* I, 487)

The equation of human body and body politic is here made concrete; in a sense, too, this last meditation casts a retrospective shadow over Benjamin's collection as it evokes the revolts of 1918 – the attempt to find a new bodily form – and their failure: the body is convalescent. Yet this dreaming, procreative, Surrealist collective can emerge only on the basis of a new, constructivist mastery of technology and its deployment in a non-linear, montage-like form: "In technology, a *physis* is being organized through which mankind's contact with the cosmos takes a new and different form from that which it had in nations and families" (*SW* I, 487). The body politic can be constituted anew, Benjamin argues here, only if it builds itself up from the smallest basic units, two humans uniting agapaically and erotically, with new progeny who are at once the figure and the very material of the new state. As always for Walter Benjamin, that new state is imaginable only as the product of a dangerous, critical reading, the reading of new textual forms. The textual forms of the European avant-garde.

NOTES

1. On the notion of the historical avant-garde and its differentiation from high modernism, see esp. Peter Bürger, *Theory of the Avant-garde* (Minneapolis: University of Minnesota Press, 1984).
2. For a general introduction to these aspects of the culture of the Weimar Republic, see John Willett, *Art and Politics in the Weimar Republic: The New Sobriety* (New York: DaCapo Press, 1996).
3. For a facsimile of the journal that includes translations and a critical apparatus, see Michael Jennings and Detlef Mertins, eds., *G. Journal for Elementary Form Production* (New York: Monticelli Press, forthcoming).
4. It has been assumed in the Benjamin literature that the famous trip to Russia which produced the *Moscow Diary* was motivated solely by his attempt to woo Asja Lacis. As both the diary itself and especially the essays associated with it – "The Political Groupings of Russian Writers"; "On the Present Situation of Russian Film"; and "Reply to Oscar A.H. Schmitz" – attest, Benjamin was also driven by the need to experience first hand the milieu from which the ideas of Lissitsky and his fellow constructivists had emanated.

5. See, for example, the collections "Short Shadows," "Ibizan Sequence," "In the Sun," and "Thought Figures," all in Walter Benjamin, *SW* II.

6. Karl Marx, *Capital*, "The Fetishism of Commodities and the Secret Thereof," quoted from Robert C. Tucker, ed., *The Marx–Engels Reader* (New York: Norton, 1972), 215–16.

7. For a superb introduction to constructivism, see Maria Gough, *The Artist as Producer: Constructivism in Revolution, 1920–26* (Berkeley: University of California Press, forthcoming).

8. See, for example, Moholy-Nagy, "Production-Reproduction," in *Photography in the Modern Era*, ed. Christopher Phillips (New York: The Metropolitan Museum of Art, 1989), 79–82; on the "New Vision" see Michael W. Jennings, "Agriculture, Industry, and the Birth of the Photo-Essay in the Late Weimar Republic," *October* 93 (Summer 200), 36–39.

9. For a superb introduction to Berlin Dada and photomontage, see Brigid Doherty, *Montage* (Berkeley: University of California Press, forthcoming).

10. For a reliable overview of Surrealism, especially in its relationship to Dada, see Matthew Gale, *Dada and Surrealism* (London: Phaidon Press, 1997).

2

JAN MIESZKOWSKI

Art forms

Film today articulates all problems of modern form-giving...
Walter Benjamin, *Arcades*

It is a foregone conclusion for me that there is no such thing as art
history.
Walter Benjamin, Letter to F. C. Rang

Scarcely any twentieth-century author rivals Walter Benjamin's influence on
the contemporary understanding of art and the aesthetic implications of new
media. His thought has left its mark on all areas of contemporary theory and
practice, from architecture, painting, and sculpture to installation art, photography, and film. From his research as a graduate student on truth and
experience in idealist philosophy to the enormous study on the nineteenth
century, the Paris *Arcades Project*, that consumed him for the last decade
of his life, Benjamin investigated the formal, historical, and political dimensions of visual phenomena with unparalleled creativity. In a similar vein,
the academic discipline of art history preoccupied him from an early age
and, throughout the course of his life, he would continue to reflect on its
methodologies and practices.

At the same time, it would also be accurate to describe Benjamin's œuvre as
a sustained engagement with a tradition in German letters in which the poetic
word, defined in contradistinction to visual media, is the centerpiece of aesthetic experience. As Benjamin explains in the curriculum vitae he wrote in
1925, "[In my studies] I have been concerned with the meaning of the connection between the beautiful and appearance (*Schein*) in the realm of language"
(*SW* I, 422). Even with his famous theory of dialectical *images*, "the place
where one encounters them is language," not the plastic arts (*Arcades*, 462;
N2a, 3). In this regard, a cursory glance at Benjamin's collected works will
reveal that the majority of his texts explore the theory of representation in
literature. His dissertation, *The Concept of Art Criticism in German Romanticism* (1919), opens with the clarification that "in the work that follows,
the term 'art' will always be understood to indicate literature...the term
'artwork' indicates individual works of literature" (*SW* I, 118). Similarly, his
famous endorsements of the avant-garde are of poets, not cabaret artists;

when he discusses the Surrealists, he considers novelists like André Breton and Louis Aragon, rather than painters such as Hans Arp, Max Ernst, or Salvador Dalí. For Benjamin, moreover, the study of literature addresses not only the ways in which linguistic representation must be distinguished from visual or auditory media, but the possibility that all art may constitute a negation of expression as such. In the lyrics of the German poet Friedrich Hölderlin, for example, he locates that "caesura, in which, along with harmony, every expression simultaneously comes to a standstill, in order to give free reign to an expressionless power inside all artistic media" (*SW* I, 341).

Confusion about these conflicting tendencies in Benjamin's work may arise in part from our own uncertainty about the nature of aesthetics as a doctrine of the arts and the privileged place it has historically accorded to poetry. The word "aesthetics" is rarely used today without its counterpart, "politics," something for which Benjamin is partly responsible thanks to his widely cited pronouncement in "The Work of Art in the Age of its Mechanical Reproduction" (1935–36) that "the logical result of Fascism is the introduction of aesthetics into political life," whereas "communism responds by politicizing art" (*SN* IV, 269–70). The call to study aesthetics together with politics can mean more than one thing. It frequently identifies an interest in debunking an old-fashioned idea of art as autonomous of social or political reality, in which case the major task in studying "aesthetics and politics" is to situate works of art in their cultural and historical contexts. Others go further and ask whether aesthetic paradigms actually organize social and political reality, for example, the performative mechanics of power may be based on theatrical paradigms drawn from drama or on structures of narrative self-understanding derived from the epic or the novel. If in the former approach art is viewed as the product of a reality external to it, in the latter art itself proves to be a paradigm for human agency and communal existence.

In his dissertation, Benjamin argues that the Romantics were the first to consider fully the ramifications of the idea that a work of art is an entire system unto itself, i.e., it does not need to be understood with reference to a theory or moral doctrine that it represents or exemplifies, but is comprehensible as a conceptual system in its own right. This insight would above all prove to be of enormous significance for Benjamin's understanding of art as an historical entity. In December of 1923, he wrote to a friend of his conviction that connections between works of art are more like those between philosophical systems than genealogical relationships among people:

> It is a foregone conclusion for me that there is no such thing as art history. The concatenation of temporal occurrences, for example, does not imply only things that are causally significant for human life.... In terms of its essence,

[art] is ahistorical. The attempt to place the work of art in the context of historical life does not open up perspectives that lead us to its innermost cores as, for example, the same attempt undertaken with regard to peoples leads us to see them from the perspective of generations and other essential strata. The research of contemporary art history always amounts merely to a history of the subject matter or a history of form, for which the works of art provide only examples, and, as it were, models.   (C, 223–24)[1]

For Benjamin, art is of crucial importance for any political project because it forces us to evaluate what we mean when we say we understand something historically. While his letter may appear to propound a purely formal understanding of aesthetic phenomena, Benjamin's claim is not that art is simply ahistorical. "The historicity of works of art," he writes, "is the kind that can be revealed not in 'art history' but only in interpretation" (C, 224). The core of such an "interpretation" is an effort to think about art not as a product of aesthetic or social systems external to it, but as a process, an event, of representation. To treat it in any other terms is to turn the artwork into a model or instance of something it is not. "In interpretation," says Benjamin, "relationships among works of art appear that are timeless yet not without historical relevance" (C, 224). The key is that these relationships are organized less according to a hierarchy in which determination is a factor of sequence – e.g., "the past determines the present, the present determines future" – than according to a logic of form. A project that is truly responsive to these tensions – a "historical materialism" – can begin only at the point historicism ends, at the point that the authority of what is understood as prior is challenged – the authority of memory, of remembering, and above all the authority of the "eternal image of the past."[2]

What distinguishes art from other kinds of representation, then, is the way in which it facilitates precisely such a confrontation with a model of history as pure past. While Benjamin's concerns with the limits of an historicist approach to art would be articulated in the early 1920s, it was not until more than a decade later that he would fully expound the implications of his theory by considering the relationship of artworks not simply to the past, but to the future, as well: "One of the foremost tasks of art has always been the creation of a demand which could be fully satisfied only later" (SW IV, 266). Art becomes art by making demands for which there is as yet no form or paradigm with which to situate or contextualize them. These are demands that cannot yet be understood, demands that are literally not yet demands because they impose demands on the very form of what can currently be recognized as a demand. With this formulation, Benjamin means not simply that art is forward-looking rather than nostalgic, but that it is a discourse that exceeds itself, that exists in the present only as a demand for, or better, on, the future. As art always distinguishes itself from a representation of what is with its demand for something that is not yet, it is clear to Benjamin that one cannot study art simply as the expression of the social, cultural, or political reality of its time. Art "is" never art in the present, but always art that cannot yet be; it is a demand for what in our time remains impossible.

If art is always an art that lies ahead of existing artworks, in advance of what art is or can be, then the very notion of a contemporary art, an art of the "now," is called into question. At the same time, Benjamin insists in a number of texts that the project of historical materialism must understand the contemporaneity of its objects before it can engage fully with their history. It is precisely this confounding task of confronting the present of something that by definition has no present that Benjamin undertakes in "The Work of Art in the Age of its Technological Reproducibility." Written in 1935, this essay necessarily confronts the contemporaneity of European historical experience as the experience of fascism:

> The concepts which are introduced into the theory of art in what follows differ from the more familiar terms in that they are completely useless for the purposes of fascism. They are, on the other hand, useful for the formulation of revolutionary demands in the politics of art. (*SW* IV, 252)[3]

Both here and at the close of the piece, Benjamin appears resolute in his conclusion that technological change serves to facilitate the politicization of art rather than the "introduction of aesthetics into political life." At the same time, he stops short of conferring a purely positive teleology on the changes taking place in aesthetic production, and, when he stresses that the concepts which currently serve fascism ("creativity, genius, eternal value and mystery") are "at present almost *uncontrollable*," he seems to be hinting that the prospect for their utter dissolution is a hope, but not a guarantee (*SW* IV, 252; emphasis added). The crucial question, then, is whether there is something about the relationship between art and technology that is inherently resistant to a destructive politics, or whether the opposite is, in fact, the case, i.e., whether the crucial *historical* insight into the twentieth century is that the relationship between art and technology is essentially unstable.

In terms of the purely aesthetic implications of new media, the conclusion would seem to be unambiguously favorable. "The Work of Art" is responsible for much of Benjamin's popularity among scholars of photography and film, as he vigorously rejects what he calls, in his "Little History of Photography" (1931), "the philistine notion of 'art' in all its overweening obtuseness, a stranger to all technical considerations, which feels that its end is nigh with the alarming appearance of new technology" (*SW* II, 508). The question remains, however, precisely how the relationship between art and politics is to be understand. Benjamin describes the "Work of Art" essay to a mutual friend, the philosopher and social theorist Max Horkheimer, in the following terms: "These reflections attempt to give the questions raised by art theory a truly contemporary form; and indeed from the inside, avoiding any *unmediated* reference to politics" (*C*, 509). At the heart of this "unmediated reference" will be Benjamin's account of a crucial figure of mediation: the aura. The "contemporary" form of art theory is defined by the idea that the aura of artworks "withers (*verkümmert*) in the age of technological reproducibility" (*SW* IV, 254). Changes in technologies of reproduction have accentuated the reproducibility of artworks to such a degree that their reproductions can become truly independent of their model and enter "into situations which would be out of reach for the original itself" (*SW* IV, 254). Benjamin partly characterizes this shift in terms of the ways in which reproductions of artworks today "meet the beholder or listener in his own particular situation," thereby reactivating the experience of the artwork in previously unrealized ways (*SW* IV, 254). He also describes changes in the way the viewer understands his encounter with the representational mechanics of the medium, for instance, in the case of film, whose audience, he argues, identifies with the camera rather than with the actors as one might in the theater. At the same time, Benjamin readily allows that "in principle a work of art has always been reproducible" (*SW* IV, 252). His historical point is not merely that people once saw only the unique canvas of the Mona Lisa in the Louvre, whereas today they encounter photos of it everywhere. Technical reproduction has become an artistic process in its own right, hence, "the work of art reproduced becomes the work of art designed *for* reproducibility" (*SW* IV, 256 – emphasis added). The challenge in understanding the contemporary production of art is thus how to move from a paradigm of individual creativity to one not simply of reproduction, but of reproducibility: a model in which the very possibility of producing something artistic depends on its being produced "as" an exemplar of reproducibility.

The political thrust of Benjamin's argument thus centers on the question of whether the change in the aura in the age of technological reproducibility is a change in what art is or in what we think about it; or, in other words, is the object of aesthetic inquiry something inherent to the material work or the ideologies of its audience? Benjamin attempts to explain the aura in terms of an artwork's "authenticity," the "here" and "now" of the work, its singular existence (*SW* IV, 253). The viewer of the artwork does not, however, bask in the unmediated revelation of its presence. Rather Benjamin describes an encounter with the authority that the work's presence acquires from its position in the highly ritualized network that organizes models of tradition and cultural heritage – systems, even cults, of beauty that present us with works of the past as treasures of civilization. In these terms, the experience of the authenticity of the work of art is as much a factor of how the presence of the work is framed or situated as it is an immediate experience of that presence; it is in essence a social experience, and for this reason is always open to a political cooption over which the individual viewer may have little control.

As a way of clarifying this point, Benjamin insists that authenticity is dependent on everything in the artwork that is transmissible, which includes its "material duration" and its function as "a testimony or witness to history (*geschichtliche Zeugenschaft*)" (*SW* IV, 254). Reproducibility challenges the authority of this material duration, literally freeing the work from its status as a carrier of something prior; it could even be argued that it frees the experience of art from its basis in the material existence of the artwork. But precisely what are the criteria of transmissibility, and how can one characterize the relationship between "material duration" and historical witnessing that clarifies them? Benjamin writes: "The concept of aura which was proposed above with reference to historical objects may usefully be illustrated with reference to the aura of natural ones. We define the aura of the latter as the unique appearance (*Erscheinung*) of a distance, however close it may be" (*SW* IV, 255). This definition, he adds in a footnote, "represents nothing but the formulation of the cult value of the work of art in categories of space and time perception" (*SW* IV, 272n11).[4]

It is by no means clear why it should be obvious that cult value can be expressed in the categories of space and time.[5] As the phenomenon of irreducible distance, the aura is not so much a construction of the artwork's presence, of what is here and now, as a name for its resistance to being here and now, a resistance to whatever outline or model would fix the artwork's presence at anything but a definite remove. The very notion of contemporary art vanquishing the aura – of putting it, if you like, at a distance – is thereby confounded, for the aura, as the authority of the artwork's presence as transmissibility, is nothing if not the keeping-at-arm's-length of the artwork, "however close it may be." The authority of "here" and "now" is realized only when "here" and "now" are "then" and "there." Defined as unapproachability incarnate, the aura confirms that the authentic art object has always-already taken leave of its viewer, always-already being on its way (*SW* IV, 272n11). However we understand reproducibility to lead to the withering of the aura, it is not because it introduces a difference or distance that was lacking in the original, since distance is precisely what is cultivated by the rituals of auratic art, mediacy rather than immediacy.[6]

To have a perspective on the contemporaneity of art is thus to reflect on objects whose authority as present is at present always at a remove. As a consequence, some critics have argued that the aura emerges precisely in and through resistance to it, or perhaps, that it appears only in its withering, only in the epoch in which the distance that it organizes is in retreat.[7] Samuel Weber, for example, has proposed that Benjamin's underlying concern is that the media responsible for the aura's demise, in a particular film, are potentially the site of its inevitable, even vigorous, reemergence.[8] The key to Benjamin's account of the relationship between art and politics is that the change in the aura heralds not simply a transformation in our ideas about art or in the nature of the works being produced, but "changes in the medium of contemporary perception" (*SW* IV, 255). Superficially, this does not appear to be a provocative point. Arguing that the contemporary mode of reception is one of "distraction" (*Zerstreuung*), Benjamin writes: "The film makes the cult value recede in the background not only by putting the public in the position of the critic, but also by the fact that at the movies this position requires no attention. The public is an examiner, but an absent-minded one" (*SW* IV, 255). From this perspective, we might conclude that his ultimate point is merely that today's technology gives individuals art that requires less concentration and hence makes them less prone to notice systems of authenticity, even when they are still there. The more fundamental change, however, is in the nature of the "audience" itself, which is no longer the individual but the mass: "The mass is a matrix from which all traditional behavior toward works of art issues today in a new form" (*SW* IV, 267). There is an extraordinarily close parallel in "The Work of Art" essay between the mass as viewer and the massive or mass-like quality of reproductions that are said to overwhelm the singular original.[9] In this respect, it is less a question of choosing between a subjective and an objective account of the aura than of seeing how both viewer and what is viewed exist within a broader massification of the world. It is within this framework that the political character of art must be evaluated.

Some of Benjamin's accounts of this mass-mediation can sound somewhat gnomic, as when he writes, "Mechanical reproduction of art changes the reaction of the masses toward art. The reactionary attitude toward a Picasso painting changes into the progressive reaction toward a Chaplin movie" (*SW* IV, 264). It is on the basis of such claims that Benjamin has continued to be influential for left-wing media scholars who strive to reject the unambiguous valorization of high art and validate the political and social worth of mass culture. Yet, why should the mass "reaction" toward Chaplin be progressive rather than reactionary, or worse? As Theodor Adorno – Benjamin's colleague and sometime benefactor – rather bluntly puts it, Benjamin could

be accused of placing "blind trust in the spontaneous powers of the proletariat within the historical process," for the laughter of a cinema audience
at the funny tramp with his hat and cane may simply be bourgeois sadism
(*CA/B*, 130). Moreover, Adorno worries that Benjamin's argument goes too
far in making all art potentially counter-revolutionary, without acknowledging that some works resist collapse into taboo or fetish and continue to
exhibit "the sign of freedom" (*CA/B*, 129).

However we choose to evaluate the psychological verisimilitude of these
claims about audience response, it is arguable that they only touch the surface
of Benjamin's real interest in mass movements. A succinct expression of his
position can be found in the quote from Marx and Engels that he provides
as an epigraph to a section of a 1939 essay on Paris: "It is easy to understand
that every mass-type 'interest' which asserts itself historically goes far beyond
its real limits in the 'idea' or 'imagination,' when it first comes on the scene"
(*Arcades*, 16). For Benjamin, the aims of what is massive are never fully
governed by or identical with a form, model, or plan that defines or prescribes
them. The mass becomes historical not by actualizing an idea of the mass, but
by exceeding, even negating, such an idea. The mass is reproducibility that
has fled its original. It is thoroughly "massive" – hence, always potentially
"uncontrollable" – even with respect to itself.

Nevertheless, Adorno's objection retains some urgency: does Benjamin's
theory of art in the age of technological reproducibility reduce art to a craft
or mechanical technique? Should one conclude that his faith in the trans-
figuring power of reproducibility occludes his faith in art, or even that it
opens the door to the fascist nightmares he fears? Benjamin's theory of artistic transformation can only be understood if we grasp the way in which
form – frequently used as a catch-all term for everything atemporal and
transhistorical – becomes for him a genuinely historical paradigm. To begin,
we must note that Benjamin's approach to art as an act or a system rather
than an object is entirely in line with the doctrines of Kantian aesthetics, in
which art is the basic model for the coordination of intellectual and material labor. Today, of course, the word "aesthetics" can mean many different
things. Derived from the Greek *aistheta* (perceptions), the term classically
refers to a problem central to Western philosophy since its inception: what
is the relationship between sensation and thinking, between the sensible and
the supersensible? In its modern form, the word first appears in Alexander
Baumgarten's *Aesthetica* of 1750, where the science of sensuous knowledge
whose aim is beauty, "aesthetics," is distinguished from the science of rational knowledge whose aim is truth. In the nineteenth century, a focus on
taste as a system of values threatens to displace the discussion of perception
per se, and art gradually replaces nature as the central paradigm of beauty.

Aesthetics thus comes increasingly to be understood as a discourse of subjective preferences rather than the study of how the act of judgment articulates the mental with the material realm of human existence. This is why to speak of someone's "aesthetic" is to refer to their likes and dislikes in fashion or entertainment, not their assumptions about how the mind makes sense of perceptions.

For Benjamin, the seminal aesthetic treatise in German letters is Immanuel Kant's *Critique of Judgment* (1791). In Kant, the problem of how we judge an object to be beautiful is central to understanding how the human being as an entity that cognizes sensory data can have anything to do with a human being who exercises the transcendental authority of a metaphysical category called a "will." In defining art as "production through freedom," Kant rejects the prescriptive tenets of eighteenth-century poetics with its rules for the composition of fine verse, instead basing the creation of the beautiful on the imaginative power of singular genius.[10] In these terms, art is the act whereby the crafting of a sensible medium (paint, canvas, stone) is linked with the spontaneous designs of a free mind. For Kant's successors G. W. F. Hegel and Friedrich Schelling, art is characterized as nothing less than the grounds of self-knowledge as such, the event whereby the self can encounter its own intelligible design or intuit itself as an auto-productive entity. At the same time, one of the chief tenets of Kantian doctrine is the notion that the singular mysteries of artistic genius resist thorough explanation. There may be no way to explain how the artist "does" art, which therefore remains a prime example of doing something productive without knowing precisely how one is doing it, even if what one is doing is producing oneself. This inherent check on the study of art – this sense that art may be the construction of self-knowledge although this knowledge is not possessed by the self – haunts the philosophy of aesthetics and continues to distinguish art from discourses of knowledge or "know-how," from science or craft.

If the aesthetic is the category that is to coordinate the freedom of the mind with the sensible constraints of material existence, a vision famously captured by Kant's claim that beauty is the symbol of the morally good, then it is only a small step to the development of a full-blown aesthetic model of society. Such a project is undertaken in Friedrich Schiller's *Letters on the Aesthetic Education of Man* (1795), where the coordination of beauty and morality is envisioned as the basis for a pedagogy that teaches sound community organization. Today, the implicit political orientation of Schiller's work, particularly his conception of art as the popularization of philosophy, is frequently condemned as reactionary. Yet, on an even more fundamental level, his attempt to establish a smooth transition between philosophical and political reality via an aesthetic model in which the arts manifest themselves to the senses is hampered by the difficulty of accounting for the nature of poetry. If painting, sculpture, and music are distinguished from one another by their different material media, then what is the material medium of the word? The question is all the more pressing since Kant, Schelling, and Hegel leave no doubt that poetry is the art of art; it and it alone "sets the imagination free," as a result of which the question seems to be less how poetry differs from the other arts than how all art can be shown to be essentially poetic.

In his dissertation on the German Romantic theory of art, Benjamin emphasizes that the "immanent structure" of the work of art as it is understood by Friedrich Schlegel or Friedrich von Hardenberg (Novalis) is a structure of reflection rather than of self-consciousness (*SW* I, 155). In these terms, reflection is not, as we might think, a psychological act of introspection or a communal process whereby a society grasps its own identity through an examination of its cultural products. Benjamin writes:

> A distinction between the Kantian concept of judgment and the Romantic concept of reflection can be indicated in this context without difficulty: reflection is not, as judgment is, a subjectively reflecting process; rather, it lies enclosed in the presentational form of the work and unfolds itself in criticism, in order finally to reach fulfillment in the lawful continuum of forms.
>
> (*Concept of Criticism, SW* I, 165)

The precise nature of this "presentational form" is not, Benjamin insists, "a rule for judging the beauty of art" or a parameter or precondition for art "being pleasing" (*Concept of Criticism, SW* I, 158). Analogies with physical objects fail, for this form is not a mold, framework, or outline, but the act whereby the artwork reflects on itself and thereby divides against itself, into subject and object. In reflection, the work of art gives itself a form rather than following some externally determined rule or pattern prescribed for it. At the same time, Benjamin insists it is also crucial for the Romantics to consider the "limitedness of any finite reflection" (*Concept of Criticism, SW* I, 156). Through reflection, the artwork becomes art, but as such it necessarily acknowledges that it is "merely" a work within the overall unity of Art itself. To "reach fulfillment in the lawful continuum of forms" is to realize the "presentational form of the work" as the establishment and dissolution of the very authority of the work's form.

In Friedrich Schlegel's Romantic poetics, poetry is characterized as an unending process in which language examines the limits of genre, poetry, and indeed of language itself. Such a discourse is, in Schlegel's famous dictum, "forever becoming and never perfected." For Benjamin, the crucial lesson of Schlegel's poetry – language that ceaselessly evaluates its own status as language – concerns the artwork's peculiar relation to its own necessity:

> [E]very single reflection in this medium can be only an isolated and fortuitous
> one, the unity of the work vis-à-vis the unity of art can be only a relative unity;
> the work remains burdened with a moment of contingency. It is precisely the
> function of form to admit this particular contingency as in principle neces-
> sary or unavoidable, to acknowledge it through the rigorous self-limitation of
> reflection. (SW I, 156)

Form is both the act whereby the work of art affirms its own autonomy, its
independence from any external standard or rule that would govern it, and
the act whereby it acknowledges the inevitable fact that any given form is
contingent. Benjamin thus concludes that the lesson of the Romantic artwork
is that "the unconditioned arbitrary is necessary" (SW I, 157). As he understands it, form is the possibility of reflection, hence the possibility of art, but
it is also the confirmation that the form of any given artwork is arbitrary.
Insofar as every form confirms its own contingency, it confirms its own dissolution, which is to say that every form is also the form of what it could also
be; it is a form only as the form of the possibility that it could be something
else. Only when reflection has reached the point that it can admit its own
contingency does it become art, which is to say that form is the triumph and
ruin of the artwork, a work for which being is always being-as-other, and
becoming is simultaneously becoming-absolute and becoming-contingent.

In the context of Benjamin's later essays, these ruminations may seem
unnecessarily abstract. Yet this idea of art as a form of presentation that is
always also a presentation of what might be "otherwise" lies at the heart of
one of Benjamin's major preoccupations: the allegorical nature of language.
Allegory – etymologically, "speaking otherwise than one seems to speak" –
names the fact that language can signify two things at once, saying one
thing and yet meaning something else. By nature, allegories are reflexive,
that is, they call attention to the ways in which their meanings are produced
as much as to what those meanings may be. Where questions of style and
diction are concerned, allegory has traditionally been understood as one
representational mode among others and, in the late eighteenth and early
nineteenth centuries, it was often disparaged as too mechanical, capable of
only an abstract depiction of its original meaning.

It is precisely this hierarchy of forms that concerns Benjamin in the final
section of *The Origin of the German Tragic Drama* (1924–25), his study
of the German baroque *Trauerspiel* (mourning play). Benjamin deplores the
tyranny of the symbol as the privileged model for art theory in the nineteenth century. At that time, symbolic representation was championed for
the supposed continuity it provided between a symbol and the totality it

"symbolizes," most commonly as the idea of a unity between the perception and thought (or imagination) of beauty.[11] In more prosaic terms, the symbol suggests that one can make a smooth transition from a sensible representation to a supersensible idea, i.e., that there is a substantive connection between form and content. Benjamin's objection is that the very insistence on the indivisibility of form from content "fails to do justice to content in formal analysis" and to "form in the aesthetics of content" (SW I, 160). He therefore proposes a more dynamic model in which allegory and symbol are understood not as different modes from which a writer may choose depending on his or her stylistic preferences, but as features of language that are inevitably co-present in any discourse. In this sense, allegory names not a code to be deciphered – for example, a set of emblems or personified figures, the meanings of which one can look up in a book – but a disjunction potentially inherent to all artistic media between the mode and meaning of an expression. With the symbol, image should coincide with substance; allegory, by comparison, calls attention not, as is often thought, to the ways in which language fails to signify, but to the strange co-presence of distinct semantic levels of a text, levels whose relationship to one another is not easily clarified with an aesthetic or semiotic model.

For Benjamin, one of the central difficulties in studying allegory is the fact that any analysis of a given example of an allegorical discourse will immediately revert to a predictable set of general complications about the nature of language. In this respect, he sees allegory as being like a moral discourse because it treats specificity as a function of universals rather than particulars, a tension he famously captures with the claim: "Allegories are, in the realm of thoughts, what ruins are in the realm of things" (Origin, 178). Allegory "ruins" thought not because it interrupts syntheses of the understanding, but because it seems to render the analysis of individual examples irrelevant: whatever approach you take, the same general account of representation obtains. What allegory presents, then, is not a hidden meaning, but an overtly negative relationship between content and mode of expression. At the same time, it is representational. As Benjamin puts it, allegory "holds fast to ruins; it offers the image of petrified unrest."[12] Allegory represents not the loss of sense or meaning, but the inability of a medium to account for the nature of its own presentation. Throughout Benjamin's œuvre, we find a preoccupation with models of experience – shock, dream, melancholy – for which there is an overt disjunction between the claim to the immediacy of representation – *this* image, *this* vision, etc. – and the claim to specify the identity of what is confronted. In each case, the relevant representational field – sight, consciousness, memory – threatens to collapse. Even mimesis, ostensibly the privileged trope of resemblance, is revealed to be predicated on disruptions of the dialectic of similarity and difference, failing to provide us with an identity we could ever hope to "see." In the final analysis, likeness proves to be a coordination of what is unlike or dissimilar.[13]

Benjamin's exploration of these problems in the philosophy of aesthetics culminates in a thoroughgoing challenge to the priority of expression. In his text on Goethe's novel *The Elective Affinities* (1919–22), he interrogates a concept that has been central to the aesthetics of beauty since Kant and Hegel: *Schein* (appearance, semblance, shine). Attempting to explain the appearance of beauty in this text in which the manifestations of different characters form and dissolve in a murky dynamic, Benjamin begins with the relatively conventional claim that "everything essentially beautiful is always and in its essence bound up, though in infinitely different degrees, with *Schein*" ("Elective Affinities," *SW* I, 350). He immediately qualifies this definition, however, insisting that *Schein* "does not comprise the essence of beauty. Rather, the latter points down more deeply to what in the work of art in contrast to the semblance may be characterized as the expressionless (*das Ausdruckslose*)" ("Elective Affinities," *SW* I, 350). For Benjamin, beauty is not the animation or enlivening of the work of art, the spirit or pneuma that brings paint or stone to life. On the contrary, beauty is life in arrest: "The life undulating in [the artwork] must appear petrified and as if spellbound in a single moment"; otherwise, the work will lapse into mere *Schein* or unstructured chaos ("Elective Affinities," *SW* I, 340). Art is beautiful in the suspension of the very emergence-into-view – in German, the *Er-scheinung* – that ostensibly constitutes its manifestation. The beautiful is not the shining-forth of truth or reality, but the disruption of the revelatory unveiling of an object – an object that remains beautiful, says Benjamin, only as long as it remains veiled. In these terms, the work of art is not a symbolic representation of a world; it is not one moment that smoothly modulates into a unified whole. The artwork is "complete" only in the very negation of expression that is its destruction: "Only the expressionless completes the work, by shattering it into a thing of shards, into a fragment of the true world, into the torso of a symbol" (*SW* I, 340). Such a beauty is neither the perceptible manifestation of truth (Neoplatonism), the symbol of the morally good (Kant), nor the sensible appearance of the idea (Hegel). It is something much closer to what idealist thinkers would term the sublime:

> The expressionless is the critical violence which, while unable to separate semblance from essence in art, prevents them from mingling. It possesses this violence as a moral dictum. In the expressionless, the sublime violence of the true appears as that which determines the language of the real world according to the laws of the moral world. (*SW* I, 340)

Criticism is not something brought to bear on the artwork by an external judge; it is a violence internal to the artwork that constitutes it as an event with form. Criticism thereby prevents the simple collapse of essence into appearance (or vice versa) that would destroy either the work's capacity to give itself form or its capacity to acknowledge its own contingency.

In late eighteenth-century German letters, the violence of the sublime, characterized in Kant as the imagination sacrificing itself for the sake of reason, is commonly discussed as the power of divine speech in the Hebrew Bible. In this vein, Hegel's *Aesthetics* explicitly identifies the impossibility of fashioning an image of the divine (and the prohibition attendant on it) as the violence of the word, the word as pure iconoclasm.[14] The divine word is the sublime event of beauty because its articulation cannot be understood as an image, a perception, or a vision of the imagination, which is to say that the utterance of the divine word can never be grasped as something that could manifest itself in the order of *Schein*. As iconoclasm, the word is the negation of representation as the expression of something that could be seen or heard or felt; it is the assertion of a verbal authority that gains a moral voice in rejecting any identification of the medium and the message.

In identifying the presence of this iconoclastic violence, this expressionless force, as a crucial moment in *all* art forms, Benjamin makes perhaps his most far-reaching contribution to the discourse of aesthetics. From this perspective, we can now consider his final attempt to coordinate the political and historical dimensions of artistic events, the *Arcades Project*. In the last version of "Paris, Capital of the Nineteenth Century," the essay that prefaces the English edition of the volume, Benjamin describes the goal of his enterprise:

> Our investigation proposes to show how, as a consequence of this reifying representation of civilization [the history of civilization, the inventory of all life forms & creations], the new forms of behavior and the new economically and technologically based creations that we owe to the nineteenth century enter the universe of a phantasmagoria. These creations undergo this "illumination" not only in a theoretical manner, by an ideological transposition, but also in the immediacy of their perceptible presence. They are manifest as phantasmagorias. Thus appear the arcades – (*Arcades*, 20)

Today, the *Arcades Project* is regarded with great enthusiasm as an example of what a radical interdisciplinary approach to culture might be. Yet, it could be argued that Benjamin's analyses strive to situate themselves between rather than across traditional fields of study. In this respect, the "universe of a phantasmagoria" is not simply a collection of visions or images – true or false, natural or artificial – but an entire system of relationships poised uneasily on the borders between public and private space, past and future, dream and waking. As with the problem of beauty in Goethe, the goal is not to "unveil" these phenomena to expose their underlying mechanism or design, but rather to understand precisely how they "linger on the threshold" between the formation and destruction of expression (*Arcades*, 13). Even more than in the earlier texts we have considered, Benjamin is explicit that any particular aesthetic phenomenon – be it painting, sculpture, photography, or film – emerges at and as the collision of representational and material orders. Art is not, as Hegel might have described it, the excess of intelligible sense over physical substrate, but the clash of the one register with the other, their resistance to mutual coordination.

At first glance, this claim may appear extreme. Benjamin's individual efforts to coordinate the relationships described above between ideologies and the "immediacy of their perceptible presence" seem to follow "The Work of Art" essay in identifying technological shifts in material processes as the motor of artistic change:

> It is worth considering – and it appears that the answer to this question would be in the negative – whether at an earlier period technical necessities in architecture (but also in the other arts) determined the forms, the style, as thoroughly as they do today, when such technological derivation seems actually to become the signature of everything now produced. With iron as a material, this is already clearly the case, and perhaps for the first time. (*Arcades* 157; F3a 5)

The arcades themselves exist only in virtue of the appearance of iron and innovations in the production of glass. Benjamin's point is not, however, simply that material conditions dictate aesthetic styles. He also stresses that the emergence of new media is a genuine attack on the concept of art, a point he makes repeatedly in the case of photography, which he describes as a challenge first to painting, then to art as such. Benjamin also allows that new processes and materials allow classical art forms to unsettle their own generic boundaries: "Just as architecture, with the first appearance of iron construction, begins to outgrow art, so does painting, in its turn, with the first appearance of the panoramas" (*Arcades*, 5). Popular until the mid-nineteenth century, panoramas were precursors of photography, continuous narrative scenes or landscapes painted to conform to a flat or curved background that surrounded or were unrolled before the viewer (*Arcades*, 5). Like iron, they cannot simply be understood as a new material or process that dictates a new form of expression, nor as a mere advance in craft or engineering. The panoramas transform the relationship between art and technology – between creation and production, artists and engineers – because they are a new form of transformation: "Forerunners of the moving picture [they] mark an upheaval in the relation of art to technology," but they "are at the same time an expression of a new attitude toward life" (*Arcades*, 6). Newly emergent technical practices are thus to be grasped as disruptions rather than as the simple coordination of human expression and technological expertise. These practices threaten to outgrow the bourgeois aesthetic by making it impossible to understand art as a set of given forms or processes, yet these new forms of construction are never fully emancipated from this aesthetic. They "stop halfway," never fully heralding the emergence of a new social or political order (*Arcades*, 898).

In this regard, Benjamin's discussion of *Jugendstil* is exemplary. This turn-of-the-century design movement was known primarily for its floral patterns rooted in Art Nouveau Japanese art. "According to its own ideology," claims Benjamin, "the *Jugendstil* movement seems to bring with it the consummation of the interior. The transfiguration of the solitary individual appears to be its goal. Individualism is its theory" (*Arcades*, 9). Upon closer examination, however, it proves to hide a more fundamental conflict: "But the real meaning of *Jugendstil* is not expressed in this ideology. It represents the last attempted sortie of an art besieged in its ivory tower by technology. This attempt mobilizes all the reserves of inwardness" (*Arcades*, 9). The ideology of individual interiority is only a tool in the reactionary struggle against the onslaught of technology, which *Jugendstil* strives to "sterilize" by "ornamentalizing it," severing "technologically constituted forms from their functional contexts" and turning them into "natural constants" (*Arcades*, 557–58; s8a, 1 and s8a, 7). Benjamin will also locate this tendency in a movement whose fascist essence is far more obvious: futurism. In these terms, the fascist impulse in art always involves the effort to separate the possibility of form from technology, to determine form not as something "natural," but as the hyper-technical, a super-technology that could control its own formation and dissolution while remaining formless. Still, Benjamin hesitates to condemn *Jugendstil* entirely, adding that it "represents an advance, insofar as the bourgeoisie gains access to the technological bases of its control over nature; a regression, insofar as it loses the power of looking the everyday in the face" (*Arcades*, 559; s9a, 4). The struggle against technology is always a struggle in the grasp of technology, never a struggle in spite of it; technology proves intractable not because everything that was allegedly natural is revealed to be artificial, but because technology names the mode of form-giving that is peculiar to art in the age of technological reproducibility as a *massive* mode, that is, a mode of experience not entirely within our control.

For Benjamin, technology is art as the fruition of technique; it is also where art founders, where art exceeds itself or loses itself, unpredictably, as the art of the future or as the future of something other than art. For this reason, technology is never to be confused with mechanicity:

> The effort to assimilate [the superabundance of technical processes and new materials that had suddenly become available] more thoroughly led to mistakes and failures. On the other hand, these vain attempts are the most authentic proof that technological production, at the beginning, was in the grip of dreams. (*Arcades*, 152; F1a, 2)

Dreams constitute a break, an intervention, in the authority of consciousness as the purveyor of human experience. They also mark an interruption of authority itself – hence, in the case of art, an interruption of authenticity. "In the grip of dreams" means that technology is never the technology of technology; it is never fully self-determining, nor simply reducible to material or process. Technology is the excess of concept over material. It appears – dream-like – because the two will never be perfectly coordinated. It is in this sense that Benjamin proposes that dreams are what cannot be *"thought away,"* i.e., they are located where thought as the mechanics of ratio confronts the possibility of another form of thought that it will never think (*Arcades*, 391 K1a, 6).

Ultimately, the study of the Paris of the nineteenth century is "the critique not of its mechanism and cult of machinery but of its narcotic historicism" (*Arcades*, 391; K1a, 6). This historicism is not an approach to art from without, but a movement from within that seeks to reduce the power of formation and deformation to a canon of accepted molds and practices. The force that counters this movement – what in the Goethe study was called "the expressionless" – emerges in the *Arcades Project* as the central figure of its principal poet: the Baudelairean motif of death. Under the petrifying gaze of the allegorist, death "merges," says Benjamin, "with the image of Paris," but death itself never becomes an image, nor an event of creation or destruction (*Arcades*, 895). Like the expressionless that "shatters" the artwork into shards, death suspends the revelatory emergence of any icon of presence or absence, gain or loss. Death is art as pure iconoclasm, art that holds us spellbound between essence and appearance, between matter and form. Through this counter-force, art comes into its own by proving itself to be the destruction of expression. In the terms of "The Work of Art" essay, the relation between art and technology can be clarified by describing reproducibility as the rendering contingent of production itself. Art is "politicized" when it challenges the authority of what already exists to serve as a standard for what has a right to be. The error Benjamin calls "fascism" is thus the confusion of reproducibility with the power to confirm that the absolute is contingent and the contingent absolute. This latter power is what we call "art."

NOTES

1. Already in a letter to his friend Ernst Schoen at the end of 1917, Benjamin writes of "the repellent phenomenon that, nowadays, inadequate attempts at a theoretical understanding of modern painting immediately degenerate into contrastive and progressive theories in regard to earlier great art" (*C*, 114).
2. Benjamin argues this point most famously in his "On the Concept of History" of 1940 (*SW* IV, 389–400).
3. I will be quoting from the third version of the text (1939), which was the source for the first publication of the essay in German in 1955. An earlier version of the essay was published in a shortened form in French in 1936. On the history of the manuscript, see the editor's notes in Benjamin's *Selected Writings*, III, 122; IV, 270.
4. In his "Little History of Photography," Benjamin writes something similar: "What is aura, actually? A strange weave of space and time: the unique appearance or semblance of distance, no matter how close it may be" (*SW* II, 518).
5. It has been argued that this is an indication of the fundamentally Kantian conception of experience underlying the demonstration. See Rodolphe Gasché, "Objective Diversions: On Some Kantian Themes in Benjamin's 'The Work of Art in the Age of Mechanical Reproduction,'" in *Walter Benjamin's Philosophy: Destruction and Experience*, eds. Andrew Benjamin and Peter Osborne (New York: Routledge, 1994), 183–204.
6. The aura would appear first and foremost to be a structure of mediation, so it is not surprising that on this particular score Adorno praises Benjamin for disparaging the aura's mystifying authority. It is notable, however, that in making this point Adorno explicitly maintains that the aura is analogous to what Benjamin calls the symbol in *The Origin of the German Tragic Drama*. Against Adorno's gloss, it is possible to argue that the aura is precisely not a pretension to the seamless coordination of image and content, of substance and mode. See *CA/B*, 128.
7. On these difficulties, see David S. Ferris, "Introduction: Aura, Resistance, and the Event of History," in *Walter Benjamin: Theoretical Questions*, ed. David S. Ferris (Stanford University Press, 1996), 1–26; Eva Geulen, "Zeit zur Darstellung. Walter Benjamin's *Das Kunstwerk im Zeitalter seiner technischen Reproduzierbarkeit*," *Modern Language Notes*, 107:3 (1992), 580–605.
8. See Samuel Weber, *Mass Mediaurus: Form, Technics, Media* (Stanford University Press, 1996), esp. 76–107.
9. To my knowledge, this point has most clearly been made by Weber (*Mass Mediaurus*, 84).
10. Immanuel Kant, *Critique of Judgment*, trans. Werner S. Pluhar (Indianapolis: Hackett, 1987), 170.
11. The most famous contemporary treatment of this problem is Paul de Man's "The Rhetoric of Temporality," *Blindness and Insight* (Minneapolis: University of Minnesota Press, 1983) 187–228.

12. "Central Park," trans. Lloyd Spencer, *New German Critique* 34 (Winter 1985), 38.
13. See "Doctrine of the Similar" and "On the Mimetic Faculty" (*SW* II, 694–98, 720–22).
14. On Hegel's sublime, see Paul de Man, "Hegel on the Sublime," *The Aesthetic Ideology*, ed. Andrzej Warminski (Minneapolis: University of Minnesota Press, 1996), 105–18.

3

BEATRICE HANSSEN

Language and mimesis in Walter Benjamin's work

Language is the "alpha" and "omega" of Benjamin's thought, forming an elaborate, ornate mosaic that encompasses all of his writings, from the early essay "On Language as Such and on the Language of Man" (1916) to the materialist work of the mid and late thirties. Even the image-oriented, iconographic *Arcades Project*, dedicated to the exegesis of dialectical images, was to find its epistemological justification in the statement that the historian eminently chanced upon such images in language. Laboring untiringly on a comprehensive philosophy of language, in which the whole proved larger than its composite parts, Benjamin wove comments on language into almost every single essay, faithful to his early belief that it constituted the "arche," or origin, of all intellectual expression.

Like the Early Romantics, who used fragments and "mystical terminology," or Nietzsche, who wrote aphorisms as a way of developing a new, seemingly antisystematic system, Benjamin produced reflections on language that appeared to defy conventional codes of systematization. Averse to the overly abstract discourse of philosophy, he was to become one of modernity's preeminent essayists, critics, and philosophical storytellers, using a language replete with poetic and mystical images, rhapsodic figures of speech, laconic *aperçus*, literary parables, and historical allegories – a storyteller, who, toward the end of his life, hoped to resort to the method of literary montage, "the art of citing without quotation marks" (*Arcades*, 458), as a way of calling authentic historical and political experience (*Arcades*, 473) by its name. But, for all the methodological and ideological approaches Benjamin espoused over the years, his writings on language as a whole displayed a remarkable unity; they all enacted – performed – an unwavering critique of rationalistic, instrumentalist, or aestheticizing conceptions of language and rhetoric *in* the medium of language. Whether he embraced a language mysticism informed by the kabbalah and Hamann, admired Mallarmé's *poésie pure* as the illumination of language's magical side (in his early years, at least), or supported Brecht's materialist conception of a language of gestures,

Benjamin did not cease questioning the reduction of language to a handy tool, to the instrumentality of logic and discursivity, or to the technical view of linguistics.[1]

Benjamin's earliest work confidently labeled semiotic theories (including classicist theories of the sign) as bourgeois constructs that turned language into an external, referential vehicle or means for the mediation of values and (truth) contents. Early on, the stories of the Fall and Babel emerged as Benjamin's favorite parables to catch the fated dialectic of the modern condition in language. Challenging modernity as a fallen culture promoting linguistic dispersion, he deplored its departure from the origin of pure language, the creative word, and the name, as it idolized the logical proposition and the secular "magic of judging." Inspired by Kierkegaard's critique of modernity, he attacked the tyranny of its universal history of progress no less than the bourgeois information age and its sensationalist journalism, which degraded language's authentic communicative power to a difference-obliterating, idle chatter, or prattle ("On Language," *SW* I, 71; *Origin*, 233). Indeed, while Benjamin's comments on language fall into four broad categories – metaphysical, mystical, epistemological, and materialist – what distinguishes all of his language work is that, from its inception, it was guided by a large-scale theory about the changed structure of experience (*Erfahrung*)[2] and of perception. Pursuing this theory, he meant to release a more authentic existentialist way of being in the world. To be sure, in the early thirties, Benjamin hailed a destructive, antihumanist avant-gardism or "positive (artistic) barbarism" (as opposed to political barbarism), whose violent method of destruction greeted the disappearance of aura and "poverty of experience" as a "freedom from experience," the latter considered as the excess of an outworn humanist culture ("Experience and Poverty," *SW* II, 732, 734). Yet, in other work from the thirties, he resolutely returned to a negative assessment of modernity's "increasing atrophy of experience" ("Motifs," *SW* IV, 316). Baudelaire's parrying lyrical poetry exemplified the attempt to recover a world of correspondences in poetic experience (*Erfahrung*), but also displayed the traumatic signs of a time marked by shock experiences (*Erlebnisse*), which, by hardening the shield of consciousness and intellectual memory, risked losing the vast repository of tradition, aura, and lived experiences (*Erfahrung*).

Contemporary vitalistic philosophy, represented by Dilthey, Klages, and Jung, devalued *Erfahrung* to *Erlebnis*. This philosophical leveling of experience continued a trend that had started with (a certain) Kant and the neo-Kantian relegation of *Erfahrung* to the calculations of the positivistic, scientific mind-set. For Benjamin, language, once released from the correspondence model of truth, might provide the path to another realm of possibilities, to the recognition of altogether different "correspondences." Set free from the nefarious effects of instrumental reason, language was to regain some of its lost aura. Once humans recognized language's unfathomed revolutionary potential, perhaps it might field a blow, issue a redemptive shock, undoing the numbing anaesthetic and aestheticized shock effects of modernity's culture of dispersal.[3]

It seems timely, therefore, to address Benjamin's complex language theory – sometimes neglected in favor of more accessible work, such as the technology essay – in order to unlock how modernity's progressive aestheticization of the cultural field occurred at the expense of an unalloyed purity of language. A reading of the 1916 essay, "On Language as Such and on the Language of Man" paired to an analysis of the 1933 "Doctrine of the Similar" and "On the Mimetic Faculty" will demonstrate how the category of mimesis emerged as one of the quintessential modes of human cultural production in Benjamin's intellectual development. Through an analysis of the mimetic faculty – the perception and production of sensuous *and* nonsensuous similarities – Benjamin hoped to forge a synthesis between his earlier language philosophy and the concerns of the cultural critic committed to historical materialism. Where Benjamin's earliest thought championed a "spiritual" language-magic, his later work posited a magical, mimetic, and corporeal phase antedating the acquisition of (verbal) language. In language's sanctuary, this mimetic impulse was to find a new abode, but perhaps – as the later essay, "On the Mimetic Faculty," in contradistinction to "Doctrine of the Similar" seemed to suggest – at the cost of blotting out an earlier stratum of magic.

Mystical language, pure language

Benjamin's earliest mystical view of language reads like a peculiar amalgam of Kantian "mysticism," Early Romanticism (Schlegel and Novalis), Hölderlin's poetry, Hamann's aphorisms, and the kabbalah. Following the Romantic critic Friedrich Schlegel, he devised an intricate "system" of "mystical terminology,"[4] which, by overcoming the antinomy between conceptual mediacy and intuitive immediacy, was to realize a language-based, "noneidetic" mysticism in the midst of philosophical discourse (*Concept of Criticism*, *SW* I, 139–40). The mystical terms that formed part of this new lexicon were *Sprachmagie* (language-magic *and* the magic of language), pure language, word, name, symbol, and, significantly, system – a term stripped of its rationalistic connotations. Writing within and at the margins of logic, as a philosophy student Benjamin crafted not a few formal, quasi-systematic essays, which in the end meant to demonstrate that all system was to be thought of as symbol. Like the original broken symbolical ring that constituted its totality through the merger of its broken parts, so Benjamin's symbol pointed to a harmonious participatory relation among fragments and the whole of which they were a part. All languages existed in a symbolical intentionality toward pure language, which in turn shone forth through multiple languages, much as the kabbalistic *Zohar*, or book of splendor, exalted the luminous presence of the creative Word in the vessel of language-shards.[5]

Enigmatic as the term the "magic of language" at first might seem, Benjamin enlisted it to resist the degradation of language to a neo-Kantian concern with concepts and cogitation as well as the activist flaws he detected in Martin Buber's political philosophy, or what Gershom Scholem referred to as its "blood and *Erlebnis* arguments" (*Friendship*, 29). Eulogizing language's unmediated magic, or mediate immediacy (C, 80), Benjamin favored the sober, "objective writing" of the Early Romantics' journal *Athenaeum* over Buber's *The Jew*. Rather than set up a strategic, causal or instrumental link between words and political action, objective, political style pointed to a radically different sphere, whose silence was that of the intrusive, ineffable caesura, the interval between words; for, "only where this sphere of speechlessness reveals itself in unutterably pure power can the magic spark leap between the word and the motivating deed, where the unity of these two equally real entities resides" (C, 80).

In this description of language's magic spark, the core of Benjamin's early mystical language philosophy shone forth. He would subsequently capture the essence of this philosophy in one of his beloved tropes, a chiasm of sorts: if the Absolute inhabited pure language, then pure language in turn was the immediate medium of the Absolute. Pure language existed as immediate mediality, as a language movement encompassing different centers, stadia of being or existence, which were infinitely completed and consummated in the Absolute. Benjamin identified the workings of this immediate mediacy in the Early Romantics' theory of "I-less" reflection, whose interlocking reflective centers "[hung] together infinitely (exactly)," as Hölderlin's gloss of his *Pindar* translation had put it (*Concept of Criticism*, *SW* I, 126). Holding the middle between philosophy and poetry, Benjamin's language at the time aimed at a Hölderlinian balance between sobriety and ecstasy (*mania*), a non-subjective ecstatic language, in which the cadence of discursive language was interrupted by the caesura. Borrowed from Hölderlin's annotations to Sophocles, this prosodic figure signaled the silent, forceful, potentially terrific and sublime incursion of divine power – the expressionless – in the midst of language. As it disclosed the sphere of the ineffable, the caesura at once prompted the dissolution of the mythical layer of information, meaning, and subjective intention (see, "Task," *SW* I, 261).[6]

Neither scientific, political, nor ordinary linguistic communication captured Benjamin's imagination but an entirely different magical communicability, which manifested itself in an organic language movement that transpired among God and humans, humans and things, nature and God. The name of this magical communication among various layers, registers, realms, states of existence, and levels of intentionality, was translation, or translatability, a term that was to receive its earliest account not, as is commonly assumed in Benjamin's 1921 translation essay, but in the 1916 "On Language as Such and on the Language of Man." As this title already indicates, the essay is concerned with language "as such" and with human language, denoting that the two were not necessarily identical. Where the essay's first part focused on language-magic, that is, language's immediate mediacy and infinity, the second, longer half disclosed the tremendous task that lay encapsulated in human language, namely, the task of (Adamic) naming. In the name – or "the language of language" – pure language came to word ("On Language," SW I, 65). In it, the divine, infinite spirit spoke, a spirit very much like the *eyn sof*, the pure Infinite of the *Zohar*, whose splendor radiated through the words, the texture, of the Torah, at once creation and revelation in and "through" language.

Taking on secular humanism, Benjamin's language theory corrected the common view that only humans, unlike animals or plants, were endowed with language. Language communicated spiritual contents but in such a way that the latter communicated themselves reflexively, that is, not *through* language but *in* language.[7] Resisting, moreover, a *rationalistic* logocentrism, Benjamin questioned the predominance of human reason, the privileged organ of the *animal rationale*, as he stretched the notion of *Geist* (spirit) to everything, including mere objects. Yet, to extend the "existence of language" to all things animate and inanimate did not mean to turn language into an inauthentic metaphor.[8] "This use of the word 'language,'" Benjamin cautioned, "is in no way metaphorical" ("On Language," SW I, 62). For, regardless of the level of consciousness (or even lack of consciousness) that a being or thing possessed, each communicated spiritual content, in keeping with the Scholastic model of gradation among levels of spiritual being ("On Language," SW I, 66). Allied, moreover, to Jacob Boehme's natural philosophy, such reflexive self-communication resembled the mystical theory of Revelation at the core of his *De signatura rerum* [Of the Signature of Things, 1682], according to which all things great and small revealed themselves in an original natural language, thus participating in the language-spirit of Revelation (*Origin*, 202).

At the core of Genesis 1 lay an original covenant between God and humans, a symbolical contract forged in language. For, if divine Revelation transpired in the "creative omnipotence of language," then in humans God "set language, which had served *him* as medium of creation, free" ("On Language," *SW* I, 68). Through the name, "the frontier between the finite and infinite," human language participated "most intimately in the divine infinity of the pure word" ("On Language," *SW* I, 69); conversely, all the finite (secular) human word could render was second-order knowledge. Saturated with the divine language-spirit, the name furthermore connected to the world of mute things, ruled by the magic of matter. The bond among these various levels of existence was ensured through intercommunication in translation ("On Language," *SW* I, 69), a harmonious process of spiritual transposition in non-mediate mediation. In the dynamic movement of language, human naming acted as the medium – not vehicle or means – of translation between God's infinite creative word and unspoken, nameless things. Just as the human name remained deficient unless it was the echo of, or response to the divine word, so things – distinguished by a mute "magic of matter" ("On Language," *SW* I, 67, 69) – remained incomplete, unless they were named by humans. Thus, though Benjamin sought to resist anthropocentric philosophies of language, he still held fast to *Genesis* according to which Adam was "the lord of nature" ("On Language," *SW* I, 64, 65), whose naming language amounted to the medium in which *"the [spiritual] being of man communicates itself to God"* (*SW* I, 65). As the interplay between reception and spontaneity, the name bound humans to things, exposing both bourgeois linguistic and most mystical theories to be wrong, the former for turning language into an arbitrary referential sign system, the latter for identifying the word with the essence of the thing (see "On Language," *SW* I, 69). Humans' magical community and communication with things was immaterial and purely spiritual, a pneumatic contract or covenant of which the sound was the spiritual symbol. This, Benjamin averred, was the "symbolic fact" that *Genesis*'s second account of creation rendered in God's breathing his breath into Adam, a breath "at once life and spirit and language" ("On Language," *SW* I, 67).

Spurning rationalism's reverence of the *logos* as the seat of human reason, Benjamin paid tribute to the "language spirit," a mystical term dear to Jacob Boehme (see *Origin,* 201–02). Benjamin's persistent use of the sonorous word "echo" reverberated with Boehme's conception of the Spirit as a divine, polyphonically tuned organ, in which every voice and every pipe, in piping out its own tone, echoed the eternal Word. If creation through language preeminently entailed the foundation of language community, then it followed that the polyphonic and harmonious translation among several strata in the great chain of language defied "abstract areas of identity and similarity"[9] ("On Language," *SW* I, 70), including the figurative similarity brokered by metaphor. To be understood neither figuratively nor metaphorically, harmonious translation among languages transpired as a transformative process among "media of varying densities," involving the "transportation of one language into another through a continuum of transformations" ("On Language," *SW* I, 70; trans. modified). Translation did not express unbridgeable difference, nor the bridging of separate registers in metaphoric transposition; instead, language's "secret password" was deciphered as it gradually passed into the singular language of the sentry standing at the gates of a higher sphere of creation. Yet again, Benjamin here appeared inspired by Hamann, whose rhapsodic *Aesthetica in Nuce* had described creation as "speech to the created (*die Kreatur*) by the created; for one day tells it to another day, and one night to another; the password of creation runs through every climate until the end of the world, and in each one hears the voice of creation."[10]

In Benjamin's ontotheology, the original act of foundation or positing was that of the divine Word, a position most succinctly voiced in "The Task of the Translator," which cites the opening words of St. John's gospel from the New Testament: *en archēi ēn ho logos* (*In the beginning was the Word*) ("Task," *SW* I, 260). For Benjamin, this was an original gift whose extraordinary "giving" humans could only realize by reciprocating through naming language. Fundamentally, he thus dismissed both rationalistic and poetic theories of human spontaneity in language, as neither the concept (Kant and neo-Kantianism) nor the metaphor (Nietzsche) constituted humans' most creative act. Language could never find its determination and fulfillment in the aesthetic, productive force of human creation through metaphor, whose relativism Nietzsche had made transparent when he interpreted truth as a maneuverable army of tropes (see Nietzsche's "On Truth and Lies in an Extramoral Sense"). Long before Nietzsche, Hölderlin's poetry had already unraveled the hubristic, aestheticizing claims of German idealism to such thetic positing. However, at this early stage of his work, Benjamin did not dwell on how idealism's positing of meaning had found its response in Nietzsche's post-Hegelian philosophy, which replaced "meaning" with the positing of pluralist "values." Only later, in *The Origin of the German Tragic Drama*, would Benjamin address the consequences of such relativistic, nominalistic pluralist values in the context of his new theory of allegory. In the 1916 essay on language, by contrast, he framed the spontaneity of the human mind by making it subservient to a more original receptivity to the divine Word, whose soundings echoed in human names. Rather than signaling the exchange of meanings, semantics, or a contingent economy of values – all philosophical equivalents of the Fall – pure language escaped such mundane circuits of distribution and exchange, initiating an altogether different economy of the gift and restitution. Thus, the human act of naming did not proceed *ex nihilo* but required a receptive (though hardly passive) attitude, consummated in the response to the divine Word. Human creativity itself was restricted to the proper name, the act of naming one's offspring ("On Language," *SW* I, 69), in light of which the mechanics of metaphor merely corresponded to inauthentic analogy or bad mimetic similarity. To engage in the act of naming – including the gift of a second, secret name ("Agesilaus Santander," *SW* II, 712–16) – meant to accept one's duty as a human. To do so did not amount to reproducing the divine Word mimetically; rather, it meant to listen to, to echo, and hence to activate divine creation through the acoustics of the spoken (not yet written) word which alighted upon things like a tender breath. In these "spirited" speech acts, each and every word seemed to stream from the divine "Sprachgeist" or "spirit of language" – a word that also alludes to the Hebrew concept of *ruah* ("divine breath").[11] Indeed, what else but this breath accorded humans and objects their "aura" (Latin, "breath of air"). For though the word "auratic" never expressly appeared in the language essay, it would pour forth from the later (iconographic) work, as if the latter were still suffused with the breath of the language-spirit.

Just as creation transpired through pure language, so the fall occurred in language, affecting its purity as well as the language-spirit. Now removed from its root origin, the power of the name hardly survived in the mundane everydayness characterizing the merely finite *human word* ("On Language," *SW* I, 71). As the playing field of an "infinitely differentiated" and dispersed knowledge, this word simply expressed an inferior degree of "external magic." In its wake arose another form of translation, more precisely, the postlapsarian multiplication of translations among various languages and registers of knowledge.[12] Again, it was Hamann who had grasped the operations of this "mediate" mode of translation, when he likened the transposition of angelic language into human language to the reverse side of a carpet, showing "the stuff, but not the workman's skill," and to an eclipse of the sun that is perceived mediately, in a vessel of water (Hamann, *Aesthetica*, 142). Charting the same transition from "one language" and "perfect knowledge" ("On Language," *SW* I, 71) to the imperfections of mere mediacy, Benjamin posited that the name made way for the external communications of the human word and a derivative realm of judgment (rendered in Genesis by the snake's "nameless" knowledge). This inferior "knowledge of good and evil" – of the level of Kierkegaard's "chatter" – had found its just response in God's judging, purifying word, driving the first humans out of paradise ("On Language," *SW* I, 72). At bottom, Benjamin concluded, the Fall initiated an idolatrous practice of mimesis (here: inauthentic similarity), the spectacle of parody, in which fallen, mediate language imitated original immediacy. Abstraction now ruled in logical and philosophical propositions no less than in the judgments and sentences dispensed in the name of the secular law whose "mythic origin" Benjamin was to pursue with a tenacity rivaled only by Kafka's allegories and parables about the Law. Years later, in the 1931 Kraus essay, Benjamin would write the postscript to this narrative, setting Kraus up as the latter-day judge, who, in taking on the platitudes and otiose phrases of modernity's information technology, not only proved that "justice and language remain founded in each other" but thus also consecrated his Jewishness ("Karl Kraus," *SW* II, 444).

Whether Benjamin invoked the Romantics' model of reflection, the acoustic register of the echo, or translation as a work's "afterlife" ("Task," *SW* I, 254), language never amounted to a monolithic flux of words, articulations or signs; rather, it disclosed an intricate texture of "communication," in which different strands, reflection centers or texts (original and translation), interacted polyphonically. Much as criticism, especially art criticism, brought the work to reflective completion, so translation did the same to the original, so "naming language" returned the gift of Revelation in communicative receptivity, an order altogether different from the trafficking in linguistic coins or the Babel-like accumulation of inauthentic translations. Thus, while it is not impossible or necessarily ill-advised to do a rhetorical reading of Benjamin's early writings illustrating how the work of language undoes the text's overt organic claims, from a historico-philosophical perspective it seems important to acknowledge that the early Benjamin unambiguously embraced an organic, pure language that claimed to be neither metaphorical nor allegorical but if anything was symbolical.

Everything depends here, then, on the status of the fragment, much as it did in the Early Romantics' aesthetics and epistemology. In Benjamin's early thought, the fragment never existed in and by itself, but always was the shard that helped complete symbolical intentionality. Thus, while his acclaimed "The Task of the Translator" (1921) stood in dialogue with (secular) discussions of a translation's "fidelity" to or "freedom" from the original, the essay proffered the hope of a *symbolic* approximation of pure language, evoked in the interlinear, or word-by-word, translation of Holy Writ. The "hallmark" of bad translations was external communication ("Task," *SW* I, 253), the transmission of inessential contents, which assumed that a translation's telos was the reproduction or imitation of the original's meaning. Dismissing a purely philological theory based on external family relations among languages, Benjamin posited a "suprahistorical kinship," a common purposiveness among all languages, which were "interrelated in what they express" ("Task," *SW* I, 257, 255), that is, in their common intentionality toward pure language. If languages existed in a "constant state of flux," then pure language would emerge, in Revelation, at "the Messianic end of their history," "from the harmony of all the various ways of meaning" ("Task," *SW* I, 257). The translation, as a form, ensured the afterlife, the survival of the original work, by transporting it into "a more definitive language realm" ("Task," *SW* I, 258; trans. modified), rebounding with the original's echo. Consequently, the translator's task consisted in the integration of "many tongues into one true language," thus "ripening the seed of pure language in translation" ("Task," *SW* I, 259) – an organic image that recalled the *Zohar*'s "garden of nuts," the multiple layers and shells around the innermost kernel, whose essence Hamann hoped to render when he set out to compose an aesthetics *in nuce*. Rather than relating to one another as production did to (mimetic) reproduction, original, and translation participated in a model of incorporation, making them "recognizable as fragments of a greater language, just as fragments are part of a vessel" ("Task," *SW* I, 260). Shunning once again the realm of metaphor and inauthentic analogy, Benjamin embraced the technique of *Wörtlichkeit* – in truth an untranslatable term that meant "literalness" but (when taken literally) also spelled fidelity to the Word. Enacted in Hölderlin's all too literal Sophocles translations, such literalness emanated from a higher truth, the higher awareness that "in the beginning was the Word." Complementing the original in sonorous harmony, the real translation was transparent, for "it does not cover the original, does not block its light, but allows the pure language, as though reinforced by its own medium, to shine upon the original all the more fully" ("Task," *SW* I, 260). Through a literal rendition of syntax, authentic translation managed to bring the word to the foreground. "For if the sentence is the wall before the language of the original, literalness (*Wörtlichkeit*) is the arcade" ("Task," *SW* I, 260). For all their uncanny strangeness, Hölderlin's translations uncovered the profundity of "the harmony of languages," to the point where in stooping to the abyss, they risked losing (external) meaning "in the bottomless depths of language" ("Task," *SW* I, 262). Translations, then, assisted in turning language's symbolizing force into the symbolized, without, however, collapsing them into the same. True translations helped to bring home pure language from its exile in alien tongues, helped to release it by transposing it into a new language. Realized in such sonorous harmony, pure language no longer "means or expresses anything but is, as expressionless and creative Word, that which is meant in all languages – all information, all sense, and all intention finally encounter a stratum in which they are destined to be extinguished" ("Task," *SW* I, 261). Only in Holy Writ was the conveyance of meaning not the "watershed for the flow of language and the flow of revelation." For, in the word-by-word transliteration of Holy Writ, the literalness or non-figurative nature of the divine Word appeared. Lacking any need for mediate mediation, the Word was unconditionally translatable, as testified by the interlinear transliteration of the Scriptures, in which all tongues, overcoming the brokenness of their vessel, together rendered the purity of Revelation in language.

Even in the secular present, riddled with shards, language fragments, ruins, linguistic rubble, and dross, the eventual soldering of the shards constituting the symbol lingered as a powerful potentiality. For such reconstitution to come about, humans would need to recollect (*anamnesis, Origin, 36–37; SW* II, 718) the Adamic language of the name, allowing its echo to reverberate in the present. Modernity therefore existed as the possibility of *tikkun*, that is, in Gershom Scholem's words, as "the Messianic restoration and repair which mends and restores the original being of things, and of history as well, after they have been smashed and corrupted by the 'breaking of the vessels.'"[13] Until this potentiality materialized, the condition of modernity could then, by implication, be defined as the rupturing of the organic community of pure (as opposed to derivative) translation. In the life of humans, this condition manifested itself as secular chatter, the fall from the origin in pure language; in natural life, it took the form of nature's mourning at the excesses and abuse experienced at the hands of humans, more particularly their language. Combining his mysticism with a Romantic philosophy of nature, Benjamin's early 1916 essay thus introduced yet another central motif that would recur in his work as a whole: the language of nature, always at a risk of being silenced, alienated, objectified, and suppressed in and through human language. In the face of so much man-made over-naming, nature relinquished itself to the silence of melancholy.

Language's mimesis

Benjamin never entirely renounced his early language mysticism, retaining its frame of reference even as he adopted the historical-materialist method of cultural analysis, which, anchored in an exegesis of allegory, was to find its culmination in the *Arcades Project*. When in February of 1938 Scholem and Benjamin met for the last time in Paris, Scholem was perplexed that the main topic his friend chose to discuss was the connections between "On the Mimetic Faculty" and the 1916 language essay (see Scholem, *Friendship*, 205 ff.). Benjamin remained convinced that his early metaphysics of language could securely ground his new theory of a pivotal anthropological category and human faculty, namely, a primordial and authentic mode of *mimesis*, whose sediments were to be found in language. Scholem, for his part, very much doubted that Benjamin's early theological language-magic could coexist with a materialistic (Brechtian) theory of language committed to the very elimination of magic, or even with the work on history in progress in the *Arcades Project*. Scholem, impatient with what he considered to be Benjamin's "Janus face" (Scholem, *Friendship*, 209), had little understanding for the synchretic Judeo-Marxism that his friend, like Bloch, embraced, holding that a union between the two was impossible.

As his letters amply show, Benjamin never questioned the feasibility of a mediation between his earlier language philosophy and later style of dialectical materialism (*C*, 372) – though he readily admitted that the new study of mimesis was "perhaps a peculiar text" (*C*, 406). Language, Benjamin now declared, amounted to an "archive of nonsensuous similarities" and "nonsensuous correspondences" (*SW* II, 695, 722), the last resort of an original, primitive, more potent and encompassing human gift for mimesis. Bordering on the esoteric and occult, the study mined contemporary anthropological research on mimesis to disclose the quasi-religious experience of a world suffused with nonsensuous, spiritual similarities. Moving between anthropology and religion, Benjamin coupled his new theory of mimesis to Freud's idea of a phylogenetic telepathic mode of communication, preceding the origin of language (*GS* II.3, 953). At the same time, he claimed to have encountered the phenomenon of "nonsensuous similarity" in the *Zohar*, specially in "the manner in which [its author] considers the sound formations, and even more the script signs, as deposits of world connections," being careful to reject the *Zohar*'s view that such correspondences flowed forth from emanation rather than from a "mimetic origin" (*C*, 512). Perhaps the competing programs of these two sources – the more sober psychoanalysis, the spirited kabbalah – partially help to explain the striking discrepancies that existed between the earlier, longer version of the study – "Doctrine of the Similar" (Berlin, 1933) – and the revised, cut draft that Benjamin readied just a few months later on Ibiza, now labeled "On the Mimetic Faculty."[14] Where the first version unambiguously aligned itself with mystical and theological conceptions of language, the second proposed a more "naturalistic" account of the phenomenon – to use the felicitous term suggested by Schweppenhäuser and Tiedemann (*GS* II.3, 950). Blotting out references to mysticism, theology, and, crucially, the residue of magic in language, the later "On the Mimetic Faculty" ended with the statement that language's higher "level of mimetic behavior" had liquidated the earlier powers of magic (*SW* II, 722) – a position that may have reflected Benjamin's effort to come closer to Scheerbart's and Brecht's praxis of a pared-down, non-auratic language, stripped of all magic (*SW* II, 733).

Despite his dislike of Cassirer's neo-Kantian framework, Benjamin may well have taken note of his influential *Language and Myth* (1925), which regarded metaphor to be the earliest concoction of a mythical thinking immersed in language, in other words, a mode of translation rooted in the power to generate similarity. Yet, the differences were considerable. Not only did Benjamin expand the scope of mimesis to the point where it acquired ontological dimensions, spelling a primeval, enchanted state of natural correspondences in which even objects were endowed with mimetic power; he also thoroughly revised his own initial negative appraisal of mimesis as an inauthentic mode of being, whose falseness formed the foil against which the purity of language earlier had acquired shape. Such earlier, sometimes covert, references to "bad" mimesis may have been informed by the Judaic prohibition against idolatry as well as the Platonic critique of mimesis in *The Republic*. The first significant work by Benjamin to break explicitly with this refusal of the mimetic was *The Origin of the German Tragic Drama*, whose study of allegory anticipates his theory of the dialectical image. For the first time, Benjamin here seriously weighed the dialectical relations between image and language, in advance of his later full-blown fascination with the image culture of photography and film. However, the mimesis study ventured even further since it proved willing to postulate a mimetic stage predating the acquisition of language. Freed of its negative Platonic connotations, the mimetic faculty was modeled on Aristotle's *Poetics*, which had isolated mimesis as a fundamental human activity. For humans to be endowed with the mimetic capacity meant that they possessed the ability not just to recognize (reception) but to produce similarities (spontaneity). Reworking his 1916 understanding of human reception as echoing, Benjamin now defined the world of natural correspondences as the "stimulants and awakeners of the mimetic capacity which answers them in man" ("Doctrine," *SW* II, 695).

Having an ontogenetic and phylogenetic history, mimesis, when studied according to the first perspective, could be seen to manifest itself in the everydayness of children's play, in keeping with Aristotle's observation that "from childhood it is instinctive in human beings to imitate."[15] Benjamin's autobiographical *Berlin Childhood Around 1900* offered up several examples from his own youth, while his adult collection of children's picture books sought to conserve the power of the mimetic illustrative image in the present. A phylogenetic account of mimesis, by contrast, uncovered the historical wear that had befallen the mimetic capacity, its frailty in the present, and the sparsity of magical correspondences – all in all a state that unfavorably distinguished moderns from ancient peoples. Once, the horoscope was not just a handy interpretive tool but also an astrological nexus that held together micro- and macrocosm, an experiential totality that mapped how the heavenly constellations were to be repeated and imitated by individuals and collectives. Fundamentally, the diminished capacity of mimesis reflected a dulling of the perceptual apparatus, which increasingly became unable to perceive similarities announcing themselves immediately, instantaneously, flashing up in the moment of the *Nu* (now, instant). Only language, in fact, nothing more nor less than the highest manifestation of the mimetic genius, remained in the place of our earlier ability to recognize similarities among astral constellations and ourselves.

Up to a certain point, linguistic theory had always acknowledged language's mimetic capacity in onomatopoeia.[16] But Benjamin refused to take onomatopoeia merely in its empirical, philological sense, that is, as the sensuous imitation of a natural sound. Instead, he considerably expanded it, first of all, to include the registers of echo and rhyme, whose playful resounding of a more original language were central to *The Origin of the German Tragic Drama* and the Kraus essay (*Origin* 210; *SW* II, 451–54).[17] Benjamin did not stop there. Going further, his theory of similarity expanded onomatopoeia to include the nonsensuous similarities through which words of different languages were grouped around the same signified. What else, then, did Benjamin do here than implicitly reinterpret the 1921 translation essay on which he now projected the doctrine of similarity? What is more, to similarity at the level of sound needed to be added a nonsensuous similarity at the level of writing and script. Confirming that the most intriguing instance of a nonsensuous similarity was that between the written and the spoken, graphology uncovered the images, or picture puzzles, deposited in handwriting to be the repository of the unconscious. Original writing for Benjamin, then, was not the production of conventional signs but an ideographic activity, as the discussion of hieroglyphs in *The Origin of the German Tragic Drama* had already intimated. Just like spoken language, script itself was an archive of nonsensuous similarities or correspondences (on this aspect, see also Benjamin's fragment "Astrology," *SW* II, 684). Divination relinquished its power to the (non-mediate) medium of language, so that things were now present immanently, living as essences in language (a truth condensed in the Hebrew word *beth*, which was the "root" for "house," *SW* II, 696), waiting to be snapped up by the attentive glance of the studious reader. "Collecting [*herauslesen*: gathering, collecting, gleaning, extracting from] on the basis of similarity," Benjamin noted in a preliminary draft, was to be considered "the primal form of reading [*lesen*]" ("Antitheses Concerning Word and Name," *SW* II, 718; trans. modified). Whether profane or magical (as in astrology), reading was the gift that enabled the spirit to participate in another temporality, in which similarities flashed up out of the flood of things. Such acts of illumination required, however, that the mimetic come to appearance in and through language's semiotic, communicative side. Only in and through the materiality of letters, the "magical function of the alphabet" ("Antitheses," *SW* II, 718), could the picture puzzle, or rebus, be rendered visible. This magical union of matter and spirit, or so, at least, "Doctrine of the Similar" seemed to suggest, was to correspond to the absorption of reading, a state in which the reader dwelt in, or literally (*wörtlich*) inhabited, a world of similarity through words. A "thought image" (*Denkbild*) from 1933 best captured the dynamics of this enchanted style of reading. In this image Benjamin linked the ability of children to treat words as "caverns, with the strangest corridors connecting them" to everyday acts of reading, when texts are read not for the meaning but "for the names and formulas that leap out of the text at the reader," "meaning" being "merely the background on which rests the shadow that they cast, like figures in relief." However, a second thread led to commentaries of sacred texts, for in their interpretation the student would "fix on particular words, as if they had been chosen according to the rules of the game," knowing that, in the end, they had been "assigned" to him as "as a task" ("Thought Figures," *SW* II, 726).

Weary, in the end, of the Platonic ban on mimesis, Benjamin thus developed a redemptive concept of imitation, which no longer had anything to do with the production of a "transportable" aesthetic copy snatched from an external object. Ultimately, our gift to see similarities proved the weak rudiment of a more "powerful compulsion to become similar and to behave mimetically" ("On the Mimetic Faculty," *SW* I, 720). Compelled by this forceful drive, the child Benjamin had acted out the word *Mummerehlen*, changing into the word he could not understand – an episode recounted in his memoirs, *Berlin Childhood*. Interested in the process of becoming and being one with the object world, Benjamin thus returned to the magical moment preceding the sharp division between object and subject in instrumental reason and technology.[18] It is this very attunement to a magical world that overwhelmed young Benjamin in *Berlin Childhood*, a vignette that allegorically illustrated how a radical alterity came to shape the subject.

Similar to Adorno's equally complex conception of a beneficial mimesis, Benjamin's theory described an encounter with the otherness of nature that preceded its melancholic stage of lamentation – a register of nature that wholly escaped the objectifying worldview of the natural sciences. It was this very interplay between mimetic *perception* and *(re)production* that Benjamin felt to constitute poetic experience (*Erfahrung*). Nothing less than the "impassioned cult of similarity" shaped the literary *intérieur* of the French mystic-writer of self-absorption, Marcel Proust, who, as an "aged child," proved "homesick for the world distorted in the state of similarity" ("On the Image of Proust," *SW* II, 239–40). If the Romantics were the first to have comprehended that this state of similarity was the realm of *correspondances*, and if Baudelaire had most passionately conjured up their aura, then it was still only Proust who had succeeded in revealing these correspondences "in our lived life." His was "the work of *la mémoire involontaire*, the rejuvenating force which is a match for the inexorable process of aging" ("On the Image of Proust," *SW* II, 244). Only when gauged in the context of this intricate web of connections can one make sense of a puzzling line Benjamin jotted down in the early thirties: "Experience (*Erfahrung*) consists of lived similarities" ("Experience," *SW* II, 553; tran. modified). This gnomic statement, however, loses its air of mystery when it is linked to an entry from an early draft for the *Arcades Project*, in which Benjamin, musing about his own proper name, "W.B.," defined the name as the "realm of the similar," while similarity was the "organon of experience (*Erfahrung*)" (*Arcades*, 868). As "the object of mimesis," the name simultaneously brought together its bearer's past and future, as it both "preserves, but also marks out in advance" "the habitus of a lived life" (*Arcades*, 868). Finally, these various strands of reference all came together in the 1933 notes, "Antitheses Concerning Word and Name," which aimed to reconstruct the hidden pathways between the 1916 language theory and the doctrine of mimesis. Closing the circle, these notes looped back from language to the realm of auratic similarities, ending in a sublime theory of recollection: "Historically," Benjamin mused, "the fleeting appearance of similarity has the character of an anamnesis – that is to say, of a lost similarity, free from the tendency to become dissipated. This lost similarity, which existed in time, prevails in the Adamite spirit of language" ("Antitheses Concerning Word and Name," *SW* II, 718), that is, in the recollective power of the name. In the end, then, mimesis, or the recognition and production of sensuous and nonsensuous (language-based) similarities, required an altered mode of perception, not unlike the sensibility that marked the poet or theologian.

At once an allegorist and collector of language, Benjamin throughout the years of his research sought to set language free, reviving its original, productive, and poetic force. Conforming to the physiognomy of the collector, on display in the *Arcades Project*, he gathered unalloyed, unmined, pure specimens of language, hoping to avert language's reduction to a mere means of communication, the trafficking in worn-out coins, exploited for their exchange value – whether perpetrated by the jargon of neo-Kantianism or the empty slogans wielded by at least part of modernity's mass media culture. Conforming to the figure of the allegorist, however, Benjamin remained entangled in a double, dialectical relation to language: seeking to recapture some of its primeval meaning *(Sinn)* and symbolic nature, which he perused with the profundity of the melancholic brooder, he also recognized the necessary alienating, defamiliarizing allegorical operations of language. The same duality, in the end, marked his proposals for an altered way of reading and for the observance of a swift tempo, able to seize the "critical moment" ("Doctrine," *SW* II, 698), something profane reading had in common with its older, magical variant. For, as his writings on language indubitably suggest, if language's reality required a style of reading that could cope with its interruptive, caesura-like force, it also called for another gift: the ability to recognize the flash of lightening, the magic of similarities and correspondences, in poetic, historical, and secular no less than in sacred texts.

NOTES

1. Benjamin proved indebted to Hamann's *Aesthetica in nuce*, subtitled "A Rhapsody in Kabbalistic Prose," as well as to his "Metakritik" of Kant. Important references by Benjamin to this anti-Enlightenment critic and philosopher can be found in "On Language" (*SW* I, 67, 70), and in "On the Program of the Coming Philosophy" (*SW* I, 108). An early positive appraisal of Mallarmé appears in the 1921 "The Task of the Translator: An Introduction to the Translation of Baudelaire's *Tableaux parisiens*" (*SW* I, 259), and in a 1925 fragment, "Reflections on Humboldt," which argued that the philologist [Humboldt], in distinction to Mallarmé, neglected "the magical side of language" (*SW* I, 424).

2. Benjamin discusses this change in the structure of experience in "Motifs," (*SW* IV, 313–14). The word used for experience here, *Erfahrung*, along with *Erlebnis*, which is close to yet distinct in meaning from *Erfarhung*, are key words running through all of Benjamin's thought. Among Benjamin's most important texts on the topic are "On the Program of the Coming Philosophy" (*SW* I, 100–10); "Experience" (1931 or 1932; *SW* II, 553); "Experience and Poverty" (1933; *SW* II, 731–36); "The Storyteller," and "On Some Motifs in Baudelaire" (*SW* III, 143–66 and *SW* IV, 313–55). For the English translator, the pair *Erfahrung* and *Erlebnis*, which both can be rendered by "experience," poses inordinate translation difficulties since there exists no corresponding English pair that captures the varying German connotations. In a note to a sentence from Benjamin's 1929 text, "The Return of the Flâneur," the Harvard edition proposes the following demarcation: *Erlebnis*, "a single, noteworthy experience"; *Erfahrung*, "'experience' in the sense of learning from life over an extended period" (*SW* II, 267n). Although appropriate in this context, the translation cannot be maintained in all instances. Often, for Benjamin, the term *Erlebnis* signaled a negative condition, the irrationalist "experience cult" of vitalism taken to task in section 1 of "On Some Motifs in Baudelaire." His earliest use of the term *Erfahrung* sought to uncover – in Nietzschean fashion – the "mask" of experience, often worn as a solace by elders and "spiritless philistines," who were blind to higher values that remained "inexperiencable" (see "Experience," *SW* I, 3–5). Subsequently, the term *Erfahrung* came to represent the attempt to retrieve a more authentic, non-scientific concept of experience, which would include "absolute experience" and the "experience of the Absolute." As such, it frequently appeared in conjunction with a heightened state of perception. Perhaps

the most helpful distinctions between the pair *Erfahrung* and *Erlebnis* emerge in "On Some Motifs in Baudelaire," where both were securely linked to Benjamin's theory of memory and where authentic *Erfahrung* was tantamount to the ability to countenance the auratic. *Erfahrung* in this context meant the conjunction between the individual past and the collective past.

3. On the anaesthetic in Benjamin, see Susan Buck-Morss, "Aesthetics and Anaesthetics: Walter Benjamin's Artwork Essay Reconsidered," in *October* 62 (Fall 1992), 3–41. For an early study of Benjamin's language-magic, see Winfried Menninghaus, *Walter Benjamins Theorie der Sprachmagie* (Frankfurt am Main: Suhrkamp, 1980); see also Richard Wollin, *Walter Benjamin: An Aesthetic of Redemption* (Berkeley, Los Angeles, London: University of California Press, 1994), 29–77.

4. The term "mystical terminology" was coined by A. W. Schlegel in a letter to Schleiermacher to describe how his brother's genius was "concentrated" in "self-coined phrases." Using the term positively, not just for Friedrich Schlegel but also for Novalis, Benjamin saw it as the Romantic attempt to acquire a "noneidetic intuition of the system" in language (*Concept of Criticism, SW* I, 139–40).

5. *Zohar, The Book of Splendor: Basic Readings from the Kabbalah*, ed. Gershom Scholem (New York: Schocken Books, 1977), *passim*.

6. The figure of the caesura not only structured Benjamin's Hölderlin essay, *SW* I, 18–36, but played an equally cardinal role in his "Goethe's *Elective Affinities*," *SW* I, 297–360.

7. In what follows, Benjamin's "geistig" and "Geist" are rendered as "spiritual" (instead of "mental") and "spirit" (instead of "mind," suggested by the extant translations of the essay).

8. "On Language," *SW* I, 62. Benjamin's early writings seem strewn with caveats not to read his statements metaphorically instead of literally. See, for example, "The Task of the Translator," *SW* I, 254, discussed below. However, by no means does it follow from this that he rejected metaphor *as such*, as is clear, for example, from his correspondence with the Austrian writer Hofmannsthal (*C*, 286), which offered a raving appraisal of Proust's use of metaphor in "A propos du style de Flaubert." See also *GBr* III, 116, where Benjamin lauded the virtues of literary metaphor in reply to a now lost text by Hofmannsthal about "Gleichnisse."

9. The words Benjamin uses here, "*Gleichheits- und Ähnlichkeitsbezirke*," indicate external or abstract similarities. Here, Benjamin still deployed the word "similarity" (*Ähnlichkeit*) negatively, a practice far removed from his later texts, "On the Mimetic Faculty," and "Doctrine of the Similar" (discussed below).

10. J. G. Hamann, "*Aesthetica in Nuce*," in *German Aesthetic and Literary Criticism*, ed. H. B. Nisbet (Cambridge University Press, 1985), 141; trans. modified.

11. Benjamin's use of the German "Sprachgeist" also makes use to the Latin, *spiritus*, and the Greek, *pneuma*. For a clear discussion of the differences between these various terms, see Jacques Derrida, *Of Spirit: Heidegger and the Question* (University of Chicago Press, 1989).

12. Another fragment from 1920–21, "Language and Logic" (*SW* I, 272–75), fine-tuned this initial position. This short text went against the mystics' view that the "degeneration of the true language" defied a "primordial and God-willed unity," ending in its "dissolution into many languages" (*SW* I, 273). Instead, the multiplicity of languages was to be comprehended as a "multiplicity of essences,"

while postlapsarian "degeneracy" meant a decrease in "the integral power to rule." The original language expressed itself in harmony through the multiplicity of spoken languages, so that its power was infinitely greater than that of any singular, individual language.

13. Gershom Scholem, "Walter Benjamin and his Angel," in *On Walter Benjamin*, ed. Gary Smith (Cambridge, MA: MIT Press, 1988), 84.

14. The text "Doctrine of the Similar" was retained in a notebook from the years 1931 to 1933, which included versions of the mystical "Agesilaus Santander," also written on Ibiza. Faced with the horrors of National Socialism, Benjamin here reflected on the significance of the Jewish practice to give children secret names. See Gershom Scholem's account in "Walter Benjamin and His Angel," 55, as well as an early entry about Walter Benjamin's name from the *Arcades Project* (*Arcades*, 868; Q°, 24), discussed below.

15. *Aristotle's Poetics*, ed. James Hutton (New York: Norton, 1982), 47.

16. Citing Rudolf Leonhard approvingly, for whom every word not to mention the whole of language was onomatopoetic ("Doctrine," *SW* II, 696), Benjamin in fact pursued his earlier discussion of onomatopoeia in *The Origin of the German Tragic Drama* (*Origin*, 204) and the 1931 Kraus essay. He also reconsidered the issue in a long review essay on language sociology commissioned by the Institute for Social Research. Mostly a dry, reproductive account of prevailing research in the area, which was to earn him Brecht's warm approval, the essay ended on a lively, enthusiastic note, attesting to Benjamin's fascination with a non-linguistic, mimetic, and corporeal mode of expression that also fueled his admiration for Klages's dubitable science of graphology ("Graphology Old and New," *SW* II, 398–400).

17. For a more detailed interpretation of the Kraus essay, see my *Walter Benjamin's Other History: Of Stones, Animals, Human Beings, and Angels* (London, Berkeley, and Los Angeles: University of California Press, 1998), 114ff.

18. My reading here is indebted to Michael Weller's "Imitating Truth: Mimesis in Adorno's *Ästhetische Theorie*" (2001 Harvard University thesis). For further study of the dialectic of mimesis, the reader is referred to Max Horkheimer and Theodor W. Adorno, *The Dialectic of Englightenment*, trans. John Cumming (New York: Continuum, 1991).

4

HOWARD CAYGILL

Walter Benjamin's concept of cultural history

> There is no document of culture that is not at the same time a document of barbarism.
>
> Walter Benjamin, "Theses on the Philosophy of History"

The famous sentence from Benjamin's seventh thesis on the philosophy of history describing documents of culture as documents of barbarism appears in the context of a reflection on culture as the plunder of history's victors. Faced with the barbaric documents of culture and their transmission to the present, Benjamin continues, it is the task of historical materialism to "rub history against the grain." The general references to historicism and historical materialism in the seventh thesis obscure the original significance of the sentence as part of a specific reflection on the limits of cultural history. The same phrase also appears at a crucial point in the 1937 essay on the Marxist cultural historian "Eduard Fuchs: Collector and Historian." At this point the sentence, "There is no document of culture which is not at the same time a document of barbarism," continues: "No cultural history has yet done justice to this fundamental state of affairs and it can hardly hope to do so"(*SW* III, 267). The burden of Benjamin's critique of previous cultural history rests on its never having done "justice" to the negative or barbaric aspect of culture, an act of reparation for past injustice that he thinks it can "hardly hope" to achieve. Nevertheless, in spite of this stricture, Benjamin's 1937 prognosis for cultural history is not entirely bleak: some small hope remains for what he calls a "dialectical cultural history." The analysis of the concept of a dialectical cultural history will thus give a concrete illustration of what it might mean to "rub history against its grain."

Benjamin's critique and redefinition of the field of cultural history involves a number of deeper conceptual issues. The various approaches to cultural history that he criticized shared a common lineage in the critique of Hegel. Given his professed distaste for Hegel's philosophy, Benjamin's call for a dialectical cultural history cannot be simply construed as a return to the Hegelian dialectical philosophy of history. It involved instead a renegotiation of the relationship between philosophy and history, one in which philosophy instead of providing the reason of history suffers its rationality to be disrupted by it. The historical documents of barbarism put into question the civility of reason. Not only the materials but also the philosophical structures that shape historical narrative, whether those of religious or secular progress, must themselves be questioned. Benjamin sees the greatest openness for this process in the then new tradition of cultural history, whose object was less rigidly defined than those of political, art, or religious histories and thus more open to material that questions the narrative forms of history. Benjamin will describe as "dialectical" (but not in the Hegelian sense of this word) a practice of cultural history that admits evidence while negating given historical narratives. Benjamin's understanding of the concept of cultural history is thus crucial not only to his historical practice and his philosophy of history, but also to his pursuit of what may be described as a non-Hegelian but speculative philosophy.[1]

Benjamin's concept of cultural history may best be described by means of his responses, favorable and critical, to the varieties of cultural history that developed during his lifetime. The previous cultural historians who had not, in Benjamin's opinion, done justice to the barbaric aspect of culture are easily identified from his writings and polemics with them. Prominent among them are Heinrich Wölfflin, Alois Riegl, Aby Warburg and his school, along with Eduard Fuchs and the historical materialists; less prominent but nevertheless significant are Jacob Burckhardt, Johan Huizinga, and Franz Mehring. The key figure in formulating the discipline of cultural history as an antidote to Hegelian philosophy of history was of course Jacob Burckhardt, and it was the achievement but also the unresolved tensions of his work that inspired the tradition of cultural history in which Benjamin was educated and with which he took issue.

Jacob Burckhardt and the origins of cultural history

The motivation for Benjamin's call for a "dialectical" cultural history is best understood by a glance at the origins of the discipline. The beginnings of cultural history may be traced to Jacob Burckhardt's period of study at the University of Berlin during the early 1840s. This was a time when the university was in full reaction to the influence of Hegel, a turn evident in the objective historical approach of Ranke and the philosophy of the late Schelling (the latter expressly called to Berlin to "root out the dragons teeth of Hegelianism"). Burckhardt's concept of cultural history emerged in this climate of full opposition to Hegel's philosophy of history, but remained marked by the negation of a Hegelianism that it never fully overcame. Benjamin greatly admired Burckhardt's work, especially the creation of a non-Hegelian historical narrative that made lateral links across a period rather than progressive links between periods. Yet, he was sensitive to the risks of empiricism and lack of discrimination latent in this non-philosophical approach to history, risks which were avoided, in Benjamin's judgment, in Burckhardt's work on late antiquity *Constantine the Great* (1853) but not in the *Culture of the Renaissance*.

In spite of Benjamin's perception there was never a serious risk of Burckhardt's cultural history recoiling from the excess of theory in Hegel's philosopy of history to an historical empiricism. Burckhardt's very opposition to Hegel ensured that cultural history would remain sensitive to issues in the philosophy of history, for it was necessary to criticize Hegel not only historically but also philosophically. As a consequence, Burckhardt inverted both the philosophical method and the historical judgments of Hegel's philosophy of history. He not only rejected the "teleological" character of Hegel's view of history as the realization of the idea of freedom, but defended judgments on the significance of ancient Greek culture, the role of the Emperor Constantine in the Christian transformation of the Roman Empire, of the Renaissance, and the Reformation that were diametrically opposed to those of Hegel.[2] Yet, this opposition to Hegel left a number of tensions and ambiguities in Burckhardt's cultural history that were bequeathed to his heirs and which continued to trouble Benjamin. The first was an unresolved tension between philosophy and history, and the second an ambiguity concerning the object of cultural history, most evident in the place of art in culture and thus of art history within cultural history. These and other tensions and ambiguities were resolved in diverse ways by Burckhardt at different stages in his career, as well as by the succeeding generation of cultural historians.

With respect to the relation of philosophy and cultural history, or more broadly to the role of theory in history, Burckhardt was patently contradictory. His position in the *Weltgeschichtliche Betrachtungen* is at first glance unequivocal. The systematic philosophy of history is "a centaur, a contradiction in terms; for history, that is coordination, is not-philosophy [*Nichtphilosophie*] and philosophy, that is subordination, is not-history [*Nichtgeschichte*]."[3] The critique of Hegel as subordinating the material of history to the progress of the idea of freedom is couched in terms of the "more modest" historical enterprise of coordination. For Burckhardt, cultural history consists not in the subordination of historical events to a given scheme, but their coordination. Yet, under closer examination the historical work of coordination is by no means as philosophically innocent as it professes to be. The work of coordination assumes prior decisions as to what are the relevant historical features to be coordinated. Benjamin will later, in his concept of "constellation" locate these decisions in the interests of the present, a move that Burckhardt anticipates but not as an explicit methodological presupposition.

In the second chapter of the *Weltgeschichtliche Betrachtungen*, Burckhardt systematizes his concept of coordination in terms of the three "potencies" [*Potenzen*]: of the state, religion, and culture. The task of historical research and historical narrative is to coordinate material falling within these potencies. Yet the term "potency" itself is by no means philosphically neutral, potency being a central category of Schelling's philosophy where it denoted the attempt to introduce a dynamic quality into Kantian categories. Indeed, for Burckhardt the three potencies function as a system of dynamic categories for the coordination of historical materials into a narrative. Cultural history analyses the mutual relationships between the three potencies, themselves concealing a further intra-categorial distinction between the *static* potencies of state and religion and the *dynamic* potency of culture.

As a consequence, Burckhardt's cultural history both denies and relies upon a philosophy of history. It testifies to the inevitable presence of a philosophy of history even at the moment that it is most denied: the apparently modest historical project of coordination is a dissembled philosophical subordination. The role of prior conceptual work in historical research is considered vital to the definition of the field of cultural history, but it is also denied. Cultural history as inaugurated by Burckhardt has an inherent philosophical blindness which makes many of its choices and exclusions arbitrary and unreflexive. Benjamin will seek a "dialectical cultural history" capable of reflecting upon its conceptual choices and exclusions but without lapsing into an Hegelian sacrifice of historical material to conceptual organization.

Perhaps the most significant example of a problem in the conceptual organization of Burckhardt's cultural history involves the place of art. In the preface to the *Die Kultur der Renaissance in Italien – Ein Versuch* [The Culture of the Renaissance in Italy – An Experiment] (1860), Burckhardt refers apologetically to the fragmentary character of his "experiment" and to cultural history's "most essential difficulty" of reducing "a vast spiritual continuum to specific and apparently often arbitrary categories in order to bring it somehow to presentation."[4] The necessity of such reduction is never reflected upon, but its main victim in the experiment in the cultural history of the Renaissance is the history of art. Burckhardt confesses the exclusion of art to be "the greatest gap in the book" even if he did deal with the art history of the period elsewhere, in the earlier "guide book" presentation of Italian art in *Der Cicerone: Eine Anleitung zum Genuss der Kunstwerke Italiens* [The Cicerone: A Primer for the Enjoyment of Italian Artworks] (1855), a number of drafts written in the 1860s, and the posthumous *Beitrage zur Kunstgeschichte von Italien* [Lectures on the Art History of Italy] (1898).

The precedent of excluding art from cultural history would be developed in two opposed directions by Heinrich Wölfflin and Aby Warburg – the former insisting on a discrete history of art without explicit links to cultural history, the later pursuing a synthesis of cultural and art history on the basis of psychology. Both developments would be guided by implicit but identifiable philosophical orientations. Benjamin's response to the two developments of Burckhardt's separation of art and cultural history was crucial for the development of his own concept of the discipline.

Wölfflin, Riegl, and the separation of cultural and art history

In 1893 Heinrich Wölfflin succeeded Burckhardt to the Chair of Art History at the University of Basel. Although Burckhardt's student, Wölfflin's interests inclined more toward philosophy and art history than to cultural history; and, while he professed that "the best part of what he was and wanted to be" he owed to Burckhardt,[5] his work showed a steady movement toward the purification of art history from its links with cultural history. What made possible the secession of art from cultural history was Wölfflin's neo-Kantian aesthetic. This allowed him to stress the integrity and the importance of the formal properties of works of art over their links with artistic psychobiography or culture. The process of separating art from culture, increasingly evident from *Renaissance and Baroque* (1888), *Classic Art* (1899), and the *Principles of Art History* (1915), made possible a formal art history separated from the considerations of cultural history.

Wölfflin's work marked a revolutionary departure for the discipline of art history, creating an object – the formal properties of works of art – capable of independent study. Yet, the return to a Kantian philosophical position behind the Hegelian and Schellingesque approaches to art and culture was by no means unproblematic. Wölfflin's formalism created problems for the historical narrative of art history – either the forms had to be themselves historical (a position adopted by Riegl and his concept of "artistic will") or the works of art reduced to the historical exemplifications of timeless patterns. As Panofsky noted in his early critique of Wölfflin, tying a formal pattern to an historical epoch "is not an explanation, but requires explanation."[6] These explanations were often smuggled in covertly: in *Renaissance and Baroque*, Wölfflin disqualified the psychological, technical and "cultural historical" explanations for formal regularities as offering a "pale image of the whole,"[7] while in the *Principles of Art History* he supplements considerations of style with "*the style of the school, the country, the race.*"[8] With the latter admission Wölfflin opened the way for a return to a unified cultural and art history, but without precise examination of what might it might mean to propose "school," "nation," and "race" as explanatory principles. Wölfflin's turn from a vague biographical or "cultural historical" history of art to a "science of art" or *Kunstwissenschaft* based on the study of the formal properties of artworks carried with it an unthematized dependence on cultural history.

Benjamin's attitude toward Wölfflin and the development of cultural history that he represented was equivocal. Very early, in 1912, Benjamin praised Wölfflin's *Classical Art*, but on hearing Wölfflin's lectures in Munich he considered his work a catastrophe for the German university. A more balanced assessment of the significance of Wölfflin's contribution is to be found in his 1932 review of the first volume of the *Kunstwissenschaftliche Forschungen* [Research in the Study of Art] for the newspaper, the *Frankfurter Zeitung*. This review, entitled "The Rigorous Study of Art," begins with a critical appreciation of the revolutionary gesture made by Wölfflin's *Classical Art* in bringing together art history and philosophical aesthetics. For Benjamin, the way in which Wölfflin tried to achieve this, by dividing the work into historical and systematic counterparts, "reveals not only the aims but also the limits of an endeavour which was so epoch-making in its time" (*SW* II, 666). The aim was to take art history beyond "mere biographical anecdotes or a description of the circumstances of the time" but, for Benjamin, the use of "formal analysis" left a dichotomy between "the history of art" and "an academic aesthetic" (*SW* II, 666). The gesture was revolutionary in constituting a new object for the "science of art" but incomplete in not bringing together abstract formal qualities with the history of discrete works.

The dichotomy between timeless formless qualities and the history of art that Benjamin saw as vitiating Wölfflin's achievement promised, in his judgment, to be overcome by the focus of the contributors to the *Kunstwissenschaftliche Forschungen* on the individual work. While Wölfflin had a keen appreciation of the significance of the individual detail in a work, his formal method required that such details be understood as differentials or units of comparison. The detail is compared with other details, the work with other works, the œuvre with other œuvres and the stylistic epoch with other epochs. The alleged "formal qualities" of a work are evoked by comparative analysis, a method that both Benjamin and Panofsky suspected for imposing an arbitrary formal difference rather than discovering it through a process of analysis. By focusing upon the given work, the contributors to the *Kunstwissenschaftliche Forschungen* do not simply compare the formal properties of the work with other works but consider instead the problem of "the formal incorporation of the given world by the artist" ("Rigorous Study of Art," *SW* II, 667). The contributors had learnt from Wölfflin not to assume the nature of the relationship between work and world, but instead of separating them had taken the nature of this relationship itself to be the object of their inquiry.

Benjamin notes later in the review that the focus on the individual work and its "formal incorporation of the given world" shifts the emphasis of art historical study from an emphasis on form to one on incorporation. The focus on how the given world is incorporated in a work lends significance to those elements that make up the individual materiality of a work rather than its formal universality. The "precursor" of this approach and thus "of this new type of art scholar is not Wölfflin but, Riegl" (*SW* II, 668). The new art history that Benjamin here welcomes gains its inspiration from a body of work that was contemporary with Wölfflin's, that shared many of its aims, but which did not pursue the latter's formal method.

For Benjamin, the manner in which art and cultural history were to be integrated was to be the problem of research rather than its methodological premise. Indeed, when considering Eduard Fuchs's materialist critique of Wölfflin's formalism, Benjamin regarded the latter as having more heuristic value for an integrated art and cultural history than the former's dogmatic materialism. In *Eduard Fuchs: Collector and Historian* he cites Fuchs's critique of a passage from Wölfflin's *Classic Art* that claims "concepts of style cannot be exhausted by their material characterization." In response to Wölfflin's claim, Fuchs retorts that, "precisely these formal elements cannot be explained in any other way than by a changed mood of the times" ("Fuchs," *SW* III, 270). Benjamin strongly objects to Fuchs critique on the grounds that it assumes the existence of a link between style and epoch instead of making this link the object of research. In this respect, Wölfflin's extreme formulation of the autonomy of style is more heuristically useful since it leaves open the nature of the links between stylistic and economic and technological change.

In his defense of Wölfflin against Fuchs, Benjamin suggests that works of art contribute materially to creating the "mood of the times." Benjamin takes as an example changes in building and patterns of dwelling during the Renaissance:

> One could hardly fail to benefit from asking what economically conditioned changes the Renaissance brought about in housing construction. Nor would it be unprofitable to examine the role played by Renaissance painting in projecting the new architecture and in illustrating its emergence, which renaissance painting made possible.[9]

Benjamin here assumes a position that is between a formal idealism and materialism. Heuristically, he suggests the latter is of more value because it leaves in question the link between style and epoch rather than presuming to know the nature of the link in advance. Yet, apart from their relative heuristic values, both formal and materialist positions, if taken to their limit, absolve works of art from any responsibility for historical change. They are either formally above historical change or the simple reflection of it. In each case, culture is absolved of any responsibility for history and thus of any possibility of a cultural history calling culture "to justice" for its historical responsibility. In Benjamin's example, Renaissance painting can be considered in part responsible for changes in patterns of dwelling and public space, and by extension of responsibility for historical change.

Benjamin's defense of Wölfflin against Fuchs's materialism underlines his pursuit of a "dialectical" cultural history that makes problematic the notion of culture and the link between works of culture and their historical epochs. He refuses to accept either the scission of art and cultural history proposed by Wölfflin or Fuchs's dogmatic integration in a crude form of historical materialism. The work of Alois Riegl as he intimated in "The Rigorous Study of Art" provided for him an alternative model to both Wölfflin's formalism and to vulgar materialism.

Benjamin's admiration for Riegl's masterpiece *Late Roman Art Industry* (1901) was of long standing; he featured it in an article of 1929 on "Books that Remain Alive" along with Lukács's *History and Class Consciousness*, Rosenzweig's *Star of Redemption*, and Alfred Meier's *Building With Iron*. The article summarises the grounds for his claim that "no other work in art history has had the same fruitful influence in terms of both content and method" and that its author was "the precursor of a new type of art historian" (GS III, 170). In terms of content, Riegl's work was revolutionary for its dissolution of the hierarchy of fine art and craft products – considering a range of late antique artifacts that encompassed architecture, statuary, mosaics, and jewellery. Perhaps more significant for Benjamin was the break "with the theory of 'phases of decadence'" and Riegl's recognition "in what was previously called a 'lapse into barbarism' of a new feeling for space and a new artistic will [*Kunstwollen*]" (GS III, 170). Art works previously considered documents of decline with respect to what preceded them were now to be understood not in terms of a progressive history of art but in terms of being informed by different but no less valid concepts of spatiality and "artistic will."

The procedure developed by Riegl is in complete contrast with the formal method perfected by Wölfflin. The latter developed his aesthetic categories by means of comparing works of art with each other while Riegl's categories are developed by situating works of art with respect to the expression of an "artistic will." The concepts of style developed by both Riegl and Wölfflin are directed against Semper's identification of stylistic traits with technological exigency, but while Wölfflin stresses the formal autonomy of style Riegl links its development to the expression of "artistic will." The virtues of this approach are apparent: the concept of "artistic will" is able to explain both the apparent autonomy of style and its historical development. The dangers are equally evident, for "artistic will" might very easily become a transhistorical metaphysical principle, simply a dynamic equivalent of a timeless form. This danger was amply demonstrated in the work of Wilhelm Worringer which went so far as to link dynamic artistic wills with epochal and even human types.[10]

In *Late Roman Art Industry*, Riegl makes effective use of the concept of artistic will without ever giving a theoretical definition of it. He uses it most frequently to dissolve the boundaries of artistic genres – late Roman sculpture and painting share the same artistic will as do mosaics, miniatures, and costume. Works of art of all genres are related by Riegl to "a unified *Kunstwollen* which takes in its service all raw material and every technique rather than being dominated by them."[11] In its most extreme formulation, the artistic will is said to govern all "creative activity of man."[12] After having established the general concept of the artistic will, Riegl develops its historical variants. He distinguishes between three types – primitive "tactile," classical balanced "tactile and optical," and late Roman "optical" artistic wills. Each in turn is linked to a particular configuration of perception – "close up view [*Nahsicht*]," "normal view [*Normalsicht*]," and "distant view [*Fernsicht*]" as well as an "artistic intention" (*Kunstabsicht*) whose formal characterizations are uncannily similar to Wölfflin's basic formal principles.[13]

While the link between formal characterization (*Kunstabsicht*) and dynamic principle (*Kunstwollen*) is elaborated in terms of modes of perception, the place of the dynamic principle within a broader concept of culture remains obscure. Riegl admits as much himself toward the end of the *Late Roman Art Industry* in an ambiguous footnote on the relationship between "art history" and "iconography" with their respective objects "the history of the *Wollen* in the visual arts" and the "poetic and religious *Wollen*." Riegl acknowledges that there is a "bridge between the two" but that "a deeper knowledge" of the connection requires the separation of the two inquiries – he concludes programatically by seeing in "the creation of a clear separation between iconography and history of art . . . the precondition of any progress of art historical research for the near future."[14] In the final analysis it seems as if Riegl is as rigorous as Wölfflin in his separation of art and cultural history, but at the same time acknowledging the necessity of their being reintegrated in future work.

It is interesting to reflect on the reasons for Bejamin's interpretative charity with respect to Riegl. It was certainly not shared by the group of cultural historians associated with the school of Aby Warburg who, shrewdly, recognized no great difference between the approaches of Wölfflin and Riegl. Panofsky's 1920 essay "Der Begriff des Kunstwollens [The Concept of Artistic Will]" is sensitive to the dangers of the concept of "artistic will," notably the possibility that if made into a transcendental category "artistic will" might generate a dynamic formalism comparable to the static version developed by Wölfflin. Edgar Wind, writing in 1930 on "Warburg's Concept of 'Kulturwissenschaft' and its Meaning for Aesthetics" regarded the work of Wölfflin and Riegl, "despite differences in detail" as "both informed by a polemical concern for the autonomy of art history, by a desire to free it from the civilization and thus to break with the tradition associated with the name of Jacob Burckhardt."[15] Benjamin's judgment of Riegl is at first sight by no means as categorical as his Warburg School contemporaries. As we have seen, he spoke favorably of Riegl and of the concept of *Kunstwollen*. Yet, when his use of Riegl's work is inspected more closely, it becomes clear that what he took from it were a number of methodological prescriptions that for Riegl himself were not central.

Benjamin's use of Riegl in the "Epistemo-Critical Prologue" of *The Origin of the German Tragic Drama* underlines his innovative application of the concept of "artistic will." For Benjamin, as for Riegl, the concept of artistic will is important for dissolving generic and critical notions of value – in this case between classic and baroque – and for dissolving the concept of "so-called periods of decline." Yet, Benjamin prizes this discovery for making it possible to study genres and epochs excluded from the canon and thus to put into question canonicity itself. This was not one of Riegl's primary concerns, nor was another methodological prescription adopted by Benjamin, namely the focus on incompleteness or the imperfect realizations of the artistic will – artistic "failures" such as the German Tragic Drama rather than the traditional focus on fully realized work (*Origin*, 55). Benjamin ignored Riegl's scruples concerning the links between art and cultural history, and pragmatically took from him what was useful for his concept of cultural history. This is consistent with the comment on Riegl as a "precursor" in "The Rigorous Study of Art" – the "new type of art scholar" is now able to practice what Riegl felt he could not – namely, the fusion of iconography and art history. This fusion is most effective in the marginal and uncanonical case, as Benjamin observes, "it is precisely in the investigation of the marginal case that material contents reveal their key position most decisively" (*SW* II, 669).

Far from rejecting the turn from cultural to art history, Benjamin approaches the work of Wölfflin and Riegl pragmatically, prizing the heuristic value of the formalism of the one and the suggestive methodological prescriptions of the other. Their work contributed to his concept of cultural history, but the critical encounters were to be with the two most powerful examples of the integration of art and cultural history, those of Aby Warburg and his school and historical materialism.

The integration of art and cultural history: Warburg and Benjamin

Kurt W. Foster begins his introduction to the English translation of Aby Warburg's collection of essays *The Renewal of Pagan Antiquity: Contributions to the Cultural History of the European Renaissance* (1932)[16] by comparing Warburg and Benjamin. The grounds of comparison – their postwar influence and the "academic industry" now devoted to them – underestimates the affinity between their concepts of cultural history: both were fascinated by transitional periods such as the Renaissance and the Reformation; both sought a theoretically informed and integrated cultural history that paid close attention to the individual artifact or text; and both were driven by the need to establish constellations between the present and the past, between modernism and tradition. Fascinatingly, neither Warburg nor Benjamin were able to complete their final projects, both dedicated to evoking "dialectical images" of historical memory: Warburg's MNEMOSYNE Atlas[17] and Benjamin's *Arcades Project* file. Yet, in spite of the broad similarities between the basic projects, the details of their execution differed greatly. The two concepts of cultural history that they represented seemed to approach each other most closely in Benjamin's *The Origin of the German Tragic Drama*, sufficiently for Benjamin to make an approach to Warburg by sending him a copy of the book.[18] Unfortunately nothing came of this approach, perhaps less because of the unfavorable influence of Erwin Panofsky, as is often claimed, than because of the already evident differences between Warburg and Benjamin's methodologies.[19]

In the preface to his now classic essay "The Art of Portraiture and the Florentine Bourgeoisie" (1902), Warburg situates his work within the divided heritage of Burckhardt's cultural history. He points to the distinction between the discussion of "the psychology of the individual in society without reference to visual art" in *The Culture of the Renaissance* and the "introduction" to works of art in *The Cicerone*, and notes that "Burckhardt was content . . . to examine Renaissance man in his most perfectly developed type, and art in its finest manifestations, separately and at leisure, without

worrying whether he would ever have time for the comprehensive presentation of the whole culture."[20] Having evoked the separation of the histories
of art and culture, Warburg does not follow Wölfflin and Riegl in endors-
ing their divorce but seeks to reintegrate them. He finds in Burckhardt's
posthumously published essays on "The Altarpiece," "The Collector," and
especially "The Portrait in Painting" the inspiration for "yet a third empirical
path to the great objective of a synthesis of cultural history" (*Renewal*, 186).
The new synthesis of art and cultural history can be achieved by means of
the method "of examining the individual work of art within the immediate
context of its time, in order to interpret as "causal factors" the ideological
and practical demands of real life" (*Renewal*, 186). The study that follows
attempts to apply this method through an analysis of the Ghirlandaio fresco
in the church of Santa Trinità (Florence).

Warburg's methodological preface and the essay that follows it already
demonstrate the points of meeting and divergence between his and
Benjamin's concepts of cultural history: both subscribe to the integration
of art and cultural history and both agree that this is best achieved by means
of the close analysis of an individual work, whether of visual art or literature. It might be expected that Benjamin would be sympathetic to viewing
the "immediate context of [an artwork's] time" in terms of "the ideological and practical demands of real life." Yet, Warburg's understanding of
the latter differs subtly, but widely, from what Benjamin would accept. The
clue to Warburg's understanding of the significance of "ideological and practical demands" was already revealed earlier in the preface in his characterization of Burckhardt's *The Culture of the Renaissance in Italy* as a study
of "the *psychology* of the individual in society." This is by no means an
accurate formulation of Burckhardt's experiment, but it was one consistent
with Warburg's own cultural historical training under Karl Lamprecht.[21]
The latter attempted to ground cultural history in psychology, categorizing
the periods of German history in his *Deutsche Geschichte* in terms of psychological epochs and the periods of crisis that accompanied the transition
from one epoch to another.[22]

In Warburg's "The Art of Portraiture and the Florentine Bourgeoisie" it is
quickly evident that the "ideological and practical demands" are construed
in terms of individual and group psychology. In many ways the translation
of the "demands" into psychological terms proved very fruitful, especially
in permitting a link between the individual artist, their milieu and the social
and economic forces that created the milieu. Indeed, the turn to psychology
provided for Warburg the key to that "great objective of a synthesis of cultural history" uniting the individual work with its culture. Warburg regarded
Renaissance Florence as a period of transition characterized by practical and

ideological tensions with their correlates in group and individual psychology. He describes the "citizen of Medicean Florence" as uniting "the wholly dissimilar characters of the idealist – whether medievally Christian or romantically chivalrous, or classically Neoplatonic – and the worldly, practical, pagan Etruscan merchant" (*Renewal*, 190). This tension and the conflicts and compromises it provoked were translated by Warburg into psychological correlates, as in his general observation that, "When conflicting worldviews kindle partisan emotions, setting the members of society at each other's throats, the social fabric inexorably crumbles; but when those views hold a balance within a single individual – when instead of destroying each other, they fertilise each other and expand the whole range of the personality – then they are powers that lead to the noblest achievements of civilisation" (*Renewal*, 190). Works of art in this view of cultural history become the privileged sites for the harmonious reconciliation of the real and psychological tensions that attack the fabric of a given society. The Ghirlandaio fresco is then persausively read in terms of this tension and its resolution.

The integration of cultural and art history by means of the translation of practical and ideological demands into psychological tensions that are brought to resolution in works of art implies an affirmative concept of culture. Social tension and their psychological correlates may be resolved in art – the role of the art work is to heal and provide psychological and social balance. Warburg's acknowledgment of social and psychological tensions and the threat they pose to the social fabric was accompanied by a sometimes desperate affirmation of culture as the site of psychological and social healing. His work exemplifies the difficulty that cultural history faced in accepting that a document of culture – the site of the reconciliation of social and psychological tension – was, by definition of being such a site, also a document of barbarism. For, at the limit, Warburg's position would require that a civilized society without tension and conflict would have no need of art, and that the existence of art is thus an index of barbarism.

Benjamin's "dialectical" concept of cultural history differs considerably from that of Warburg in embracing the negative aspect of works of art and culture. He also criticized the psychological approach to cultural history pioneered by Lamprecht and developed by Warburg for dissolving social into psychological tensions and then prescribing culture as the remedy for these tensions. For these reasons, the apparent confluence between his and Warburg's approach to cultural history in *The Origin of the German Tragic Drama* already contains large methodological and substantive disagreements.

The differences between Warburg and Benjamin's concepts of cultural history may be illustrated by their discussions of melancholy and in particular

Dürer's allegorical engraving "Melancholia I." The interpretation of this image became one of the set pieces of the Warburg School, departing from the demonstration by Carl Giehlow in his essay, "Dürers Stich 'Melancholia I' und der maximilianische Humanistenkreis" (1904), of the image's indebtedness to the ancient and medieval medical tradition of the diagnosis and treatment of melancholy. Warburg critically extended Giehlow's interpretation of the image in one of his finest essays, "Pagan–Antique Prophesy in Words and Images in the Age of Luther" (1920), whose approach was broadened and confirmed by Panofsky and Fritz Saxl in a study "'Melancholia I.' Eine quellen- und typengeschichtliche Untersuchung" (1923) that became the basis of the later *Saturn and Melancholy*. All of these interpretations, with the exception of the last, were referred to by Benjamin in his own discussion of the engraving in *The Origin of the German Tragic Drama*.

Warburg begins "Pagan–Antique Prophesy in Words and Images in the Age of Luther" with a reference to "the history of art in the widest sense (insofar as the term covers image making in all its forms)" (*Renewal*, 598). He proposes to examine images that "lack aesthetic appeal" and are thus "unpromising material for the purely formal concerns of present-day art history" (*Renewal*, 598). While this taking of distance from Wölfflin may seem a departure from the earlier focus upon a work of art as a site of the harmony of the tensions of a given age, it is in reality a confirmation of it. For the essay culminates in an interpretation of an indisputably "aesthetic" work of art – "Melancholia I" – on the basis of the astrological imagery that preceded it. Warburg's subtle and beautiful interpretation of the Dürer engraving reads it as a therapeutic diagram. Focusing on the "magic square of Jupiter" prominent in the upper left of the image, Warburg criticizes Giehlow's claim that it is a symbol of inventive genius. He argues instead that the magic square has its roots in therapeutic magic opposed to the influence of Saturnine melancholy. Warburg, however, does not leave his interpretation at this point, but takes it another step:

> The truly creative act – that which gives Dürer's *Melancholy I* its consoling humanistic message of liberation from the fear of Saturn – can be understood only if we recognise that the artist has taken a magical and mythical logic and made it spiritual and intellectual. (*Renewal*, 644)

As in the essay on "The Art of Portraiture and the Florentine Bourgeoisie" the vocation of art is to sublimate the psychological tensions of an age into an image of harmony. In this case, the magical and mythical logic that was evident in the "non-aesthetic" images discussed in the article prior to the Dürer is made "spiritual and intellectual." The "cosmic contest" between Saturn and Jupiter evoked by magic is "humanised and metamorphosed by

Dürer into the image of thinking, working human being" (*Renewal*, 644). The humanistic transformation of mythic and magical forces through the work of art is here once again affirmed by Warburg in terms of the creative working through of the tension between Saturnine depression and and Jovial elation, and not, as in Giehlow, the affirmation of genius.

In their development of Warburg's reading of "Melancholia I," Panofsky and Saxl focus on the allegorical character of the engraving. Their reconstruction of the tradition of medical and astrological knowledge that was visually reassembled in the allegory is informed by Warburg's view that the allegory presents an "image of thinking, working human being" or the unity of the thinker and the artist. In the work of allegorical art the demands of truth and the demands of beauty are brought together into a "spiritual and intellectual" transfiguration. Panofsky and Saxl's work plumbs some of the depths of this synthesis, showing how "scientific" and "artistic" traditions fuse in the engraving to produce a new allegorical art. Although any reference to the Nietzschean origins of the unity of knowledge and art (the "artistic Socrates') are carefully ignored both in their essay and in the later *Saturn and Melancholy*, the attempt to reconcile the Apollinian and the Dionysian remains central to their and to Warburg's research. The intense fascination shown by Warburg and his followers for the person and the work of Dürer follows from the view that he represents a moment in which the drives for knowledge and for beauty find themselves in a rare equilibrium.

Although Benjamin's interpretation of "Melancholia I" pays overt homage to the work of Giehlow, Warburg, Panofsky, and Saxl, it is hard to imagine a more resolute inversion of their aims, methods, and results. In *The Origin of the German Tragic Drama* allegory, far from reconciling and sublimating opposed forces, instead presents their irreconcilability. For Benjamin, only "symbolic" art offers the possibility for reconciliation, and this under specific conditions. Consequently, for him the Dürer engraving does not represent a moment of transfiguration – of myth into knowledge and knowledge into art – but instead a moment of tension and potential collapse. Allegory does not offer therapeutic consolation, but the spectacle of ruin and even, in an ironic reference to the Warburg School's fascination with the history of medicine, the *facies hippocratica* of the signs of death. Allegory is the contemplation of bones, an anatonomical art form that does not bring life, as it did for Warburg, but only death and dispersion.

The view of allegory as a "mortuary art" is as far removed from Warburg's interpretation of its therapeutic powers as it is from the humanistic core of Warburg's interpretation. Warburg sought in Dürer's allegory a "humanistic message of liberation from fear of Saturn" in which transfigured humans overcome fear of the cosmos and the objectivity that surrounds and oppresses them. His interpretation of the image focuses on the Jovial magic square that has overcome the assembled emblems of Saturn and melancholy – "the salvation of the human being through the countervailing influence of Jupiter has already taken place...and the magic square hangs on the wall like a votive offering of thanks to the benign and victorious planetary spirit" (*Renewal*, 645–47). The image is interpreted as the outcome of a millennial psychodrama between the forces of Saturn and Jove. In Benjamin the humanistic element is completely absent. Emblematically his focus rests upon the dog and the stone – precisely the non-human elements of the images – creatures and things.[23] They remain in the image as emblems of natural and creaturely melancholy. The focus follows from Benjamin's concept of melancholy, which is less a psychological state than an ontological property of things. For Benjamin, it is not humans that are melancholy before physical and creaturely nature, but nature that is melancholy under the gaze of the human.

The origins of Benjamin's theological antihumanism can be found in the texts of 1916 that form the "conception" of *The Origin of the German Tragic Drama*, in particular "On Language as Such and on the Language of Man." In the latter Benjamin describes how human language effects an imperfect and even violent translation through "the Fall" of the language of nature into the language of mankind, depriving it of expression. This deprivation, for Benjamin, produces the "great sorrow of nature" – its mourning for a non-human, divine expression and its consequent melancholy, "how much more melancholy it is to be named not from the blessed paradisical language of [divine] name, but from the hundred languages of man" ("On Language," *SW* I, 73). Melancholy is in the world and the creature, not necessarily in the gaze of man: human melancholy, as Benjamin is at pains to show in *The Origin of the German Tragic Drama*, is but an aspect of a general ontological melancholy, not its source and privileged centre.

The shift of the locus of the melancholy from the human to the cosmos severely disrupts the humanistic agenda of Warburg's cultural history. The work of allegorical art no longer provides the therapeutic synthesis or "consoling message of human liberation" from Saturn and melancholy, but the fragmented image of a shattered nature in a state of mourning. The emblems of melancholy assembled in Dürer's engraving remain in a state of fragmented mourning from which there is no exit that is within human power. The fragments gathered in the engraving are not symbolically reassembled in a "spiritual and intellectual transfiguration" but perform an allegorical *Trauerspiel* or "play of mourning." The work of art presents the shattered emblems of allegory for contemplation, but not for healing or completion. The melancholy of objects cannot be redeemed by human knowledge or work since it is precisely human knowledge and work that has condemned them to melancholy. The most the work of art can do is to bear witness to this predicament. While Warburg sees "Melancholia I" as both the presentation and an act of human liberation, Benjamin sees it as the presentation and an act of mourning.

Warburg and Benjamin's opposed views of art as therapeutic liberation and act of witness and mourning are carried over into their concepts of cultural history. Warburg's cultural history attempts to perform the very act of human liberation from the forces of melancholy and the cosmos that is its object. The work of knowledge and of culture consists in rediscovering and conveying to the future the consoling vision of a balance between freedom and destiny or Jove and Saturn. Knowledge and art are thus dedicated to the human transfiguration of the forces of nature. Yet, from the point of view of Benjamin, this understanding of cultural history as the affirmation of life and human freedom over death and natural destiny remains a document of barbarism, since such affirmation in history and in art does not bear witness to the price of this affirmation in natural, creaturely and human suffering.

Benjamin's concept of cultural history

The role that is played by the Warburg School's humanistic concept of culture and cultural history in *The Origin of the German Tragic Drama* is ascribed in the *Arcades Project* to historical materialism. In *The Origin of the German Tragic Drama* the cultural history and underlying humanistic philosophy of Warburg and his school served as a point both of orientation and of criticism. The method and the results of historical materialism play a similar role in the *Arcades Project*, both orienting the method and program of research and serving as its critical foil. Both projects share the concern to reject the notion of periods of decline and progress, to achieve a constellation of the past and the present, and to apply the theory of allegory (*Arcades*, 458–59). In both projects these concerns are aspects of a broader "theological" critique of humanism. This emerges clearly in Benjamin's statement of his concept of cultural history developed against the humanism of historical materialism.

Benjamin's work on the *Arcades Project* generated a number of accompanying articles that reflected on the broader project or applied some of its theses. The first third of "Eduard Fuchs: Collector and Historian" from 1937 can be read as a reflection on the concept of history underlying the work on the *Arcades Project*. Benjamin took the opportunity of a commissioned essay on the leading Marxist cultural historian of the period of the Second International to state a thorough critique of Marxist cultural history. After some introductory comments on Fuchs, Benjamin cites a passage from Engels that criticizes the compartmentalization of history and the notion of historical development. He then proceeds to make it yield a number of unexpected conclusions that add up to a devastating critique of precisely the historical materialism that Engels and his followers thought they were defending.[24] The critique and the concept of a dialectical cultural history that emerges from it are based on the philosophical concept of experience developed by Benjamin in other writings, and on the symptomatic difficulties posed by the experience of art.

First of all, Benjamin identifies in the Engels passage a "critique of the convention in the history of ideas which represents a new dogma as a 'development' of an earlier one" ("Fuchs," *SW* III, 261). Engels's rather modest claim is taken by Benjamin as an occasion for a critique of historicism and the statement of an experiential concept of historical knowledge. Historicism's assumption of continuous historical development is criticized for the contemplative character of its experience of the historical object and representation of this object within epic narrative forms. Against this, Benjamin proposes an image of "historical materialism" that foregrounds the present experience of the past and its presentation in constructivist forms of narrative that create constellations between past, present and future:

> Historicism presents the eternal image of the past whereas historical materialism presents a given experience with the past – an experience that is unique. The replacement of the epic element by the constructive element proves to be the condition for this experience. The immense forces bound up in historicism's "once upon a time" are liberated in this experience. To put to work an experience with history – a history that is original for every present – is the task of historical materialism. The latter is directed toward a consciousness of the present which explodes the continuum of history.   ("Fuchs," *SW* III, 262)

The first distinction between historicism and historical materialism is couched in terms of the temporality and modality of the experience of the past. Historicism has an experience *of* the past, regarding it as an object eternally present, while historical materialism has an experience *with* the past that is a unique and transient constellation. In the latter, the historical object ceases to be an object *of* and becomes a participant *in* an historical experience. The condition for this experience of the present with the past is a "constructive" rather than epic narrative – as exemplified in the modernist "montage" narrative form adopted in the *Arcades Project*. The "consolidation" of experience and history is not an Hegelian synthesis of experience and history, in which the present recognizes itself in its past, but the experience of shock in which neither present not past can contain each other in a coherent experience. If the past and present were continuous, then the present could narrate the past without difficulty and this narration would be the fused experience of past and present bequeathed to a future that is continuous with it. Benjamin instead describes the consolidation of experience as an original and unique constellation, intending originality in the sense of the "Epistemo-Critical Prologue" to *The Origins of the German Tragic Drama* as "an eddy in the stream of becoming." Experience of the past is blocked, producing a disturbance or "eddy" that has consequences for the future. Thus with respect both to past and future, the incomplete experience of the past with the present "explodes the continuum of history."

These reflections on the experience of history owe more to Benjamin's concept of experience than to Engels, and certainly to Fuchs whom Benjamin immediately after dismisses for his "old dogmatic and naïve idea of reception" ("Fuchs," *SW* III, 262). However, Benjamin draws further and even more radical conclusions from Engels concerning the historical object. Engels's critique of the separation of the specialized fields of history from each other is taken much further by Benjamin who claims "that it placed the closed unity of the disciplines and their products in question" ("Fuchs," 226). He exemplifies his thought with a reference to art history, with whose claim for autonomy in the hands of Wölfflin he was deeply familiar. Benjamin's argument has two steps – the first is that the consequence of critique of the closed unity of the history of art and its object "art" "challenges the unity of art itself, as well as that of those works which purportedly come under the rubric of art" ("Fuchs," *SW* III, 261). The unity of the object "art" – secured by Wölfflin in terms of its form – is here dispersed spatially into the world which contained and is contained in works of art. The identity of the work of art – what it is that makes this object or practice in the world "art" – is thus put into question, as is the discipline that claims to study such objects and practices.

Benjamin goes even further with his dissolution of the concept of art, dispersing it not only spatially into the world, but also, temporally, into history. The work of art for him is never complete: "For the dialectical historian concerned with works of art, these works integrate their fore-history as well as their after-history; and it is by virtue of their after-history that their fore-history is recognizable as involved in a continuous change" ("Fuchs," *SW* III, 261). The work of art is never completely present – its process of embodying and distinguishing itself from the world is continued in the interpretations of it, which change its identity. The experience of a work of art is ineluctably historical for Benjamin, it "does not depend on an encounter just with the work of art but with the history which has allowed the work to come down to our own age" ("Fuchs," *SW* III, 262). This history is a question not just of the reception and the transmission of work but also of the history that was the condition of this continued reception.

After these preliminary statements of the consequences of viewing the past as an active partner in an historical experience – the experience *with* rather than *of* the past – Benjamin goes on to reflect on their implications for the concept of culture and cultural history. His two-page digression on cultural history encapsulates his concept of culture and his view of the possibility of a "dialectical" cultural history. His discussion is preceded by locating the work of Fuchs in the "problematic" of the epoch of German Social Democracy and identifying this "problematic" with that of cultural history: "his work participates in a problematic that is inseparable from cultural history" ("Fuchs," *SW* III, 267). The "problematic" of the epoch had been described in terms of historicism, particularly in respect to technology. Benjamin argued that the Social Democrats believed in the continuity of history according to which the proletariat would become the heirs to the culture and the technological achievements of the past. The Social Democrats "saw the past as having been gathered up and stored forever in the granaries of the present. Although the future held the propect of work, it also held the certainty of a rich harvest" ("Fuchs," *SW* III, 267). It was relationship to the past that Benjamin also held to be "inseparable from cultural history."

Benjamin returns to the quotation from Engels and now critically describes its "true meaning" as the "*locus classicus* which defines historical materialism as the history of culture" ("Fuchs," *SW* III, 267). Benjamin criticizes Engels's view of the unity of the study of history as flowing together "into the study of cultural history as the inventory which humanity has preserved to the present day" ("Fuchs," *SW* III, 267). As the inventory of the past "stored forever in the sheds of the present," cultural history/historical materialism, while claiming to serve progress, in fact subscribes to "barbarism." The first way in which culture is said to be barbaric involves the production of the objects of culture: "Historical materialist surveys in art or science have, without exception, a lineage he cannot observe without horror. The products of art and science owe their existence not merely to the effort of the great geniuses who created them, but also, in one degree or another, to the anonymous toil of their contemporaries" ("Fuchs," *SW* III, 267). It is in following this claim to the unacknowledged labor implicit in objects of culture that Benjamin states: "There is no document of culture which is not at the same time a document of barbarism. No cultural history has yet done justice to this fundamental state of affairs, and it can hardly hope to do so" ("Fuchs," *SW* III, 267). In this context the reparation of cultural history would seem to consist in naming the unnamed, in acknowledging their contribution, but, while important, for Benjamin "the crucial element does not lie here" ("Fuchs," *SW* III, 267).[25]

The "decisive element" is not the restitution of past suffering by the present, which would be for the present to come into complete possession of the past, but rather the impossibility of ever possessing the past. For Benjamin, "Historical materialism sees the work of the past as still uncompleted. It perceives no epoch in which that work could, even in part, drop conveniently, thing-like, into mankind's lap" ("Fuchs," *SW* III, 267). The objects and events of the past are not conveyed as complete and autonomous objects to the present but retain a reserve, whether of unacknowledged labor or of a potential that is yet to be realized. It is this reserve, akin to the melancholy of objects in *The Origin of the German Tragic Drama* that make it impossible for the past to be fully possessed by the present. Something of the past escapes the present, leaving the past as an incomplete task, already in the future.

A "dialectical cultural history" would be one capable of acknowledging the reserve of the past, but this would also be to acknowledge that the past can unsettle and disrupt the present. This position was consistent with Benjamin's speculative concept of experience which maintained that the objects of experience will always exceed, trouble and even destroy the established limits of experience. The objects of the past, because they cannot be fully possessed, will always disrupt the efforts of the present to contain them within its categories or forms of narrative. Yet, Benjamin considers that a dialectical cultural history capable of respecting and transforming itself before the past is fragile, even "devoid of sense," "since the continuum of history – once blasted apart by dialectic – is never dissipated so widely as it is in the realm of culture" ("Fuchs," *SW* III, 268). The inclusive character of the concept of culture reduces the potential for reserve of the objects of the past, and by so doing makes it possible for all of everything of the past to be possessed: cultural history "may augment the weight of the treasure accumulating on the back of humanity, but it does not 'provide the strength to shake off this burden so as to take control of it'" ("Fuchs," *SW* III, 268). Yet, it is precisely this senselessness that offers the chance to cultural history to do justice to the past.

A dialectic cultural history is possible if it adopts "the destructive element which authenticates both dialectical thought and the experience of the dialectical thinker" ("Fuchs," *SW* III, 268). The "destructive element" does not refer to the destruction of the past by the present but rather the possibility that the reserve of the past will destroy aspects of the present and open it to the future. The "decisive element" is the notion that the past is incomplete and cannot be completed in the present and consequently that the encounter of the past with the present will transform the present. Ultimately, Fuchs and historical materialism fail to achieve the status of a dialectical cultural history since they prescribe in advance the relationship between past and present, selecting what is relevant and why it is relevant and reducing the past to items in an inventory of the present. It is at this point that Benjamin finds even the strictures of Wölfflin's formalism to be more dialectical, since by its formal rigidity it endangers its own conceptual structure in the face of historical objects.

Rubbing history against the grain

The concept of a dialectical cultural history is speculative, but not in an Hegelian sense of the objects and events of the past being contained within a conceptual narrative which always exceeded them (the promise of freedom) and which is realized in the present. For Benjamin, the incompleteness of the objects and events of the past is not recuperated by the present but serves to unsettle and threaten its conceptual frameworks. Unlike Warburg, Benjamin's cultural history does not try to preserve the present from the barbarism of the past by showing the therapeutic sublimation of destructive forces in works of culture, but rather by showing that objects of culture exceed the concept of culture and in this excess possess a destructive moment of barbarism.

The objective focus of Benjamin's speculative concept of experience and of the dialectical concept of cultural history that follows from it is far removed from any humanism, whether that of Warburg or of historical materialism. The underlying theological rather than humanistic character of his cultural history is fully owned in his correspondence with Horkheimer on the subject of the Fuchs essay. In a letter of 16 March 1937, part of which Benjamin excerpted for the *Arcades Project*, Horkheimer objected to the idea that the past is incomplete: "Past injustice has occurred and is completed. The slain are really slain. In the end, your affirmation is theology. If one takes the lack of closure entirely seriously, one must believe in the Last Judgment."[26] For Horkheimer, doing justice to the past is to acknowledge that it and its injustices are irreparable and to be mourned; anything else is "idealistic" and "theological."

Benjamin's response is to admit and deny Horkheimer's objection. The "corrective" to Horkheimer's view of the closure of the past is "the consideration that history is not simply a science but also and not least a form of remembrance [*Eindenken*]" (*Arcades*, 471). The past only exists for remembrance and can be modified for it – the complete made incomplete, the incomplete complete. Benjamin continues: "This is theology; but in remembrance we have an experience that forbids us to conceive of history as fundamentally atheological, little as it may be granted us to try and write it with immediately theological concepts" (*Arcades*, 471). While history cannot be written according to the theological structures of the progress of Messianism, the experience of the past in remembrance contains an excess that is not, as in Hegel, the humanistic concept of freedom, but the theological concept of incompleteness. The incompleteness of the past forces the present to face its own fragmentation. The task of the historian to "rub history against the grain" destroys not only the lustre of completeness that attends the past but also the shine of invincibility of the present.

NOTES

1. For a detailed analysis of Benjamin's philosophy in these terms see my *Walter Benjamin: The Colour of Experience* (London: Routledge, 1998), esp. ch. 1.
2. For a more detailed analysis of Burckhardt's anti-Hegelianism see my inaugural lecture "Philosophy and Cultural History," Goldsmiths College, London.
3. Jacob Burckhardt, *Weltgeschichtliche Betrachtungen* [1905] (Stuttgart: Alfred Kroner, 1978), 4.
4. Burckhardt, *Die Kultur der Renaissance in Italien* [1869] (Stuttgart: Alfred Kroner, 1988), 3.
5. David Marc Hoffmann, *Jacob Burckhardt 1818–1897: Geschichte – Kunst – Kultur* (Basel: Schwabe 1997), 86.
6. Erwin Panofsky, "Das Problem des Stils in der bildenden Kunst" [1915], in *Aufsatze zu Grundfragen der Kunstwissenschaft*, eds. Hariolf Oberer and Egon Verheyen(Berlin: Wissenschaftsverlag Volker Spiess, 1998), 25.
7. Wölfflin, Heinrich, *Renaissance and baroque* [1888], trans. Kathrin Simon (London: Collins, 1964), 76.
8. Wölfflin, *Principles of Art History: The Problem of the Development of Style in Later Art History* [1915], trans. M. D. Hottinger (New York: Dover Publications, 1950), 6.
9. Ibid., 6.
10. See Worringer's *Abstraktion und Einfuhlung* (Bern, 1907) and, perhaps more tellingly, *Formprobleme der Gotik* (Munich, 1911).
11. Alois Riegl, *Late Roman Art Industry*, trans. Rolf Winkes (Rome: Giorgio Bretschneider, 1988), 145.
12. Ibid., 169.
13. In an astonishing contrast, Riegl illustrates the differences between artistic wills, perceptions, and artistic intentions in the terms of the representation of folds in clothing – Egyptian representation was "tactile and without folds" while the Greek – both tactile and optical – achieved "clear division and yet harmonious necessary connection between the parts" (169). The typology of artistic wills is used in a different context by Benjamin in his essay "The Work of Art in the Age of its Mechanical Reproduction."
14. Riegl, *Late Roman Art Industry*, 227.

15. Edgar Wind, "Warburg's Concept of 'Kulturwissenschaft' and its Meaning for Aesthetics," in *The Art of Art History: A Critical Anthology*, ed. Donald Preziosi (Oxford University Press, 1998), 207.

16. *The Renewal of Pagan Antiquity*, trans. David Britt (Los Angeles: Getty Research Institute Publications, 1999). Subsequent references to this work will be given parenthetically in the text.

17. For a discussion of this project see, E. H. Gombrich, *Aby Warburg: An Intellectual Biography* (Oxford: Phaidon Press, 1986), 283–306.

18. This annotated copy of *The Origin of the German Tragic Drama* is still held in the Warburg Institute Library, London. My thanks to Alex Coles for bringing it to my attention.

19. For the version citing the unfavorable influence of Panofsky, see the "chronology" in Walter Benjamin, *SW* II, 827.

20. Warburg, in *Renewal*, 186.

21. For the influence of Lamprecht on Warburg, see Gombrich's chapter, "The Psychology of Culture," in *Aby Warburg: An Intellectual Biography*, 25–37. The links between Warburg and Lamprecht deserve closer examination. It is evident in the famous example of the American Indian children's drawing of lightning in Warburg's 1923 lecture "Images from the Region of the Pueblo Indians of North America" in which Warburg asked the children "to illustrate the German fairy tale of "Johny-Head-in-the-Air" (see, *The Art of Art History: A Critical Anthology*, ed. Donald Preziosi [Oxford University Press, 1998], 204). This was, in fact, a contribution to a comparative research program into the psychology of children's art initiated by Lamprecht in which researchers were asked to collect children's illustrations of "Johny-Head-in-the-Air." Warburg's copy of Lamprecht's research program is to be found in the Warburg library.

22. For Benjamin's critique of Lamprecht, see "Fuchs."

23. *Origin*, 145–56; for the interpretation of the dog, p. 152, of the stone pp. 153–55.

24. The citation is from a letter from Engels to the Marxist cultural historian Franz Mehring dated 14 July 1893, cited by Benjamin in "Fuchs," 226.

25. This is underlined in the *Arcades Project* where Benjamin writes in Convolute N that, "Barbarism lurks in the very concept of culture – as the concept of a fund of values which is considered independent not, indeed, of the production process in which these values originated, but of the one in which they survive" (*Arcades*, 467–68; N5a, 7).

26. Horkheimer, letter to Benjamin, 16 March 1937; the third sentence of the citation is omitted by Benjamin in his excerpt in *Arcades*, 471; N8, 1.

5

ANDREW BENJAMIN

Benjamin's modernity

Any argument that starts with the claim that it concerns a theory of modernity is constrained to account for the nature of modernity's inception. Even in working with the assumption of modernity's presence there would still have to be a description of that which was located in its differentiation from the modern. Part of the argument to be developed here is that for the major thinkers of modernity its occurrence is thought in terms of a break or an interruption. Here, the particular project is to locate that thinking in the writings of Walter Benjamin. A context therefore is set by those writings and the presence within them of attempts to develop a relationship between modernity and its necessary interarticulation with a philosophical conception of historical time. Given this context, the opening question has to concern the specificity of interruption within those writings.

How is interruption to be thought? What is the conception of interruption at work within Benjamin's writings? Although it appears as a motif in his engagement with Romanticism and is then repositioned – if not reworked in the later writings in terms of a thinking of historical time – interruption as a mode of thought within Benjamin's work can be identified under a number of different headings. In each instance what insists is the question of what interruption stages. In Benjamin, as will become clear, interruption is the term through which a theory of modernity can be thought. This is not to argue that it is identical with the conception of modernity located in Benjamin's writings as such. Rather, it is modernity as an interruption, one that has to be maintained and which will vanish within the resurgence of historicism understood as the insistence of continuity in the face of discontinuity, that marks the move from a specifically Romantic motif to a thinking of historical time. The Romantic motif of interruption will allow for such a thinking of historical time. The direct consequence of this is that to the extent that this latter point is the case then a theory of modernity will owe as much to a Romantic heritage as it will to one coming from the Enlightenment.[1] Indeed, it can be further argued that thinking the particularity of modernity as an interruption depends upon the successful distancing of the conception of historical time within the Enlightenment tradition.

Interruption is named in different ways. Perhaps the most emphatic, and the one that will allow this theme to be traced here, is the "caesura." The aim of this chapter is to develop an understanding of interruption both in terms of the "caesura," and to note the effective presence of this specific mode of thought within a number of different texts. Often interruption will be named differently. Rather than attempt a synoptic exercise, two particular moments will be taken up. The first concerns the work of the caesura in Benjamin's essay "Goethe's *Elective Affinities*" and the second is the recurrence of the term in Convolute N of the *Arcades Project* (*Arcades*, 475; N10a, 3). In regard to Benjamin's own chronology these texts mark the beginning and the end of his writing career. While Benjamin writes both his doctoral dissertation and his essay on Hölderlin prior to the Goethe essay, the latter can be seen as the point of departure both for his development of the concept of criticism developed in the dissertation and his sustained engagement with the Romantic heritage. The *Arcades Project*, while not finished in a literal sense, always brought with it the possibility of never being finished. As such it was the work that truly marked the end of Benjamin's writings.

Almost at the end of Benjamin's extraordinary study of Goethe's novel, he writes that a particular sentence contains what he describes as the "caesura of the work." Analyzing this claim will open up the way the caesura is staged in his early writings. The passage in question is the following:

> In the symbol of the star, the hope that Goethe had to conceive for the lovers had once appeared to him. That sentence, which so to speak with Hölderlin contains the caesura of the work and in which, while the embracing lovers seal their fate, everything pauses, reads: "Hope shot across the sky above their heads like a falling star." They are unaware of it, of course . . .
>
> ("Goethe," *SW* I, 354–55)

The presence of the star cannot be divorced from its presence as a symbol. The text is clear, "*Denn unter dem Symbol des Sterns*" ("In the symbol of a star"). Introduced with the symbol is the split that works within the caesura and which is registered in the lover's non-registration of the star – as the symbol of hope. Understanding that split means paying attention to the complex relationship between time and the Absolute as it figures in the symbol insofar as the symbol is evidenced in this passage. (At this stage in Benjamin's development he is yet to formulate a sustained distinction between symbol and allegory.) Benjamin has allowed here for a conception of the symbol that departs both from the simultaneity of the relation between symbol and the symbolized, and equally from the hermeneutic demands of surface/depth as the setup through which the symbol is constrained to be interpreted. The opening up of the symbol occurs within what could be described as a destruction entailing ontological and temporal considerations. Destruction figures in the Goethe essay in a number of different places. One of the more significant is in terms of the "torso."

Benjamin refers both in the Goethe essay and in the doctoral dissertation to the "torso." In the case of the dissertation the term is used to argue that the particular "can never coalesce with the Ideal" but has to remain "*als Vorbild*" ("as a prototype"). In the Goethe essay the symbol is also linked to the "torso." It is presented in relation to the work of "the expressionless." Benjamin writes: "Only the expressionless completes the work by shattering it into a thing of shards, into a fragment of the true world, into a torso of a symbol" ("Goethe," *SW* I, 340). What is a "torso of a symbol"? The first part of the answer to this question is that it is a result; the consequence of the work of the "expressionless." The work is completed in its being fragmented. The mistake would be to read this as a literal claim. There are not any shards; there will not have been any fragments. Rather that moment (and it is a moment, Benjamin writes *in einem Augenblick*) is that in which the most severe form of irreconcilability occurs. The torso of a symbol, however, is not given within the structure of necessity demanded by diremption since it does not envisage its own overcoming or resolution. Rather, it is the staging of an opening that can only ever be maintained as this opening. Being maintained in this manner it defines a predicament in which the problem of closure and thus resolution is staged without an end being envisaged.

What then of the "torso" in this predicament? As a torso the symbol has been stripped of the structure and thus of the possibility of temporal simultaneity: nonetheless this cannot be interpreted as opening up a field of infinite deferral. The work is still completed. The expressionless completes. Again the text is clear, Benjamin states, "*vollendet das Werk*" ("completes the work"). It is completed by the occurrence within it that is the work of a temporal register that cannot be assimilated to the temporality of expression. This means that what completes the work is integral to the work's formal presence and not to the "content" of its narrative. The "expressionless" is not the interruption of continuity nor is it simple discontinuity. It completes the work by showing, on the one hand, the perpetual vacuity of expression if expression were thought to voice the all, and, on the other, by demanding of the work that it recall – recall within and as its work – its separation from the eternal. While more needs to be said, the introduction of time allows the problem of the nature of the caesura, and in this context its relation to hope, to be staged. In the passage already noted the caesura enters with a particular purpose. The expressionless understood as "a category of language and art" – though not of a work or genre – "can be no more rigorously defined than through a passage from Hölderlin's 'Remarks on Oedipus'" ("Goethe" *SW* I, 340) to which Benjamin adds that the deployment of the caesura beyond its use in a theory of tragedy has not been noticed, let alone pursued with adequate rigor.

Two points therefore. The first is that the caesura allows for a rigorous definition of the expressionless. Secondly, the caesura is to be used other than in its employment within a theory of tragedy. The caesura is precisely not an emblem of rhetoric. On one level the caesura and the expressionless are different names for the same possibility, namely an interruption that yields completion. It is this possibility that needs to be pursued by a return to the passage in which the completion of Goethe's novel is identified as occurring in a single sentence. How could it be that a sentence might "contain the caesura of the work"? What is shattered in this case? Where are the shards? Here there are no twitching limbs vainly gesturing at what remains, i.e., to the torso. How then is this claim to be understood? Moreover, the passage in which this phrase – "which will complete the work" – is presented, does not occur at its completion. It may set the seal for what will occur, and yet it occurs pages from the end. How then does it work to complete the work? For Benjamin this has to be the question proper to criticism if only because the answer would "provide detailed knowledge of the work."

It is essential therefore to return to one of Benjamin's formulations of criticism. Only with an understanding of criticism will it become possible to follow the role attributed to the caesura in the Goethe essay. The essay is, after all, a work of "criticism." The passage in question moves criticism through a number of vital stages. While the passage is detailed – containing in addition an important reference to Schlegel's own criticism of Goethe's *Wilhelm Meister* – its detail is essential:

> The legitimization of criticism – which is not to posit criticism as an objective court of judgment on all poetic production – consists in its prosaic nature. Criticism is the preparation of the prosaic kernel in every work. In this, the concept preparation is understood in the chemical sense, as the generation of a substance through a determinate procedure to which other substances are submitted. This is what Schlegel means when he says of *Wilhelm Meister*: "the work not only judges itself it prepares itself." The prosaic is grasped by criticism in both of its meanings: in its literal meaning through the form of expression, as criticism expresses itself in prose; in its figurative meaning through criticism's

object, which is the eternal sober continuance of the work. This criticism, as process and as product, is a necessary function of the classical work.

(*Concept of Criticism*, *SW* I, 153)

Criticism is that approach to the work in which the identification of its particularity allows for its incorporation into what Romanticism would have identified as "the realm of the Absolute." The move, in the most direct sense, would be from the "prosaic kernel" to the prose of criticism. The extent to which a work is criticizable is the extent to which it prepares itself (is prepared) for this possibility. The complicating factor in the passage is how the distinction between the "literal" and the "figural" is to be understood. For Benjamin "prosaic" has two meanings. The first refers to its presence defined within the context of the passage as "unmetrical language." The prosaic expressed in the prose of criticism. However, the prosaic is also "grasped by criticism in a figurative sense" as "the eternal continuation of the work." What that means is that criticism holds to particularity while, at the same time, allowing for the particular's absorption into the Absolute.

Criticism is able to allow for the completion of the particular work to the extent that the work is criticizable. As it is formulated in the Goethe essay this signals the presence of the possibility of showing "in the work of art the virtual possibility of formulating the work's truth content" as the "highest philosophical problem." The latter is, of course, the staging of the Absolute and its impossible possibility. The moment that brings this together is the caesura. As has already been intimated, the first reference in Benjamin's text to this term that is worth noting concerns his identification of the caesura as it figures in Hölderlin's *Remarks*. It is important to return to the actual text he cites. The Hölderlin text, as cited by Benjamin is as follows:

> For the tragic transport is the actually empty and the least restrained. – Thereby in the rhythmic sequence of the representations wherein the transport presents itself, there becomes necessary what in the poetic metre is called caesura, the pure world, the counter rhythmic rupture – namely, in order to meet the onrushing change of representations at its highest point, in such a manner that not the change of representation but the representation itself soon appears.
>
> ("Goethe," *SW* I, 340–1)

Hölderlin's formulation is more complex than suggesting a form of interruption that would only ever be a counter-rhythm. Metre does not measure the interruption. That would make the caesura a literal breaking apart. Rather, such a rupture must take place on the level of representation and presentation. The site of interruption is the "sequence of the representations" and their movement is that of the "onrushing change of representations."

The sequence and the movement produce the site of interruption. This sequence cannot be straightforwardly conflated with plot. Sequence and movement need to be viewed in temporal terms. They involve a particular form of unfolding; one which articulates a sequential temporality. The caesura is positioned by place – insofar as it can be located – while it is not the work of place. Thus, it is not another occurrence. The complicating factor here is that interruption is both the interruption of a certain temporal sequence, and equally the interruption of the possibility of reading that sequence as the unfolding of the purely transcendental. In other words, the work is neither regulated nor caused by that which is external to it. The former element is the one that comes to dominate Benjamin's later writings. Nonetheless, the other element is important as what is refused by it is the possibility of an eternal other, either as God, idea, or myth, to provide the artwork with its legitimacy and, though this is probably to reiterate the impossibility of legitimacy, to offer the locus and thus determine the nature of critique. Critique is not a relation between an external element and internal components that causes these components to receive a specific determination.

What remains elusive in this presentation of the caesura – and here it cannot be restricted to the caesura since it involves the other forms of interruption – is how such an event can "give free reign to an expressionless power inside all artistic media." The answer to this question is there in the almost possible object of attainment identified by the use of the term "sobriety." It marks the point of connection between measure and the measureless. As such it is the return of the problem of particularity. This time, however, it is posed in a different way. Rather than the particular, it is the Absolute that has centrality. Absolute here is marked by an impossible possibility. At the same time it is also generative. However, despite being productive, the Absolute cannot be produced. It can be neither made nor shown. Read back though the caesura – and while not wishing, again, to conflate them – it marks the interruption that yields an artwork. It presents that which is proper to art. This is the "expressionless power inside all artistic media"; i.e., the Absolute. The Absolute, the nature of its presence, already turning within semblance cannot be reduced to that to which "mere semblance" gestures.

How is semblance to be delimited? In a discussion of "Goethean figures" and thus as an integral part of the work's critique, Benjamin, drawing on the critical apparatus he had already established, writes of those figures:

[They] can appear to be not created or purely constructed but conjured. Precisely from this stems the kind of obscurity that is foreign to works of art and that can be fathomed only by someone who recognizes its essence in semblance. For semblance in this poetic work is not so much represented as it is in the poetic representation itself. It is only for this reason that the semblance can mean so much; and only for this reason that the representation means so much. ("Goethe," *SW* I, 345)

At work in this formulation is that which arises from the operation of critique. In the first instance, there is an appearance of figures having one source rather than another. Here, again, the detail is necessary. The formulation is precise. Goethean figures "can appear" to have arisen through an act of conjuring and if that were then the case the critique of conjuring as "having nothing in common" ("Goethe," *SW* I, 340) with the generation of art would have been rendered otiose. The problem of this appearing is the problem inherent in the work. Its presence attests to the necessity of critique, and thus to critique as an activity done in relation to a work that sanctions it. Rather than taking what appears as appearance, in the end mere appearance, the reverse situation needs to occur. There has to be the recognition of what is essential to art in the semblance; the "Wesen" in the "Schein." With the *Elective Affinities*, and it should be noted that Benjamin specifies that, in this work, there is not a "presentation of semblance," it is the presentation itself. This is the reason why semblance can have the meaning that it does and, reciprocally, this is why the presentation itself is imbued with such meaning. Again, it is essential to see what is being distanced. Not only is there a sustained refusal to interpret appearance as representational and therefore as standing for something other than itself, there is also a distancing of the possibility that semblance acts out what it can only gesture at in action without being such an action.

Understanding the import of this claim concerning the presence of semblance depends upon accepting Benjamin's identification of the two elements that determine the interpretation. The first is that "the subject of *The Elective Affinities* is not marriage," and the second is that "belief in Ottilie's beauty is the fundamental condition for engagement with the novel" ("Goethe," *SW* I, 338). This is not "the appearance of the beautiful," rather it is the "semblance-like beauty" that is central. This shift has to be recognized as a move from content to truth, that is, from a concern with the "material content" to a concern with "truth content." It is not as though marriage and the concerns of bourgeois gentility are absent. Rather they only figure within the work of truth. Before pursuing this move to semblance and thus to the complexity surrounding semblance, it is essential to note that the emergence of beauty occurs as part of the process of critique. Underlining the importance of this shift is not, therefore, a mere passing remark. It delineates how Benjamin's essay is also a work of critique.

Once critique is linked to an engagement with truth rather than content, then content has to be repositioned in relation to truth. The detail of Benjamin's engagement with the constitutive elements of the novel is, though only in this instance, not necessary. What has to be retained however is the direction of that engagement. Benjamin's move is to reposition semblance and thus give it its full philosophical force. Semblance opens up the realm of the Absolute and the relationship between the particular and the Absolute once it is understood that semblance stages both itself and the Absolute. (The presence of the latter is to be thought in terms of the impossible possibility of the Absolute's presence.) Precision is essential here. Benjamin's claim is that critique works within the opening between particular and Absolute. It needs both elements – particular/Absolute – since the interrelationship of these elements comprises the work of art. This is why in regard to the treatment of beauty in Goethe's novel, in which beauty becomes "the object in its veil," Benjamin will write that:

> The task of criticism is not to lift the veil but rather, through the most precise knowledge of it as a veil, to raise itself for the first time to the true view of the beautiful. To the view that will never open itself up to so-called empathy and will only imperfectly open itself to a purer contemplation of the naive: to the view of the beautiful of that which is secret. Never yet has a true work of art been grasped other than when it ineluctably represented itself as a secret.
>
> ("Goethe," *SW* I, 351)

The opening line contains the key to this passage. There would seem to be a twofold possibility. The first links criticism to the process of revelation and thus the uncovering of an inner truth. This is precluded since criticism is not concerned with lifting the veil. In the same way a fetishism of the veil generating an interpretive mysticism would still attribute to the veil the quality of harboring depth. This would imply that the veil is literally the veil. Both these possibilities are curtailed since criticism is already informed. Benjamin is clear: the veil is known. It is an object of knowledge. Intuition or empathy would fail to interrupt the work of the infinite. Knowledge rehearses the petrification of the object: the object of knowledge. Knowledge does not provide access to the secret. Knowledge is knowledge of the artwork as the secret. Knowledge maintains the secret, though as known. The limit is established by the effective nature of the Absolute. While accounting for presence – and allowing for its present incorporation as part of the particular's presence – it can never be present as itself.

If there is a way of generalizing what is at work in the complex relationship between interruption and criticism, then it can be captured in the claim that what the caesura allows is the relationship between the particular and the Absolute to be thought. In doing this the artful nature of the artwork is presented. Criticism in the context cannot be thought other than in its relationship to the work of the Absolute. The complex presence of the Absolute and the way it figures within, if not providing the very ground of, Benjamin's engagement with Early Romanticism, opens up the move to his later concerns with history. That concern is not with the detail of history – Rankean "facts" – but with the temporality that such facts display and within which such facts are able to be displayed. History cannot be thought other than as a philosophy of time.

In moving from a concern with criticism to the concerns of Benjamin's *Arcades Project* the difficulty any commentator faces is how to account for the repositioning. Perhaps the key interpretive question is: is there a retention of the Romantic conception of the Absolute? (In sum, a conception in which a particular work is both itself and the Absolute at the same time.) Prior to any attempt to answer this question, what has to be addressed is the move from interruption in the writings directly concerned with Romanticism to a more generalized sense of interruption. Prior to turning to the passage from the *Arcades Project* in which the term "caesura" figures, two specific formulations of interruption need to be noted. The first comes from "The Work of Art in the Age of Its Technological Reproducibility" and the second from "On the Concept of History."

As a text, Benjamin's essay "The Work of Art in the Age of Its Technological Reproducibility" is full of remarkable moments, shock insights that attest to the interruption that yields the work of art within modernity. One of the most emphatic occurs in the following passage:

> Let us assume that an actor is supposed to be startled by a knock at the door. If his reaction is not satisfactory, the director can resort to an expedient: he could have a shot fired without warning behind the actor's back on some other occasion when he happens to be in the studio. The actor's frightened reaction at that moment could be recorded and then edited into the film. Nothing shows more graphically that art has escaped the realm of the "beautiful semblance" which for so long was regarded as the only sphere in which it could thrive.
>
> (*SW* IV, 261)

What is this "beautiful semblance" where art was thought to "thrive," and in which it can "thrive" no longer? What type of change has occurred such that this dislocation and thus subsequent relocation comes to pass? The reference made in this 1936 text is both to the Early Romantics (and thus to Benjamin's own engagement with that heritage) and to a sustained engagement with the topic of beauty that reappears throughout his work. A significant instance of that engagement is the long footnote on beauty in the essay "On Some Motifs in Baudelaire" (*SW* IV, 352). This footnote signals a historicization of beauty that was not as evident in his earlier writings. As has already been intimated, the most sustained discussion of beauty as "beautiful semblance" appears in the final section of his essay "Goethe's *Elective Affinities*." In the final pages of that text Benjamin introduces – perhaps reintroduces – the task of criticism in relation to beauty. This relation is central. All of Benjamin's work on art has been concerned with detailing the task of criticism. Criticism is the key to the doctoral dissertation. Indeed the complex relationship between philosophy and criticism is evident in the opening line of the Preface to *The Origin of the German Tragic Drama* (*Origin*, 27–56). In the published version there is an important modification of the earlier drafts. The change introduces the problem of philosophical style by inscribing the problem of presentation into the presentation of philosophy itself. The first passage is from the draft and the second is from the published version.

> Es ist der philosophischen Erkenntnis eigen, mit jeder Wendung von neuem vor der Frage der Darstellung zu stehen.
> [It is characteristic of philosophical knowledge that it must continually confront the question of presentation.]   (*GS*, III, 840)

> Es ist der philosophischen Schrifttum eigen, mit jeder Wendung von neuem vor der Frage der Darstellung zu stehen.
> [It is characteristic of philosophical *writing* that it must continually confront the question of presentation.]   (*Origin*, 28; emphasis mine)

While the shift from knowledge to writing is of great significance in terms of the development of Benjamin's text, what is interesting for these concerns is that writing becomes a practice stemming from a particular formulation of philosophical activity. The initial use of the term "knowledge" (*Erkenntnis*) creates the link to criticism, for it is at the end of the Goethe essay that criticism and knowledge are interconnected. What is important in the move from Benjamin's early texts to the later ones is that the conception of art is inextricably bound up with the task of criticism once criticism is defined in relation to knowledge. A shift in the nature of art enjoins a concomitant shift in the activity of criticism and thus of the philosophy of art. While that shift occurs, what is not lost is the link to knowledge.

Does this mean, however, that the shift from the "realm of beautiful semblance" detailed in the passage cited above is at the same time a move away from a thinking of art conditioned by the Absolute? Drawing such a conclusion would be too hasty. Clearly, what Benjamin can be interpreted as suggesting is not that the Absolute no longer figures in how the work of art is to be understood, but that the locus of art and thus what counts as art's work has changed. The move from the identification of art with poetry – or at least if not with poetry then with literature in the broadest sense of the term – and thus the capacity to generalize about art based on that identification, has ceded its place to a definition of art in terms of what produces it. In regard to the work of art, what is occurring can be reformulated as a move from *poesis* to *technē*. Even in allowing for this reformulation the question that returns is the extent to which such a move rids itself of the Absolute. And yet this question cannot be posed as though the answer were all or nothing. It is more likely the case that in the move from one to the other – *poesis* to *technē* – the Absolute rather than vanishing comes to be redefined. While art will continue to be defined via the activity of criticism, understood either implicitly or explicitly, in relation to the Absolute, the shift of the content of that definition will yield a differing understanding of the Absolute.[2]

As a generalization, the contrast is between two different possibilities for art and criticism. The nature of that difference is to be understood in terms of the relationship between time and the object. *Poesis* involves a different relationship than the one at work in art defined as *technē*. Indeed, it is because the relationship is formulated in this way that the temporal considerations at work in the latter – the conception of the work of art determined by *technē* – are such that they open up as historical concerns; not the concerns of history as such but in terms of the temporality proper to that conception of history that is constrained to undo the identification of history with the temporality of historicism. (The latter being the temporality of continuity that is sustained either in terms of simple chronology or in terms of the endurance through time of concepts – for example: beauty, genius – that are taken never to change.) Both the need for, as well as another sense of interruption, occur at this precise point. Prior to looking at passages from "On the Concept of History" and the *Arcades Project* in which the conception of interruption figures – and in the case of the latter is identified by the use of the term "caesura" – it is essential to note, if only in passing, the nature of the shift.

What determines Benjamin's initial sense of interruption is the necessity that the activity be internal to the work. The work "prepared" itself to be criticized. There is an extent to which the work has an autotelic nature. The link between the work of the "expressionless" and the activity of criticism – both are involved in differing forms of the work's ruination – is that they are defined in relation to an activity that originates in the place and presence of the Absolute. Once a work can be construed as criticizable then there is little that stands in the way of the practice of criticism. While it is true that Benjamin has harsh words to say concerning Gundolf's interpretation of Goethe and, while there is a growing awareness of the political nature of criticism, it remains the case that there was no theorization of that which stood in the way of the activity of criticism. In other words, it was not the case in the early writings that there was any recognition of the need for a preliminary move, one which would allow for criticism. Such a move is not preliminary in the sense that it is prior to the activity of criticism. Rather, criticism means dealing both with the way in which a given work of art worked as a work of art while also stripping that work of its insertion into the temporality of continuity – what Benjamin identifies as "historicism" – and thus disrupting the structures that accompanied that hold.

Two points need to be made here. The first is that what the identification of the possibility of inserting, or cutting, a segment into a work – a possibility signaled in the citation from "The Work of Art in the Age of its Technological Reproducibility" given above – indicates is that there is a shift in how the art object is understood. Part of the change is that the way the work of art works as criticizable changes. The second and related point is that the possibility of the work's absorption into the temporality of continuity is now a possibility that is inherent in the work itself. In the shift from *poesis* to *technē* the work of art does not prepare itself to be identified as something particular. In the move from *poesis* something else takes place. Henceforth, the work of art is always prepared for its absorption into the realm of continuity. As has been indicated, what this means is that the activity of criticism – and perhaps it is possible to go further and argue that this is the task of the progressive critic – necessitates the interruption of that enforcing continuity; an enforcing that is inherent in the technical nature of the object.

Benjamin identifies the problem of historicism – understood as the temporality of sequential continuity – in the following passage from "On the Concept of History." Of central importance in this passage is the use of the imagery of the rosary beads. It provides a clear example of the way continuity has to be interrupted in order that the potential within and for art be released. Of equal importance is that instead of writing about the critic Benjamin will now write of the "historian." The passage in question is the following:

> Historicism contents itself with establishing a casual connection between various moments in history. But no fact that is a cause is for that very reason historical. It becomes historical, posthumously, as it were, through events that may be separated from it by thousands of years. A historian who takes this as

his point of departure stops telling the sequence of events like the beads of a rosary. Instead, he grasps the constellation which his own era has formed with a definite earlier one. Thus he establishes a conception of the present as the "time of the now" which is shot through with chips of Messianic time.

(*Ill*, 263)

A beginning can be made here with the interruption signaled by the use of the rosary. The question has to be – what does it mean to "stop telling the sequence of events"? Here, there is a decisive formulation of interruption. And yet within the formulation what is interrupted has a more complex quality. It is the projection of unity or synthesis – or what Benjamin will identify elsewhere as "universal history" having Kant rather than Hegel in mind – that has to be undone. No longer is this destructive move made in the name of anything other than an intervention within temporal continuity. Precisely because it is an interruption that involves a specific orientation that can be as much philosophical as it is artistic, the demands of that orientation, itself demanding a decision, allow what is taking place here to be described as a politics of time.[3]

Interruption as a figure within Benjamin's writings is linked to the dominance of historicism. Again, this is not a simple concept of the historical and thus of historical time. What takes place within historicism is the naturalization of chronology, on the one hand, and the naturalization of myth, on the other. Working within both is a continuity that effaces the question of whose history is being told or narrated and thus for whom and for what end a given history is being constructed. The act that denaturalizes both myth and chronology is the interruption. The immediate consequence of this interruption is the reconfiguring of the present. With that reconfiguration the present emerges as the "now" – a temporalized and historicized now – that generates the nature of the philosophical and therefore, and at the same time, the political task.[4] What this means is that in Benjamin's later writings a twofold register is added to the locus of interruption. In the case of the earlier work, the locus was the work of art itself. Marking the move is the incorporation of the work of art into a time of the present in which whatever determines the work's specificity can be effaced. Effacing specificity occurs because what marks the work is its capacity to interrupt the time of the present. This interruption occurs as long as the temporality of the present is thought in terms of continuity. What this means, in addition, is that the present is not thought outside its insertion into continuity. This accounts for why Benjamin argues for the urgency of making something a concern for the present. If this does not occur, then the present does no more than form part of the "appearance of permanence" (*Arcades*, 486; N19, 1).[5] As such the present is lost from the present. Thinking the present is already an interruption; an interruption yielding the present.

The interruption occurs when the historian stops "telling the sequence of events like the beads of a rosary." Here, there is a decision that interrupts. This position is made possible by a shift that can be traced from the work of the art defined in terms of "beautiful semblance" to the art work's inescapable connection to reproducibility and thus to technology. The methodological consequences of this interruption redefine how destruction and therefore ruination are to be understood. This other possibility is signaled in the *Arcades Project* as follows: "Historical materialism has to abandon the epic element in history. It blasts the epoch out of the reified 'continuity of history.' It also blasts open the homogeneity of the epoch. It saturates it with ecrasite, i.e. the present (*Gegenwart*)" (*Arcades*, 474; N9a, 6 [trans. modified]). Signaled in this passage is the decision to abandon continuity. That abandoning allows for, and at the same time, is the opening up of the epoch's homogeneity. What is meant by epoch is rescued and transformed in the process. The blasting open allows the fallout to contain the elements of historical work. The position being staged here needs to be run both ways. In the first instance it has to be argued that in the detritus of history – what has been cast out of epic history – there lies the potential to interrupt continuity. Continuity may have been founded on just such an elimination. In the second, it is by blasting apart continuity that what looks to be insignificant, or merely awaits incorporation into a form of continuity or totality, may contain the potential to redefine the present and, more significantly, to have consequences that are potentially as much political as they are philosophical or historical. Occurring in this process is an act of rescue in which images of the past have a capacity to define the present. The rescue is the release – or attempted release – of that potential. In defining it – and again it should be remembered that such an act of definition is the result of a decision – the present comes to be established in contradistinction to the present of continuity. In the formulation of "On the Concept of History," "every image of the past that is not recognized by the present as one of its own concerns threatens to disappear irretrievably" (*Ill*, 255). While it is clear that the methodological import of this procedure involves what it is premised on and the different conception of interruption and destruction it involves, what endures as the open question is the relationship all of this has to the Absolute, even if it is a reworked, perhaps even reconfigured, conception of the Absolute. Does this other history of destruction entail the effective presence of the Absolute? This is a question that cannot be ignored.

The passage from the *Arcades Project* that opens up the interruption demanded by the caesura and which will allow for the question of the Absolute to begin to be posed is the following. It should be remembered that bringing the Absolute into focus is not to add on an extra element. Criticism, as noted already, is unthinkable except in relation to the Absolute. The obvious question is: does this remain the case given the already noted move from the criticism to the historian? Were critics, and therefore criticism, a form of historical materialism *avant la lettre*?

> Thinking involves both thoughts in motions and thoughts at rest. When thinking reaches a standstill in a constellation saturated with tensions, the dialectical image appears. This image is the caesura in the movement of thought. Its locus is of course not arbitrary. In short it is to be found wherever the tension between dialectical oppositions is greatest. The dialectical image is, accordingly, the very object constructed in the materialist presentation of history. It is identical with the historical object; it justifies its being blasted out of the continuum of the historical process. (*Arcades*, 475; N10a, 3 [trans. modified])

The significance of this passage is twofold. Not only does it reinforce the interconnection between interruption and the historical object, there are also intimations of how a reworked conception of the Absolute can emerge. (These intimations will need to be connected to another passage from the same Convolute [460; N2.3] in which the nature of "historical understanding" is redefined in temporal terms.) Despite being interrelated each of these moments needs to be treated in turn.

The "dialectical image" is an interruption. As a dialectical image rather than as a simple image it involves the co-presence of what can neither be reconciled nor rendered synthetic. The image becomes a type of temporal montage and therefore should not be understood within the conventions of the image. Those conventions will always privilege sight over language. The "tensions" inherent in the image are there precisely because of the impossibility of the image's incorporation into the temporality of historicism or into the procession of concepts and activities that are articulated within that temporal unfolding. This image is described as "the caesura in the movement of thought." What does this mean? Any answer to this question has to begin with the recognition that, for Benjamin, the dialectical image is the true historical object. Even though that will be a contested assertion, it is the ineliminability of the conflict that directly confirms the impossibility of withdrawing the historical object from questions concerning for whom, and in whose name, a given history is being formulated. Historicism will always try and incorporate "events" into its own conception of continuity. The caesura is the interruption of that attempt. What that interruption demonstrates is that destruction reconfigures both the historical object and what can count as historical. In the same process, it indicates that continuity (whether it be in terms of the naturalization of chronology or the incorporation of myth into and as history) is always a secondary effect whose primary intent is the elimination of conflict – even if that elimination is only ever putative. Chronology, myth, and nature would be terms deployed within the desire for what is always the same. The claim here is that not only does the "caesura" overcome that possibility, it also shows the "always the same" to be a politically charged aspiration and not one that contains the truth of time. In other words, the caesura, in overcoming all that which is entailed by continuity, achieves this end by staging the truth of time. It is precisely this staging that opens up the Absolute.[6]

Truth is not being counterposed to appearance. Even though continuity is an appearance and even though the truth of time emerges with the interruption of that appearance, there are two additional points that need to be noted. The first is that the move from *poesis* to *technē* allows for the presentation of time in this way since reproducibility is already implicated in the reconfiguring of time. Second, the reason why there is no straightforward opposition between truth and appearance is that there is no presentation of truth that has the same status as any given narrative of continuity. There is no narrative of truth. There are only moments of interruption. These moments are fleeting; appearing and disappearing as sites of philosophical and political activity.

There will be no final summation. And this lack of finality is not the identification of the Absolute with a domain of unfettered freedom. How then, in this context, will the Absolute figure?

The answer to this question should now be clear. The Absolute is time. Neither chronological time nor clock time, the Absolute is given within the interruption in which the truth of time is presented. Interruption is only possible because what can be known and therefore what functions as the ground of what can be known are not identical with what appears. Knowing what appears, allowing it to be reconfigured as an object of knowledge, necessitates understanding appearance as an effect. There is the inevitability of interruption. It is connected to the way Benjamin defines "historical understanding" as what is "to be viewed primarily as an afterlife (*Nachleben*) of that which has been understood: and so what came to be recognized about works through the analysis of their after life, their fame, should be considered the foundation of history itself" (*Arcades*, 460; N2, 3). The point being made here is a redefinition of history. Within that redefinition history becomes the continuity of the reworking of what is already there. This reworking is occasioned by the interruption of the given. With that interruption what is given comes to be given again and in so doing has an "afterlife." It is, of course, never given again as the "same." This is a process without conclusion. Or at least it is a process whose conclusions are always strategic and provisional. The Absolute is therefore that which allows for the interruption; but equally it is what is evidenced by that interruption. There can be no attempt to present the Absolute, nor even to state the truth of time. The Absolute as time is what allows for the "dialectical image" while precluding any image of time. The absence of the latter is, of course, the moment in which modernity appears as secular.

Interruption as a defining motif in Benjamin's thought dominates both his engagement with Romanticism and his move to the writing of another construction of history. In both instances the interruption – analyzed in this context in terms of the caesura – is unthinkable outside its relation to the Absolute. In regard to Romanticism, the presence of the Absolute is explicable in terms of a retention of key elements of Schlegel's philosophical and critical project.[7] In the case of the *Arcades Project* the Absolute returns as time. Two important conclusions can be drawn from this setup. The first is that it must force a reconsideration of the role of the Absolute within philosophical thinking; even that thinking whose ostensible concern is a theory of modernity. The second is connected insofar as what must be taken up is the extent to which a theory of modernity will depend upon a philosophy of time that has its point of departure in Early Romanticism, rather than in the march of teleological time implicit, for example, in Kant's construal of the relationship between history and the Enlightenment. In sum, interruption will continue to figure since the hold of continuity makes modernity an unfinished project.

NOTES

1. For an important discussion of Benjamin's work that pays attention to his relationship to Romanticism see Howard Caygill, *Walter Benjamin: The Colour of Experience* (London: Routledge, 1998).
2. While not defining its presence in relation to the Absolute, Carol Jacobs indicates the extension of "criticism" in her treatment of the relationship between criticism and translation. See *In the Language of Walter Benjamin* (Baltimore: Johns Hopkins University Press, 1999), 286–87.
3. See Peter Osborne, *Politics of Time* (London: Verso, 1997) for an important development of this theme that stems from a consideration of Benjamin's work.
4. I have tried to develop this argument in my *Present Hope* (London: Routledge, 1997)
5. The full quotation is: "It could be that the continuity of tradition is only an appearance. But if this is the case, then it is precisely the persistence of this appearance of permanence that establishes continuity of appearance."

6. This is a complex and perhaps difficult claim. The argument is, however, straight-forward. Forms of continuity rather than being either natural or inevitable are forms of time. Time is given such forms for specific ends. Interrupting such concepts of time works, first to restrict the realization of those ends; second, to show that such concepts are neither natural nor inevitable; and finally to show that time is a site of contestation. The conflict between continuity and discontinuity is the truth of time. Interruption, precisely because it reveals the work of construction, stages time's truth.

7. This position has been worked out in considerable detail in my *Philosophy's Literature* (Manchester: Clinumen, 2001).

6

SARAH LEY ROFF

Benjamin and psychoanalysis

> Perhaps without being aware of the fact . . . you find yourself . . . in the
> most profound agreement with Freud; there is certainly much to be
> thought about in this connection.
>
> Theodor W. Adorno, Letter to Walter Benjamin, June 1935

Psychoanalysis is a science that attempts to explain normal and pathological states in the human mind, as well as a clinical practice of treatment for the latter. It began with Freud's rejection of hypnosis and shock therapy as cures for hysteria and his development with Josef Breuer of the "talking cure," a technique of analyzing patients' free associations that was to become a central feature of the psychoanalytic session. In Freud's account, psychoanalysis did not truly come into its own until he began to analyze the network of associations that arise in dreams; this was the breakthrough of his first major work, *The Interpretation of Dreams*. Describing dreams as the "royal road to . . . the unconscious," Freud insisted that their images arise from the interaction between whole systems of repressed thoughts, as a result of which no single meaning can be affixed to any image.

Although this approach may seem reminiscent of the structuralist linguistics emerging around the time Freud was writing, nothing like it had existed before in the realm of dream interpretation. Indeed, while the idea of an unconscious region of the mind that influences our actions most often surprises readers who encounter Freud's work for the first time, it is present in many nineteenth-century theories of psychology which influenced him. The notion that we produce dreams as a result of the struggle between conscious and unconscious wishes is thus less original to Freud than his structural approach to analyzing the relations between them. In psychoanalytic theory, this strategy shifts the relation between form and content from the individual element onto the whole system. This, in turn, suggests an important point of contact between psychoanalysis and early twentieth-century theories of language and literary criticism, in particular Walter Benjamin's.

While Benjamin criticism is an ever-growing field, scholars have only recently begun to pay attention to his relation to Freud or Jung. Ordinarily, the relation between a writer (Benjamin) and a movement (psychoanalysis) would be thought of as a problem of influence. Discussing Benjamin and Freud would thus require us to practice source criticism, examining the former's references to Freud's works as a way of establishing his place within psychoanalytic discourse. As Sigrid Weigel has observed, however, "It is . . . difficult to reconstruct exactly Benjamin's reading of Freud's work, since he only seldom makes explicit reference to it."[1] As she proposes, the limited number of allusions to psychoanalysis in Benjamin's work can be accounted for in terms of the way in which he thought, proceeding less by exposition than by practices such as image and citation. Weigel argues that Benjamin "is perhaps least inclined to [mention Freud] where the traces of Freudian thought-figures are most influential in his work," an approach taken a step further by Rainer Nägele when he introduces Benjamin's own concept of a "constellation," noting that "the possibility of talking about [Benjamin and Freud]" in these terms "is not established by the mere fact that there are explicit references to Freud in Benjamin's writing" since "a constellation is not a question of influence."[2] As Weigel puts it, it would therefore be simplistic to reduce the question of Freud's influence on Benjamin to the number of citations of psychoanalytic works we can discover, since "a reconstruction of 'influences' or philosophical traditions in which [Benjamin's] thought may be considered will always fail to grasp its specificity" (Weigel, xi). Indeed, examining the relationship between Benjamin and psychoanalysis may serve to highlight modernist transformations in concepts of authorship and work to which both Benjamin and Freud contributed.

At this point, we would, however, clearly have left behind the narrow problem of influence, and it might be useful to invoke the term "intertextuality," an idea that has gained currency in literary criticism over the past thirty years as a way of designating the relations between texts that exceed the organizing concept of authorship. Growing out of the connections between post-structuralism and psychoanalytic approaches to literature, the notion of intertextuality assimilates the author "Benjamin" and the movement "psychoanalysis" to a general concept of text. Just as Freud displaces the meaning of the individual dream image onto a larger network of associations, intertextuality calls into question the author's mastery over the production of his or her work and places it within the larger field of "discourses" and their transformation. In these terms, it becomes possible to examine significant areas of contact between Benjamin's and Freud's thought despite the fact that it may not be possible to trace them back to the explicit influence of one author on the other.

Interestingly, Benjamin's best-known discussion of Freud, arguably the only one that is more than a fleeting textual reference, appears at the end of his life. The problem of trauma was at the forefront of his concerns in his 1939 essay "On Some Motifs in Baudelaire," a problem that had also preoccupied Freud since his initial studies of female hysterical patients in the 1890s, becoming particularly acute with his attempts to develop a theory of shell shock in male soldiers during the First World War. Indeed, the problems of trauma and memory could be said to provide one of the clearest points of contact between the two. Focusing on the passage in Freud's 1921 essay "Beyond the Pleasure Principle" in which he clarifies the theoretical underpinnings of his approach to the problem of trauma, Benjamin's 1939 discussion points to Freud's insistence on the incompatibility between consciousness and memory, relating this to Proust's notion of the *mémoire involuntaire* famous from his discussion in *Remembrance of Things Past* of the memories evoked by biting into a tea biscuit. Benjamin correctly diagnosed a phenomenon many readers of Freud have observed, his removal of functions of awareness from consciousness and their relocation to what he terms the "preconscious," a sort of vestibule area between the unconscious and the preconscious where functions of censorship actually take place. In Freud's notion of the memory trace, memory therefore becomes an effect of the impact of the outside world on the unconscious and preconscious registers, while consciousness is reduced to providing the first line of defense against external stimuli. In the simplest sense, trauma results from a rupture in the protective shield of consciousness; Freud nonetheless proposes that it is less likely to occur in cases where the subject has prepared himself for the onslaught of external stimuli through mechanisms that occur in the unconscious–preconscious system such as anxiety and narcissism. Ultimately, Freud understands the trauma victim's constant rehearsal of unpleasant past events in his dreams as a means of trying to establish these mechanisms of preparedness after the fact.

In his essay "On Some Motifs in Baudelaire," Benjamin's goal is less the attempt to establish the validity of Freud's highly speculative hypothesis than the desire to put his ideas to work in a new context, a form of decontextualization belonging to his theory of the constellation. He thus insisted that he should "content [himself] with investigating [the idea's] fruitfulness in situations far removed from the ones Freud had in mind when he wrote" (*SW* IV, 317). The new context was his own shock theory, the notion that the basis of late nineteenth-century lyric poetry was the individual's confrontation with the crowd in the big city, "an experience for which the shock experience has become the norm" (*SW* IV, 318). For Benjamin, the "special function of psychic mechanisms under present day conditions" lay in their increased capacity to accept shocks. Rather than retreating into the domestic sphere as had the early nineteenth-century bourgeoisie, the late nineteenth-century poet confronted the crowd directly. As a consequence, Benjamin drew an analogy between Freud's neurological conception of consciousness and the way in which Baudelaire placed "the shock experience at the very center of his artistic work" by "making it his business to parry shocks" (*SW* IV, 319). Taking up Freud's account, Benjamin observed that preparedness for anxiety was a task for which consciousness was particularly suited, since it was located in a portion of the cortex "frayed by effect of the stimulus" (*SW* IV, 318). Baudelaire, whose shocking poems and disturbing personal appearance were confrontations with the shock experience, was the poet of a consciousness that served a crucial psychological function despite the fact that it might no longer be the locus of awareness.

One of the most interesting question we can ask about Benjamin's late reading of Freud was why it took him so long to arrive at it. Weigel has proposed that we can locate in Benjamin's scattered but increasingly frequent allusions to psychoanalysis between 1935 and 1939 a systematic working through of the implications of the psychoanalytic conception of memory. She also describes an earlier phase around 1928–29 in which Benjamin's reception of Freud is "less systematic and conscious, but . . . no less intensive." To this phase we may add an even earlier period around 1918 when Benjamin seems to have first become acquainted with psychoanalysis (Weigel, 117). The very scattered nature of these earlier allusions seems marked, however, by a mechanism of deferral that deserves our attention, since the psychoanalytic notion that appears to have closest bearing on Benjamin's thought, that of melancholia, contains a structure of deferral we may also trace within the level of Benjamin's reception of psychoanalysis.

Benjamin's first references to Freud betray considerable skepticism or resistance. In 1918, he took a seminar at the University of Berne with the psychologist Paul Haberlin on "The Problem of Body and Soul." We know from the catalogue of his reading that Benjamin became acquainted with three of Freud's texts around that time, namely, "Jokes and their Relation to the Unconscious," "On Narcissism," and the "Rat Man" case history. However, his friend Gershom Scholem reports that his assessment of Freud was at this point "negative."[3] Scholem's claim seems borne out in the allusion to Freud's jokes book in a satirical seminar catalogue he and Benjamin concocted for an imaginary university. They proposed two works by "Prof. Sigmund Freud" for a physics seminar to be held in the philosophy department, neither of which actually exists and both of which seem to be (perhaps somewhat juvenile) jokes about psychoanalysis: "Where do Little Children come from?" and "Explications of Selected Jokes" (*GS*, IV, 442). The joke about joke interpretation may have been in perfectly good humor, since Scholem's report of Benjamin's negative assessment of Freud seems belied by the fact that the latter returned to the jokes book in the preparatory notes for his 1931 study of the Viennese satirist Karl Kraus (*GS*, II.3, 1097).

The book does not, however, seem to have played a significant role in the final version of that essay, suggesting that Benjamin's initial approach to Freud was, indeed, cautious.

According to Scholem, it was Freud's famous "Rat Man" case that initially made the strongest impression on Benjamin. Here again, Scholem raises doubts about Benjamin's initial enthusiasm for psychoanalysis, reporting that Benjamin was more impressed by Daniel Paul Schreber's *Memoirs of a Neuropath*, the book written by a schizophrenic patient on which the case history was based. Scholem insists that Schreber's book "appealed to [Benjamin] far more than Freud's essay on it" (*Friendship*, 57). However, we should hesitate before treating Scholem's report of his friend's indifferent initial encounter with psychoanalysis as completely reliable, not least since it was Freud's study rather than Schreber's memoirs that were recorded in the catalogue Benjamin kept of works he had read. "I do not remember his ever contradicting my expression of profound disappointment at Freud's *Interpretation of Dreams*," Scholem writes, perhaps revealing more about his own stance toward psychoanalysis than Benjamin's (*Friendship*, 61). A more complex picture is provided by Benjamin's own remark in a 1928 essay about his collection of books by the mentally ill when he states that he was not certain whether the fascination he felt for Schreber's book when he purchased it in a second-hand bookshop in Berne arose before or after he had read Freud's case history:

> Then, in 1918, in a small antiquarian bookshop in Berne, I came across Schreber's famous *Denkwurdigkeiten eines Nervenkranken* [Memoirs of My Nervous Illness]...Had I already heard of this book? Or did I read about it a few weeks later in the essay on it by Freud...? No matter. I was at once spellbound by it. (*SW*, II, 24)

For Freud, expressions of uncertainty during conscious recall are evidence of a process he terms secondary revision, the further censorship of unconscious thoughts by the conscious mind at the moment an event is remembered. For Freud, such revision is symptomatic of a high degree of repression. While Scholem adopts the role of the outright opponent of psychoanalysis, Benjamin's hesitancy about Freud suggests a more ambivalent mode of resistance. Scholem also appears to simplify the dynamics at work in Benjamin's early reception of Freud when he observes that he "never" heard the latter discuss his interest in the insane "in connection with the technique of psychoanalysis" (*Friendship*, 67). In the essay on "Books by the Mentally Ill," Benjamin was clearly concerned, as Scholem states, with the theological dimensions of the world view of mentally ill people. Here again, Schreber plays an important role. Discussing the interrelation between the pathological and theological aspects of Schreber's mania, Benjamin remarks: "references to the 'countermeaning of primal words,' a theme treated sporadically by Freud, also appear in this remarkable document. 'Juice' is called 'poison,' 'poison' is called 'food,' 'reward' is called 'punishment,' and so on" ("Books by the Mentally Ill," *SW*, II, 124). This passage suggests at least a working knowledge of Freud's famous thesis that the unconscious does not respect the law of non-contradiction and readily reverses the meanings of words into their opposites. In this, Benjamin's first substantial reference to Freud, he was thus already aware of an issue to which considerable attention must be paid: the affinity between Freud's interest in the connection of ancient symbols and archaic forms of language to unconscious modes of thought and Benjamin's own philosophy of language, in which the archaic also plays a crucial role.

As Nägele observed, "writers who link their writing most explicitly to Freud...[often] have little to do with what is at stake in Freud's writing, whereas [those] who assume a defensive or even hostile attitude toward Freud may touch precisely on the sphere from which Freud's thought emerges" (Nägele, 57). If this suggests one way in which we can understand Benjamin's early resistance to psychoanalysis, another way of assessing his connection to Freud would be by reversing the problem and considering his reception by the psychoanalytic movement. Four years after its appearance in 1928, Benjamin's first major published work, *The Origin of the German Tragic Drama*, was reviewed in *Imago*, the journal of the International Psychoanalytic Association devoted to discussing applications of psychoanalysis to the humanities. Although little known, this review is remarkably prescient in its concern with problems in Freud's conception of language that are still considered important by literary critics today. In *The Origin of the German Tragic Drama*, Benjamin undertook a study of allegory in the German Baroque theatre. Recently, critics like Nägele and Julia Reinhard Lupton have observed that Benjamin's distinction between the classical tragedy and the baroque mourning play, which is crucial to the book, can be understood in terms of Freud's account of mourning and melancholia, two different responses to the loss of a beloved object.[4] The similarities between Benjamin's and Freud's interest in melancholia were also noted by the 1932 reviewer, Alexander Mette, a Berlin psychoanalyst who was himself to become the author of a Nietzschean study on the psychological bases of tragedy which bears similarities to Benjamin's.

Similar to the rest of his generation in viewing the First World War as a crucial traumatic experience, Benjamin would later take the impoverishment of experience in the modern era as a predominant theme in essays such as "The Storyteller." The same concerns can be seen in his account of the role of melancholia in the baroque plays written during and after the

Thirty-Years War, a period of extended religious strife between Protestants and Catholics in the mid-seventeenth century. Related to the fact that he had been influenced by early phenomenology in his student days, mood or temperament is a central concept in Benjamin's thought; it is present in his account of melancholia in *The Origin of the German Tragic Drama*, and is also strongly in evidence in his later studies of Surrealism and in the unfinished *Arcades Project* that occupied his attention during the 1930s. For his part, Freud was also interested in the role of mood in the trauma neuroses that became so common during the First World War, devoting several studies to the problem including an important section of "Beyond the Pleasure Principle," the essay we have already discussed. Attentive to this common concern, Mette examined the way in which Benjamin treated the baroque tragic drama's replacement of the classical tragic hero with a constellation of characters at the center of which were two personality types, the tyrant and the intriguer, both of whom belonged to a single, deeply pessimistic and contemplative mood.[5] Benjamin and Freud shared a quasi-scientific interest in producing a typology of temperament.

For Benjamin, the melancholia characteristic of a war-torn era sometimes found expression in typical behaviors of the baroque's dramatic figures, for example, the indecisiveness of the tyrant or the playfulness of the intriguer. In addition, Mette drew special attention to the way in which Benjamin analyzed the bombast of the baroque as a "planned linguistic gesture" (Mette, 538). Arguably the greatest critic of German expressionism, Benjamin conceived of baroque linguistic practices as an *expression* of melancholia, giving it an underlying psychological basis. Mette's most intriguing move was to connect this to Freud's discussion of the way in which schizophrenics treat language. According to Benjamin, baroque stylistic practices produced "hieroglyphics" or imagistic language symbols behind which a melancholy pathology could be discerned. Rooted in a theological conception of an irredeemably fallen world in which access to the essence of things had become impossible, the baroque's insistence on the extreme concretion of language led to an increasing number of neologisms as well as a tendency to dismember words and other bits of language while scattering them throughout the text. Mette describes the effect of this concretion as follows: "on the one hand, writing is elevated over the sound of words to an extraordinary degree, while language is dissolved, on the other, into fragments that become the realm for an altered and intensified form of expression" (Mette, 538). Mette regarded it as particularly significant that Benjamin drew comparisons between such stylistic practices and the disconnected juxtaposition of syntactic elements in the late Sophocles translations of the German poet Friedrich Hölderlin, who succumbed to madness in the latter half of his life. We may also see a connection to Benjamin's discussion of the theological dimensions of pathology in his study on the works of the mentally ill.

Basing himself on Freud's analyses of schizophrenia, Mette's ultimate conclusion was that "the peculiar juxtaposition of melancholy and mania [in the baroque drama] and the strange way in which they coincide with the phenomena of schizophrenia point to a difficult struggle for the validation of the Super-Ego and the maintenance of object cathexes" (Mette, 538). In his book, Benjamin had noted that the explicit presentation of physical torture on the baroque stage departed from the classical conventions of tragedy in leaving nothing to the imagination. For Mette, these dramatic elements could be seen as the baroque's internal image of the Counter-Reformation, which had once again gained the upper hand and had reassumed its position as the father-imago. As a consequence, it had become what he regarded as the sadistic object of Oedipal frustration, an allusion to what Freud termed the castration complex, the child's fear that he would be punished by his father for desiring his mother and his transformation of this fear into aggression of his own. It was this fear which led to the predominance of fantasy and the turning of aggression onto the medium of expression itself, i.e., language, characteristic of schizophrenia. Proposing, in effect, that history made the same kind of imprint on baroque literature as infantile experience did on a person who was mentally ill, Mette thought Benjamin had revealed baroque stylistic peculiarities to be fundamentally pathological symptoms.

Interestingly, Mette also noted that some of the dramatic practices Benjamin described could be regarded as instances of the reappearance of totemic thinking, a subject of particular interest to Freud. As a consequence, his review not only offers insight into the relation between Benjamin's account of the baroque and Freud's diagnosis of the linguistic symptoms of psychopathic disturbances, it also suggests one way in which Benjamin's collection of works by the mentally ill can be brought together with another of his interests, the occult. The common thread lies in the archaic nature of the linguistic phenomena described, an issue that raises larger questions about Benjamin's theory of dialectical images.

If this thoroughgoing analysis of the connections between Benjamin and Freud seems somewhat radical, Mette's comments on Benjamin's form of criticism are also worthy of attention. Observing that *The Origin of the German Tragic Drama* was different from conventional literary histories of the period in its attempt to produce a philosophical tractatus that would penetrate, as Benjamin had put it, the very "idea" of the tragic drama, Mette observed that Benjamin's contrast between classical tragedy and baroque dramatic form focused on problems of stylistic analysis, at the same time as historical content continued to take precedence over form. He saw this procedure as analogous to the way Freud's theory of dream interpretation subordinated form to meaning and attempted to extrapolate encodings of actual events in the dreamer's waking life from the mythic formations of the dream (Mette, 538). Like critics today, Mette thus pointed to the similarities between the ways in which Benjamin and Freud read texts. This issue is essential for a full consideration of Benjamin's reception of Freud.

One model of intertextuality is Julia Kristeva's notion of transposition, which replaces the conventional study of sources with an analysis of textual interactions derived from Freud's rejection of a one-to-one transformation of conscious into unconscious thoughts. For Kristeva, texts constitute systems of signs that can refer to earlier texts at the same time as they constitute sites for the interaction between larger discourses.[6] Kristeva stresses that every system of signs is a field of transpositions rather than the neat transformation of one system into another, just as, for Freud, pushing thoughts into the unconscious produces interactions which themselves lead to a return of the repressed in symptom-formations such as dreams. Although every discourse strives to establish itself as a new position, none can ever avoid this dynamic, in which repression is an imperfect mechanism and the return of the repressed is ongoing. As a consequence, texts and discourses become sites for the displacement and redistribution of the values attached to elements within the discursive systems they take up.

Intertextuality encourages us to pay particular attention to the role of individual texts or œuvres as sites of competition between and interaction among discourses, an approach which may provide one way of understanding the role of psychoanalysis in Benjamin's thought. As it remains today, psychoanalysis was only one theory about how the mind worked in the first half of the twentieth century, and far from the least controversial. It is worth examining Benjamin's deployment of it in relation to two other major psychologies of his day, German academic psychology and Soviet behaviorism. Following Kristeva, Benjamin's texts may be understood as attempts to establish a new position in relation to these discursive fields that ultimately bears the traces of its own repressions and compromises.

This approach is particularly helpful in understanding Benjamin's use of psychoanalysis as a counter-weight to contemporaneous German academic psychology. Although he was active in the German youth movement before the First World War, Benjamin became increasingly critical of the reactionary politics of the "philosophy of life" movement that emerged out of it, devoting a considerable portion of his 1922 essay on "Goethe's *Elective Affinities*" to a critique of the poet Stefan George and his circle, about whose ideas he grew increasingly concerned throughout the 1920s as their relation to the rising tide of fascism became more evident. His objections to the theories of Ludwig Klages, a psychologist associated with the George circle, and his related polemic against Freud's apostate disciple Carl Jung are important both to his critique of fascism and to his theory of dialectical images.

In addition to his general philosophical works, Klages was the author of several books on graphology, the study of handwriting. While traces of it can still be seen today in the role personality tests continue to play in the way corporations hire employees, this is an area no longer viewed as a reputable scholarly field, except in linguistics, where it refers to the study of the relation among elements within and among writing systems inspired by the same structuralism we have seen at work in Freud's theory of dreams. However, speculations about the connection between handwriting and character played a significant role in the early development of ergonomic theories about the optimal workplace. Despite the fact that Benjamin sought to free graphology from "the moralistic assessment of character," it may be difficult for us to understand how he and Freud could have participated so eagerly in the widespread enthusiasm for converting occult disciplines into scientific fields at the end of the nineteenth century. It should be related to the problem of the archaic image. According to the graphologists, handwriting could be viewed as a kind of hieroglyphics that embedded images into letters. An unusually short line on an "h" or a "t" could thus be seen as evidence of a person's tendency to abase himself before authority, i.e., as an unconscious depiction of his own inability to stand up straight.

Benjamin's relation to Klages's graphology was complex. Benjamin acknowledged the importance of late nineteenth-century French graphology, which attempted early semiotic analyses of handwriting by studying individual letters as signs to which fixed character traits could be assigned, however, he also appears to have endorsed Klages' critique of this approach, which is remarkably close to Freud's rejection of the attachment of fixed meanings to dream images. Just as Freud regarded this mode of interpretation as too static, Klages objected that French graphology made use of "stereotypes on which to construct interpretations" (SW, II, 399). Instead, he interpreted handwriting as gestural. As Benjamin puts it, "there is no talk in [Klages'] writings of specific signs; he speaks only of the general characteristics of writing, which are not restricted to the particular form of individual letters." He regarded this approach as insufficiently structuralist or materialist. Benjamin thus had two important critiques of Klages: first, he objects to his lack of precision in the interpretation of the individual aspects of handwriting, and, second, he proposes that handwriting should instead be analyzed "in terms of unconscious graphic elements and unconscious image fantasies" (SW, II, 399).

This approach, first developed at the Berlin Central Institute for Scientific Graphology, appealed to Benjamin because it combined a semiotic theory of handwriting as a kind of material sign with an ideographic conception of script related to his interest in archaic images. It was Freudian psychoanalysis, he pointed out, which underlay the Berlin graphologists' approach (*SW*, II, 399). As he observed in his 1933 essay on "The Doctrine of the Similar," Klages was a "vulgar proponent" of the study of handwriting, however, for Benjamin, the Berlin graphologists had a different conception:

> [I]t is worth noting that script, perhaps even more than certain combinations of sound in language, clarifies – in the relationship of the written form [*Schriftbild*] of words and letters to the signified … the nature of nonsensuous similarity. Thus, for instance, the letter *beth* [in Hebrew] is the root of the word meaning "house" … The most recent graphology has taught us to recognize, in handwriting, images – or, more precisely, picture puzzles – that the unconscious writer conceals in his writing. (*SW*, II, 696–97)

In the unconscious, words are transformed into images, a process Freud terms *Bilderschrift*, literally "image-writing." For Benjamin, psychoanalytic graphology reveals the relationship between the *Schriftbild*, the image that writing produces in words and letters, and their meaning. This conception is intimately connected to the use of the term "graphology" in modern linguistics to designate a structural comparison of elements within writing systems. Psychoanalysis thus became crucial for Benjamin as the most advanced approach to the ideographic study of script: it was "a systematic attempt to construe the handwriting of even civilized people as a set of hieroglyphs. And the authors have," he declared, "managed to preserve contact with the world of images to a hitherto unprecedented degree" (*SW*, II, 133).

Benjamin's effort to make use of psychoanalysis against the right-wing ideologies informing Klages's work (in which the notion of gesture stands in for a kind of transcendental ineffability Benjamin regarded as the fundamental principle of philosophical fascism) can also be seen as an example of the way Benjamin's texts function as staging-grounds for struggles between discourses. His deployment of psychoanalytic graphology as a critique of Klages's conception of archaic images is typical of his strategy of taking up elements of Freud's thought not so much with an eye to their function within psychoanalytic debates but as a means of strengthening his own positions. This strategy is related to his practice of citation, in which passages are deliberately torn from their original context to be arranged in new constellations. In this respect, it would be an exaggeration to call Benjamin a Freudian. Rather, he was a tactically astute reader of Freud who weighed the advantages and disadvantages of deploying psychoanalytic ideas and approaches for a larger theoretical agenda.

Benjamin's interest in graphology gives a particularly good example of such a deployment. In a 1928 review of Georg Mendelssohn's *Der Mensch in der Handschrift* [Man in his Handwriting] Benjamin writes, "One day it may be possible to exploit graphology to investigate telepathic events" (*SW*, II, 134). Benjamin's interest in the occult, in particular, telepathy, may strike us as strange, yet it marks an important point of contact with Freud who shared this same interest. An entry from Benjamin's unpublished notebooks in which he records a passage from Freud's 1934 "On the Problem of Telepathy" points to the nature of this contact. In this passage, Freud makes a speculative connection between telepathy and group psychology, thus opening up the larger question of Benjamin's interest in psychoanalytic notions of collective consciousness. Observing the inexplicable commonality of purpose found in beehives and ant-hills, frequently taken as metaphors for human society in Enlightenment thought, Freud makes the following observation:

> One is led to a suspicion that this is the original, archaic method of communication among individuals and that in the course of phylogenetic evolution it has been replaced by the better method of giving information with the help of signals which are picked up by the sense organs. But the older method might have persisted in the background and still be able to put itself into effect under certain conditions – for instance, in passionately excited mobs.[7]

As we know from a letter Benjamin wrote in October 1935 thanking Gretel Adorno, the wife of his colleague Theodor Adorno, who had sent him Freud's essay, he regarded this passage as closely related to the philosophy of language he elaborated in his 1933 essay "On the Mimetic Faculty." In this letter, Benjamin writes:

> In the course of his reflections, Freud establishes a connection between telepathy and language in which he makes the first a phylogenetic forerunner of the second as a means of communication – he points to the insect state as illustration. I recognize here ideas I examined in a small sketch from Ibiza – "On the Mimetic Faculty." (*GS*, II.3, 953)

Around the time he was engaged with the problem of war trauma discussed in "Beyond the Pleasure Principle," Freud also became interested in the problem of group psychology, a topic that brought him back to his earlier studies of hysteria in Charcot's clinic, particularly to the problem of the seemingly telepathic communications among hysterical patients. Benjamin seems to have been intrigued by the way in which Freud both constructed an historical theory of telepathy as a forerunner to language and imagined a possible return to the more archaic means of communication in crowds. In a letter to the essayist and poet Werner Kraft, he remarked that he had been "very surprised to find significant correlations" between psychoanalysis and his own language theory.[8] In comparison to the vague hesitancy he expressed with respect to his reading of Freud and Schreber, this confession of surprise suggests the kind of sudden jolt of recognition he himself regarded as important in the production of dialectical images.

Freud's emphasis on the phylogenetic or ancestral aspects of language forces us to turn our attention to the new question of Benjamin's concern with the theory of collective phenomena, an issue that was increasingly central to his thinking after 1928. As even Scholem is forced to concede, Benjamin's interest in French Surrealism, a movement heavily influenced by Freud and about which he wrote an important essay in that year, provided "the first bridge to a more positive assessment of psychoanalysis" (*Friendship*, 134). In Surrealism, we find a convergence of Benjamin's interests in dreams, the occult, and even in graphology as a form of automatic writing. 1928 also marks an important break in Benjamin's work as a whole, for it was at this time that he returned from his trip to Moscow and began work on the *Arcades Project*, his never-completed study of nineteenth-century bourgeois commodity culture. Likewise, it is in 1928 that he records in the catalogue of books he had read his first encounter with Freud's "Beyond the Pleasure Principle."[9] In the same year, he refers to this reading in a discussion of the need for a new examination of children's play from the child's perspective:

> Such a study would have to explore the great law that presides over the rules and rhythms of the whole world of play: the law of repetition. We know that for the child repetition is the soul of play, that nothing gives him greater pleasure than to "Do it again!" The obscure urge to repeat things is scarcely less powerful in play, scarcely less cunning in its workings, than the sexual impulse in love. It is not an accident that Freud has imagined he could detect an impulse "beyond the pleasure principle" in it.
>
> ("Toys and Play," *SW*, II, 120)

In "Beyond the Pleasure Principle," Freud did indeed examine a series of cases he thought revealed a flaw in his theory that the purpose of dreams lay in the fulfillment of a unifying wish. If one example was the dreams of trauma victims we have already discussed, another was the child's desire for repetition during play. As Benjamin recognized, Freud's discussion of this issue established a connection between repetition and desire, the principle Freud saw as the basis for the death drive, the mechanism he understands as "beyond" the pleasure principle. In the later Benjamin, the problem of desire becomes increasingly important, particularly in relation to the social collective.[10]

To understand the importance psychoanalysis was to acquire in Benjamin's thinking after his return from the Soviet Union, it is important to know something of the politics that surrounded the Bolshevik attitude toward Freud. In fact, Benjamin's return to Paris and his interest in Surrealism can be best understood in the context of his response to Soviet Marxism.

At the time, Surrealism was the most important art movement to embrace psychoanalysis. In many ways, it was ahead of Freud himself, who famously expressed his discomfort with the experiments being carried out in his name, illustrating that his thought sometimes had broader implications than he realized. The Surrealists also regarded themselves as Marxists. Benjamin's engagement with them may thus have been his first encounter with Freudo-Marxism, a synthesis of the two movements that was also becoming a topic of discussion among his friends at the Institute for Social Research, what we today know as the Frankfurt School. Although it is an intellectual tradition with a long history that continues to the present day, in the 1920s and 30s Freudo-Marxism was a splinter movement that never gained legitimacy with either the Comintern or the International Psychoanalytic Association. Despite a brief curiosity about progressive psychoanalysis during the attempts to deal with problems of social dislocation after the Civil War, the Soviets had by 1926 come to regard Freudianism as a dangerous bourgeois deviation, rejecting it in favor of the reflex behaviorism of Ivan Pavlov, which was seen as more appropriate for dialectical materialism.[11] For its part, the International Psychoanalytic Association was to expel Wilhelm Reich, a Freudo-Marxist who travelled to the Soviet Union in 1929; he was excluded from the German Communist Party at the same time.

When Benjamin became interested in Surrealism, he was thus becoming involved with a movement that was being rejected as a double heresy on both sides. This was precisely the kind of stance that appealed to him. "The ability to free [oneself] from sectarianism," he had observed in his discussion of psychoanalytic graphology [in his review of Mendelssohn's *Der Mensch in der Handschrift*], "is a matter of life and death at the present time" (*SW*, II, 133). In the case of Freudo-Marxism, the movement's doubly decontextualizing violence corresponded well to his practice of blasting citations out of their original context.

As with Klages and Jung, Benjamin's use of psychoanalysis can thus be seen as part of his response to the materialist psychology of the Soviets. His return to Paris and his engagement with Surrealism in 1928 followed his failed visit to Moscow to see his lover Asja Lacis, during which he considered making a commitment to Soviet orthodoxy. Even if he was ultimately to reject this,

Soviet psychology continued, as Miriam Bratu Hansen has suggested, to play an important, if buried, role in his work, particularly in his theory of film. It is likely that it was through Lacis, an active member of the proletarian theater, that Benjamin became acquainted with the acting theory of Sergei Eisenstein, the great Soviet filmmaker and theoretician of a materialist film aesthetics. Curiously, Eisenstein's theory of audience reception, in which the effects of shock and anaesthetization could be undone by the way an actor used his body to evoke liberating psychological effects in his audience, was partly influenced by Klages.[12] Benjamin was interested in precisely such passages between mind and body. He seems to have taken to this idea, basing his notion of "collective innervation" on it (Hansen, 315–16).

Although "innervation" was a term also used by Freud in his description of somatic conversion, the production of psychosomatic symptoms by hysterical patients, Hansen holds that Benjamin's deployment of this concept is not primarily psychoanalytic. As she points out, the term "innervation" had been in use in neuropsychology since the 1830s as a description for transfers of energy between the neurological system and the mind. Like Freud, whose study of the constant rehearsal of painful memories by trauma victims during the First World War played an important role in the development of his theory of the death drive, Benjamin was, as we have seen, interested in the shock produced by modern trauma. Yet, whereas for Freud, psychosomatic symptoms were the product of a process in which mental disturbances were expressed through their transformation into motor symptoms such as paralysis, for Eisenstein, it was two-way dynamic. Following Eisenstein, Benjamin saw the possibility for a reversal of psychosomatic conditions.

Hansen sees this structure as particularly important for Benjamin's account of film reception, in which the "first technology" of the individual actor's use of his body was converted into a "second technology" in the audience, i.e., the group. Hansen makes a strong argument to suggest that Benjamin's relation to psychoanalysis could at times be subordinate to other, more materialist approaches. Still, she concedes that the theory of collective innervation, most evident in the second (and for Benjamin authoritative) draft of "The Work of Art in the Age of its Technological Reproductibility," is suppressed in the final version of the essay (Hansen, 314). She also points out that Benjamin refers in his 1931 "Little History of Photography" to Freud's psychopathology of everyday life, comparing what he called photography's "optical unconscious" to "the discovery of the instinctual unconscious through psychoanalysis" (SW II, 512). This suggests that psychoanalysis had in fact become a model for his conceptualization of film.

As a consequence, we must consider the possibility that Benjamin had made a deliberate turn to Freud late in his career as an alternative to Soviet psychology, a process that can be compared to his use of psychoanalytic graphology as a means of countering Klages. In an unpublished fragment from 1934, for instance, we find him critiquing a work on *Psychiatry and Civilization* by the French author Henri Damaye because his "scientific positivism" prevented him from "gaining access to the many achievements of psychoanalysis" (*GS*, VII, 89). Unfortunately, this process is to some extent obscured by Benjamin's vexed relation to the Freud debates within the Frankfurt School. In the final years of his life, he was dependent on the School's patronage, which offered him remuneration for his work – increasingly difficult for a left-wing writer on the eve of the Second World War – as well as hope of emigration to the United States, where the Institute had relocated. The multiple revisions of many of his late essays, most famously the "Work of Art" piece, were partly motivated by his efforts to fit his thought to the sometimes doctrinaire views of his patrons.

In some ways, this helped him to articulate his thinking on psychoanalysis. Although Adorno, for instance, warned him away from Reich and his group, his responses to early proposals for the *Arcades Project* nudged Benjamin in the direction of a more direct engagement with Freud. Motivated by his own recent examination of psychoanalysis, Adorno proposed in 1934 that Benjamin "might find *Freud's* debate with Jung an appropriate vehicle" in relation to his "materialist doctrine of ideas":

> for although Freud himself is quite unconcerned with our own question, he does confront Jung with the serious nominalistic challenge that is certainly required for any genuine access to the primal history of the nineteenth century itself... Freud's individualistic but dialectical critique can actually help to break the archaizing tendency of the others, and then itself be used, dialectically, to overcome Freud's own immanentist standpoint. (*CA/B*, 62)

A few months later, Adorno reiterated the possibility of using Freud, to which Benjamin replied:

> Amongst all the things in your letter, none struck me more forcibly than the position you seem to take up with regard to the question of the "mediation" between society and psychology. Here we are both pulling at the *same* rope, although I was unaware of the fact in this particular form – though it is hardly an ideal situation to find Fromm and Reich are both pulling hard at the other end. I shall be looking at Freud soon... and then, after Freud, I shall take up Baudelaire. (*CA/B*, 99)

Notably, the same structure of deferral we encountered in the early stages of Benjamin's engagement with Freud can be seen again here. A few months on, Benjamin finds himself in the midst of a study of Jung that has to be postponed in favor of Baudelaire. Strikingly, he never uses the name Freud in his discussions of Klages and Jung in the *Arcades Project*: instead, he refers to "psychoanalysis" as an alternative approach to the archaic dimensions of the nineteenth-century collective mind. He does not return to Freud until 1939, when he records a rereading of "Beyond the Pleasure Principle" in his catalogue of books.[13] Still, Adorno had in effect laid out for Benjamin the work he was to do in Convolute K, where he would use Freud against Jung but also go on to critique him.

The fact that Benjamin's study of psychoanalysis never properly took off can perhaps be attributed to Max Horkheimer's lack of enthusiasm for the project. In June 1935, at the same time as Adorno was advocating further Freud study, Horkheimer was insisting that Benjamin complete an essay on the cultural historian Eduard Fuchs, whose historical orientation Horkheimer regarded as "much more far-sighted for social psychology than Freud ... despite his psychologically far more primitive apparatus" (*GS*, II.3, 1319). Interestingly, Nägele has proposed, however, that what Benjamin wrote about Fuchs reverses Horkheimer's preference, revealing Fuchs's evasions and silences to be symptomatic of a failure to free himself from a moralistic account of society in the way that Freud had:

> Fuchs avoid[s] as much as possible the theory of repression and of the complexes that might have modified his moralistic conception of social and sexual relations. The erotic world of images as a symbolic one, which Freud discovered in his *Interpretation of Dreams*, appears in Fuchs only at moments when his inner participation is most intense. In that instance, it permeates his presentation even when every allusion to it is avoided.   (*GS*, II.2, 498–99)

Here, Benjamin returns to the importance of desire he raised in connection with the drive to repetition in his essay on children's play. The problem of desire is also at issue in his discussions of free love in the *Arcades Project*, a work stamped by a call for the liberation of desires and affects characteristic of both Freudo-Marxism and Surrealism. In treating Fuchs's silences as symptomatic, Benjamin takes up the psychoanalytic notion of resistance of which we have also made use in relation to his own early ambivalence about Freud. It is a technique similar to the one found in his later discussion of the crowd as a presence pervasive in its absence in Baudelaire's poem "A une passante."

There is, however, a further twist to the tale. While Benjamin's use of Freud in the "Baudelaire" essay produces a different version of the shock theory than his use of Soviet psychology for the theory of collective innervation, his emphasis on the position of consciousness in the cortex strikingly highlights Freud's reconciliation of psychoanalysis with a neurological conception of the brain, a tendency which many of his followers might have been more in-clined to downplay, as Frank Sulloway has pointed out.[14] In fact, Benjamin's suggestion that Baudelaire parried the shocks with his body stands in con-trast to Freud's own emphasis on psychic mechanisms such as anxiety and narcissism. Arguably, this is an example of the impact of Soviet materialist psychology on Benjamin's thought. In Kristeva's terms, we could see it as an instance in which a psychoanalytic idea is subtly displaced as it comes into contact with another discourse with which it may even be in conflict.

On the level of what we might call conscious intention, it is clear that Benjamin was aware of the connections between Freud's conception of dream images and his own theory of the dialectical image. Despite the fact that it plays a crucial role in his reception of Freud, it is less obvious that he saw their shared concern with the problem of war traumas. It would not be an exaggeration, however, to describe intertextuality as a fundamental mode of Benjamin's thought. His practice of citation – most famous in the *Arcades Project*, but also repeatedly in evidence in his allusions to Freud – can be un-derstood as a case of both allusion and pastiche. Both his theoretical essay on "The Task of the Translator" and his actual translations of Proust are examples of a complex conception of translation; and his practice of dispers-ing letters and phonemes throughout his texts, most famously in his plays on the connections between the German term for violence, *Gewalt*, and his own name, can be seen as instances of anagram.[15] The notion of intertextuality – which focuses, like that of schizophrenic language-disturbance, on language practices determined by unconscious rather than logical thought-processes – thus provides insight into the ways in which multiple fields converge in his texts.

This also suggests something of the impact of Benjamin's manner of read-ing on his writing practices. On the one hand, our use of a term such as "intertextuality" to describe how references to Freud are scattered through-out Benjamin's texts implies that his relation to psychoanalysis cannot be treated simply as a problem of one-to-one translations between one system (Freud's) and another (his own). This would fail to take into account the fact that psychoanalysis is never more than one position amongst many in Benjamin's writings and that, as it comes into contact with these other po-sitions, it undergoes various kinds of displacement. On the other hand, it allows us to understand why we can speak of a psychoanalytic influence on Benjamin's thought despite the fact that direct allusions to Freud and his followers often emerge fleetingly and without warning. While psychoanal-ysis seems gradually to have come to serve as a strategic ally in Benjamin's increasingly polemical work, his allusions to Freud are citations torn from their original context, their meanings altered as they are deployed for new purposes. Benjamin's use of psychoanalysis reveals a double process of annihilation and reinscription that marks his relation to texts and textuality as a whole, revealing a fragmentation that means the translation between discourses can never be seamless or complete.

NOTES

1. Sigrid Weigel, *Body and Image-Space: Re-reading Walter Benjamin*, (New York: Routledge, 1996), 116. Subsequently cited in the text as "Weigel."
2. Rainer Nägele, "Beyond Psychology: Freud, Benjamin, and the Articulation of Modernity," in: *Theater. Theory. Speculation: Walter Benjamin and the Scenes of Modernity* (Baltimore: Johns Hopkins University Press, 1991), 57. Subsequently cited in the text as "Nägele."
3. *GS*, VII.1, 440–41, nos. 540 and 549. Gershom Scholem, *Friendship*, 57.
4. See Julia Reinhard Lupton and Kenneth Reinhard, *After Oedipus: Shakespeare in Psychoanalysis* (Ithaca: Cornell University Press, 1993), 34–59.
5. Alexander Mette, review of Walter Benjamin, *Ursprung des deutschen Trauerspiels* [*The Origin of the German Tragic Drama*], *Imago* 7:4 (1931), 536. Subsequently cited in text as "Mette."
6. Julia Kristeva, *Revolution in Poetic Language* (New York: Columbia University Press, 1984), 59–60.
7. Sigmund Freud, *Standard Edition*, XXII, 55.
8. Walter Benjamin, *Correspondence 1910–1940* (University of Chicago Press, 1994), 521.
9. *GS*, VII.1, 460, no. 1076. Based on surrounding evidence, this undated reference cannot have been recorded before 1928.
10. There are two further references to Freud in Benjamin's discussions of childhood in this period, one in a review of children's primers where he alludes to Freud's "doctrine of the unconscious" and the other in a discussion of colonial pedagogy in which he mentions Freud's study of narcissism, a work he had entered into his catalogue a decade previously (*GS*, III, 271 and *GS*, III, 273).
11. On the history of psychoanalysis in the early Soviet Union, see Alexander Etkind, *Eros of the Impossible: The History of Psychoanalysis in Russia* (Boulder: Westview Press, 1997), 179–225.
12. Miriam Bratu Hansen, "Benjamin and Cinema: Not a One-Way Street," *Critical Inquiry* 25 (Winter 1999), 317. Cited in the text as "Hansen."
13. *GS* VII.1, 475, no. 1680, probably from 1939 based on surrounding evidence.
14. See Frank Sulloway, *Freud Biologist of the Mind: Beyond the Psychoanalytic Legend* (New York: Basic Books, 1979).
15. For examples of this approach, see Werner Hamacher, "The Word 'Wolke,' If It Is One," in *Benjamin's Ground*, ed. Rainer Nägele (Detroit: Wayne State University Press, 1988), 147–76, and Thomas Schestag, *Asphalt* (Munich: Boer, 1992).

7

REBECCA COMAY

Benjamin and the ambiguities of Romanticism

When the young Benjamin finally decides, in 1917, to jettison Kant for the Romanticism of Friedrich Schlegel and Novalis as the topic for his doctoral dissertation at the University of Berne, the choice reflects no arbitrary shift of interest. Benjamin had already been struggling to rescue Kant's thought from what he perceived to be its fatal slide into scientific positivism in the hands of the neo-Kantians of his time. Whether it was the failure of this rescue or another reason (according to a letter from Benjamin to Scholem, it was the "very unpleasant" experience of finally getting around to reading the philosophy of history expressed in Kant's essays on "Ideas for a Universal History" and "Perpetual Peace"), this shift toward the Romantics marks a clear break with the dominant philosophic thought of his day. Moreover, since this was a movement away from the various ideologies of progress espoused both by the neo-Kantians (and also used by one of them, Hermann Cohen, to justify the German war effort) and by the German youth movement with which Benjamin had been involved during the years preceding 1917, the stakes are immediately high.

If Benjamin's renunciation of Kant during the war years is linked, at least in his own mind, to the conformism he sees implicit in the latter's portrayal of history as an endless inexorable progress toward a pre-established goal – the "infinite task" – it is also crucially informs his rehabilitation of the Romanticism that flourished at Jena under the influence of Novalis and Friedrich Schlegel in the late 1780s and early 1790s. Through this rehabilitation, Benjamin resists the then current German nationalist appropriations of Romanticism (whether in the form of mythic appeals to *Volk* culture or the contemporary vitalist reworking of Romanticism's precursor in *Sturm und Drang*). It is therefore *early* Romanticism – emphatically quarantined from its later (and earlier) mutations – which is at issue for Benjamin in 1917–19. Indeed, in the very concept of "early" Romanticism [*Frühromantik*], Benjamin perhaps finds the radical resources of youth which he had previously and vainly sought in the German youth movement. In a letter from 1913, Benjamin had given voice to this potential as follows: "In every individual who is born, no matter where, and turns out to be young, there is, not 'improvement,' but perfection from the start" (C, 54). The opposition between "improvement" and "perfection" strikes out, in the first instance, against the ideology of progress in its various historicist formulations: whereas the appeal to improvement posits a transcendent goal which would function as ideological justification of the present (which it would secretly buttress by way of otherworldly compensation), the persistence of an already immanent fulfillment would, conversely, expose the present to the constant pressure of self-transformation. The contrast itself rests on the philosophical difference between two kinds of infinite. Despite Benjamin's abiding reservations, Hegel's distinction between the "true" and "bad" infinite is here fundamental. In the "fulfilled infinite" of Schlegel and Novalis, Benjamin sees a passage beyond what he identifies as the empty infinite – the endless accumulation of repetitive acts, events, or occasions – implicit in the project of transcendental idealism (from Kant to Fichte). The passage beyond the infinite task becomes the essential project of philosophy. In Romanticism, Benjamin detects a resource previously hidden.

The passage itself, however, is fraught with ambiguities. For, while the Romantic infinite is praised precisely for bringing "Messianic" closure to bear on an otherwise indifferent, infinitely "progressive" – because self-perpetuating – continuum, its actual logic seems at first rather to exacerbate the very condition it would address. The "bad infinite" is here identified as the serial reflexivity of consciousness itself, which now bears the burden once assigned to the infinite task. How is this to be arrested? Benjamin's argument is complicated but displays the following schema. On the one hand, in a first twist, Benjamin explores the Romantic attempt to move beyond the dogmatism implicit in Fichte's project of a transcendental self-grounding: the securing of identity within the self-positing of the self-knowing ego. Fichte's very attempt to bypass the bad infinite of reflection – thinking about thinking about thinking... – proves, in this first moment, only to entrench him in the vertiginous reflexivity which he would surmount. Novalis and Schlegel pursue this strand by exposing precisely where Fichte's own project rests on a prior self-differentiation that dissolves the unitary self into an infinity of reflections. The unacknowledged truth of Fichtean dogmatism is therefore infinite, serial self-reflection: Jena Romanticism reveals the secret truth of Fichte. On the other hand, in a second twist, Benjamin's Romantics argue that this infinite is said to contract or "fulfill" itself so as to arrest the very endlessness to which it attests. By this means, Romantic reflection culminates in a new absolute, which both is and is not that of the transcendental subject. The Romantic absolute expresses at once, paradoxically, both the hypertrophy of reflection and its arrest or caesura. If the structure of this double twist appears to be resolutely dialectical with respect to Fichtean dogmatism – negation, negation of the negation – Benjamin's formulation lacks the resolution that this Hegelian structure might otherwise suggest.

This chapter will attempt to draw out some of the ambiguities of Benjamin's rendering of the Romantic infinite – ambiguities which will continue to inform his project to the very end. After sketching out some of the technical issues at work in Benjamin's account of the Romantic revision of Fichte's transcendental idealism, I will suggest where these issues resurface in his later work as well as what is at stake. The first section addresses Benjamin's account of the Romantic critique of Fichte; the second and third sections address the two poles of the ambivalence informing this critique; the fourth (and final) section points to the residues of this ambivalence in Benjamin's own later writings.

From idealism to criticism: antinomies of reflection

Fichte had attempted to fulfill the foundational project of modernity – to vindicate an autonomous subject as philosophical first principle – by closing the fatal fissure that he had detected in the classic formulations of both Descartes and Kant. He reproaches his predecessors for having introduced opacity into the translucent identity of the self-knowing self. Fichte complains of Descartes: "The addition of *cogitans* is completely superfluous: one does not necessarily think if one is, but one necessarily is if one thinks."[1] And, to Kant, he objects: "The consciousness of my thinking is not something which is just incidental to my thinking, something which is only added onto it afterwards and which is thus [only] linked to it, but is rather inseparable from it." At the source of the modern philosophy of the subject, in other words, Fichte detects a split that condemns consciousness to a Sisyphean process of self-reflection. According to Fichte's startling revision of Kant, only "intellectual intuition" would offer the means to arrest the infinite regress latent in the Cartesian–Kantian project by providing an immediate unity of subject and object. By such means, the self would retrieve itself in a timeless present uncontaminated by the deferral characteristic of conditioned, temporal experience. According to Fichte, in the intuitive immediacy of the subject's self-encounter, reflecting and reflected consciousness were to coincide with neither delay nor remainder, leaving no residue which would either solicit or permit further reflection.

Applying Fichte's own critique of his predecessors to Fichte himself, Novalis and Schlegel draw out the inconsistency of Fichte's "original insight" by drawing attention to the mediation implied in the very immediacy of self-positing. Novalis's rejoinder to Fichte is, for Benjamin, paradigmatic: "The statement 'a is a' is nothing but a positing, a differentiating, a linking. It is a philosophical parallelism . . . The essence of identity can only be put forward in a pseudo-proposition. We leave the identical in order to represent it."[2] For Novalis, the statement of identity performatively contradicts, as statement, the truth of the unmediated identity it would announce. The very representation of identity involves its mediation, and as such, its self-betrayal. Through this inevitable lapse into representation, the ultimate truth of Fichte's "fundamental proposition" is revealed to be an unending mirror-play of doubles and negatives, the very grounding of the self revealed to be a vertiginous leap into an abyss.

Fichte himself had already hinted at such an inconsistency in his rigorous effort to recuperate for subjectivity the very heterogeneity that would seem most to vitiate it. His admission of an "originary duplicity"[3] within the innermost interior of the self – "the self is to encounter in itself something heterogeneous, alien, and to be distinguished from itself" – had already exposed the autonomous subject to a fundamental passivity which Fichte himself had gamely attempted to appropriate as the final measure of the subject's most heroic sublimity: self-possession in the very event of self-dispossession:

> The self must originally and absolutely posit in itself the possibility of something operating upon it; without detriment to its absolute positing of itself, it must leave itself open, as it were, to some other positing . . . this alien element is to be encountered in the self, and can only be encountered therein. If it lay outside the self, it would be nothing for the self, and nothing would follow for the self from this. Hence, in a certain respect, it must also be cognate to the self; it must be capable of ascription thereto.   (*Science of Knowledge*, 239f.)

Here, Fichte promises to resolve "the apparent contradictoriness" of this immanent alterity – to think through what he calls the "unthinkability" of this actively produced passivity – an aporia that would indeed threaten to compromise the autonomy of the subject's own self-positing. In their various attacks on the residual dogmatism implicit in Fichte's appeal to intellectual intuition, Schlegel and Novalis pull away the "transcendental anchor" which would arrest the regress of thinking about thinking (about thinking . . .), thus unleashing the serial infinity of a "Fichteanism without check" (Novalis cited by Benjamin, *Concept of Criticism*, SW I, 132).

This is not to say that the *desire* for self-identity is simply extinguished for the Romantics. Novalis stresses that the "need" for grounding is

"eternal" – if unsatisfiable – and that the drive to unity is indeed the supreme
ethical imperative of the self-alienated self. The fractured subject is said to
"resist" its own inevitable dispersal by generating the "necessary illusion"
of a self-coincident self.[4] Unity is therefore postulated, but as a fiction which
knows itself as a fiction: such a simultaneous positing and undermining of
belief indeed constitutes the essence of Romantic irony. This postulate, however, only results in a further split, this time between the self-alienated subject
and the subject that "feels" the possibility of reconciliation. "Hovering" or
"suspended" (*schweben*: a ubiquitous term in Jena Romanticism) between
its escapable knowledge of difference and its desire-driven belief in unity or
identity, the Romantic subject curiously satisfies to the letter the Freudian
formula for fetishism: *I know* (about lack and difference), *but nonetheless
I believe* (in my own unmutilated perfection). Such a grammatical disjunction allows the subject to sustain contradictory attitudes through a rigorous
partitioning of experience. To what extent does the Romantic "hovering"
between unity and difference exemplify a perverse splitting of experience and
what might be at stake here? The issue ultimately concerns the two aspects,
perhaps irreconcilable, of the Romantic infinite.

Benjamin himself alludes to the ambiguity of the Romantic gesture, indeed to its "purely logical, unresolvable contradictions" (*Concept of Criticism*, SW I, 192n46). The ambiguity, for Benjamin, concerns the question of final closure: does the hypertrophy of reflection imply an ultimate
skepticism that preempts the possibility of eventual grounding? Conversely:
does every effort to determine the infinite entail a dogmatism that would
furtively reinstate the supremacy of the self-assertive subject? How does
the antinomy between unity and fragmentation express itself? The question will continue to resound through Benjamin's corpus with increasingly
charged implications. The status of the absolute is at stake. Does the unending movement of reflection sever any relation between the contingent, the
profane and the relative on the one hand and the absolute on the other –
a severance which would threaten to congeal the existent as the ultimate
measure of both thought and being? Conversely, does every positing of a
relation presuppose a premature reconciliation between contingency and
the absolute which would, equally, reify contingency by granting it eternal
being?

Despite Benjamin's own praise of Romanticism for bypassing the sterile
opposition between skepticism and dogmatic rationalism, his actual exegesis
of Schlegel and Novalis seems to point simultaneously in two contradictory
directions (which may, in the end, turn out to be merely two sides of the same
coin). His reading emphasizes, on the one hand, an insistent acknowledgment
of irresolvable contingency: fragmentation, negativity, deferral; and, on the

other hand, the desire for closure, totality, fulfillment. Can such a tension sustain itself without collapsing under the weight of its own abstraction?

The stakes are high. The antinomy Benjamin traces in early Romanticism will reverberate throughout his own later writings and indeed stamp this otherwise heterogeneous corpus with its own peculiar consistency of tone. Such a tension has been traditionally articulated in terms of Benjamin's own abiding ambivalence between an idealistically inflected Messianism and the radical materialism that would appear to subvert this: the promise of (total) redemption pitted against the irreparable fragmentation born of historical loss; the redemption of all souls in Paradise pitted against the famous rubble heap of history. In his final essay on history Benjamin will famously argue for the essential intertwining of these two irreconcilable poles: "historical materialism" is to annex the "theology" which will, in turn, manipulate it. How might such a chiasmus of idealism and materialism be traced in the dissertation Benjamin wrote at the very beginning of his career? Two conflicting strands of Benjamin's exposition of the Romantics will be elucidated in the following two sections.

Potentialities

Benjamin comments that whereas Fichte had attempted to "arrest" or "transfix" reflection, the Romantics saw reflection as something that "expands without limit or check," such that "the thinking given form in reflection turns into a formless thinking which directs itself upon the absolute" (*Concept of Criticism*, *SW* I, 129). Since, as Benjamin continues, it is "only with reflection [that] the thinking arise[s] on which reflection takes place" (*Concept of Criticism*, *SW* I, 135), there arises the paradox of a redoubling preceding the unitary original to be reflected – a duplicity which will, by Benjamin's account, demolish the very primacy of the Fichtean subject as epicenter of reflection: "In the thinking of thinking no consciousness of the 'I' is understood" (*Concept of Criticism*, *SW* I, 134). No longer checked or limited, as in Fichte, by the non-I or the object, the self finds itself in a world of reciprocal glances, echoes, and specular reflections. Benjamin cites Novalis: "The eye sees nothing but eyes..." (*Concept of Criticism*, *SW* I, 145). If Benjamin's later theory of aura is already latent here (the utopia of the returned gaze), the spectre of a dizzying hall of mirrors is also lurking, a spectre that evokes the nightmarish dreamworld of nineteenth-century glass architecture (a phantasm also to be richly explored by Benjamin during his Paris sojourn in the 1930s).

Such an intensification of reflection implies a relocation of its theater of operation. For the Romantics, "art" (its essence still to be determined) assumes the reflexive role formerly assigned to the transcendental ego of idealism. The unitary subject having been evacuated, reflection is now best realized by the proliferation of metatextual palimpsests, rewritings, commentary – the "endless succession of mirrors" famously described in the *Athenaeum Fragment* 116 and epitomized for Benjamin by Schlegel's self-described "*Übermeister*" essay (also in the *Athenaeum*) whereby the original work is found to transcend or "heighten" itself in the critical reflection it occasions. Here, Novalis's technical term becomes crucial: the work "potentiates" itself, as in a mathematical squaring or raising to a higher power.

Criticism is in this sense stripped of its juridical, validating role, whether as foundational transcendental discipline (as in the Kantian "tribunal" assessing the lawful claims of reason) or as arbiter of taste and connoisseurship (as in the neoclassical normative aesthetics of Gottsched, Lessing, and Winckelmann). Antonio, a character in Schlegel's "Dialogue on Poetry" sharply clarifies the stakes when he remarks on how the Enlightenment project of evaluative critique had drawn its secret energy from the free-market ideology of commodity exchange: "The principles underlying their criticism . . . were to be found in [Adam] Smith's writings about the wealth of nations. They were happy only when they could put another classical writer into the public treasury."[5] Abandoning its traditional legitimating or legislative role, Romantic criticism instead comes to realize itself as an inexhaustible process of supplementation of the individual work through the repetitive recycling of prior texts. Schlegel explicitly links such "unceasing, repeated reading"[6] to the very possibility of tradition. As Benjamin notes, for Schlegel, the "essence of critique" is to link history and philosophy through the reconstruction, reinterpretation, and retransmission of lost, damaged, incomplete, inaccessible, or otherwise absent (neglected, unread, unreadable) objects.

Criticism in this way is seen to enter into the very production of art itself, which thus takes on an inherently collective and historical dimension. Through criticism, individual artist and individual artwork, as well as the individual genres (epic, lyric, drama, etc.) and forms of art (painting, poetry, music, and so on) are transcended through the anonymous "sociability" of intertextual connection. The specificity both of individual works and of the autonomous artistic mediums is absorbed and effaced within the invisible unity of the "absolute work" (*Concept of Criticism, SW* I, 169) – Schlegel's "single, indivisible, perfected poem" (cited in *SW* I, 167) – whose essential character is to expose the continuous coherence of art. The plural arts are brought back to the transcendental "idea" of Art-in-general, now inflected as a mediating continuum, or, in a term highlighted by Benjamin, quite simply, "medium." Benjamin summarizes: "In this medium all the presentational forms hang constantly together, interpenetrate one another and merge into the unity of the absolute art form, which is identical with the idea of art" (*Concept of Criticism*, SW I, 165).

Indeed, "criticism" becomes constitutive of the work it would seem to feed upon. In this respect, a work of art is recognized as a work of art through its "criticizability," through the posthumous elaboration it both demands and renders possible, leading to a chiasmic blurring of writing and reading, original and translation, production and reproduction. Hence, Schlegel: "Poetry can only be criticized through poetry."[7] Benjamin here contrasts Goethe's efforts to insulate the work from criticism (by way of an archetypal poetics of content grounded in a neoclassical appeal to antiquity posited as "fact") with the Romantic perception that reflection itself essentially creates and supersedes the work to which it clings (*Concept of Criticism*, SW I, 182). Schlegel writes: "For the Moderns, or at least for us Germans, criticism and literature are born at the same time; and the first, in fact, almost a little earlier." Benjamin remarks: "not only is criticism, in Romantic art, possible and necessary, but in the theory of Romantic art one cannot avoid the paradox that criticism is valued more highly than works of art" (*Concept of Criticism*, SW I, 185).

A further paradox lurks within this paradoxical chiasmus: the critical supplement that "completes" and "perfects" the work simultaneously undermines and fragments the latter by exposing (if not indeed producing) the work's irreparable lack or insufficiency – that is, its inherent need for criticism. Totalization and fragmentation thus reveal themselves as two sides of the same coin: the fragment points toward a negative horizon of completion just as the activity of perfection humiliates what it would enhance. (Indeed the ambiguity is crucial in the critical term *Vollendung* or "completion": both teleological perfection and dissolution or termination.) Benjamin quotes Novalis: "Only the incomplete can be understood, can lead us further. What is complete can only be enjoyed. If we want to understand [something], we need to posit it as incomplete" (*Concept of Criticism*, SW I, 154). Thus, no doubt, the "contempt" and "cruelty" which Schlegel, or a character in his *Lucinde*, attributes approvingly to the aesthetic culture of his day – an aggressivity palpable also in the explosive energy which Schlegel senses in Lessing's "shattering" criticisms of those he most reveres, as well as in the savage literalism of his own pronouncements. Schlegel quotes Lessing with approval: "'one does not scold a pitiable poet; one is lenient with a mediocre one; but one is merciless toward a great poet.'"[8]

The Enlightenment split between taste and genius, between the judging faculty and the productive faculty reaches at once its culmination and its overturning. Criticism comes to eclipse the work to which it nonetheless owes its very being: it becomes the shadow of a shadow, nourishing itself on the phantom that it vindicates only by superceding and erasing it. The work becomes work only through the criticism that "unworks" it. The work of art lives on only as a ghostly residue of itself, mortified by the very response to which it owes its continued life. The very condition of the possibility of criticism is thus the condition of its own impossibility, insofar as it necessarily effaces the very object on which it simultaneously depends. This paradox will find logical fruition in Hegel's own well-known pronouncement on the essential pastness of art – its inevitable mortification at the hands of the criticism to which alone it owes its own survival as art: "thought and reflection have spread their wings above fine art."[9] Despite his famous animosity to every form of Romanticism, Hegel's description is utterly Romantic in its radicality: "the statues are now cadavers from which the living soul has flown, just as hymns are words from which the living soul has flown... Our active enjoyment of them is therefore not an act of divine worship through which our consciousness might come to its perfect truth and fulfillment; it is an external activity – the wiping off of some drops of rain or specks of dust... – [an activity] that erects an intricate scaffolding of the dead elements of their outward existence."[10]

Such a mausoleum-like condition marks at once the triumph and the very ruination of tradition. In a letter to Scholem written in June 1917, Benjamin remarks, "Romanticism is the last movement to preserve and transmit [*hinüberretten*] the whole of tradition again" (C, 89; trans. modified). The "saving" [*retten*] which transmits what it redeems simultaneously evacuates or finishes off the latter – "*hinüber*" means both, spatially, transitively, "over against," and, colloquially, "over, finished off, dead, done with" – as if a lethal excess arises in the very moment of the work's transmission (an excess, however, through which the work's indestructibility is signaled in the very moment of its self-erasure). Through criticism, the work "dissolves" within the singular universality of art as such: art-in-general, the "idea of art," art in its character as medium or vehicle of transmission. Indeed transmissibility, pure motility, becomes the defining property of the "perfected" or "potentiated" artwork. Judgment subordinates the content or signified of the work, its truth or meaning, to the work's inexhaustible productivity as a signifier among and of other signifiers. "Nothing is to be done with the object; it is a medium, nothing more" (Novalis). Benjamin explains this in terms of the supremacy of form: he is here elaborating Schlegel's well-known statement in *Athenaeum Fragment* 116, regarding the "hovering" of the work between its mode of presentation and what is thematically presented. In a much later context, Benjamin will come to speak of Kafka's own sacrifice of truth to the hollow form of its sheer transmissibility. The eclipse of meaning by the material form of its presentation – a "Jewish" literalism is implicit here: Schlegel's "apology of the letter"[11] – defines, for Benjamin's Kafka, at once the "sickness" of tradition (the complete evacuation of any determinate content to be handed down) and, paradoxically, the latter's supreme vindication (a transmission that occurs in the absence of anything to transmit and which indeed transmits essentially this very absence). Transformed by criticism into pure medium or "mediality" – a medium that ceases to mediate, ceases to communicate, and ceases ultimately to mean or signify – the work unworks itself. It strips itself of both purpose and referentiality, suspending itself as "a means without end."[12] Reduced to a pure gestic thrust, without object or orientation, language comes to exhibit the "special purposiveness" to which Benjamin refers in "The Task of the Translator," (*SW* I, 255) and to which Kant was perhaps alluding in his well-known doctrine of aesthetic purposiveness without purpose. Benjamin's claim in his earliest meditations on language that "all language communicates itself" ("On Language," *SW* I, 64) thus finds immediate confirmation for him in Jena and, as we shall see, beyond. By suspending intention, expression, reference, as well as the various exteriorities of utility and power, language comes to reveal itself as pure potentiality: communicability in (and indeed of) the utter absence of anything to communicate – at its limit, communicability of the incommunicable.

Such dissolution of the work into the singular plurality of "art" suggests, paradoxically, at once an extreme vindication of art and its eventual overcoming as a privileged autonomous event. At its limit, the thought of medium displaces the very opposition between instrumentality (means toward ends) and aesthetic autonomy (ends without means) it simultaneously invokes. The criticism that "mixes" and dissolves the heterogeneous works, genres, and art forms in the medium of "art as such" inevitably comes to dislodge the ultimate specificity and privilege of art even while it assumes this. Through criticism, "prose" comes to invade the inspired geniality of "poetry" just as the boundaries come to blur between "art" and "life" – between poetry and the social groups which defined the literary culture of Jena – and even eventually, perhaps, between elite or autonomous art and the popular forms of mass entertainment which Romanticism never stopped reviling.

There are profound ambivalences within Romanticism that Benjamin does not quite, and perhaps could not yet, in 1919, make fully explicit. Does the commitment to the mediality of the medium logically commit Romanticism to embrace the "endless chain"[13] of purposes, reasons, and products – what Friedrich Schlegel disparages, elliptically, as the "minus univ[ersality]"of "money, lust and so on"[14] (it is the "and so on" which is of particular interest here) – and thus signal the eventual contamination of the pure medium by that from which it necessarily (as medium) sets itself apart?

In his *Characteristics of the Present Age* (1808), Fichte equates the critical hypertrophy of his day with the mass market of the book trade churning out its "stream" of fashionable, self-obsolescing products whose ultimate source and destination is the abyss of journalism (associated by Fichte with the narcotic, narcoleptic passivity of reading): "This stream of literature is always renewing itself and bursting forward so that every new wave will push aside the one that preceded it; hence the reason why things were printed in the first place is suspended ... everything past will be forgotten ... the person who has no particular desire [to read] or doesn't have a great deal of extra time, no longer needs to read any books whatsoever ... in this system books are printed only so that they can be reviewed, and there would be no need for books if there could be reviews without them."[15] Does the aesthetic ideology of Romanticism come to fulfill itself by effacing the very boundary between the aesthetic and the "anaesthetic" realm of commodity culture, a boundary on which the very possibility of criticism as such depends? Such a result would, paradoxically, perfect criticism by undermining its condition of possibility: perfect criticism would come to absorb even the "nugatory" – abject, uncriticizable non-art – as fodder for the absolute work.[16]

The Romantics themselves come close at times to saying this. In terms suggestive of Benjamin's own eventual recycling of Origen's heretical doctrine of *apokatasis* (the admission of all souls to Paradise on the Day of Judgment), August Schlegel briefly considers the possibility of a higher (divine) criticism which would extend the boundaries of art as such so as to incorporate the very dregs and deformities which seem most revoltingly to oppose it: "However repulsed we are by the barbarism and non-art produced in many epochs, including even perhaps our own, who can tell if the genius will not take these myriad distorted and deviant forms and figures of humanity and mold them into a great work of art."[17] Benjamin praises the "radicalism" of the thought that embraces even the banalities of commerce from which it simultaneously recoils. A string of bare quotations – a habit to be perfected by Benjamin in the *Arcades Project* – makes the point without elaboration. Observe Benjamin piling up the citations from Novalis: "'Truly artistic poetry is remunerable.' 'Art ... is mechanical.' 'The seat of genuine art is solely in the understanding.' 'Nature engenders, the spirit makes. *Il est beaucoup plus commode d'être fait que de se faire lui-[sic!]même*'" (*Concept of Criticism*, *SW* I, 176). Does the "entirely positive" concept of criticism Benjamin finds in Jena Romanticism logically undermine the very aestheticism to which it is simultaneously committed? The implications of the question will become clear when we come, in our final section, to consider the Romantic vestiges informing Benjamin's later reflections on mass culture. Does the infinity of reflection lead simultaneously to an "auratic" privileging of art and to the ultimate undermining of such a privilege at the hands of technological reproduction?

Fulfillments

Despite (or because of) the vertiginous negativity of reflection, the Romantic infinite is to be distinguished – Benjamin insists on this – from the Hegelian "bad infinite" of endless, linear advance. "Obviously" (but maybe not so obvious to a long line of readers of Romanticism, from Hegel through Szondi to de Man and beyond) "reflection, with its thinking of thinking of thinking and so forth, *had to* be for them more than an endless and empty process" (*Concept of Criticism, SW* I, 126; emphasis mine). Benjamin's later polemic against the fantasy of "homogeneous empty time," the (liberal, Social Democrat, fascist, Stalinist, etc.) ideology of infinite progress along an inert temporal continuum he will eventually deride as the consoling "rosary" of historicism (see "On the Concept of History") is no doubt already stirring. "Empty" is here ideologically loaded: it signifies a neutral vacuum susceptible to the arbitrary projections of already existent power. It is worth recalling again that Benjamin's decision to write a dissertation on Romanticism comes sharply upon the heels of an abandoned research project on Kant's "Ideas for a Universal History" and follows an intense disillusionment with the conciliatory optimism of the German youth movement with which he had initially cast his lot. A misguided confidence in the inevitability of progress – the Kantian "infinite task" – had culminated in a catastrophic embrace of the German war effort.

Benjamin is emphatic that the Romantic renunciation of Fichte's intellectual intuition in no way commits Romanticism to a sterile ontology of deferral – "a progress into the void, a vague advance in writing ever-better poetry" (*Concept of Criticism, SW* I, 168) – an abstraction which would threaten both to reify the absolute (as absent telos or destination) and to congeal the given (as unsurpassable horizon of existence). Rather than, like Fichte, limiting reflection in order to retrieve a point of unmediated fulfillment, Benjamin's Romantics claim to find "fullness" in the very infinity of reflection. This fullness assumes, and Benjamin underlines this, explicitly Messianic dimensions. The reflection that threatened Fichte with the specter of infinite regress becomes here the mark of an essential progress, or, rather, to cite Benjamin's jarring neologism, as "progredibility" [*Progredibilität*] (*Concept of Criticism, SW* I, 168). With this strange word, "progress" is emphatically distinguished from the Enlightenment kind, which Benjamin disparages as nothing more than a "merely relative connection of cultural stages to one another" and as a "mere becoming." For Benjamin, what is "progressive" about the "progressive universal poetry" advertised in the *Athenaeum* (*Fragment* 116) – and we have intimations here of what Benjamin will later vindicate as the "genuine concept of progressive universal history" – is the work's immanent connection to the absolute, revealed (alone) by criticism. Benjamin thus implicitly links the mirror-play of Romanticism to a Leibnizian monadology whereby each reflection contains within itself the infinity of all other reflections (including its own reflection on this). This connection to Leibniz becomes evident in "On the Concept of History," where the Messianic moment, contracting itself into the potential and the burden of all history, is explicitly characterized as a monad. Benjamin writes: "This interconnection can be grasped in a mediated way from the infinitely many stages of reflection, as by degrees all the remaining reflections are run through in all directions" (*Concept of Criticism*, *SW* I, 126). This is the philosophical underpinning of the Messianism Benjamin gingerly locates in Jena Romanticism and which he will eventually appropriate as his own in his later reflections on history. This Messianism is sharply distinguished by Benjamin from the political theology of later Romanticism[18] and even, for that matter, from certain religious gestures of early Romanticism itself.[19] What is "Messianic" here pertains to the inherent possibility of redemption in and of the present: the absolute nestles in the cracks and deformities of finite existence.

Questions inevitably arise with this introduction of Messianic fulfillment – arguably the most difficult topic in Romanticism (as well as in Benjamin), and all the more difficult in Benjamin's own revision of Romanticism since the very notion tends to be tucked away in footnotes, concealed as the "esoteric" content of the dissertation, just as, at the end of Benjamin's life, theology as such is presented as the secret, dwarflike presupposition of authentic historical consciousness. Does dogmatism return in the critical effort to transcend it? Does the "mystical thesis" of the Idea threaten to fold back the Romantic project within the idealist trajectory from which it had initially appeared to spring free? Does the absolute work (despite or because of its own self-unworking) perform the stabilizing role of the erstwhile subject? Such a result would, ironically, join Benjamin's version of romanticism with the Hegelian philosophy that had notoriously reviled it. In this sense the "mingling" of genres announced under Schlegel's banner of *menstruum universalis* would find a curious parallel in Hegel's own notorious commitment, in the *Aesthetics*, to the ultimate interconvertibility of all the arts – a model of translatability premised, in this latter case, on the priority of signified to the signifier and thus implying a radical dematerialization of the work. Infamously, poetry in this context enters as the "total art" which alchemically metabolizes the other arts into its own medium; more precisely, the medium has in fact become irrelevant. Reduced to a sonorous orifice "entirely saturated" with spiritual content, the poetic medium is seen by Hegel to degrade to a "mere external designation" or "means of communication" which can thus "dissolve" or "evaporate" without residue in thought.[20] Does the Romantic commitment to art-as-medium in the end relapse into a kind of covert Hegelianism that effaces the very "mediality" of the medium in the face of thought? Does the very intensification of the medium thus amount to the latter's ultimate erasure?

Is there, in another register, a secret return to Fichteanism in the Romantic urge to "fulfillment" – a disavowal of the abyssal void opened up by the very process of reflection? Is there a voluntarism in the Romantics' determination to "force their way to the absolute" (*Concept of Criticism*, *SW* I, 130)? Despite Benjamin's attempt to shield Romanticism from Hegel's notorious objections – the much-vaunted "arbitrary will" of the creator is, he insists, a "paltry metaphor" for a will which is only indirectly (and problematically) subjective (*Concept of Criticism*, *SW* I, 162) – the language of force is conspicuous wherever Benjamin attempts to characterize the Romantic absolute. Does the "potentiation" of criticism revert to a form of power? Benjamin quotes Schlegel: "To transpose oneself at will now into this sphere, now into that sphere . . . is possible only for a mind that . . . contains within itself an entire system of persons" (*Concept of Criticism*, *SW* I, 183). Does the will relinquish or recover its authority by becoming properly "systematic"? If one is "free," as Benjamin puts it, to "ascribe to the indifference-point of reflection whatever metaphysical properties one likes" (*Concept of Criticism*, *SW* I, 134), does a certain decisionism creep in which would in the end buttress the regime of the existent? Does the criticism that fulfills by annihilating the work equally render it untouchable?

Schlegel's well-known "porcupine" metaphor is revealing: "A fragment, like a miniature work of art, has to be entirely isolated from the surrounding world and be complete in itself like a porcupine" (*Athenaeum Fragment* 206). Setting aside the vexing hermeneutic question of how to even begin to read this fragment (should it be isolated from its surroundings? from the adjacent fragments which might and in many cases do contradict it?), the formulation suggests a possible self-suturing of the fragment into a new totality, all the more inviolable in its prickly self-enclosure. What is disturbing here is perhaps not so much the contradiction between the radical fragmentation unleashed by reflection and the unity that appears to contain it (the unifying flash of wit, the organic unity of the Book, and so on). It is rather the logical permeability between fragmentation and unity as such that is disconcerting. Does Romanticism collapse the distinction between fragment and totality by reifying fragmentation within the monadic sufficiency of the moment? Schlegel's formulation in *Fragment* 53 of the *Athenaeum* is provocative in its ambiguity: "It is equally fatal for the mind to have a system and to have none. It will simply have to decide to combine the two." Does the "combination" or "binding" of system and fragment function (systematically) as a harmonizing unification of the terms, or (fragmentarily) as a disparate aggregate?

If the work must assume its own "criticizability" (*Concept of Criticism*, *SW* I, 159), does it preemptively disarm the mortifying criticism it simultaneously solicits? Fragmentation as such can function defensively or fetishistically as its own denial. Critique and the absence of critique would in this instance strictly coincide; more precisely, criticism would neutralize itself precisely through its own activation. Schlegel remarks on the ambiguity of Goethe's *Wilhelm Meister* in this respect: "Perhaps one should... at once judge it and not judge it which appears to be no easy task. Luckily, it is one of those books which judge themselves, and thus spare the critic all work."[21] Is there, then, a secret positivism in the theory of criticism by which the work and by extension everything finite is stabilized precisely by virtue of its own critical self-unworking? The question will eventually have direct political implications. Does the immediacy of fulfillment imply a consecration of the existent that arrests the critical trajectory it nonetheless presupposes?

Critical after-lives

The various aporias lurking in Benjamin's explication of Romanticism will find unexpected echoes throughout Benjamin's subsequent writings, leading one to wonder whether there is not indeed a lifelong identification with the Jena circle. A letter written during the period of the dissertation stresses the intense contemporaneity of the Romantic venture – "a new concept of art that is in many ways our concept of art" – and remarks that the dissertation itself could be written "only in these times" (*C*, 136).

The most immediate after-effect emerges in Benjamin's subsequent concept of translation (elaborated shortly after the dissertation): the redemption, completion, and indeed reconstitution of the original through its supplementary afterlife in another language. In the "Task," the lapsarian multiplicity of languages is to be overcome, if only "embryonically" (*SW* I, 255), through the translation which exposes translatability as such to be the essential property of language, just as, in the dissertation, it is the exposure of the work's criticizability that unifies the disparate works and media within the singular plurality of the "absolute work." Traces of the dissertation also survive in the concept of quotation theorized later still (for example, in the essay on Karl Kraus) and put into audacious practice in the *Arcades Project* (Benjamin's unfinished, *Bouvard et Pécuchet*-style monster-compendium of bibliomanic scavengings). In each case, what is sought is a redemptive refunctioning of the original through its literalizing, parasitical repetition. An entire mimetic apparatus is at work. Through the repetitions and relays of its production language reveals itself to be a "complete archive of nonsensuous similarities" ("On the Mimetic Faculty," *SW* III, 722) – a collection of resemblances without an original – and eventually consummates itself in the mechanical exercise of habit.

It is tempting as well, though interestingly problematic, to find further residues in the later logic of reproduction, or rather, reproducibility, elaborated in the famous "artwork" essay of 1936, in which Benjamin notes the ontological displacement of the unique or original exemplar under the impact of mass technology. Schlegel's call for an activity which "merely supplements, joins, fosters"[22] here finds perhaps its most extreme, if most startling, vindication. The Romantic "medium" indeed seems to find a direct analogue in the modern media. In film, perhaps above all, the critical agenda of Romanticism is obscurely realized through the inherent tendency of this medium to negate both the isolated specificity of the traditional artforms (music, painting, poetry, drama, etc.) and – by virtue of its collective mode of production and reception and by virtue of its complex relation both to technology and to the market – the isolated autonomy of art as such. By presenting the intrinsic interpenetration of the various mediums, film, for Benjamin, reveals art as such to be a differentiated collectivity that is both an allegory and an instance of a redeemed social world. Film is the ghostly medium which promises and threatens to accomplish – threatens to unravel precisely by accomplishing – what for Romanticism remained an unthinkable and impossible ideal.

And one might speculate, finally, about the subterranean passage linking the reflexive circularity of Romantic critique with Benjamin's own eventual formulations regarding the retroactive temporality of historical (not historicist) existence. "Historical materialism" is (famously, in "On the Concept of History") to rewrite by citing the past as a reservoir of unredeemed experience rendered legible only through the "posthumous shock" inflicted in the present. To enter history is to register as a crisis for the present the shock of betrayed possibilities – thwarted futures – in the past.

Such a circularity defines the peculiar force of Benjamin's messianism: the redemption of the irredeemable through the impossible reawakening of vanished possibilities within the irreversible "one-way street" of time. Here, Benjamin's earliest and latest writings draw together unexpectedly. The "secret core" of Romanticism alluded to in the cryptic margins of the dissertation (in footnotes, letters, and in an "esoteric" appendix withheld from academic scrutiny) – its Messianic philosophy of history, associated by Schlegel with the French Revolution – perhaps indeed finds its own posthumous redemption in Benjamin's own eventual reflections on the revolutionary possibilities of the past.

Repetition in this sense becomes, by the end of Benjamin's life, the historical literalization of Romantic "potentiation": the revelation of possibility through the recognition of the very impossibility of past fulfillment. The logarithmic "squaring" of the work through criticism at Jena becomes, by the end of Benjamin's life, the excavation of betrayed possibilities precisely as possibilities: unrealized, counterfactual potentiality, the belated encounter which charges the present with its most cataclysmic urgency and despair. In the moment of revolution the past becomes "citable in all its moments" ("On the Concept of History," *SW* IV, 390). Note: "citable" rather than simply "cited." Potentiality vindicates itself in the very moment of Messianic fulfillment. And at this point one can begin to sense the accumulative force of the semantic chain of modal signifiers snaking its way through Benjamin's entire œuvre: criticizability, translatability, reproducibility, citability. The repetitive stammer speaks of the insistent pressure of the possible from which criticism draws both its energy and its most intractable burden.

NOTES

1. Fichte, *The Science of Knowledge*, trans. Peter Heath and John Lachs (Cambridge University Press, 1982), 100.
2. Novalis, "Fichte Studies" (1795–96), §1, in Jochen Schulte-Sasse et al., ed. and trans., *Theory as Practice: A Critical Anthology of Early German Romantic Writings* (Minneapolis and London: University of Minnesota Press, 1997), 90.
3. Johann Gottlieb Fichte, *Wissenschaftslehre nova methodo* (Hamburg: Felix Meiner, 1982), 185.
4. Novalis, "Fichte Studies," §566, §37, in *Theory as Practice*, pp. 109, 102.
5. Friedrich Schlegel, "Dialogue on Poetry," quoted by Jochen Schulte-Sasse, "The Concept of Literary Criticism in German Romanticism, 1795–1810," in *A History of German Literary Criticism, 1730–1980*, ed. Peter Uwe Hohendahl (Lincoln and London: University of Nebraska Press, 1988), 153.
6. Friedrich Schlegel, "Concerning the Essence of Critique" (1804), in *Theory as Practice*, 269.
7. Schlegel, "Critical Fragments," section 117, in *Theory as Practice*, 319.
8. Schlegel, "Über Lessing [On Lessing]," *Kritische Ausgabe*, ed. Ernest Behler et al. (Munich, 1958–) II, 100–25, at pp. 105 and 109.
9. Hegel, *Aesthetics: Lectures on Fine Art*, trans. T. M. Knox (Oxford University Press, 1975), 10.
10. Hegel, *Phenomenology of Spirit*, trans. A. V. Miller (Oxford University Press, 1977), 455f.
11. Schlegel, "Philosophical Fragments," §15, in *Theory as Practice*, 337.
12. This formulation owes much to Giorgio Agamben, *Means without End: Notes on Politics*, trans. Vincenzio Binetti and Cesare Casarino (Minneapolis: University of Minnesota Press, 2000).

13. August Wilhelm Schlegel, *Lectures on Fine Art and Literature*, quoted by Schulte-Sasse, "Concept of Literary Criticism," 137.

14. Schlegel, *Kritische Ausgabe*, XVIII, 307.

15. Fichte, quoted in Schulte-Sasse, "Concept of Literary Criticism," 121.

16. Hegel was perhaps the first to recognize this paradox, in the *Aesthetics*, when he lambasts Romantic irony – "the most inartistic of all principles" – for its simultaneous aestheticism and anaestheticism: on the one hand, the "divine creative genius" dissolves everything into the infinite play of art, on the other hand, art as such is humiliated to the status of pure semblance, nullity, and, indeed, the prosaic ugliness of everyday life. See *Aesthetics*, 64–69.

17. August Wilhelm Schlegel, *Lectures on Fine Art and Literature*, quoted by Schulte-Sasse, "Concept of Literary Criticism," 138.

18. Benjamin alludes to the "weakness and sedateness" of the later Romantic school – due to its curtailment of the "creative omnipotence of reflection" (*Concept of Criticism, SW* I, 150) – and sees here a retreat to an essentially Fichtean position (as evidenced in the so-called Windischmann lectures of 1804–06) (*Concept of Criticism, SW* I, 134). As is well known, Schlegel, following his conversion to Catholicism in 1808, began promoting various myths of utopian national harmony exemplified by a restorative notion of the *Volk*, and, eventually, by 1815, came to embrace Metternichian-style politics. (Nietzsche's caustic remark in the *Birth of Tragedy* on the way "all Romantics end up, namely as Christians," is well known.) Jochen Schulte-Sasse (op. cit.) argues that such a retreat was already implicit in the Jena period. See also note 19 below.

19. See, for example, *Concept of Criticism, SW* I, 156. For a rigorous reading of Romantic "religion," see Philippe Lacoue-Labarthe and Jean-Luc Nancy, *The Literary Absolute: The Theory of Literature in German Romanticism* (Albany: State University of New York Press, 1988), 59–78; and for a detailed interpretation of Benjamin's own response to Romantic Messianism, see David Ferris, "'Truth is the Death of Intention': Walter Benjamin's Esoteric History of Romanticism," in *Studies in Romanticism* 31 (1992), 455–80.

20. Hegel, *Aesthetics*, pp. 627, 964, 968.

21. Friedrich Schlegel, "Über Goethes Meister," *Kritische Ausgabe*, (Munich: Paderborn, 1967), II, 133f.

22. Schlegel, Ideas § 53, in *Philosophical Fragments*, trans. Peter Firchow (Minneapolis: University of Minnesota Press, 1991), 99.

8

RAINER NÄGELE

Body politics: Benjamin's dialectical materialism between Brecht and the Frankfurt School

The extremes as points of orientation define the *via regia* of philosophical investigation for Benjamin. The first sentence that opens the main body of Benjamin's *The Origin of the German Tragic Drama*, after the epistemological preface, categorically states the direction as "the necessary direction toward the extreme" (*Origin*, 57).[1] The extreme as point of direction and orientation, even as the "norm of conceptualization" (*Origin*, 57), is set off from a logic that defines the norm by the normal, the average, and the middle. It is in this direction toward the extreme that Benjamin finds his own intellectual procedure intersecting with that of Carl Schmitt, whose essay on the concept of sovereignty appealed to Benjamin above all because of this methodological intersection with his own mode of thought. When Benjamin, in his book on German tragic drama, explicitly quotes the one-sentence paragraph with which Carl Schmitt opens his book: "Sovereign is he who decides over the state of emergency,"[2] his own epistemological preface has already articulated the logic of the extreme that underlies Schmitt's procedure. For Schmitt, the concept of the "sovereign" is a liminal concept (*Grenzbegriff*). "A liminal concept," he writes, "is not a confused concept as it is in the popular literature, but a concept of the extreme sphere. Accordingly its definition cannot be tied to the normal case, but to the liminal case."[3] At this point the intellectual worlds of Benjamin and Schmitt come to their closest encounter; from here they will move away from each other in opposite directions. Schmitt will become and remain a fundamentalist, Benjamin will remain a marginalist, being faithful only to the liminal border lines.[4]

There is another, baroque, figure in Benjamin's logic of the extreme: the Leibnizian monad. The logic of the extreme corresponds to a monadological logic where the singular contains the universal. This is in contrast to a subsumptive and representational logic where the particular is contained in the general and represents the general. Excentricity is its mark not only in thought but also in life, or, more precisely, it is the figure of the inseparable intertwining (*Verschränkung*) of life and thought.

Excentricity is not without a relation to the circle. It is in and through the circle that excentricity is experienced, first perhaps in the figure of the engimatic Luise von Landau with whom Benjamin "sat in the circle until she died" (*Berlin Childhood, SW* III, 352). Luise von Landau was an aristocratic girl, excentric in the circle of bourgeois girls and boys gathered "in Fräulein Pufahl's circle" (*Berlin Childhood, SW* III, 359), and excentric as the one who was torn away, at an early age, into what Hölderlin called the "excentric sphere of the dead." Her name exerts a magic spell on Benjamin, not so much because of the aristocratic *von*, but because he had heard "the accent of death fall upon it." The "accent of death" interrupts the rhythmic flow of life as a caesura that fixes the name separated from the no longer living person as the inscription of a cenotaph, an empty tomb. Excentricity as the figure of the inseparable intertwining of thought and life also figures their inevitable rupture and difference as they enter the cenotaph of writing.

The empty tomb remains explicitly one of the two unsolved riddles of Benjamin's *Berlin Childhood*. As the cloudy kernel of Benjamin's life and thought, it is the crypt that excentrically marks a repetitive pattern of circles of friendships and of political constellations. Benjamin's two closest friends in later life, Gershom Scholem and Theodor W. Adorno, could already be considered at almost opposite poles in terms of thought and personality; but they shared an intense dislike, even hatred, of another friend of Benjamin in the thirties, Bertolt Brecht. Brecht was clearly the excentric figure in the circle at this point. While on a personal level Brecht was never as close to Benjamin as Scholem was (and to a lesser degree Adorno), Brecht intersected with Benjamin's life and thought all the more intimately on a level that can be reduced neither to the "personal" nor to the merely "ideological": their relation is profoundly marked by the cryptic crypt and touches the center of Benjamin's excentric thoughts and life constellations. He must thus figure as excentrically central in any account of Benjamin's political, ideological, institutional, and personal relations.

March 1933 was the beginning of Benjamin's exile without return. But, as so often in Benjamin's thought and life, the caesura was not only a rupture but also a kind of seal and signature to preceding developments that now emerged in clearer shape and form. The simultaneity of rupture and continuity is the characteristic figure that determines the relationship of Benjamin's life and thought as a ruptured continuity of repetitions of elements and ever changing arrangements of these elements. In terms of his material existence and production, Benjamin's already precarious situation since the late twenties became and remained relentlessly desperate. The absence of stable habitat was accompanied by the increasing difficulty of finding possibilities for the publication of his critical essays and book reviews which, for the most part, had become his only income by the early thirties.

It was in this situation that already existing friendships and ties, among them above all with Scholem, Gretel Karplus, Adorno, and Brecht, entered into a new constellation; and it was the desperate economic situation that defined Benjamin's precarious relationship with the Institute for Social Research that later became known as the "Frankfurt School." It was also this situation that redefined Benjamin's position in regard to Marxist thought and politics.

Benjamin's first encounters with Marxist thought accompany the writing of *The Origin of the German Tragic Drama* in 1924, a year after the beginning of his acquaintance with Theodor W. Adorno. It was not Adorno, however, who initiated Benjamin's interest in Marxism, but rather a typically Benjaminian intertwining of thought and life. In 1923, Georg Lukács published his highly influential book *History and Class Consciousness*. Benjamin discovered it through a review by Ernst Bloch in 1924, and immediately considered it a "very important book, especially important to me," as he reports in a letter to Scholem on 13 June 1924 (*C*, 244). Scholem was alarmed, fearing both for the book on the tragic drama and for his friend's political development in which he saw a parallel to his own brother's political engagment with the Communist party. Benjamin responds in a long letter on September 16 1924 (*C*, 246–51). He does not deny a certain danger for his book project, but he insists that he will persist, noting that, despite the difficulties, he was able to write the epistemological preface, and the first and second chapters. The problems posed by the book on tragic drama compete with the problems posed by contemporary communism; one might even say that they irrupt into the philosophical, theological, and aesthetic set of problems pursued by the book.

At this point, however, Benjamin wants to defer a discussion about communism with Scholem. Things are not quite ready yet: "the objective side (*das Sachliche*) cannot yet be clearly articulated and the personal aspect (*das Persönlich-Motivische*) is not yet ripe to be transmitted." The curious juxtaposition of the *Sachliche* and the *Persönlich-Motivische* points at another encounter, on the personal level, Benjamin's encounter with the Latvian bolshevist Asja Lacis, whom he met in Capri and with whom he fell in love. Asja Lacis, who had studied theater and film in Moscow and lived with the theater director and critic Bernhard Reich, had come to Munich in 1923 where she worked as assistant director with Brecht on the staging of "Life of Edward II." In 1924, she traveled with Reich and her daughter to Capri. There she met Benjamin, according to her own report in a store where she wanted to buy almonds. *I did not know the Italian word for almonds, and the salesperson did not understand what I wanted. Next to me stood a man and said: "Madam, may I help you?" "Please," I said. I got my almonds and went with my package out onto the piazza. The gentleman followed me and asked: "May I accompany you and carry your package?" I looked at him – and he continued: "Allow me to introduce myself – Doctor Walter Benjamin."*[5] On the following day, Benjamin showed up at Asja's apartment: *A vivacious conversation developed. I told him about my children's theater in Orel, of my work in Riga and Moscow. Immediately he was enthusiastic* [entflammt – literally, "inflamed"] *for a proletarian children's theater and for Moscow.*

A dense web of threads emerges in Asja Lacis's laconic account. When Benjamin hints at the personal component in his fast-developing intense interest in Marxism with the double expression of the *Persönlich-Motivische*, his phrasing not only points at his erotic infatuation as a personal motivational force that coincides with the impact of Lukács's book, but it also addresses a central motif that, according to Asja Lacis's account, emerged in the first conversation and incited Benjamin's enthusiasm: the motif of the children's theater. Benjamin's interest in the world of children – he was an avid collector of toys and children's books – permeates his engagement with Marxism and historical materialism no less than his increasing interest in Freud.[6] This particular interest becomes a determining factor in a constellation that defines both a specific relation and decisive distance to the Frankfurt School with its various forms of Freudo-Marxism. It also enters into a particular relation to one of the central motifs of Lukács's book: reification (*Verdinglichung*), a term that under the gaze of the child assumes qualities that Lukács could not have imagined.

There is yet another component in the *Persönlich-Motivische* of the children's theater that introduces a motif touching the core of Benjamin's thinking: the theater and the theatrical as constitutive and formative elements in his theory. The motif of the theater is also the strongest link between the work on the German baroque tragic drama and the later political, social, cultural, and philosophical investigations leading to the work on the Parisian *Arcades Project*. It is symptomatic that two of the most prominent theories of modernity in German, Nietzsche's *Birth of Tragedy* and Benjamin's *The Origin of the German Tragic Drama*, are centered in questions of the theater. While Nietzsche's book emerged in the early decades of the twentieth century as an influential force in the formation of European modernism, Benjamin's book on a rather obscure literary production of the German baroque seems at first glance far removed from modernist concerns. Only in recent decades has its significance as a theory of modernity come into full view. Its early impact was more discreet, but nevertheless decisive. If for a long time Adorno seemed to be the more obvious theoretician of modernism, his theoretical foundation is to be found in Benjamin's book. Already in the summer of 1932, Adorno used Benjamin's book as the basis of his seminar.[7]

But, while Adorno happily adopted such central terms as "constellation," the crucial function of the "caesura," of the extreme, and the theological – the theological as extreme – the function Benjamin gives to the theatrical and the gestural marks a significant difference between them. Theater and gesture provide the space and structure that allow for the specific intersection of the extremes in Benjamin's late philosophy of language, the theological vocabulary and his historical materialism; above all, they provide the space and structure for the dialectical images.

When we describe the encounter of the extremes in the theatrical space of Benjamin's theory – or more precisely, in the space that opens up between theory and praxis – as an intersection, the term is meant as a provisional counter-term to Adorno's favorite critical term: *Vermittlung* (mediation). This term had been canonized, of course, by Hegel as the center of his dialectic. When Benjamin works his way from a radical dualism, doubly affirmed by his immersion in Kantian philosophy and by what he considers the center of his Jewish experience (*Erfahrung*, in contrast to *Erlebnis* [see *GBr*, I, 75]), toward his *Dialektik im Stillstand* (dialectic at a standstill) and the dialectical image, it is more through Hölderlin's concept of the caesura than through Hegel's dialectic.

The move from pure theory to (political) praxis leads into a sphere of identity and difference between the political and the theological that, for Benjamin, can no longer be negotiated in terms of mediation. On 29 May 1926, Benjamin again is compelled to defend his increasing engagement with Marxist theory and politics to his concerned friend Scholem (C, 300f.). It is now a methodological problem for Benjamin, because he is supposed to defend theoretically a situation that demands a redefinition of the relationship between theory and praxis, and thus cannot, by definition, be purely theoretical. Benjamin understands his present situation as an "attempt to leave the purely theoretical sphere." In human terms, Benjamin writes, this is possible only "either in religious or political observance." But the "either... or" is essentially identical: "I do not concede a difference between the two in essence." No more does he concede "a mediation."[8] Benjamin tries to think of an identity of extremes that is produced not in mediation but in a paradoxical inversion and transformation of the one into the other (*Umschlag*). With the term *Umschlag*, Benjamin picks up another central term of Hegelian dialectics, but the inversion Benjamin understands in this word is not, as it is for Hegel, the result of mediation, but a paradoxical event. This un-mediated dialectical *Umschlag* is characterized already in the book on the German tragic drama as an allegorical dialectic in specific contrast to a bourgeois–humanistic dialectic where the ethical subject collapses into the individual. Against this humanistic short-circuit of ethical subject and individual, Benjamin posits the dialectic of "baroque apotheosis. It happens as an inversion of the extremes into each other" (*Origin*, 160). It is a figure that invokes another meaning of the German word *Umschlag*: as envelope, a mere external container. But, as in one of Benjamin's favorite images of the infolded stockings, where "pocket" and "content" can be flattened out with one grip into a third entity, the *Umschlag* as envelope, suggesting container and content, is the sudden inversion and unfolding in which container and contained are transformed into a third form: a readable surface. This indicates not only the categorical difference between Hegelian and Benjaminian dialects, but also Benjamin's crucial and never resolved difference to Adorno.

The consequence of this difference is a radical subversion of any totalizing consistent theory: being radical means to be radically attentive to every moment of the situation without any regard for theoretical consistency. The categorical imperative is: "To procede radically, never consistently in the most important things would also be my attitude if some day I should join the communist party (which again I would make dependant on the ultimate impulse of chance)" (C, 300). Benjamin's formulation of the relationship of theory and praxis in this letter is the most precise political analogon to the analytical praxis as it emerges in Freud's theoretical writings and in his analytical praxis.

The formulations in the letter of 1926 prepare the ground for the encounter with Brecht in 1929. Brecht's gestural epic theater and the discovery of Franz Kafka's gestural world (still the most incisive insight in Kafka's writing) constitute the major scene of Benjamin's theory and praxis of the thirties, that produces the concepts of "body space" (*Leibraum*) and "image space" (*Bildraum*) of the Surrealism-essay as well as the physiognomic–graphematic space of the work on the Parisian *Arcades Project*.

This physiognomic–graphematic space as a surreal political body space and image space emerges in unexpected places, for example, in a description of Benjamin's own living space, the last one designed in its arrangement by Benjamin himself – although the agency of this arrangement by "himself" is oddly displaced. On 28 October 1931, Benjamin describes to Scholem the arrangement of pictures in his new apartment: "Speaking of physiognomy, I wonder what an expert would make of the picture arrangement of my apartment. Although not everything has been put up yet, I realize with some shock that there are – with the exception of a little birthday portrait of

Stefan [Benjamin's son] – only pictures of saints in my communist cell" (*C*, 386). What Benjamin sees as his own arrangement, he must now account for with some shock when he reads it as the condensation of a communist cell and a monk's cell, as a kind of theo-political space, dominated by a trick image of a Jesus head that presents at the same time, depending on one's perspective, three different representations of saints. One might read the tricky physiognomy of this head of Jesus as an allegory of that *Umschlag* without mediation that defines Benjamin's monadological dialectic where the extremes of the theological and the political are extremely opposed and paradoxically identical.

The three-headed Jesus in one head also figures Benjamin's own double-faced head. In a letter to Scholem, dated 14 February 1929, Benjamin writes: "Of my writings one might, for the sake of bibliography, mention the fact that in the *Neue Schweizer Rundschau* a 'Weimar' has appeared that presents in the most lovely way the side of my Janus head that is turned away from the Soviet state" (*C*, 347). "Weimar" is a short text in three parts, written after his visit to the town of Weimar and the Goethe museum there in June 1928 (*SW* II, 148–50). The visit was supposed to give him some impulses for the Goethe article for the Soviet encyclopedia. It turned out, in Benjamin's eyes, as the other face of that article. The difference between the encyclopedia article and the Weimar essay in style, tone, and procedure demonstrates the stylistic and methodological range of Benjamin's writing of his later period. While the encyclopedia article, manifestly at least, seems to pursue a strictly sociological–materialist course, the three short meditations on Weimar belong to a genre that, in a certain sense, was a Benjaminian invention: *Denkbild*, a "thinking image" or "imaged thinking." But the term has also a venerable tradition. It is, since Herder in the eighteenth century, the German translation of "emblem," that specific Renaissance and baroque combination of image and text: an allegorical picture with a title-motif (the *inscriptio*) above it and an exegetical text underneath it (the *subscriptio*).

The "Weimar" *Denkbild* as the other face of the seemingly straightforward and, in the eyes of Scholem and others, reductive encyclopedia article is not simply its opposite or a denunciation of it. It would be a mistake to consider the encyclopedia article as a pure opportunistic disguise. For Benjamin, it was an exercise in one extreme form of materialist analysis, for which, then, the "Weimar" *Denkbild* delineates the other face as the other, no less materialist, extreme. One might call this mode a spatial physiognomy, a reading of spatial arrangements as Benjamin suggests it as a revealing possibility for an understanding of himself and of his own room. It is, to a certain degree, a foreplay to his work on the Parisian *Arcades Project*.

The first of the three short texts paradigmatically sets up a theater. The typically broad window sills in small German towns, particularly broad in the famous Weimar hotel, *Zum Elefanten*, become for Benjamin balconies in a theater presented by the marketplace of Weimar below the window. The morning market turns into an orgiastic musical ballet. But what seems like an allegorical mystification of the market events serves at the end as its revelation: "Now it [the market/theater] lay buried under paper and refuse. Instead of dance and music only exchange and business" (*SW* II, 148). The translation of the market economy and its events into the artistic forms that have their origins at feudal aristocratic courts reveals the irretrievable past-ness of these forms: "Nothing can be so irretrievably gone like a morning." Benjamin now reads the abyss of allegory, i.e., the abyss between literal and figurative meaning, as the abyss opened up by the commodity and its phantasmagoric scenarios.

Benjamin sees the spatial arrangements and decor of the Goethe–Schiller archives, where everything is white, as hospital rooms for the manuscripts. The range of expression of hospitalized bodies is reduced to an intensified mimic that becomes all the more expressive and readable. It is this setting that makes the manuscripts readable physiognomically not only in terms of what is written on them, but as physical entities in a specific spatial setting. And, finally, it is the arrangement of Goethe's study and adjacent bedroom that opens up a specific relation between writing and death ("And when he slept, his work was waiting in the next door, in order to pray for his liberation from the dead" [*SW* II, 150]). At the same time it allows for a reading of the historical difference between Goethe and the twentieth-century visitor as an inversion of the relationship between world and interiority in writing: "He who has the opportunity, through a happy chance, to gather himself in this room, experiences in the arrangement of the four rooms in which Goethe slept, read, dictated, and wrote the forces that called forth a world as re-sponse when he touched his innermost self. We, however, must make a world resound in order to bring forth a weak tone in our interior" (*SW* II, 150).

Benjamin's shocked accounting of the arrangement of pictures in his apart-ment can also serve as a model for a new arrangement in the relationship of theory and praxis. In the previously quoted letter to Scholem of 29 May 1926, Benjamin states the difficulty of giving a theoretical account of a situ-ation that is marked by a necessity to leave the purely theoretical sphere. In the following years, this problematization of the theoretical sphere is inten-sified to the point of a seemingly total renunciation of theory. Thus he writes to Martin Buber on 23 February 1927: "One thing I can affirm to you most decisively – the negative: all theory will be excluded from my presentation" (*C*, 313).

Yet, Benjamin's move is determined neither here nor earlier by a simple and naive faith in a pure praxis outside of theory and reflexion. What emerges in the late twenties and in the writing of the thirties is a rethinking of the relation of theory and praxis that also defines Benjamin's ultimate distance to the "Frankfurt School," to Horkheimer from the beginning on, and more and more to Adorno, who in some ways represented those aspects of the Frankfurt School with which Benjamin had the closest affinities.[9]

Already the letter to Martin Buber delineates the difference to any naive faith in pure praxis. After asserting that all theory would stay at a far distance from his presentation, Benjamin continues: "By doing so [i.e. keeping theory at a far distance], I hope to succeed in letting speak the creaturely dimension: as far as I have succeeded in grasping and holding on to this new, alien language that resounds loudly through the resonating mask [*Schallmaske*] of a completely changed environment" (C, 313; trans. modified). This is how Benjamin proposes to report about his trip to Moscow and his impressions of the new Soviet state in Buber's journal *Die Kreatur*. The title word of the journal, or rather a slight variant of it, *das Kreatürliche*, becomes in Benjamin's letter the speaking historical subject whose voice should not be obliterated by any theory. At the same time, however, by designating *das Kreatürliche* as the speaking historical subject, Benjamin introduces a discourse that is, in a curious way, both alien and familiar. It stands in an odd, if not opposing, relationship to the official Marxist discourse in the common self-representation of the Soviet state. While the philosophy of Marx articulates the human condition in a complex dialectic, where the human subject is both the product of its world and the producer of that world, the dominant communist rhetoric in the Soviet Union and elsewhere tended to pick up and intensify the nineteenth-century rhetoric of linear progress, technocratic delirium, and a fantasy of unlimited productivity. One of the most consistently recurring motifs in Benjamin's later writings is the attempt to separate Marxism and historical materialism from this ideology.

Human existence as *Kreatur* and *kreatürlich* emphasizes the human condition in its physical subjection to death and decay, the human subject as created rather than creator. This is in contrast to both a dominant bourgeois rhetoric of individual creativity and to the communist rhetoric of a promethean collective creativity. These terms belong to a theological vocabulary, in which the human condition is entangled in a nature overshadowed by guilt, expelled from the garden of Eden into the garden of the flowers of evil.

Yet this theological dimension of the *Kreatur* has developed its own dynamic which, in the extreme, turns against theology; one might even say: it becomes the only real force against a theology that the bourgeois secularization process only repressed and never overcame. For Benjamin, this other secularization in the name of the *Kreatur* finds one of its first powerful expressions in the baroque. In the early nineteenth century, the German poet and playwright Georg Büchner, whose *Woyzeck* returns in the twentieth century in Alban Berg's opera *Wozzeck*, emerges, in Paul Celan's words, as "the poet of the creature." Woyzeck, Danton, and the eighteenth-century writer Lenz, hero of Büchner's novella, are different figures from Büchner's *Kreatur*. In Büchner's work, the *Kreatur* enters at the same time into a potentially revolutionary and political dimension. Benjamin refers to Büchner's world as an "anthropological materialism" (*BA/B*, 108; *CA/B*, 81). When Benjamin devotes some of his major literary critical analysis to Baudelaire and Kafka, it is in an attempt to delineate the extreme outlines of *Kreatürlichkeit* in all its layers of anthropological and historical materialism. Benjamin does this in order to rethink and rewrite the discourses of both theology and radical politics. *Kreatur*, as the figure of modernity, figures human subjectivity as a sexualized body that speaks, as the flesh permeated by the word, inscribing the body in the experience of the law. Under this premise, the baroque allegorical personifications as incarnations of virtues and vices are the most precise model of a human subjectivity whose flesh can be reduced neither to a pure physis nor to nineteenth-century psychologism. It is in the *Kreatur* that, for Benjamin, the discourses of Marx and Freud intersect in a way that puts Benjamin's thinking at a far distance from the "Freudo-Marxism" of such members of the Frankfurt School as Erich Fromm and Herbert Marcuse, but also from the more subtle "mediations" of Adorno.

The language of *Kreatürlichkeit*, thus assumes a strange familiarity in a long tradition: one might call it a tradition of estrangement. But it is estranged once more in a radical way; it is a language with no precedence: "[it is a] very new, strangely stunning language that resounds loudly through the resonating mask of a completely changed environment" (*C*, 313). The *Kreatürlichkeit* that speaks here speaks in the medium of a resonating mask. It is, in the most literal sense, a *persona*. It is a form of allegory, a personification that assumes the character of a person demanding a radical rethinking of the speaking subject. The stunningly strange new language that resounds through the changed environment has to be read and heard before any theory can reemerge from the depth of this language.

However, insofar as there is a gaze that opens up to the image that praxis puts forth, there is already theory in the literal sense of the word. Theory in this sense is a praxis of seeing that is very close to Freud's free-floating attentiveness that renounces all Theory in order to allow theory to emerge from its praxis. The suspension of Theory as the paradoxical condition for theory is the structural analogy to the state of emergency as a state of the possibility of a radical exception. The exception irrupts as a signal from the real into the coherence of Theory.[10]

In the late twenties and early thirties, Benjamin saw himself again and again challenged, above all by his friend Scholem, to account for his engagement with Marxism. Two major traits emerge in these accounts: Benjamin insists that for him Marxism is not an ideology of fixed ideas but a mode of thought, a way of taking position in relation to the changing situation. He does not want to be seen "as a representative of dialectical materialism as a dogma, but as a researcher to whom the posture (*Haltung*) of the materialist seems to be more fruitful, scientifically and humanly, in all things that concern us, than the idealist attitude" (*C*, 379f.). Thinking in this sense is not simply a theoretical attitude, it implies positioning one's being in relation to the world. Benjamin uses the Brechtian term *Haltung*. The word means "attitude" or "posture," but it also contains the word *Halt*, meaning something to hold on to, but, at the same time, it is the imperative of *halten*, "stop!" *Haltung* as the result of a caesura in the flow of events allows for the thinking image, the *Denkbild*, to emerge from the praxis. Praxis is experienced in the most concrete terms by Benjamin in the thirties when the means of production for him as a writer and critic begin to disappear.

It is in this situation that the Institute for Social Research, on the one hand, and Brecht, on the other, enter into their particular constellation in Benjamin's life and work. In 1932, Benjamin's situation becomes increasingly precarious. On 10 November 1932, he writes to Adorno: "It is extremely important to me to see Horkheimer. And this for a precise reason. If anything should and can be done by the Institute to support my work, this is the moment, at a time when my work is sabotaged from all sides" (*GBr*, IV, 143; *CA/B*, 19). A couple of months later, on 15 January 1933, he writes to Scholem: "I have attempted recently to create new connections and have thus discovered, on the one hand, the *Vossische Zeitung* and, on the other, the Frankfurt Journal for Social Research. The latter has partly offered me some commissions, partly has promised me future commissions" (*C*, 400). In 1934, Benjamin publishes his first essay, "Zum gegenwärtigen gesellschaftlichen Standort des französischen Schriftstellers" (On the present social position of the French writer) in the Journal for Social Research. The rigorous materialist argumentation of this essay irritated both Scholem (who took it for a communist "Credo") and Adorno. In 1935, the Institute offered Benjamin a small stipend in support of his work on the Parisian *Arcades Project*; in 1936 the regular payment by the Institute is slightly increased, and since fall 1937,

Benjamin is officially listed as *Mitarbeiter* (member and coworker) of the Institute.[11] As welcome and necessary as the support of the Institute was for Benjamin, both Benjamin and Adorno were well aware of the potential dangers and restrictions such a support could involve. Adorno, who had initiated the Institute's support of the work on the Parisian *Arcades Project*, was at the same time worried about the restrictive effects on the work: "I know very well that the Institute and a journal that is still mainly controlled by Löwenthal will have difficulties to adopt anything else but a historical–sociological work. You will not take it badly, however, if I would like to see the work on the Arcades not as a historical-sociological investigation, but as prima philosophia in your specific sense" (*CA/B*, 83; trans. modified).

Among the members of the Institute, Adorno certainly had the closest affinity with Benjamin on an intellectual level. The relationship with Horkheimer was deeply ambivalent and overshadowed by the humiliating dependency on the Institute and the unbridgeable difference in their modes of thought. As an assistant of Professor Cornelius in Frankfurt, Horkheimer had played his part in the failure of Benjamin's habilitation.[12] Nevertheless, a meeting between Horkheimer and Benjamin in 1937 in Paris made a great impression on Horkheimer, who reported to Adorno: "Among the most beautiful things were a few hours with Benjamin. He is by far the closest to us among all the others."[13]

This closeness was, as far as Horkheimer was concerned, a very limited one. Benjamin's explorations at the extreme edges of Marxism and theology were utterly foreign to Horkheimer, as was also Benjamin's increasing interest in Freud and the relation of Freud's work with his own explorations of the working of memory. The more profound affinities with Adorno also had their limits, and the relationship was colored by its own tortuous ambivalences. Adorno's inaugural lecture of 1931 and his seminar on Benjamin's book on the German tragic drama of 1932 mark the points of closest intersection between the two – to the point where Adorno adopts Benjaminian ideas in a way that borders on plagiarism.[14]

From Benjamin's point of view, 1931 and 1932 are the years of closest rapprochement between himself and Adorno, and, while moments and points of affinity will continue to emerge in their relationship until Benjamin's death, it is only here that Benjamin talks of a "circle" that includes him and Adorno. This circle will soon be strongly disturbed by Benjamin's "excentricity," although its outlines remain readable, most of all in the common interest in the theological. There are even moments when Adorno feels himself called to defend Benjamin's "theological kernel."[15]

In a paradoxical way, Adorno's invocation of the sphere that constitutes their common "circle" is also the point of the excentric deviation. The rupture of the circle happens in its "dialectical" center. Benjamin's constellation of extremes escapes the circle. Another, excentric circle, formed between Benjamin and Brecht delineates the moves and motifs of Benjamin's writing.

Benjamin's first acquaintance with Brecht's work seemed to occur around 1927. In 1929, they meet for the first time personally. Benjamin reports it as a noteworthy meeting to Scholem: "I have made some noteworthy acquaintances. To name one, a closer acquaintance with Brecht (about whom and about which there is much to say)" (C, 350). A couple of weeks later, Benjamin writes of "friendly relations": "You will be interested in the fact that recently very friendly relations have been formed between Brecht and me, less on the basis of what he has produced so far, and of which I know only the *Threepenny Opera* and the ballads, as on the well founded interest one must have for his present plans" (*GBr*, IV, 469). The "present plans" refer to Brecht's most radical experimentations, his *Lehrstücke*, "teaching" or "exercise" plays, that are didactic not in the sense of transmitting political or ideological knowledge, but in the sense of an "apprenticeship" or as Brecht called it: *Einübungen in Haltungen*: experimental exercises in postures. Brecht presented these new forms as experimental arrangements in a series of publications called *Versuche* (Essays). Benjamin took a passionate interest in these essays, finding in them an affinity with a side of his work that he could share neither with Scholem nor Adorno.[16]

Benjamin's first publication on Brecht appeared in 1930 in the *Frankfurter Zeitung* under the title "From the Brecht Commentary," indicating that these notes were part of a larger work. Benjamin's writing and commentaries on Brecht continued throughout the thirties until shortly before his death. Symptomatically, the first sentence of "From the Brecht-Commentary" refers to Brecht as a "difficult phenomenon" (*SW* II, 374). The phenomenon Brecht is difficult because it does not fit the conventional bourgeois notion of the "free," "original" writer: Brecht, Benjamin writes, "refuses to use his great poetic talents 'freely.'" What interests Benjamin is this different position of the writer in relation to his production and to society. The different position of the writer becomes itself the most important production: "The main product is: a new posture" (*eine neue Haltung*). With the word *Haltung*, Benjamin picks up one of the key words that constitute the strong link between his and Brecht's thinking; the other word follows immediately: "'The second experiment [*Versuch*], Stories of Mr. Keuner,' the author says, 'are an attempt to make gestures quotable'" (*SW* II, 375).

Haltung (posture, attitude) and gestures are the terms that define a writing, thinking, pedagogy, and teaching that embrace theory and praxis in a new constellation. *Haltung* can be learned (*erlernbar*), gestures can be quoted (*zitierbar*): both open up possibilities and abilities, indicated in the German suffix *-bar* (equivalent to the English -able: learnable, quotable). This potentiality of the *-bar* in *Haltung* and gesture is more important than their content; although there are certain contents that have more potentiality than others. They are defined in negative terms: "the gestures of poverty, ignorance, impotence"; but in their negativity lies their power and potentiality. "Poverty," Benjamin writes in a fragmentary note, "is a mimicry that allows it to step closer to reality" (*GS*, IV, 655).

Haltung and gestures are terms that are not reducible to either body or spirit: they indicate a new definition in the relationship of these heavily charged terms. They are pedagogical instruments in Brecht's *Lehrstücke* precisely because they work on a level beyond (or perhaps one should better say: before, on this side of) consciousness and knowledge. Gestures can take the form of words, but these words are "learned" and "exercised" before they are understood. They are pedagogical innervations that position body and spirit in a radically changing world.

The full critical potential of the terms Benjamin develops in his interchange with Brecht and with Brecht's work proves its power not only in the direct commentary on Brecht's work (for example in the seminal essay on the "epic theater") but even more in the interpretation of an œuvre that seems far removed from Brecht's political theater: in Benjamin's Kafka essay of 1934. Benjamin's attentiveness to the gestural and theatrical character of Kafka's world and figures allows him to bypass the dominant pious theologization as well as the more or less vulgarized psychoanalytic and sociological reductions of Kafka's work, and to penetrate to its "cloudy kernel" precisely because Benjamin's reading remains faithful to the surface and its ostentatious theatricality that is perhaps the "deepest" enigma of Kafka's writing. Gesture and theatricality undermine a conventional metaphysics of spirituality versus materialism that make, in Benjamin's words, both the "natural" and the "supernatural" interpretations of Kafka a failure.[17] Outside of the conventional alternative of the "natural" and "supernatural," the gestural bodies and the theatrical world of Kafka suggest a structure in which the traditional terms are both opposed in stark extremes and intersect at the same time in the most violent ways. It is this other "dialectic" that brings Kafka's work, through Benjamin's reading, in a close constellation with the theater of Brecht as well as with that of Artaud. It is the staging of the body that speaks, of the flesh penetrated by the word, of a field of action and gestures that are not so much expressions of individuals, but interactions of bodies in a space that is both physical and structured by the rules of symbolic games.

The anxiety that is part of the world of *Kreatürlichkeit* is also a major part in Benjamin's relation to Brecht. Despite the close affinity – or perhaps because of it – Brecht remains a "difficult phenomenon" not only for those (outside of the "circle") who are used to the conventional bourgeois figure of the artist as individual creator, but also – and in a much more troubling way – for Benjamin. This aspect emerges precisely in the moment when Brecht, himself an exile, offers to Benjamin what none of his other friends could or would offer him, a temporary refuge in Denmark, a roof for one who had no fixed domicile.

However, entering under that roof, so much needed, evokes a layer of the relationship to Brecht, for which the word "horror" is not too strong. Twice on the same day, on 30 December 1933, in letters to his closest friends Scholem and Gretel Karplus, Benjamin uses the word *grauen*, a verb often associated with the uncanny, indicating horror and shuddering. In both letters, the *grauen* is ambiguously linked with other, opposite feelings. In the letter to Gretel Karplus it is linked to waiting for something and to hope, and, in the letter to Scholem, the departure of Brecht makes the city (Paris) seem dead and the anticipation of his presence in Denmark inspires horror.

Benjamin's three closest friends, Adorno, Scholem, and Gretel Karplus (Adorno's fiancée and later wife), were in agreement about one thing: their fear of Brecht's influence on Benjamin. There was apparently something in Brecht's ways that evoked strong responses in all three of them. But, while Adorno more or less rationalized his response by reducing Brecht to a "vulgar" Marxist and Scholem simply registered his by refusing to read the texts that Benjamin kept sending him, Gretel Karplus addressed hers in a letter full of concern to Benjamin. And Benjamin responded for once on the same level in a long letter of June 1934 (*GB*, IV, 440f.).

In contrast to his letters to Scholem, where Benjamin vigorously defends his interest in Brecht's work and its affinity with his own mode of thought on political and ideological grounds, the letter to Gretel Karplus approaches the cloudy kernel of the relationship. Benjamin recognizes first a pattern of repetition: "What you say about [Brecht's] influence on me recalls for me a significant and ever returning constellation in my life." He mentions two precedents: the friend of his youth, the poet C. F. Heinle, who committed suicide at the beginning of the First World War, and a little later the somewhat dubious Simon Guttmann, whose influence Benjamin's wife passionately opposed. Her opposition culminated in the reproach that Benjamin was under some kind of hypnotic influence. Benjamin makes no attempt to refute such a suggestion, but instead attempts another analysis: "In the economy of my existence, a few relations, that can be counted, play indeed a role that allow [*sic*] me to assert a pole that is opposite my original being." It is no longer a simple question of ideology, but one that concerns both existence (*Dasein*) and being (*Sein*). Benjamin's concept of "thinking in other people's head," his mimetic ability to occupy the most extreme opposite positions, finds here its most radical expression. The repetitive pattern of Benjamin's excentric circles of friendship opens up to a *Haltung* that involves an existential positioning of one's innermost being in the extremes. It is the most radical ex-position of one's existence. Benjamin is well aware of the protest of his friends: "These relations have always provoked a more or less violent protest in those closest to me, as now the relationship to B[recht] – and much less diplomatically expressed by Gerhard Scholem."[18] Benjamin can only plead for an understanding of the incomprehensible: "In such a case, I can do little more than ask my friends to trust me, that these ties (*Bindungen*), whose dangers are obvious, will reveal their fruitfulness." And once more, Benjamin invokes the necessity of moving in extremes – but also the liberating potential of such a movment: "It is not at all unclear to you that my life as well as my thought moves [*sic*] in extreme positions. The expanse that it [*sic*] thus asserts, the freedom to move side by side things and thoughts that are considered irreconcilable, assumes its face only through the danger. A danger that generally appears also to my friends only in the form of those 'dangerous' relations." The inseparability of life and thought appears in a grammatical deviation of the verb in the singular: life and thought moves as one, and the following pronoun "it" asserts once more the oneness of life and thought. Danger appears as a physiognomic force that gives face to the otherwise faceless; and the face is the figure of a readability of physiognomic traits. Thus danger is also the condition that the "dialectical image" appears as a moment of readability.

What is presented here in the letter to Gretel Karplus in the form of a condensed analysis of Benjamin's life and thought through the motif of a repetitive pattern, reveals its fruitfulness in the critical praxis of the thirties, of which the Surrealism essay is a particularly telling example.

The essay "Surrealism" states a crisis of the European intelligence.[19] The crisis is specifically the crisis "of the humanistic concept of freedom" (*SW* II, 207). The experience of this crisis is, for the German critic, not simply an intellectual idea, but the experience of an "exposed position between anarchistic fronde and revolutionary discipline, experienced on one's own body." This exposition and experience, leaving traces on the body, defines Benjamin's position – perhaps at the opposite pole of his "original" being, at a far distance from his own source – in relation to Brecht and to Adorno.

It positions him in the uncanny proximity of Brecht, who "refuses to use his great poetic talents 'freely,'" who is no longer caught in the traps of the "humanistic concept of freedom"; and it distances him from Adorno whose insistence on the autonomous work of art, the kernel of his aesthetics, remains grounded, beyond all dialectical twists and tricks, in the humanistic concept of freedom.

The critique of the humanistic concept of freedom clears the way for a more radical concept of freedom that emerges later in the essay: "Since Bakunin there has been no radical concept of freedom in Europe. The Surrealists have it again. They are the first ones to get rid of the liberal, moralistic–humanistic sclerotic ideal of freedom" (*SW* II, 215). However, there is and remains another question at the center of Benjamin's essay and at the center of his politics that seems to remain a question without answer. Benjamin poses it in regard to Surrealism, but it is one that keeps returning in different contexts: "But do they succede to weld this experience of freedom with the other revolutionary experience, that we must acknowledge because we experienced it: with the constructive, dictatorial element of revolution? In short – to tie the revolt to the revolution?" (*SW* II, 215).

At the time when Benjamin writes his essay on Surrealism, the movement is already falling apart, but, in its decay, its energies are liberated. What began as "a circle of closely tied together people" (*SW* II, 208) explodes. Benjamin writes this at a time, when he is acutely aware of his own dangerous relations and ties (*Bindungen*). He has experienced the dangerous ties on his own body, and his posture and the gestures of his writing are profoundly marked by this experience.

The explosion is set off by a specific constellation and confrontation of the profane with the sacred or pseudo-sacred. The mystifications within the Surrealist group that make it similar to a secret society (a *Geheimbund*), not unlike the George circle (whose spell Benjamin strongly felt), explode "in the sober (*sachlichen*), profane battle for power and domination." The explosion makes possible the transformation of the Surrealist dream into the critical reading of the dream. This transformation is possible only from within. Dream and intoxication (*Rausch*) are necessary conditions: they undo the illusionary center of bourgeois humanism, the I. "This loosening up (*Lockerung*) of the I through intoxication is at the same time the fruitful, living experience that made these people step out of the magical circle of intoxication" (*SW* II, 208). Again we can read the parallel to Benjamin's *liaisons dangereuses*, which are, in the most literal sense, an almost complete "loosening up" (*Lockerung*) of the I, the center of humanistic intellectual identity, in favor of a thinking in other people's head and a mimetic exposition to extremely opposed positions. The *Lockerung* thus achieved is the condition for its "fruitfulness," that must prove itself in the ability to step out of the magical circle and to read it excentrically. The critical procedure is close to that of Brecht's epic theater: an exorcism of the ghosts through ghosts. Brecht likens the use of film on the stage to "the role of those appearances of ghosts without which for a long time – and they were the best times – great drama could not exist. Thus it [film] plays a revolutionary role because as spirit/ghost [*Geist*] it brings the naked reality into apparition, the good godhead of revolution."[20] Ghosts exorcise ghosts, phantoms expel phantoms, intoxication prepares the ground for sobriety. The role of the ghost's apparition for Brecht is a radical critique of the seeming evidence of reality which itself is phantom and phantasmagoria, produced by the world of commodities. Through the apparition of the ghost "naked reality" is supposed to appear, for it is the ghost that points out what the appearance of reality is: namely mere appearance. The ghost plays the role of the caesura that, according to Hölderlin, interrupts the precipitous sequence of representations and shows them as representation. The theatricality of the Surrealist manifestations, their "bluff" and "falsification" is the condition for a real, true experience in a world where reality is dominated by phantasmagorias.

The Surrealist experimentation with drugs, intoxication, and ecstasies situates it in the unexpected proximity of religious ecstasy. Both "opiates" – the secular intoxication through drugs as well as the religious opium – need to be overcome. While some of the Surrealists saw in the secular illumination provided by drugs the overcoming of religious illumination, Benjamin proposes instead "a profane illumination" in the form of "a materialist, anthropological inspiration" (*SW* II, 209). Drugs and religion as intoxicating forces are (almost) on the same level, neither can cancel the other, but each can be a kind of "preparatory school" (*Vorschule*) for profane illumination. As such, both can be fruitful, but also dangerous (just as Benjamin's dangerous ties of friendship that sometimes seem to take the form of an intoxication). Of the two, religion is probably more dangerous, but, according to Benjamin, also more effective as *Vorschule*, because it is stricter and more disciplined (*strenger*). Insofar as religion (and its codification in theology) is more disciplined, it might be the most effective preparation for the transformation of the revolt into revolution. Revolution has to go beyond intoxication, which, for Benjamin, is the limitation of Surrealism; it needs for its radical freedom "the methodical and disciplined preparation" (*SW* II, 216).

This is the point where Benjamin's critical distanciation from Surrealism is articulated: the Surrealists were seduced too easily by their own mystifications and intoxications. Benjamin's articulation of his critique is paradigmatic of his critical procedure: it follows the twisted, associative paths of his critical object – and above all the twists and turns of language. In order to demonstrate that Surrealism was not always "at the height" of its own secular claims, Benjamin follows its labyrinthian moves on the heights of the Parisian roofs. Benjamin takes off from a passage in Breton's "Nadja," where Breton extols "the ravishing days of looting in Paris under the sign of Sacco and Vanzetti" (*SW* II, 209). Under the sign, names as signs point the way. Breton sees in the Boulevard Bonne-Nouvelle, one of the centers of the demonstrations, the place that "made true the strategic promises of the revolt that its name had always already contained." But, under the sign of Sacco and Vanzetti, Benjamin notices also a Mme. Sacco appearing in the text; and this woman has nothing to do with the victim of American class justice, but is a fortune-teller who warns Paul Eluard that Nadja is a dangerous woman.[21] This is the point where Benjamin inscribes his critical distance while still following the dangerous paths: "We concede the neck-breaking path of Surrealism, leading over roofs, lightning rods, rain gutters, balconies, weather-vanes, stuccoworks – the climber of façades must use all the ornaments to his advantage – we concede to it that it reaches also into the damp backrooms of spiritism. But we don't like it knocking gently at the window in order to ask about its future" (*SW* II, 209).

The profane illumination (like all true illuminations) begins with a radical exposition of oneself, exposing oneself to the point of "moral exhibitionism" (*SW* II, 209). Benjamin remarks the uncanny (*unheimlich*) effect and shock he experienced in a Moscow hotel during a congress of Buddhist monks who all left the doors of their rooms ajar. The shock of an existence that has renunciated all privacy is particularly intense for an individual as private and discrete as Benjamin was. The "moral" that emerges from this "moral exhibitionism" propels Benjamin into the perhaps most radical opposition to his "original" being: "To live in the glass house is a revolutionary virtue par excellence" (*SW* II, 209).

The exposition of the self gives room to the profane illumination of things that inspires Benjamin's work on the Parisian *Arcades Project*. He finds the models for this other gaze in Aragon's *Paysan de Paris* and his presentation of the "Passage de l'Opéra" (*SW* II, 210) as well as in Breton's texts that "bring to an explosion the immense forces of 'moods' (*Stimmungen*) that are hidden in things" (*GS*, II, 300; *SW* II, 210). Benjamin is careful to differentiate this violent, materialist, and at the same time profoundly spiritual gaze, from the traditional bourgeois tendency to put things into a "symbolic light" (*SW* II, 213). In Benjamin's profane illumination, things are not symbols for something, they are revelations in that literal and radical sense that sacred texts are revelations in religious traditions. It is here where Benjamin's historical materialism intersects with and takes its ultimate leave from theology.

Theology is a kind of disinfection of romanticism in which Surrealism with its celebration of dreams and intoxication is still entangled. It is the preparation for the truly profane which is, for Benjamin, "a dialectical optic that recognizes the quotidian as impenetrable and the impenetrable as the quotidian" (*SW* II, 216). This new optic, instead of celebrating telepathy and intoxication through drugs (or religion), recognizes everyday acts, such as reading as telepathic acts, thinking as a narcotic, and, in Benjamin's eyes, loneliness as the most terrifying drug (*SW* II, 216).

This new optic implies at the same time a specific Benjaminian concept of language. It brings us back to the difference between the conventional bourgeois tendency to see things in a symbolic light (with a correspond-ing political rhetoric that resembles a "bad spring poem" (*SW* II, 216) and "things" – everyday things – as unmediated, explosive revelations. *Alles nur Bilder* ("Nothing but images"), Benjamin says of the bourgeois and social-democratic, humanistic political rhetoric. But then, in a quintessential Benjaminian twist, he does not discard the images, but saves them as the central term of his new optics.

Benjamin follows a distinction of Aragon and expands it on the basis of his own early philosophy of language: "the difference between compar-ison (*Vergleich*) and image" (*SW* II, 217). The conventional image in po-litical rhetoric is based on a comparison between ultimately two different spheres: the political reality and the linguistic, poetic, rhetorical "flowers," metaphors, and symbols. Benjamin's philosophy of language, articulated al-ready in his early essay "On Language as such and on the Language of Man," allows for no such separation because language is not something outside of the real or beside it, but it "extends not only over all regions of human spir-itual utterance that is inhabited by language, but it extends over absolutely everything" ("On Language," *SW* II, 62). In this sense, there is nothing out-side of language, everything is under its extension, which is not the same as saying that everything is language. It allows for a different distinction: lan-guage is not a medium of expression, "through which" we express things, but "it is the immediate expression of that which communicates itself in it. This 'itself' is a spiritual essence. This implies evidently that the spiri-tual essence that communicates itself in language is not language itself, but something to be distinguished from it" ("On Language," *SW* II, 63). With this rejection of mediation, the ground for Benjamin's later difference from Adorno is prepared.

In the Surrealism essay, political action takes the place of the spiritual essence. Benjamin avoids the rhetoric of political "reality" with its meta-physical implications and instead introduces the notion of space: "To orga-nize pessimism means nothing else but throwing the moral metaphor out of politics and to discover the hundred percent image space in the space of political action" (*SW* II, 217). If the space of political action is a "hundred percent image space," there is no room left for a political "reality," on the one hand, and its representation in images, metaphors, and similes, on the other. The political space as image space is identical with a radicalized form of the Brechtian epic theater that, in its extreme, no longer knows any difference between the space of the stage and the space of the audience. In Benjamin's words: the abyss of the orchestra, that separates the audience from the stage like the living from the dead, has been leveled. Brecht's epic theater as the model for the "image space" of politics is not a metaphor, but the designation of a structure of representation – more precisely, of presentation, of *Darstellung*. As soon as we are confronted with the sphere of human life and action we stand before the question of *Darstellung* and *Vorstellung*, of presentation and representation.

The end of the Surrealism essay is a radical formulation of the sphere of human action and life, which is also the sphere of politics, as space of presentation: a "hundred percent image space." This image space is structured like a language of the unconscious, marked by jokes and "Freudian" slips. The more one situates oneself in this space "the better are the jokes he tells" (*SW* II, 217). "For also in the joke, in the insult, in the misunderstanding, everywhere where an act itself exposes the image out of itself (*wo ein Handeln selber das Bild aus sich herausstellt*) and is [...] this searched for image space opens up... " (*SW* II, 217). The image is thus not the representation of something, but its exposition in the act itself. It is a particular kind of act: the image of true presentation appears not in the intentional act but, as in psychoanalysis, in a slip, in an *acte manqué*. The veil of the *gute Stube*, the bourgeois living room and its good manners that cover up the murderous exploitation and racism underneath its smooth surface, is torn to give way to a theater of bacchanalia that recalls the Hegelian bacchanalia of truth. Another space, another scene opens up "in which political materialism and physical creature share among each other, according to a dialectical justice and in such a way that no limb remains intact, the inner human being, the psyche, the individual, or whatever we want to throw before it" (*SW* II, 217). The combination of political materialism and physical creature indicates the distance of both to any kind of idealism and to the dominant rhetoric of Socialism and Communism. Benjamin sets himself off from what he calls "metaphyscial materialism," i.e. one still based on the traditional opposition of matter and spirit, in the name of his own "anthropological materialism." In this other materialism, which is always already a space of presentation, the "image space" is at the same time a "body space" (*Leibraum*). *Leib* is, in difference to *Körper*, not merely physical body, but a "creaturely" body, above all, it is not reducible to the bodies of individuals. Collectives also have the qualities of *Leib*, they are *leibhaft* (*SW* II, 217).

The vision of this space and the ensuing praxis of reading the world mark the unbridgeable distance to Adorno, not to speak of the rest of the Frankfurt School. The extent of this distance is revealed in Adorno's helpless misreading of Benjamin's first Baudelaire essay, in which he thought to have found a "vulgar" Marxist reduction of great poetry to social facts.[22] As a *Leibraum*, Benjamin's anthropological materialism intersects with the space of Brecht's epic theater. They have common ancestors, some of whom Benjamin names: "Georg Büchner, Nietzsche, Rimbaud," and a common text that still awaits its full exposition into political reality: the communist manifesto. The common ground of these spaces does not exclude misunderstandings. But misunderstandings are, according to Benjamin, an essential part of the political image space. They can be productive.[23]

Misunderstanding is the discrepancy that opens up between the intention of an act and its understanding, but also between the intention and the act. In the space of this discrepancy something escapes the subject, the act exposes itself in this discrepancy and assumes its own life on another scene. Thus, Baudelaire standing on a street corner in Paris during the February revolution, screaming "Down with general Aupick" offers an image that becomes readable for Benjamin as a political image of the relation between revolt and revolution. Benjamin offers another image of his relationship to Brecht in a diary account of a visit at Brecht's place in Southern France (*GS*, VI, 431f.): it is an anecdote of a displaced offering of flowers. Benjamin tells this anecdote, because it exhibits an example of his behavior that remains impenetrable. It is the account of another scene, waiting to be read.

Taking a walk in southern France, Benjamin plucks a hawthorn flower (*Heckenrose*, Proust's *aubépine*), and a little later a peony, in memory of his former love Jula Cohn, while he is following a beautiful young woman. But the latter encounters another man, whom she seems to know, and Benjamin, slightly embarassed finds himself in the proximity of the Villa Mar-bello where Brecht and some of his friends live. In a state of some disorientation and lability, Benjamin decides to enter and stays for several hours. But Benjamin's journal records nothing of the approximately two-hour conversation. Instead he recounts his embarrassed attempt to offer his flowers to one of the people present: for reasons not stated, he cannot offer the peony to Elisabeth Hauptmann, he offers it instead, accompanied by ironic remarks, to Brecht, who declines and finally drops it in a flowerpot, adding the hawthorn like a "flag." The displacement of the flowers in this anecdote can be read as an allegory of the other scene that determines the enigmatic friendship between Brecht and Benjamin.

The friendship between Benjamin and Brecht is more deeply rooted in the acknowledgment of this other scene than in any intentional agreement or consensus. The language of flowers has a long tradition. Nowhere is it more elequent than in the hopelessly displaced flowers that Benjamin threw into Brecht's orderly world.

NOTES

1. For convenience, reference has been made to the Osborne translation of *The Origin of the German Tragic Drama* throughout this chapter, however, in almost every case, the translation has been modified in order to reflect Benjamin's text more accurately.
2. Carl Schmitt, *Politische Theologie. Vier Kapitel zur Lehre von der Souveränität* (Munich/Leipzig: Verlag von Duncker & Humblot, 1922), 9.
3. Ibid.
4. The political forms of the oppositions in their concrete historical appearance – fascism and Marxism – have historically both taken the form of ideological fundamentalism; but, while fascism essentially is fundamentalism, Marxism is open to the possibility of a marginalist and liminal thinking and praxis.
5. Asja Lacis, *Revolutionär im Beruf. Berichte über proletarisches Theater, über Meyerhold, Brecht, Benjamin und Piscator*, ed. Hildegard Brenner (Munich, Rogner and Bernhard, 1971), 41f. On Asja Lacis, see also: *Walter Benjamin 1892–1940. Marburger Magazin 55*, eds. Bearbeitet von Rolf Tiedemann, Christoph Gödde, and Henri Lonitz (Marbach: Deutsche Schillergesellschaft, 1990), 161–70.
6. For this constellation see also Giorgio Agamben's book on *History and Childhood* and in particular the excellent analysis of an exchange of letters between Benjamin and Adorno concerning Benjamin's first Baudelaire essay, which Agamben analyzes wonderfully through the fairy-tale story of the princess (who in Agamben's allegory curiously turns into a prince) and the frog: Giorgio Agamben, "Il principe e il ranocchio," in *Infanzia e storia: distruzione dell'esperienza e origine della storia* (Torino: Einaudi, 1978), 111–27.
7. The protocols of this seminar are now published in: *Frankfurter Adorno Blätter IV*. W. Adorno Archive (Munich 1995), 52–77.
8. To what degree Kierkegaard plays a role in this critique of mediation needs further investigation, as does Kierkegaard's discreet but decisive role in Benjamin's thought in general.
9. Adorno, too, found himself at certain times in a somewhat excentric position in relation to the Institute that was to become the "Frankfurt School." In a letter of April 25 1937, Adorno criticizes rather harshly not only Herbert Marcuse as a pedantic "Oberlehrer," but is worried that Horkheimer will consider him an incurable nagging bitchy critic of basically everyone in the Institute from Löwenthal and Erich Fromm to Neurath and Lazarsfeld (*CA/B*, 180).

10. As Carl Schmitt writes in a sentence that Benjamin could have underwritten: "In the exception the force of real life breaks through the crust of a mechanism petrified in repetition." Schmitt, *Politische Theologie*, 15.

11. For a concise history of Benjamin's relation with the Institute see Rolf Wiggershaus, *Die Frankfurter Schule. Geschichte. Theoretische Entwicklung. Politische Bedeutung* (Munich: Carl Hanser Verlag, 1986), 186ff.

12. The circumstances of this academic farce have only recently become known in more detail. See: Burkhard Lindner, "Habilitationsakte Benjamin. Über ein 'akademisches Trauerspiel' und über ein Vorkapitel der Frankfurter Schule," in *Walter Benjamin im Kontext*, ed. Burkhard Lindner (Frankfurt am Main: Athenäum, 1985), 332.

13. Letter to Adorno, 13 October 1937, quoted in: Rolf Wiggershaus, *Die Frankfurter Schule. Geschichte. Theoretische Entwicklung. Politische Bedeutung* (Munich: Carl Hanser Verlag, 1986), 186.

14. Benjamin points at this with a certain irony. Quoting a sentence from Adorno's lecture, he writes: "I underwrite this sentence. But I could not have written it without pointing at the introduction to the baroque book [*On the Origin of the German Tragic Drama*] in which this – unmistakable and, in the modest sense in which something like this can be said, completely new – thought has been expressed. I, on my part, would not have been able not to refer to the baroque book. Must I add: I, in your position, even less so." Letter to Adorno, 17 July 1931 (*GBr*, IV, 38–39; *CA/B*, 9).

15. See Adorno's letter of 2–4 August 1935 to Benjamin (*CA/B*, 104–14).

16. For a concise summary of the relationship between Brecht and Benjamin, as far as the external facts are concerned, see the commentary of the editors of the *Gesammelte Schriften* in II, 1363ff. For a further attempt at an interpretation of this relationship see my chapter "From Aesthetics to Poetics," in R. Nägele, *Theater, Theory, Speculation. Walter Benjamin and the Scenes of Modernity* (Baltimore: The Johns Hopkins University Press, 1991), 135–66.

17. "There are two ways to miss in principle Kafka's writings. The natural interpretation is the one, the supernatural is the other" (*GS*, II, 425).

18. The letter is riddled with grammatical and syntactical oddities that would need a separate analysis beyond the few observations in this essay.

19. What Benjamin does not mention is the fact that at least one French writer, Antonin Artaud, shares the same perspective, insisting on the high stakes of writing beyond the limits of aesthetic concerns. It is indeed one of the most puzzling aspects of Benjamin's essay on Surrealism and his other writings on the French scene, that, as far as I know, there is not one single mentioning of Artaud. To be sure, Artaud had ruptured his relations with the Surrealists, but precisely because he saw their potential and their limits in the same terms as Benjamin. The curious absence of Artaud from Benjamin's vision of the French cultural scene deserves all the more attention as Artaud's vision of the theater and the gestural body intersect as much with Benjamin's thinking as does Brecht's epic theater.

20. B. Brecht, *Gesammelte Werke* (Frankfurt am Main: Suhrkamp, 1967), xv, 284.

21. This Mme. Sacco also played an important role for Antonin Artaud, who addressed his *Lettre à la voyante* (*Oeuvres Complètes* [Paris: Gallimard, 1984–], I, 128–32), published in December 1926 in *la Révolution Surréaliste*, to her; it was she, who, according to a letter of Artaud to Janine Kahn, advised him to leave

France in order to gain his full power as a writer: "Mais moi pour écrire, pour pour me délivrer, pour avoir la vie plane je dois quitter la France, l'Europe, c'est en Afrique, ou en Amérique, que j'écrirai des pages capitales mais dès maintenant les choses que j'écrirai dans la peine me procureront quand même le succès." (*Oeuvres Complètes*, VII, 315).

22. For a detailed analysis of this misreading see Giorgio Agamben, *Infanzia e storia*, and R. Nägele, "Traumlektüre. Benjamins politische Baudelairelektüre," in *Lesarten der Moderne*, ed. Rainer Nägele (Eggingen: Isele, 1998), 33–54.

23. One of Brecht's last reminiscences of Benjamin is precisely about misunderstanding when he notes in his diary: "one realizes with horror how small the number of those is that are at least ready to misunderstand such things" (B. Brecht, *Arbeitsjournal 1938–1942* [Frankfurt: Suhrkamp, 1973], 294).

9

MAX PENSKY

Method and time: Benjamin's dialectical images

> It's not that what is past casts its light on what is present, or what is present its light on the past; rather, image is that wherein what has been comes together in a flash with the now to form a constellation. In other words, image is dialectics at a standstill. For while the relation of the present to the past is a purely temporal, continuous one, the relation of what-has-been to the now is dialectical: is not progression but image, suddenly emergent. – Only dialectical images are genuine images (that is, not archaic); and the place where one encounters them is language.
>
> "Awakening" (*Arcades*, 462; N2a, 3)

Reading this well-known entry from the "N" convolute of Benjamin's *Arcades Project*, even the most seasoned Benjamin expert might be forgiven a feeling of helplessness in the face of such a powerful and enigmatic array of claims. The breathtaking evocation of an alternative temporality that this quote contains in characteristically elliptical and compacted form, the glimpse at an entirely new conception of historiography that breaks with previous categories of interpretation, the notion of an image-based historical sensibility as the genuine mode of historical interpretation – these are as fascinating and compelling as any moment in modern philosophy. But, at the same time, one cannot avoid the feeling that this quote, and others like it in Benjamin's *Arcades Project*, is a theoretical promissory note that would prove difficult if not impossible to redeem. What possible philosophy of history could explicate the difference between the past and "what-has-been," between the present and the "now"? What could it mean to claim that an alternative version of historical happening depends on a "flash" of synthesis between what has been and a now: what role does such a claim leave open for the historical researcher? Why should we prefer a "constellation" to a solid work of critical historiography? Why should we understand a categorical distinction between "ordinary" temporal relations familiar to academic historiography, relations that appear indispensable for the invaluable work of historical interpretation, versus "dialectical" relations?

Seventy years after they were written, and over thirty years after they first became the object of Benjamin scholars, these claims retain the power to shock. Along with other texts in the "N" convolute, in the exposés and sketches of the *Arcades Project*, and in the "On the Concept of History," this entry extends a claim for the "dialectical image" as the methodological cornerstone of the *Arcades Project*. The problem, of course, is that the *centrality* of dialectical images for Benjamin's own understanding of the specifically new methodological foundation of the work is matched by the *obscurity* of the notion of dialectical images. Hints, clues, summations of nonexistent treatises, elliptical remarks, and a very small number of tightly packed and often hermetic doctrinal statements, such as the one above, do not add up to anything approaching a "theory" of the dialectical image, or certainly not one elaborated enough to serve as a perspicuous guide to how the thousands of pages of excerpts and citations of the *Arcades Project* were to have been used.

Benjamin regarded the dialectical image as the methodological heart of the *Arcades Project*. Yet he was unable to offer a coherent, intelligible account of what dialectical images were, what their precise methodological role should be taken to be, how they were to be related to the agency of the critical historian, what sorts of meta-theoretical and meta-methodological (in other words: theological) postulates they might imply, or indeed how, and under what conditions, dialectical images were possible at all. The dialectical image has been the subject of a good deal of dedicated scholarship.[1] Yet, at the heart of the *Arcades Project*, the "lightning flash" of the dialectical image has, to this day, remained far more a dark star, indeed a kind of theoretical and methodological black hole, a "singularity" following its own extraordinary laws and capable, apparently, of absorbing any number of attempts at critical illumination.

There are certainly two (not incompatible) explanations for this state of affairs: we may simply not yet have gotten the interpretation of the dialectical image that we need. Or, there simply may not be such a thing as a "doctrine" or "theory" of dialectical images that could serve as the object of explanation. Susan Buck-Morss, whose reconstruction of a "theory" of the dialectical image is surely the most complex and thorough to date, rightly points out that the term is simply "overdetermined" in Benjamin's own work, meaning that Benjamin tended to invoke it as often as explain it. Rolf Tiedemann, one of the editors of Benjamin's collected works, has argued that the term "dialectical image," notwithstanding its centrality for Benjamin's mature work, "never achieved any terminological consistency."[2] Are we dealing with an overly rich theoretical legacy that is still awaiting its definitive interpretation? Or does the dialectical image rather denote the failure of Benjamin's mature cultural theory? Is the legacy of the dialectical image the guarantee of Benjamin's continuing relevance, or of the limits of his relevance?

I cannot hope to offer definitive answers to these questions here. The purpose of the present chapter is the far more modest one of offering an introductory account of the salient features of the dialectical image – to summarize what Benjamin appears to have meant by the term – and to offer a brief appraisal of the role of the dialectical image in determining the continuing relevance of Benjamin's thought. In so doing, I shall organize this chapter around two intertwined perspectives on the dialectical image: the dialectical image as a radically new *method* for the conduct of a new mode of critical materialist historiography, on the one hand, and the dialectical image as part of the description of a radically alternative conception of *time* and of historical experience, on the other. As we shall see, much difficulty with the doctrine of the dialectical image arises from the attempt to reconcile these two perspectives.

Clearly, any attempt to wrestle with these questions begins with the curious construction "dialectical image" itself, which conjoins two otherwise opposed terms. "Dialectical" normally refers to the relationship of concepts or arguments to one another; "images" are, on the contrary, normally considered in terms of immediacy and singularity. Benjamin's coining of the term was meant, among other things, as a critique of available modes of historical interpretation. "Dialectics" as the Hegelian mode of analysis of the historical unfolding of Spirit devolved into a historicist fantasy: what appeared as the fated progression of historical time could be shown to be the phantasmagoric appearance of eternal repetition, mythic time, under conditions of capitalism. Images, at the same time, needed to be rescued from aesthetic discourses and endowed with a shocking, that is to say a politically effective power. Thinking in images rather than concepts is, of course, a hallmark of Benjamin's work from its very beginning. Unlike concepts, the claim to immediacy inherent in the graphic image contains the potential to interrupt, hence to counteract modes of perception and cognition that have become second nature. The primary locus of the term "dialectical image" is thus itself the establishment of a (eminently dialectical) tension between two terms which, developed to their extreme, suddenly overcome this opposition.

Hegel always made sure that appearances conformed to the logic of the concept; his method was at heart logical, and hence the phenomenology of history – what shows itself, concretely, to the gaze of the dialectical historian – is derivative of the logic of development of Spirit from which history draws its shape and meaning. Benjamin, on the contrary, begins with phenomenology, with the factual appearance of historical shapes and instances, and refuses to allow the logic of development any role except as just one of these instances. Hence, "development," the *ideal* of historical progress, is one of many different forms of appearance for the history of the rise of industrial capitalism over the course of the early nineteenth century.

The *Arcades Project* was to have been a radically new mode of materialist critical historiography: the work proposed to construct a series of images representing the philosophical truth content of the rise of capitalist culture and capitalist consciousness over the course of the nineteenth century. The vast collection of historical material that Benjamin assembled was meant to serve as a reservoir of raw materials for the construction of images: images, that is, that would "spring forth" from constructions of the historical material itself. But how should the materialist critic assemble these fragments in such a way that images would "spring forth" from them? Renouncing the formative, meaning-giving commitment to dialectical logic, however, and renouncing the commitment to the narrative of historical development that this logic made possible, Benjamin's phenomenology of the material culture of the nineteenth century clearly required some way to structure the mass of assembled material, some way of *making* a materialist historiography out of recovered bits of historical appearances. One might naturally think of a theory that would offer an account of how, and why, to make sense of the historical material; Marx's dialectical reversal of Hegel's philosophy of history, or Lukács's theory of the reification effects of the commodity form suggest themselves.

Benjamin, however, grew increasingly unwilling to commit his project to a theoretical justification. He was convinced that theories in general remained too dependent upon the intentions of the theorist. All dialectical inversions notwithstanding, Benjamin was convinced that the historical truth of the nineteenth century was *objectively* present in his assembled fragments, and that this truth would be lost, not recovered, by the imposition of a theoretical superstructure upon them. Historical truth, Benjamin came to believe, is not simply available to any theorizing subject at any given historical moment; rather historical truth becomes "legible" or "recognizable" only at specific points: "The dialectical image," he maintains, "is an image that emerges suddenly, in a flash. What has been is to be held fast – as an image flashing up in the now of its recognizability" (*Arcades*, 473; N9, 7). Under conventional terms "past" is a narrative construction of the conditions for the possibility of a present which supercedes and therefore comprehends it; Benjamin's sense, on the contrary, was that "past" and "present" are constantly locked in a complex interplay in which what is past and what is present are negotiated through material struggles, only subsequent to which the victorious parties consign all that supports their vision of the world to a harmonious past, and all that speaks against it to oblivion. Strategizing against just this approved notion of historical time, Benjamin was convinced that behind the façade of the present, these otherwise forgotten moments could be recovered from oblivion and reintroduced, shoved in the face of the present, as it were, with devastating force: "The materialist presentation of history leads the past to bring the present into a critical state" (*Arcades*, 471; N7a, 5). But this view implied that the materialist critic could not simply *will* the subversive recovery of elements of an otherwise forgotten material culture; rather, the task was to cultivate a particular capacity for *recognizing* such moments.

Beyond the methodology of hermeneutics, in which past is recovered from the perspective of a present that finds its own self-understanding only in the horizon of a recovered tradition, Benjamin sought a way to actualize historical material that would *uproot* and shock what has been constructed as "the present," that would disrupt the very relationship between past and present that hermeneutics assumes. Theory, for Benjamin, in general always requires the stability of a (theorizing) subject and the imposition of subjective intention on the structure of historical time; the invariable effect of even the best-intentioned theory is a certain pacification of history and hence the loss of the capacity for recognizing sites where past and present lose their familiar contours. Hence theory for Benjamin must be replaced by method. Benjamin was convinced that only in this way could the subjective element be removed from the construction of images; an element that he had already described in *The Origin of the German Tragic Drama* as an impediment to the revelation of truth. The claim to the objective truth of dialectical images, and the need to articulate this claim while nevertheless explaining the role of the materialist critic, was a consistent problem for Benjamin and one that his notes on the dialectical image never entirely resolve.[3]

The elimination of theory in favor of method, a project that is utterly distinctive of Benjamin's intellectual trajectory over the course of the *Arcades Project*, has more behind it than Benjamin's views on the objective nature of historical truth and his distrust of the distorting effects of the intentional subject. There is, of course, no real method without theory; no possible rule for proceeding with the historical material without some intellectual commitments that determine in advance the overall significance of the historical material, the possibility of their recovery, the purpose of their construction into images, and the shocking effect that images are intended to deploy. In fact the "theory" that Benjamin had in mind, and that he was anxious to conceal behind the historical material itself, was in fact "theory" in its oldest sense: theology. Benjamin's insistence on *not* providing an adequate theoretical justification for how dialectical images both could be constructed by critical agency and could "emerge," with a shocking force, from the assembled materials – that is, how dialectical images were both made and recognized – was to become Adorno's central criticism of Benjamin's earliest, most imagistic drafts of the *Arcades Project* (*CA/B*, 104–5).

The *Arcades Project*, as anyone who has strolled its halls knows, contains an astonishing number and variety of different theoretical orientations and resources. But if we are to get a sense of how the dialectical image was to have worked as a methodological innovation for a new mode of cultural criticism, we must turn to Benjamin's eccentric and distinctive appropriation of Marx. To an extent that is often pushed to the background in current readings of Benjamin as a literary critic, the *Arcades Project* was, centrally, a Marxist, or at the very least a Marxist-inspired, work of cultural critique. The analysis of the material conditions of the emergence of high capitalism in the Paris of the nineteenth century was intended to reveal, in microscopic detail, the gradual insinuation of a deeply oppressive form of cultural life in conformity with the economic and political imperatives of a nascent capitalist system. The work deals, fundamentally, with a form of injustice that is all the harder to grasp since it infiltrates the tiniest capillary of consciousness from the highest forms of cultural expression to the level of everyday *habitus*. For Benjamin, Marx had understood that the hegemonic character of capitalism was, like all essentially mythic modes, both all-encompassing and, for that same reason, oddly fragile. In its ignorance of authentic human needs and its blindness to the cost in human suffering it exacts, it not only requires the disenchantment of old religious–metaphysical forms of consciousness and sources of motivation, but also, in its advanced form, compels a new form of reenchantment that classical liberal political economy could not even register, let alone explain. Much of the *Arcades Project* describes this new enchantment as "sleep," and the ideology of endless newness and guaranteed progress that capitalism depended on for a new motivational basis as a form of dreamlife. "Capitalism," Benjamin writes in an unusually terse formation, "was a natural phenomenon with which a new dream-filled sleep came over Europe, and, through it, a reactivation of mythic forces" (*Arcades*, 391; K1a, 9). Awakening from this sleep is the principal task of materialist historiography, and dialectical images are, for Benjamin, the moments of waking from this collective dream.

Two quotes will help to set the parameters of Benjamin's eccentric and distinctive reception of Marx:

> Marx lays bare the causal connection between economy and culture. For us, what matters is the thread of expression. It is not the economic origins of culture that will be presented, but the expression of the economy in its culture. At issue,

in other words, is the attempt to grasp an economic process as perceptible Ur-phenomenon, from out of which proceed all manifestations of life in the arcades (and, accordingly, in the nineteenth century).

(*Arcades*, 460; N1a, 6 [cf. also 391; K2, 3])

This quote surprisingly appropriates what must count as the least promising aspect of Marxian cultural criticism – the economic determinism implicit in Marx's view of culture, and Marx's own consequent underestimation of the importance of symbolic or cultural reproduction processes, as opposed to material reproduction. By regarding the relation between material and cultural production as *expression*, rather than *determination*,[4] Benjamin claims that the distinctive cultural expressions of an epoch are simultaneously material *and* symbolic, economic *and* cultural, such that the collective consciousness of nineteenth-century European culture expresses itself in a double manner. The imperatives of capitalism are expressed both in the conscious attempts of its apologists, literary and aesthetic heroes, and statesmen to generate a dominant culture that expresses the triumphs of capitalist modernity, and in the largely unconscious *reactions* to the hellish consequences of this same modernity, which are expressed, in encoded form, in a thousand inadvertent, overlooked, or otherwise worthless cultural forms. These include: fashion, advertising, the endless ebb and flow of commodities, commercial ventures, consumer fads, popular literature, journalism and feuilletons, new building forms and materials, architectural embellishments, changes in design, and the inconspicuous emergence of new forms of bodily comportment, dress, and affect that emerge as a population finds itself obliged to accommodate new productive and commercial technologies.

Marx himself, of course, had already noticed the particular dialectical structure of the industrial commodity, and described the "fetishism" of the commodity, scornfully, as a reintroduction of pre-modern religious consciousness into the modern. As it alienates actual human beings from their own nature as free producers, the commodity at the same time assumes human qualities – hence the commodity is in itself a dialectical construction, inasmuch as it is the graphic expression of the moment where two opposed concepts, subject and object, reverse. Subjects become transformed into objects through alienated industrial labor; objects, through the same process, are transformed into subjective beings. In this sense, commodities are both nature and culture, both economic and symbolic forms, or better, are the concrete appearances of the intersection of these dialectical poles. For this reason they are sites for the disclosure of a kind of historical truth about modern capitalism. Marx, who had in mind primarily manufacturing goods and raw materials, regarded this expressive function of the commodity predominantly in terms of the alienation of free labor, and the unconscious reactivation of superseded moments of collective religious consciousness necessary to make this alienation seem natural and inevitable. In this sense "the commodity" was for Marx a general concept.

Benjamin, on the other hand, recognized that commodity fetishism appeared most clearly in objects of consumption, not of production – which register and express collective consciousness of historical experience in a far more powerful and poignant manner than industrial wares. This reveals how the dialectic of commodities remained incomplete in Marx. One could say that Marx grasped the theological complexity of the commodity, but not the commodity's status as a *phantasmagoria*; that is, as a delusional expression of collective utopian fantasies and longings, whose very mode of expression itself, as delusional, ensures that those same longings remain mere utopian fantasies. In their concentration, and reversal, of the dialectical poles of subjectivity and objectivity, commodities express *both* the hellish *and* the utopian sides of human consciousness: the transmutation of humans into objects can also be figured as the dream of a reunion with an alienated nature; the transmutation of objects into subjects recalls the religious vision of a nature endowed once again with the ability to signify. As ciphers of equivalence, "meaningful" only in the language of exchange value, commodities are expressions of the theological vision of meaningless nature, or Hell. But as markers for a continuum of unfulfilled utopian expectation, commodities also point simultaneously back toward a paradisiacal pre-history and forward toward a revolutionary interruption of the continuum that perpetuates them. As expression, commodities are phantasmagoria: Benjamin saw this point very precisely, and was thus drawn to those moments in the material culture of nineteenth-century Paris where the phantasmagoric aspect emerged most vividly – the drive toward incessant novelty with which people outfitted themselves and their city constantly, and largely unconsciously, ended up quoting the primal or the prehistoric. As Benjamin wrote in the 1935 exposé on "Paris, Capital of the Nineteenth Century":

> Corresponding to the form of the new means of production, which in the beginning is still ruled by the old (Marx) are images in the collective consciousness in which the old and the new interpenetrate. These images are wish images; in them the collective seeks both to overcome and to transfigure the immaturity of the social product and the inadequacies in the social organization of production. At the same time, what emerges in these wish images is the resolute effort to distance oneself from all that is antiquated – which includes, however, the recent past. These tendencies deflect the imagination (which is given impetus by the new) back upon the primal past. In the dream in which each epoch entertains images of its successor, the latter appears wedded to

elements of primal history – that is, to elements of a classless society. And the experiences of such a society – as stored in the unconscious of the collective – engender, through interpenetration with what is new, the utopia that has left its trace in a thousand configurations of life, from enduring edifices to passing fashions. (*Arcades*, 4–5).

However, the collective *expression* of these archaic wish images, in order to become effectively reversed into a politically shocking force, must be *represented*, and recognized, precisely for what they are; and it is this representation and recognition that the dialectical image constitutes.

We can now turn to the second of the two Marx quotes mentioned above, as Benjamin moves decisively beyond Marx to solve the problem of how this graphic representation can transform wish images into dialectical images:

> A central problem of historical materialism that ought to be seen in the end: Must the Marxist understanding of history necessarily be acquired at the expense of the perceptibility of history? Or: In what way is it possible to conjoin a heightened graphicness [*Anschaulichkeit*] to the realization of Marxist method? The first stage in this undertaking will be to carry over the principle of montage into history. That is, to assemble large-scale constructions out of the smallest and most precisely cut components. Indeed, to discover in the analysis of the small individual moments the crystal of the total event.
>
> (*Arcades*, 461; N2, 6)

Here the question of method is the question of retaining graphicness against the blurring effects of a philosophy of history. Even in its inversion of Hegel's idealism, Marx's materialist historical theory preserves Hegel's insistence on the logical structure of development, and therefore generates the significance of historical appearances without any real engagement with those appearances themselves. To realize the critical power of Marx's basic insight – the primacy of the material dimension of history, and the ideological occlusion of just this fact in capitalist modernity – Benjamin proposes a methodology entirely alien to Marxist political economy. "To carry over the principle of montage into history" means, initially, to borrow an aesthetic technique of the literary avant-garde, the French Surrealists, and to apply that method beyond the aesthetic sphere, into the practice of critical historiography.

Much reading and much interpretation of Benjamin's work has had the inevitable effect of dulling this extraordinary proposal. While the Surrealists surely desired a political effect from their projects, the technique of montage was surely one that made most sense when seen as the logical outcome of an institutionally structured history of painting: rejecting the model of the solitary creative genius, the method stuck together otherwise useless or discarded found objects – paper scraps, portions of painted canvas, newspaper, ticket stubs, cigarette butts, buttons – in a construction whose power to disorient and to shock lay to a large degree in the defamiliarization effect of seeing otherwise meaningless material objects suddenly removed from the context that determines their meaninglessness. To be sure, the shocking aspect of Surrealist montages presupposes the capacity of the audience to reflect upon the very activity of aesthetic reception and appreciation: montages "mean" in the sense that they reveal something of the essentially arbitrary nature of material signification, and the capacity of aesthetic framing to render just that arbitrary quality itself as an object of aesthetic experience, hence (as an artwork) meaningful. Moreover, despite their repeated attempts to eliminate the role of subjective intention from the constructive act of montage-building itself (often with the aid of quite extravagant notions of "objective chance," automatic writing, intoxication, dream-states, and so forth) it remains clear that the Surrealist montage, like virtually all its cognate artistic products of the aesthetic and literary avant-garde, requires rather a lot of authorial in-tention. The "principle of construction" – the series of decisions of what is to count as a fragment, how it is to be secured, whether and in what way it is to be mounted, and above all what other fragments it is to be juxtaposed to – conforms in the final analysis to a recognizable narrative of aesthetic innovation, negation, and judgment; in short, of art history from the rise of representational painting through its negation in aesthetic modernism (and subsequent rebirth in postmodern realism).

Finally, it should be remembered that the Surrealist montage still leaves undecided the *imagistic* nature of the final artistic product: the shock effect of decontextualized and recontextualized material objects does not, for the Surrealists, depend upon the construction of an image from out of the assem-bled fragments; rather, it arises from the tension inherent in the relationship of the mounted fragments to one another.[5]

Benjamin's decision to carry the montage principle over into critical histo-riography implies that *historical* fragments, like the actual physical stuff of the Surrealists, can be constructed by removing them (via historical research) from their embeddedness in a particular context (in which they are recorded only insofar as they are insignificant, the "trash of history"), and "mount-ing" them in a series of textual juxtapositions – informed by a so-far missing principle of construction – such that the juxtaposed fragments constitute a constellation. And this constellation, in turn, forms an image, not in the intu-itive sense of a visual image (which would be, in the field of art, a mosaic and not a montage), but precisely in the sense of a new, *necessary* interpretation of the fragments' relationships with one another. Finally, this interpretation would also have the shocking consequence of obliging an entirely new in-terpretation of the material culture from which they were wrested, and the relationship of that material culture to the present moment. The formerly insignificant fragments, rescued and redeployed in a critical text, would shatter the "philosophy of history" that determined them as insignificant.[6]

The methodology of "constructing" dialectical images, then, stands at the crossroads of a Marxist-inspired insight into the dialectical nature of the commodity structure, on the one side, and a notion of montage and its implicit revaluation of the world of the devalued material object on the other. The materialist critic scavenges the detritus of history for those objects that resist incorporation into a triumphal story of capitalism as endless progress and that therefore express (in their very quality as trash) the frustrated utopian fantasies of a particular generation. This detritus consists of a wide range of "commodities" taken in the broadest sense: commercial articles remembered, or half-remembered, or remembered only insofar as their use-value has drained out of them; the gadgets and "furnishings" that fade into a distinctive, faintly disreputable quaintness as they make their way from the great department stores and fashionable boutiques to the discount tables and third-rate antique shops. These things are united in their status as commodities for which the status of phantasmagoria has decayed, and which, released from the cycle of economic exchange, are available as material for construction. But Benjamin's attention was just as much focused on the "detritus" of literary experiments, popular novels, pamphlets, and feuilletons, as on contemporary accounts of rapid cultural change and innovations in architectural style and ornament. This range of poor, slightly out-of-date things is the natural medium for the materialist critic who then, in a second, destructive procedure, removes these objects from the "natural" medium in which they exist – the history of endless newness and of endless progress that capitalist modernity endlessly deploys. Violently removed from this context, the detritus can then be reconfigured into a constellation such that the *truth* of the fate of these objects, what has happened to them and what this fate says about capitalism, springs forth in a sudden, shocking image. The image is "of" the commodity: but now the commodity no longer simply "expresses" the collective hopes and fantasies of a collective. It now *represents* that hope, and the expressive quality of the commodity itself, in a reversed context: as the very fate in which collective hopes are consistently, necessarily, and brutally suppressed and denied. Represented as the medium in which collective fantasies are denied, the commodity now "means" its opposite. The fantasy world of material well-being promised by every commodity now is revealed as a Hell of unfulfillment; the promise of eternal newness and unlimited progress encoded in the imperatives of technological change and the cycles of consumption now appear as their opposite, as primal history, the mythic compulsion toward endless repetition.[7] The slight aging of the "failed" commodity, through criticism, reveals capitalism's darkest secret: the allure of the brand-new hides the essence of capitalism as an endless compulsion to repeat. Stripped of their gleam, and reconfigured, cultural goods revert to their true status: as fossils unearthed from an ongoing history of compulsion, violence, and disappointment.

The peculiar fusion of the primally old within the very heart of the most fashionably up-to-date – what Baudelaire had diagnosed as the essence of modern beauty and indeed of modernity itself – is now revealed as the dialectical explosive at the heart of the commodity itself. To ignite this charge, the dialectical image "pictures" the commodity *no differently*, in one sense, than a predominant culture does. It merely shifts the context. The dialectical oppositions or force-fields at whose frontier the commodity is forged – subject and object, history and nature, consciousness and material being – are developed into their most extreme form: at the intersecting axes of subject and object, nature and history, time and repetition, the dialectical image springs forth as a "stop" or a freeze, as the monadic crystallization of the supposedly implacable progression of historical time.[8]

Hence the *dialectics* of the dialectical image is precisely the fact that the image represents the commodity *as it truly is*, and this representation, Benjamin believes, derives its distinctive shocking quality precisely insofar as it has the capacity to awaken a collective subject from a dream-state in which it has fallen. The awakening from dream, then, is for Benjamin the quintessence of dialectical thought as such. And insofar as Benjamin is convinced that such an experience of awakening is, in dialectical terms, most intimately related to a form of remembrance,[9] we see that the method of constructing dialectical images is itself also to be understood as the development of a new form of critical memory and a new conception of the images of historical time.

The close of Hegel's *Phenomenology of Spirit* contains a famous invocation of historical time at the moment of its culmination: at the climactic moment of its self-return and full self-knowledge, Spirit remembers or "recollects" [*erinnern*] into itself the mass of historical moments that otherwise remain contingent and unrelated, dispersed through time. By bringing back within itself what had otherwise remained externalized content, Spirit annuls the distinction between past and present. It stages this recuperation of the historically contingent in a final, majestic panorama, a historical review of the images of its own self-development, presented as "a slow movement and succession of spirits (*Geistern*), a gallery of pictures, each of which, endowed with the entire wealth of Spirit, moves so slowly precisely because the Self must permeate and digest all this wealth into its substance."[10]

Time for Hegel is equated with history, and history is fully disclosed in the retrospective gathering of otherwise discrete historical images under the sovereignty of a Self, one for whom these images can now be recollected as part of a narrative drama of self-creation. Those historical moments or images that otherwise were threatened with annihilation are saved from oblivion, but saved only insofar as their significance, their correct interpretation, is produced as they are "digested" by absolute Spirit. Each of these moments, recollected and incorporated, are no longer simply images of a particular historical event, stage, or epoch; they no longer *mean* what they simply *show*. Rather, the members of this "gallery of pictures" mean what they mean insofar as they are admitted to the gallery, related to one another through their recuperation in Spirit. And this is the condition for the claim that each image contains, in microcosm, the entire wealth or Spirit or the entire span of historical time coiled within it, each from a slightly different perspective. One would also expect that a very great number of "spirits," concrete historical images, would ultimately be incapable of contributing to the goal of "the revelation of the depth of spiritual life,"[11] and would not be recollected and interiorized, and thus be irretrievably lost to memory, obliterated. Hence the imperative of full self-knowledge replicates in metaphysical language the Christian vision of a final judgment, wherein some spirits are endowed with the full richness of the historical adventure, thereby becoming not just "slow" but in effect timeless. The others receive the judgment of oblivion.[12]

The "gallery of pictures" Hegel describes at the close of the *Phenomenology of Spirit* is a vision of dialectical images – images of moments of concrete historical experience which, removed from their embeddedness in an uninterpreted and unintelligible historical medium, rescued through a fantastic memory, become capable of bearing the whole of historical time within them. This celebration of the redemptive power of memory to cancel the contingent and fleeting character of historical particularity, to bear within memory the wounds of historical suffering by rendering concrete historical moments into representations of history itself, is, as Marcuse described it in *Eros and Civilization*, "one of the noblest tasks of thought." Marcuse saw Hegel groping, with limited success, toward a radical and emancipatory vision of collective critical remembrance.[13] But Hegel's dialectical images are also encoded with a violent will to eradicate, and not merely redeem, the historically contingent. The "gallery of pictures" at the end of Spirit's "highway of despair" replicates, oddly, what Benjamin had described as the "antinomies of the allegorical" in *The Origin of the German Tragic Drama*: subjective intention seeks to redeem the contingent dimension of human experience, which otherwise remains "mere" nature, profane, horrible, but it does so only by inflicting violence upon that dimension far greater than historical time ever could have.

The *Phenomenology*'s evocation of the languid, twilit, "slow motion" of meaning-laden historical images anticipates (by only a few years) the innovation of the panorama, whose popularity in the Paris of the 1820s and 1830s Benjamin meticulously documented in the *Arcades Project*. To get a sense of how Hegel's vision of historical imagery would receive a treatment on Benjamin's terms we could do worse than image his gallery of pictures installed in a gas-lit Parisian arcade, a refuge for shoppers eager for a diversion and a rest on a rainy weekend afternoon. The capacity to remain comfortably seated while the momentous and exotic rolls gently by, framed for observation, anticipates the long railway journey that would emerge as the paradigm for the visual culture of the exotic, and offered a first rehearsal for the experience of cinema-going at the mall multiplex.[14] The panoramas allowed spectators to witness a momentous historical event, a military victory, or a famous or exotic cityscape, painted on an enormous circular wall that trundled slowly around the audience seated comfortably within.[15] The rain drums steadily on the plate-glass above, the gaslight flickers, the wooden wheels rumble gently on their tracks. The audience murmurs and exhales softly as the images roll slowly on and on, lulled by the peculiar admixture of fascination and lethargy distinctive of mass entertainment on a rainy day.

Hence a secret mechanism comes into play to ensure, through the construction of a phantasmagorical utensil for collective amusement and distraction, that the comforting vision of a progressive history (first one event, then the next following from it, then the next) is maintained precisely by not being progressive at all. The panorama revolves endlessly; its history is precisely repetition, the absence of real change.

Benjamin's recognition of the panorama as a crystallization of the commodification of the myth of historical progress is characteristic of his unique interpretation of the dynamics of historical time in the *Arcades Project* and elsewhere. Even if Hegel does not figure prominently in Benjamin's philosophical speculation on the nature of historical time and historical experience, his figure looms large in the background, and his version of "dialectical images" (not a term Hegel would have used, naturally), and the philosophy of history and the dialectic they rest upon, are the foil against which Benjamin developed his own views.[16] Benjamin was certainly aware of this context, as the following passage illustrates:

> On the dialectical image. In it lies time. Already with Hegel, time enters into dialectic. But the Hegelian dialectic knows time solely as the properly historical, if not psychological, time of thinking. The time differential [*Zeitdifferential*] in which alone the dialectical image is real is still unknown to him. Attempt to

show this with regard to fashion. Real time enters the dialectical image not in natural magnitude – let alone psychologically – but in its smallest gestalt. All in all, the temporal momentum [*das Zeitmoment*] in the dialectical image can be determined only through confrontation with another concept. This concept is the "now of recognizability." (*Arcades*, 867; Q°21)

The transmutation of wish images into dialectical images is only possible through a temporal arrest in which the dreamlike illusion of historical progress is shattered, and revealed as the hell of repetition. Sites where Benjamin was drawn to collect material for the *Arcades Project* are those where this dreamlike illusion has begun to wear thin, where "time differentials" become murkily perceptible under the surface bustle of a capitalist culture. These are sites that demand a dialectical image to be constructed: "The realization of dream elements in the course of waking up is the canon of dialectics. It is paradigmatic for the thinker and binding for the historian" (*Arcades*, 464; N4, 4).

The fading arcades themselves are, of course, the primary site, where once-fashionable shops, wares, and building styles hang on, briefly, before their destruction for Hausmann's new Paris. But Benjamin is also drawn to a fascinating range of sites where time, contra Hegel, seems to stop its steady forward flow: overheated middle-class parlors, whatever is dim, poorly lit, or rained on; boredom, waiting, idling, and distraction; the flâneur's slow tracings of the labyrinth of Parisian streets,[17] the gambler's intoxication with repetition, the endless ebb and flow of fashion. In particular Benjamin did not fail to notice that the mid-nineteenth-century figures such as Baudelaire, Nietzsche, and Blanqui speculated on the structure of an endless historical repetition or eternal return precisely as the reality of a commodity economy descended upon them. Such places and affects are invitations for interruption, and Benjamin is convinced that interruption is the truest revolutionary act.

Benjamin's work as a whole can be said to proceed from a distinctive if underdeveloped conception of an alternative temporality or historical time. His very earliest writing, as has often been noted, explores this alternative conception of historical time or historical experience in relation to the youth movement. The essay on "The Life of Students," written in 1914–15 when Benjamin was still in his early twenties, begins by dismissing a predominant conception of progressive, linear historical time, and instead advocates "a particular condition in which history appears to be concentrated in a single focal point, like those that have traditionally been found in the utopian images of the philosophers" (*SW* I, 37). This vision of historical time distilled to one single fulfilled moment, familiar from theological discourse, was, for the young Benjamin, not to be thought at all under the idea of historical progress, but rather in light of a profoundly anti-Hegelian, indeed a subversive, subterranean awareness of historical time, according to which "the elements of the ultimate condition [*Endzustand*] do not manifest themselves as formless progressive tendencies, but are deeply rooted in every present in the form of the most endangered, excoriated, and ridiculed ideas and products of the creative mind." This notion that the "trash of history"[18] – small pieces of historical experience otherwise dismissed as insignificant, beneath attention, unassimilable – is precisely the material for images of the utopian "ultimate condition," an arrest of historical time and an insight into the structure and condition of historical time as such, remained intact throughout Benjamin's career, through the widest swings of Benjamin's literary, political, and philosophical interests (*SW* I, 37).

Hence, three elements of this alternative temporality should be distinguished. First is the notion that an alternative temporality emerges, against the predominant version of continuous, chronological time, as interruptions, discontinuities, unassimilable moments, repetitions, lags, or disturbances; as unplanned or uncanny repetitions or recapitulations, in short, as "time differentials." Second and no less important is the idea that these time differentials are contained in (or expressed by) concrete historical moments or even objects that, in the "normal" context of historical time, would be dismissed as immemorable, worthless, as not candidates for meaning. Third, and more difficult, is the notion that the "trash of history" can be revealed to be a time differential only insofar as it is removed from – "blasted out of" – its embeddedness in a dominant, approved tradition of interpretation and reception, and reconfigured, rescued from the history that consigns it to oblivion, yet in such a way that it shockingly reveals just that history for what it is: Hell, a history of catastrophe.

As a collective undergoes its own history, sites emerge where an alternative history attempts to break through its oppressive surface. This alternative history is, in this context, an experience of pre-history, a history of unfulfilled wishes for a collective life free of violence, injustice, and want. These wishes are expressed as wish images sedimented in a society's material culture; in its commodities, its institutions of consumption and distraction, its building styles and architectural fashions, its popular literature. Wish images, figuring a proximate future of fulfillment, reassuring a collective of perpetual novelty in the form of a meliorist history, invariably end up quoting the ancient past. Wish images are phantasmagorical demands for release from a cycle of repetition that has grown to appear as second nature. And these wish images, under the gaze of the materialist historian, offer sites where what is expressed in the collective dream-time of capitalism can be ripped from its context and reassembled in a constellation that represents material elements in their true relation to their own mythic history. Nowhere is this dialectic of time more evident than in those commodities, places, and styles whose own fashion has waned: their exile from the cycle of consumption, their "ruining" by a commodity economy, renders their relation to the slumbering collective more visibly tense, and qualifies them as material for construction. This transformation of wish images to dialectical images serves both the redemption of the reviled object and the shocking deployment of the truth-content of commodities – their Hellish *and* their utopian core. Such a deployment marks a moment of awakening, the transformation of a "time differential," lag, discontinuity, or uneven spot in the collective experience of time into a moment of collective awakening, a "Now of recognizability": a "dialectics at a standstill." The image produced will, monadically, compact the entire span of historical time within it: the represented commodity, the "object of history" itself, contains in monadic form both the mythic history of capitalism and the tradition of the oppressed that hides beneath it.[19]

Recalling the quotation from the "N" convolute with which we began, we see how the "doctrine" of the dialectical image requires this wholly distinctive understanding of the dynamics of time: cutting through the narrative surface of past, present and future, "what-has-been," in its sudden reactualization, "crystallizes with the Now to form a constellation. For, while the relation of the present to the past is a purely temporal, continuous one, the relation of what-has-been to the Now is dialectical: is not progression but image, suddenly emergent." Hence dialectical images are things that one "encounters" in the linguistic sediment of the material culture of the nineteenth century. They are the perceptible "ur-phenomena" of history, heterogeneous moments of truth.

The time of the dialectical image, understood in this way, is in fact Messianic time, the time of the redemption of the world and the demand for the end of history understood as history's stop, rather than its culmination. This notion of dialectical images as Messianic moments of arrest, usually downplayed in the "N" convolute and in the exposés, rises to prominence in Benjamin's last "On the Concept of History." There, dialectical images are interpreted in the context of an openly theological vision of Messianic time, as the famous image of the first thesis, in which theology is pictured as a hidden dwarf pulling the strings that allow the puppet, "historical materialism" to appear to play brilliant chess (*Ill*, 253).

Clearly, a distinctive tension emerges here, between the dialectical image understood as a unique site marking the interruption of the truly heterogeneous into the continuum of repetition, that is, the dialectical image as an *event* of a new time, on the one hand, and the dialectical image as the *production* of a materialist critic who has mastered a methodology, however occluded, for the removal and recombination of recovered historical material, on the other. This tension between the subjectivity and the objectivity of the image is, of course, the repeat of the dialectics of subject and object that constitutes the possibility of the image in the first place. The Messianic conception of an alternative temporality and the notion of the dialectical image as a "Now" that "springs forth" into profane time proves difficult to reconcile with the notion of the dialectical image as the product of the painstaking application of historical method.

Benjamin's "On the Concept of History" seem to address this problem, at once drastically increasing the importance of the Messianic dimension of the dialectical images, while at the same time describing them, and indeed dialectics as such, more as a set of heuristic principles to guide the work of the historical materialist than as a historical event in its own right. "Materialist historiography" now emerges as a competing method of historical interpretation contrasted again and again to historicism. "Thinking" – a term halfway, as it were, between the passive reception of objective historical truth and the active construction of images through subjective agency – now appears as a discipline or practice that mediates between the Messianic emergence of "what-has-been" and the political demands of the present, as in this distinctive passage:

> Historicism rightly culminates in universal history. Materialist historiography differs from it as to method more clearly than from any other kind. Universal history has no theoretical armature. Its method is additive; it musters a mass of data to fill the homogeneous, empty time. Materialist historiography, on the other hand, is based on a constructive principle. Thinking involves not only the flow of thoughts, but their arrest as well. Where thinking suddenly stops in a configuration pregnant with tensions, it gives that configuration a shock, by which it crystallizes into a monad. A historical materialist approaches a historical subject only where he encounters it as a monad. In this structure he recognizes the sign of a Messianic cessation of happening, or, put differently, a revolutionary chance in the fight for the oppressed past. He takes cognizance of it in order to blast a specific era out of the homogeneous course of history – blasting a specific life out of the era or a specific work out of the lifework. As a result of this method the lifework is preserved in this work and at the same time cancelled; in the lifework, the era; and in the era, the entire course of history. *(Ill, 262–63)*

It is certainly not clear how this passage "solves" the dialectic of subjectivity and objectivity, of method and time, that lies at the heart of the dialectical image. Benjamin's final strategy was, as I have suggested, a dual one; emphasizing both the Messianic dimension of the dialectical image as a "Messianic cessation of happening" while simultaneously reformulating this dimension as part of a heuristic description of the distinctive mental features of the "materialist historian." How successful this strategy ultimately was is a question that depends on what our criterion for success is, of course. It is perhaps no accident that here, in one of Benjamin's most comprehensive (and baffling) statements of his late method, the language of the dialectical image once again consciously reverts to Hegel, both as an acknowledgement and also, surely, as a final settling of accounts. Like Hegel's, Benjamin's dialectic necessarily can never finish with the historical context, just as it can never finally establish the monadic structure of the historical object, in its radical particularity, as independent and unmediated. *Aufhebung* or sublation, the methodological necessity of preserving-as-negating-as-transcending history in the construction of the genuine historical object, involves at its heart an intractable degree of indeterminacy in any attempt to resolve or stabilize the status of the object and the subject of historical knowing. Benjamin finally defers this question by appealing to a Messianic horizon of expectation (see Thesis 18; *Ill*, 264). Such a deferral may in the end be the most appropriate response to the demand to justify, through theory, the possibility of a "Now" of recognizability. But, it also renders a range of quite pertinent questions concerning the dialectical image – can anyone other than Benjamin find and/or make them, for example – more or less structurally unanswerable.

Very like Hegel, Benjamin found himself in a deeply paradoxical position in terms of the theoretical justification of his dialectics: solving the relation between subjectivity (method) and objectivity (time) would only be possible from a perspective that took the relation as an opposition that had already been resolved. But this would entail that history, too, would be always already conceived from the perspective of its culmination. Unlike Hegel, Benjamin refuses this option: he remains, stubbornly, on the side of the unassimilated and the heterogeneous. But this means that his own account of his critical agency must necessarily remain poised at the unresolved cusp of these oppositions. "Dialectics at a standstill" also characterizes Benjamin's own elaboration of the dialectical image, and, in this case, such a frozen dialectics places some severe limits on our ability, in the present, to think with Benjamin beyond Benjamin. If the dialectical image was the quintessence of his method, this fact both establishes the continuing attraction of an imagistic approach to radical cultural criticism, and the profound difficulties in appropriating such an approach in the present. Benjamin's dialectical images are, as he meant them to be, *sui generis*.

NOTES

1. The most sustained, sophisticated and compelling interpretation is to be found in Susan Buck-Morss, *The Dialectics of Seeing: Walter Benjamin and the Arcades Project* (Cambridge: MIT Press, 1989). See also Michael Jennings, *Dialectical Images: Walter Benjamin's Theory of Literary Criticism* (Ithaca: Cornell University Press, 1987).

2. Buck-Morss, *Dialectics of Seeing*, 67; Rolf Tiedemann, "Dialectics at a Standstill: Approaches to the *Passagen-Werk*," in *On Walter Benjamin*, ed. Gary Smith (Cambridge, MA: MIT Press, 1989), 284.

3. For explorations on the problem of the objectivity of the dialectical image see Max Pensky, *Melancholy Dialectics: Walter Benjamin and the Play of Mourning* (Amherst: University of Massachusetts Press, 1993), ch. 6; Buck-Morss, *Dialectics of Seeing*, 228ff.

4. "On the doctrine of the ideological superstructure. It seems, at first sight, that Marx wanted to establish here only a causal relation between superstructure and infrastructure. But already the observation that ideologies of the superstructure reflect conditions falsely and invidiously goes beyond this. The question, in effect, is the following: if the infrastructure in a certain way (in the materials of thought and experience) determines the superstructure, but if such determination is not reducible to simple reflection, how is it then . . . to be characterized? As its expression. The superstructure is the expression of the infrastructure. The economic conditions under which society exists are expressed in the superstructure – precisely as, with the sleeper, an overfull stomach finds not its effect but its expression in the contents of dreams, which, from a causal point of view, it may be said to 'condition.' The collective, from the first, expresses the conditions of its life. These find their expression in the dream and their interpretation in the awakening" (*Arcades*, 392; K2, 5).

5. For a full account of Benjamin's relation to the Surrealists see Margaret Cohen, *Profane Illuminations* (Berkeley: University of California Press, 1993), and also *Melancholy Dialectics*, ch. 5.

6. "Balzac was the first to speak of the ruins of the bourgeoisie. But it was Surrealism that first opened our eyes to them. The development of the forces of production shattered the wish symbols of the previous century, even before the monuments representing them had collapsed. In the nineteenth century, this development worked to emancipate the forms of construction from art, just as in the sixteenth century the sciences freed them from philosophy. A start is made with architecture as engineered construction. Then comes the reproduction of nature as photography. The creation of fantasy prepares to become practical as commercial art. Literature submits to montage as the feuilleton. All these products are on the point of entering the market as commodities. But they linger on the threshold. From this epoch derive the interieurs, the exhibition halls and the panoramas. They are residues of a dream world. The realization of dream elements, in the course of waking up, is the paradigm of dialectical thinking. Thus, dialectical thinking is the organ of historical awakening. Every epoch, in fact, not only dreams the one to follow but, in dreaming, precipitates its awakening. It bears its end within itself and unfolds it – as Hegel already noticed – as cunning. With the destabilization of the market economy, we begin to recognize the monuments of the bourgeoisie as

ruins even before they have crumbled" ("Paris, Capital of the Nineteenth Century. Exposé of 1935" [*Arcades*, 13]).

7. "The 'modern,' the time of Hell. The punishments of Hell are always the newest things going on in this domain. What is at issue is not that 'the same thing happens over and over,' and even less would it be a question here of eternal return. It is rather that precisely in that which is newest the face of the world never alters, that this newest remains, in every respect, the same. This constitutes the eternity of Hell. To determine the totality of traits by which 'the modern' is defined would be to represent Hell" (*Arcades*, 544; S1, 5).

8. The notion that the dialectical image springs forth at the crossing-point of dialectical axes is the central argument of Susan Buck-Morss's *The Dialectics of Seeing*: "The dialectical image is a way of seeing that crystallizes antithetical elements by providing the axes of their alignment. Benjamin's conception is essentially static . . . He charts philosophical ideas visually within an unreconciled and transitory field of oppositions that can perhaps best be pictured in terms of coordinates of contradictory terms, the 'synthesis' of which is not a movement toward resolution, but the point at which their axes intersect . . . His unfolding of concepts in their 'extremes' can be visualized as antithetical polarities of axes that cross each other, revealing a 'dialectical image' at the null point, with its contradictory 'moments' as its axial fields" (210).

9. "There is a wholly unique experience of the dialectic. The compelling – the drastic – experience, which refutes everything 'gradual' about becoming and shows all seeming 'development' to be dialectical reversal, eminently and thoroughly composed, is the awakening from dream . . . The new, dialectical method of doing history presents itself as the art of experiencing the present as a waking world, a world to which that dream we name the past refers in truth. To pass through and carry out *what has been* in remembering the dream! Therefore: remembering and awakening are most intimately related. Awakening is namely the dialectical, Copernican turn of remembrance" (*Arcades*, 389; K1, 3).

10. G. W. F. Hegel, *Phänomenlogie des Geistes* (Frankfurt am Main: Suhrkamp Verlag, 1986), 590.

11. Ibid., 591.

12. One way of imagining the mode of this judgment is hinted at in a passage of Hegel's *Reason in History*: "One may contemplate history from the point of view of happiness. But actually history is not the soil of happiness. The periods of happiness are blank pages in it. There is, it is true, satisfaction in world history. But it is not the kind that is called happiness, for it is satisfaction of purposes that are above particular interests." G. W. F. Hegel, *Reason in History*, translated and with an introduction by Robert S. Hartman (Indianapolis: Bobbs-Merrill, 1953), 33.

13. Herbert Marcuse, *Eros and Civilization* (Boston: Beacon Press, 1955), 232ff.

14. On train journeys and the changed perception of time and visuality, see Wolfgang Schivelbusch, *Geschichte der Eisenbahnreise: Zur Industrialisierung von Raum und Zeit im 19ten Jahrhundert* (Munich: Hanser, 1977), as well as Stephen Kern, *The Culture of Time and Space* (Cambridge, MA: Harvard University Press, 1983).

15. "Setup of the panoramas: View from a raised platform, surrounded by a balustrade, of surfaces lying round about and beneath. The painting runs along

a cylindrical wall approximately a hundred meters long and twenty meters high. The principle panoramas of the great panorama painter Prévost: Paris, Toulon, Rome, Naples, Amsterdam, Tilsit, Wagram, Calais, Antwerp, London, Florence, Jerusalem, Athens. Among his pupils: Daguerre" (*Arcades*, 528; Q1a, 1).

16. In his autobiographical reminiscence of his friendship with Benjamin, Gershom Scholem recounts that, to his own surprise, Benjamin seemed very familiar with Hegel's work, and sympathetic to significant elements of it, a stance highly unusual for the predominantly neo-Kantian philosophical culture of the time. See Scholem, *Friendship*, 30–31.

17. "The city is the realization of the ancient dream of humanity, the labyrinth. It is this reality to which the flâneur, without knowing it, devotes himself" (*Arcades*, 430; M6a).

18. For the reference to the "trash" or "refuse" of history see *Arcades*, 461; N2, 6 and N2, 7, passages I will return to later in the chapter.

19. "If the object of history is to be blasted out of the continuum of historical succession, that is because its monadological structure demands it. This structure first comes to light in the extracted object itself. And it does so in the form of the historical confrontation that makes up the interior (and, as it were, the bowels) of the historical object, and into which all the forces and interests of history enter on a reduced scale. It is owing to this monadological structure that the historical object finds represented in its interior its own fore-history and after-history" (*Arcades*, 475; N10, 3).

10

MARGARET COHEN

Benjamin's phantasmagoria:
the *Arcades Project*

The *Arcades Project* is the centerpiece of what Benjamin called his "Parisian production cycle," an archeology of the emergence of high capitalist modernity that engaged him from the late 1920s until his death.[1] Begun as an essay that was to offer a historical ground for *One-Way Street*'s phenomenology of modern life (1928), the *Arcades Project* had expanded to thirty-six copious folders (known as "Convolutes") of notes and reflections by the time Benjamin was forced by the Nazi Occupation to flee Paris and the Bibliothèque Nationale where he had spent twelve years sifting through "the rags, the refuse" that he deemed his preferred materials of historiographical construction (*Arcades*, 460; N1a, 8). Benjamin was never to transform his notes into a finished work, taking his own life in September 1940, after having been denied an exit visa to Spain. On his final failed journey across the Pyrenees Mountains, he was reported to have been carrying a large black briefcase filled with a manuscript, which was never recovered. Glittering like one of the allegorical emblems dear to its owner, this briefcase gives concrete form to the simultaneous atmosphere of loss and possibility that enshrouds Benjamin's *Arcades Project*, whose notes and citations raise questions central to the entire materialist project, that, however, dissipate into pregnant and repetitive brooding, dense though evocative aphorisms, the dust of the nineteenth century.

The closest Benjamin came to offering a vision of the completed *Arcades* were two summaries of the project, a 1935 essay written for his colleagues of the Frankfurt School, and a 1939 version in French drafted to solicit funding from an American donor that is surely one of the more unusual grant proposals ever written. But if we take these exposés and the *Arcades Project*'s folders together with the tremendously influential essays that they undergird – essays such as "Surrealism – The Last Snapshot of the European Intelligentsia" (1929), "Little History of Photography" (1931), "The Work of Art in the Age of its Technological Reproducibility" (1936), "The Storyteller" (1936), "Eduard Fuchs, Collector and Historian" (1937), "The Paris of the Second

Empire in Baudelaire" (1938), "On Some Motifs in Baudelaire" (1939), and "On the Concept of History" (1940)" – it is not overstating the case to say that the *Arcades Project* has set the terms in which interdisciplinary scholars have debated the contours of cultural modernity in the last twenty years. Benjamin's contributions include the content of his analysis, such as (1) his emphasis on a distinctive temporality of progress that saturates all of modernity's cultural products; (2) his insights that the most ephemeral and seemingly trivial practices of modernity such as fashion, advertising, and mass entertainment offer privileged insights into not only the degradations of capitalism, but also its utopian possibilities; and (3) his account of the profound transformations of art, aesthetics, and sense perception itself resulting from the historical processes of industrialization and commodification. The *Arcades Project* has also informed recent critical and cultural theory with its distinctive mode of historiography that yokes the principle of writing history from the archive with the imperative to invent an alternative to grand narratives of progress. Benjamin was particularly interested in the potential of montage, a technique made famous by the European avant-garde of his time. For Benjamin, montage was not only a style but a philosophy of history: it entailed focusing on the discontinuities separating past and present, and emphasizing a utopian rather than progressive notion of historical transformation, as a way to preserve a reservoir of hope in otherwise damaged life.[2] The extraordinary impact of the *Arcades Project* across disciplines and subjects in recent years is not diminished because it dwells under the sign of failure. As Benjamin learned from Marcel Proust, another chronicler of modernity who realized the extraordinary opportunity offered when its ideological authority started to decay, failure can be a powerfully enabling pose in interrogating an episteme that apotheosizes "success at any cost," to cite the words of a Balzac hero (Rastignac) who set out to conquer Paris at the time of the city's advent to what Benjamin called capital of the nineteenth century.

Why did Benjamin choose to locate the apotheosis of modernity in Paris? For a materialist who placed economic and technological transformation at the basis of cultural expression, London might seem to have a better claim to the designation, capital of emergent modernity. England, after all, predated France in the technological innovations of the Industrial Revolution, the financial practices of speculative capitalism, and the empire building of the modern colonial project. But, as Marx pointed out, social formations develop unevenly, and Benjamin was fascinated with France's premier contribution to modernity's political and cultural contours. Across a century of revolutions centered in Paris, France invented modern republican democracy and the first modern political radicalisms; Paris was home to the genesis of mass culture, as the *ancien régime* society of the spectacle was refunctioned for post-Revolutionary society; and Paris was also the birthplace of artistic modernity in the forms of both the realist and avant-garde aesthetics that went on to global celebrity. Benjamin gave politics and culture a privileged place in his archeology of modernity because of his commitment to the political and cultural avant-garde of his own present, whose radical social aspirations he shared. As Benjamin underscores in the "On the Concept of History," history is always written from the vantage point of the present; the lost past flashes to view because it resonates with the crises and challenges that present themselves with great urgency in the historian's present.

Benjamin's point of departure for understanding modernity was Marx's account of capitalism as it had been reworked by Georg Lukács in "Reification and the Consciousness of the Proletariat" (1922), an essay Benjamin first read together with Asja Lacis and Ernst Bloch while vacationing on Capri in 1924. In the "Reification" essay, Lukács expanded on crucial but undeveloped comments in Marx concerning the effect of the triumph of the commodity form on human experience. Central to Lukács's account were Marx's observations concerning how capitalism transformed the relation between humans and things. Commodities alienated people from their labor when they separated producers from their products in the circuits of capitalist production and consumption. This labor, however, retained an uncanny power of its own which was displaced onto the commodity, and which then returned, via the commodity, to haunt humans, once the commodity's links to the producer had been forgotten.

Marx called this mystifying power of disembodied human labor commodity fetishism in the first volume of *Capital*. Lukács renamed the process "reification," proposing that it saturated all dimensions of capitalist social experience, from workers' ability to grasp their own exploitation to the proletarianization of intellectual labor and even epistemology; Lukács observed, for example, that Kant's preoccupation with the divide separating subject from object was a conceptual manifestation of the reification splitting worker from his or her product. To the extent that Lukács not only proposed but detailed how capitalist processes of production and consumption could have far-reaching effects on a society extending from the domain of economics to culture and even everyday life, his analysis was crucial to understanding the modern social formation as a totality.

Lukács renamed commodity fetishism reification in order to give a more scientific cast to the supernatural term proposed by Marx. Marx's rhetoric was, however, motivated by a crucial feature of high capitalism that he was the first to point out, though he did not theorize it fully: the fact that its thoroughgoing transformations produced phenomena which manifested an irrationality that the Enlightenment had claimed would disappear with the demise of religion. Instead, however, the emergence of modernity produced new forms of superstition and myth. Throughout his writings, Marx couches these new enchantments of capitalism in rhetoric drawn from the domain of parapsychology and the supernatural, and the fact that he replaced theory with rhetoric indicates his own Enlightenment discomfort with an aspect of modernity that he simultaneously finds enormously intriguing. Benjamin, in contrast, was nowhere more at home than in tracking such irrational processes, which he too understood as fundamental to capitalism's power. Throughout his Parisian production cycle, he sought to give his readers some sense of what he termed modernity's "fascination," as well as to explain the mystified processes on which such fascination was based. In best dialectical fashion, he allied such demystification with a moment of what he called "reversal" or "turn around" [*Umschwung*]. Benjamin emphasized these fascinating processes because they were invested with a collective's hopes and desires, as well as being mystified, and thus, he reasoned, expressed aspirations for a better life, even if in degraded and ambivalent form. One crucial task of the historiographer was to name and therefore release the utopian component swirled among the degradation in a process Benjamin called "rescue" in Convolute N.

When Benjamin sought to describe phenomena in such a way as simultaneously to convey their appeal, to dismantle their mystification, and to transform it, he pursued the three faces of historiographical analysis Hegel termed sublation [*Aufhebung*], although, as Benjamin repeatedly emphasized, he studied the refuse of history and used fragmentary methods of narration at the farthest remove from Hegel's totalizing project. But how to write rescuing critique was quite a challenge that Benjamin placed at the core of his methodological musings throughout the Parisian production cycle. These musings are concentrated most densely in Convolutes K and N, and he distilled their import for historiography with aphoristic bravura in his final "On the Concept of History." Repeatedly, Benjamin stressed that one crucial component to rescuing critique would be a distinctive form of narration constructed out of a historical moment's concrete and telling details. According to Benjamin, "a central problem of historical materialism" was whether "the Marxist understanding of history [must] necessarily be acquired at the expense of the perceptibility of history? Or: in what way is it possible to conjoin a heightened graphicness [*Anschaulichkeit*] to the realization of the Marxist method? The first stage in this undertaking will be to carry over the principle of montage into history. That is, to assemble large-scale constructions out of the smallest and most precisely cut components. Indeed, to discover in the analysis of the small individual moment the crystal of the total event" (*Arcades*, 461; N2, 6).

When Benjamin first started his arcades project in the late 1920s, he was intrigued by the possibility of a narrative that would achieve such graphicness by incorporating into its construction expressive forms from the historical moment under discussion. His initial working title for the *Arcades Project* was "Parisian Arcades. A Dialectical *Feérie*" (C, 322). The significance of the term dialectical is clear enough, but we also should not underestimate the importance of *féerie*, a word coined in the Paris of 1823 to describe a form of theatrical spectacle that enjoyed great success in the middle decades of the nineteenth century. In the *féerie*, supernatural characters were portrayed for the audience, and their irrational power was conveyed by means of extensive mechanical special effects. The fact that Benjamin elected the *féerie* out of the manifold spectacles making use of the new technology devised across the nineteenth century – spectacles like the diorama, the panorama, photography, and the wax museum – indicates his interest in Marx's perception that there was a deep link between supernatural practices and the advent of modern capitalism. In contrast to Marx, however, Benjamin not only employed supernatural rhetoric but sought to understand how, as Marx might have put it, the content goes beyond the phrase. Throughout the fragments of the project, Benjamin records details on nineteenth-century practices concerned with the supernatural, in keeping with the archaeological precept that the starting point for understanding any historical motif is recuperating how it is "embedded" in the culture that produced it.[3] Indeed, in one fragment, Benjamin explicitly asks why the nineteenth century, an era characterized by enormous technological and industrial transformations in the name of progress, was also simultaneously the century of spiritualism [*Spiritismus*].

Benjamin subsequently abandoned the notion that his project might be some form of dialectically illuminating *féerie*, commenting that he found the title too poetic. But it is perhaps more appropriate to say that he now envisioned structuring his project with the help of poetics from his own time. Above all, Benjamin was interested in the potential of Surrealism. Benjamin had heeded well the Marxian precept that a privileged moment to study the ideology of a social formation was when it was still under construction; when the raw joints and seams of its components had not yet been naturalized and/or masked. From the Surrealists along with Proust, Benjamin took the notion that an equally important moment was when a social formation's structures started to decay, as their workings once more became visible. In the *Arcades Project* exposé, Benjamin writes, "Balzac was the first to speak of the ruins of the bourgeoisie. But it was Surrealism that first opened our eyes to them. The development of the forms of production shattered the

wish symbols of the previous century, even before the monuments representing them had collapsed" ("Exposé of 1935," *Arcades*, 13). Surrealism also
interested Benjamin because the movement seized the supernatural dimension to modernity; what the movement's leader, André Breton, called the
"modern marvelous," and what its co-founder, Louis Aragon, called "modern mythologies" in his *Peasant of Paris* that first sparked Benjamin's attention to the expressiveness of the arcades. But the Surrealists refunctioned
this "marvelous" from commodity fetishism into a disruptive moment when
two hitherto separated realities with profound but hidden correspondences
came into contact, revealing a third repressed reality, or, as the movement's
founders so famously put it, a surreality. Surrealism understood this moment
as both an experience – the encounter – and a form of representation with
revolutionary potential which Breton termed the image. In Benjamin's terminology, the Surrealist encounter/image produced what he called "a profane
illumination."

When the Surrealists spoke of repression apropos of the encounter/image,
they invoked the concept with a full sense of its psychoanalytic significance.
Breton had discovered psychoanalysis while training as a neurologist, and the
Surrealists were the first thinkers to undertake the fusion of psychoanalysis
and materialism that would preoccupy materialists during the later twentieth century. In the encounters which destroyed the gray façade of everyday
banality, Breton speculated in texts like *Nadja* and *Mad Love*, material was
released where the content of the individual unconscious fused with dangerous but exhilarating repressed contents of a collective unconscious, though
Breton was not too specific about how to translate Freud's model of the
psyche from individual to society. Rather, Breton focused on the transformative potential of repressed material; he envisioned Surrealism as a kind
of rogue cultural therapy that could free modern society of its ghosts by
bringing them into what the *First Surrealist Manifesto* called "the light of
the image."[4] In *Nadja*, Breton called the moment when repressed material
was summoned up and unleashed "unchaining" [*désenchaînement*], a word
whose disruptive polyvalence harkened back to Arthur Rimbaud's notion of
poetry as a *déreglement* of sense, senses, and direction. Surrealism directed
its unchaining at once against the chains of the assembly line (*la chaîne*) binding workers, and the rigid categories of logical sequence, the *enchaînement*
of ideas.

Throughout the years he spent working on the *Arcades*, Benjamin indicated that he found the Surrealists' fusion of materialism and psychoanalysis provocative; so provocative, indeed, that one of his great tasks was to
remove his study from an "all too ostentatious proximity to the *mouve-
ment surréaliste* that could become fatal to me" (C, 342; trans. modified).

Benjamin proposed to differentiate himself from Surrealism, in particular, by remedying its lack of rigorous theorization concerning how collective and individual psychic processes interpenetrated. Benjamin's point of departure was the rhetorical affinity between the dream vocabulary Marx sometimes used to describe the mystifications of capitalism, and the importance of the dream in a Freudian schema. Perhaps the supernatural dimensions to modern life, Benjamin speculated, were manifestations of a dream sleep that came over Europe with the invention of modern capitalism; what was then needed was a way to promote awakening from the dreams of the nineteenth century. Benjamin found the notion of a dreaming collective all the more appealing because the psychoanalytic notion of dreams as the fulfillment of wishes meshed with his interest in the unrealized hopes and desires contained in the garbage of history. But Benjamin, like the Surrealists, differed fundamentally from Freud in proposing that the wishes revealed in dreams might be the basis of therapeutic social transformation. Freud emphasized the destructive power of the libido, viewing culture as based on repression. For Benjamin, in contrast, the wish images of the dreaming collective are the utopian longing for a better future whose advent could be promoted, once its content had been articulated. In its dream images, "the collective seeks both to overcome and to transfigure the immaturity of the social product and the inadequacies in the social organization of production" ("Exposé of 1935," *Arcades*, 4).

But how and why did the collective dream? Benjamin grappled with the question throughout the *Arcades Project* and above all in Convolutes K and N. Perhaps, Benjamin speculates, the nineteenth-century collective could dream because it saw a "singular fusion of individualistic and collectivist tendencies" (*Arcades*, 390; K1a, 5). Or perhaps, in the dream of the collective, two forms of the unconscious interpenetrated: "'the visceral unconscious' of the individual and the 'unconscious of oblivion' – the first of which is predominantly individual, the second predominantly collective" (*Arcades*, 396; K4, 2). Benjamin also includes fragments suggesting that the nineteenth century was "a spacetime [*Zeitraum*] (a dreamtime [*Zeit-traum*]) in which the individual consciousness more and more secures itself in reflecting, while the collective consciousness sinks into ever deeper sleep" (*Arcades*, 389; K1, 4). At other moments, Benjamin pursues transferring the Freudian divide separating unconscious and conscious to the Marxist divide separating economics from culture and ideology. Thus Benjamin speculates:

On the doctrine of the ideological superstructure. It seems, at first sight, that Marx wanted to establish here only a causal relation between superstructure and infrastructure. But already the observation that ideologies of the superstructure reflect conditions falsely and invidiously goes beyond this. This question, in effect, is the following: if the infrastructure in a certain way (in the materials of thought and experience) determines the superstructure, but if such determination is not reducible to simple reflection, how is it then – entirely apart from any question about the originating cause – to be characterized? *As its expression. The superstructure is the expression of the infrastructure* [emphasis added]. The economic conditions under which society exists are expressed in the superstructure – precisely as, with the sleeper, an overfull stomach finds not its reflection but its expression in the contents of dreams, which, from a causal point of view, it may be said to "condition." The collective, from the first, expresses the conditions of its life. These find their expression in the dream, and their interpretation in the awakening.   (*Arcades* 392; K2, 5).

In this enormously suggestive speculation, Benjamin underlines that the psychoanalytic account of the relation between conscious and unconscious processes offers a potent antidote to the simplistic notions of mimesis and causality that often regulate Marxist theorizations of the relation between superstructure and base. In addition, the dream fascinated him on account of its vividness, which had the potential to alleviate the bland and insufficiently gripping narrative mode found in much Marxist historiography. When Benjamin returned to the question of "what type of perceptibility (*Anschaulichkeit*) . . . the presentation of history [should] possess," he specified that it would be "neither the cheap and easy graphicness of bourgeois history books nor the insufficient graphicness of Marxist histories. What it has to fix in graphic form are the images deriving from the collective unconscious."[5]

Benjamin suggested that the dreaming collective produced one kind of image that offered a privileged opportunity to elucidate its contradictions and to redeem its desires, what he called the "dialectical image," in a conceptual montage yoking the Marxist method of demystification with the Freudian fondness for the realm of ambiguity and half-light. This was precisely the kind of light filtering through the frosted-glass panels of the arcades, and throughout the first half of the 1930s, Benjamin experimented with delineating the nineteenth century as a series of dialectical images. These would be carefully selected and constructed features of nineteenth-century culture which revealed the full ambivalence of modernity: its fascination and its mystification, along with the traces of utopia contained in it. In theorizing the historical content of dialectical images, Benjamin made full use of the anti-progressive temporality psychoanalysis proposed as characterizing the dream. According to Freud, individual dreams fused material from the immediate past (daily residue) with material from across an individual's conscious history as both child and adult, as well as material from the radically anti-historical unconscious. Translating the temporal schema of Freudian dream to collective history, Benjamin proposed that, "in the dream in which each epoch entertains images of its successor, the latter appears wedded to elements of primal history [*Urgeschichte*] – that is, to elements of a classless society. And the experiences of such a society – as stored in the unconscious of the collective – engender, through interpenetration with what is new, the utopia that has left its trace in a thousand configurations of life, from enduring edifices to passing fashions," i.e. in precisely the diverse range of artifacts Benjamin considered for inclusion in his Paris project ("Exposé of 1935," *Arcades*, 4–5). In *The Interpretation of Dreams*, Freud was, of course, inspired by Nietzsche's critique of nineteenth-century master narratives of progress when he articulated the anti-progressive working of the dream language, and Benjamin, too, refers repeatedly to Nietzsche's critique throughout his methodological comments.

Theodor Adorno was scandalized by Benjamin's fusion of the premier Marxist method of demystification, dialectics, with the realm of mystification, if not reenchantment.[6] Cautioning that Benjamin would fail to explain satisfactorily the link between dialectics and dream, Adorno attacked the notion of the dialectical image as pre-theoretical ambiguity rather than productive montage. Perhaps disheartened by Adorno's carping criticism, Benjamin moved away from his notion of the historian as Surrealist dream interpreter in the later 1930s, and returned, instead, to envisioning the *Arcades Project* as modeled on a spectacle from the time and place under discussion. Now, the spectacle was the phantasmagoria, a term coined in Paris to describe a new form of popular magic-lantern show that called up the dead during the Revolutionary and post-Revolutionary years when French society both awakened to utopian possibility and sought to exorcise the nightmares of its history in blood.

The centerpiece of the phantasmagoria was a mobile magic-lantern projector that the spectacle's animator, the phantasmagorian, used to project ghosts ranging from the collective heroes and villains of the Revolution to lost private loved ones reclaimed by bereaved persons in the room (whether planted or genuine was not clear). The phantasmagoria intensified the effect of these ghosts through the use of mirrors, music, smoke, projection of voices, and other illusionistic theatrical techniques, and it was so wildly successful that the term immediately passed into figurative use, where it described hallucinatory mental processes that were deluded yet that had an undeniable reality of their own. The Romantics were paramount in the cultural diffusion of this notion, and Marx bore witness to his own Romantic inheritance when he mobilized the term in *Capital* to describe the phenomenon of commodity fetishism. To characterize Marx's use of phantasmagoria, I can do no better than to cite the summary given by Otto Rühle that Benjamin included among the *Arcades Project*'s notes. Rühle writes, "Once escaped from the hand of the producer and divested of its real particularity," a commodity:

> ceases to be a product and to be ruled over by human beings. It has acquired a "ghostly objectivity" and leads a life of its own ... The commodity has been transformed into an idol, that, although the product of human hands, disposes over the human. Marx speaks of the fetish character of the commodity. "This fetish character of the commodity world has its origin in the peculiar social character of the labor that produces commodities ... It is only the particular social relation between people that here assumes, in the eyes of these people, the phantasmagorical form of a relation between things."
>
> (*Arcades*, 182; G5, 1).

An important term in Marx itself produced by the Parisian history of interest to Benjamin, the spectacle of the phantasmagoria thus offered Benjamin a thoroughly archaeological way to depict the persistence of the irrational in modern life.

The notion of the phantasmagoria accordingly took pride of place in the 1939 exposé that was Benjamin's last programmatic statement on the *Arcades Project*. In it, he comments, "The world dominated by its phantasmagorias – this, to make use of Baudelaire's term, is 'modernity'" ("Exposé of 1939," *Arcades*, 26). Accompanying the new prominence of the phantasmagoria in the 1939 resumé of the arcades is the effacement of dream vocabulary as well as the notion of the dialectical image. Instead:

> our investigation proposes to show how, as a consequence of this reifying representation of civilization, the new forms of behavior and the new economically and technologically based creations that we owe to the nineteenth century enter the universe of a phantasmagoria. These creations undergo this "illumination" not only in a theoretical manner, by an ideological transposition, but also in the immediacy of their perceptible presence. They are manifest as phantasmagorias. Thus appear the arcades – first entry into the field of iron construction; thus appear the world exhibitions, whose link to the entertainment industry is significant. Also included in this order of phenomena is the experience of the flâneur, who abandons himself to the phantasmagorias of the market place. Corresponding to these phantasmagorias of the market, where people appear only as types, are the phantasmagorias of the interior, which are constituted by man's imperious need to leave the imprint of his private individual existence on the rooms he inhabits. As for the phantasmagoria of civilization itself, it found its champion in Haussmann and its manifest expression in his transformations of Paris. ("Exposé of 1935," *Arcades*, 14, 15)

How were these phantasmagorias to be demystified? Benjamin's response was thoroughly in keeping with the antidote Lukács proposed to reification:

by showing how things are in fact the expression of processes. As artifact from the time that itself performs such dereification, Benjamin proposed Auguste Blanqui's *L'Eternité par les astres*, written while the prominent socialist was imprisoned during the Commune. Reading Blanqui's notion of a demonic universe that "repeats itself endlessly and paws the ground in place," in conjunction with Nietzsche's demystification of the ideology of progress in the notion of the eternal return, Benjamin describes Blanqui's vision as "one last cosmic phantasmagoria which implicitly comprehends the severest critique of all the others" ("Exposé of 1935," *Arcades*, 25, 26).

When Benjamin singled out the phantasmagoria as offering a privileged entrance into "Paris, Capital of the Nineteenth Century," he sought to use this spectacle in similar fashion to his use of allegory in *The Origin of the German Tragic Drama*. Indeed, the resonance of phantasmagoria with allegory goes beyond their common function as archaeological finds loaded with conceptual significance to the content of the significance itself. Both allegory and phantasmagoria traffic in enchantment, the supernatural and the dead; and both were historical antecedents to the interest in dislocation, artifice, and the inorganic characterizing the anti-Romantic avant-garde of Benjamin's own present. The nature of the enchantment at issue in the phantasmagoria and allegory is, of course, different, and this difference is intimated by the two words' strikingly expressive etymology: while allegory derives from *allos agoreuein*, to speak other than in the public place or marketplace, one plausible etymology for phantasmagoria is *phantasma agoreuein*, the ghosts of the public place or marketplace. As this etymological relation well captures, the supernatural conjured up in allegory is indeed an *other* to the marketplace; allegory is the mask taken by the divine when it appears in fallen history. The supernatural of reified human labor at issue in phantasmagoria is, in contrast, the specter *of* the market place in the senses both of firmly located there and generated by it.

As a result of this difference, Benjamin understands that a rather different notion of redemption is at stake in each form. The rescue exorcising the haunting power of allegory is a theological one, as the complete destruction of fallen history will be superseded in a final moment of reversal when the death's head becomes an angel's countenance. The rescue that will put an end to a universe of phantasmagorias is, in contrast, materialist: it is the human and historical process by which the reified forces of labor are freed from bondage.

However, although Benjamin allies such liberation with Marxist praxis, his utopian if not apocalyptic vision of the return of the repressed went well beyond the measures proposed by Benjamin's orthodox Marxist contemporaries. To put this observation another way: Benjamin's notion of rescue from what nineteenth-century contemporaries ironically called "the Hell of Parisian modernity" had a subterranean link to the theological notion of redemption at issue in his work on the German baroque. Benjamin comments: "my thinking is related to theology as a blotting pad is related to ink. It is saturated with it. Were one to go by the blotter, however, nothing of what is written would remain" (*Arcades*, 471; N7a, 7). As Benjamin makes clear in his final "On the Concept of History," his theological understanding of redemption owes much to the Jewish mysticism that he had initially discovered through Gershom Scholem and that was so important for his *Origin of the German Tragic Drama*. In Jewish Messianism, redemption was confirmed by a horrific present that would seem to negate its existence; but the Messianic twist was that this negation rather attested to redemption's possibility and power. The more horrific the present, the firmer the guarantee that a utopian future was intact, for such horror confirmed that utopia was safe, preserved from the contamination by a world in which it had no place. As the spread of Nazism precipitated Europe into the Second World War, Benjamin found the Messianic notion of redemption even more compelling than he had found it when he wrote *The Origin of the German Tragic Drama* in the aftermath of the First World War, and his "On the Concept of History" (1940) accordingly shifts the redemptive schema from the seventeenth century to the present.

In the "Concept of History" Benjamin also turned to Jewish mysticism for a model of praxis in dark times, inspired by the kabbalistic precept that the work of the holy man is an activity known as *tikkun*. According to the kabbalah, God's attributes were once held in vessels whose glass was contaminated by the presence of evil and these vessels had consequently shattered, disseminating their contents to the four corners of the earth. *Tikkun* was the process of collecting the scattered fragments in the hopes of once more piecing them together. Benjamin fused *tikkun* with the Surrealist notion that liberation would come through releasing repressed collective material, to produce his celebrated account of the revolutionary historiographer, who sought to grab hold of elided memories as they sparked to view at moments of present danger.

The historiographer as tawdry illusionist, as dialectical materialist, as Surrealist rag-picker, as Freudian dream interpreter, as allegorical brooder, as Jewish mystic: Benjamin's notion of "rescuing critique" exemplified his favorite practice of disjunctive conceptual montage. In the remainder of this chapter, I would like to set out some principal aspects of nineteenth-century modernity recovered by the *Arcades Project*, aspects that Benjamin proposed as foundational to his repertoire of dialectical images or phantasmagoria in both the 1935 and 1939 exposés. These images or phantasmagoria were not associated with a particular genre, media, or practice but rather scattered throughout what we have seen Benjamin call a "thousand configurations of life" ("Exposé of 1935," *Arcades*, 5). They comprehended new cultural genres: panoramic literature and utopian social theory; nineteenth-century canonized and uncanonized literature and art ranging from *Les Fleurs du mal* and *Les Misérables* to worker poetry and the caricatures of Grandville; commercial practices intensifying consumption like fashion and advertising; new kinds of architecture like the arcades, the department stores, monuments, railway stations, and even the streets of Paris; technological innovations like gas lighting, the railway, the wax museum, and photography; distinctive nineteenth-century forms of representation like (once more) photography and lithography; social types of great interest to contemporaries like the flâneur, the sandwich man, the lesbian, and the prostitute; and social and political events, notably those important in the history of working-class struggle, like the street revolts of the two decades between the July Revolution and 1848, the barricade fighting of 1848, and the Paris Commune, but also the celebrations of industry found in the World Exhibitions. In both the 1935 and 1939 exposés, Benjamin organized this wealth of material in sections under the aegis of a historical personage coupled with an architectural site. In 1935, his repertoire of dialectical images included "Fourier, or the Arcades," "Daguerre, or the Panoramas," "Grandville, or the World Exhibitions," "Louis Philippe, or the Interior," "Baudelaire, or the Streets of Paris," and "Haussmann, or the Barricades." In 1939, his phantasmagorias bore the same headings, though he had added a discussion of the writings of Blanqui in a conclusion and had taken out the section on Daguerre, perhaps because he had greatly expanded and developed the material found here in his "Work of Art in the Age of its Technological Reproducibility" essay published in 1936.

Fourier, or the arcades

The single phenomenon Benjamin elected as most emblematic of Parisian modernity were the covered *passages* under whose elevated iron and glasses ceilings he housed his entire project. Benjamin began his 1935 Paris exposé with a citation from an 1852 Paris guide book, *Le Guide Illustré*, that he notes, with the characteristic blank irony he brings to the garbage of history, is a "locus classicus" for this site. Calling the arcades "a recent invention of industrial luxury," *Le Guide Illustré* describes them as "glass-roofed, marble-paneled corridors extending through whole blocks of buildings, whose owners have joined together for such enterprises. Lining both sides of these corridors, which get their light from above, are the most elegant shops, so that the arcade is a city, a world in miniature" ("Exposé of 1935," *Arcades*, 3).[7]

As these comments make clear, the arcades were immersed in both the industrial and commercial aspects of capitalism. They were an innovative building form dependent on iron, the material that played a premier role in the myriad inventions of the Industrial Revolution. They were also devoted to the luxury goods that are pure surplus value and thus an embodiment of the logic animating capitalist production. Displaying the commodity as pure fetish, completely severed from its links to production and use, the arcades offered a privileged place to contemplate the commodity's powerful fascination, the pleasure and desire it inspired. In doing so, they not only revealed the workings of reification, but are linked, in however corrupted a manner, to the utopian aspirations of a dreaming collective. These aspirations are also evident in the joint ownership the arcades promoted, aspirations which can be read as a degraded yearning for a society abolishing private property, even though this yearning took the form of an activity that was decidedly for profit. Benjamin also found the arcades to contain utopian seeds in their construction principle. As a building form based on material that was purely functional, the arcades took the capitalist reduction of all relations to questions of use and profit and turned it against bourgeois notions of beauty, hearkening to an avant-garde vision of architecture freed from the separation between function and "art" that is, as Lukács made clear, itself a result of reification's divide splitting producer from product.

Benjamin coupled the arcades with the figure of the utopian socialist Fourier, because Fourier gave the arcades a prominent place in his visionary writings demystifying crucial ideologemes of capitalist society. Indeed, Benjamin cites Engels who calls Fourier "not only a critic" but "one of the greatest satirists of all time" (*Arcades*, 625; w3a, 3). Fourier modeled the *phalanstères*, the social units of his utopian society, on the arcades. But, if the arcades' ambivalent half-light facilitated the blurring of boundaries between human and commodity, thereby producing the allure of the commodity fetish, Fourier performed the gesture of blurring boundaries in such outrageous fashion that he called attention to the workings of commodity fetishism, even as he directed this blurring against fundamental boundaries underpinning bourgeois ideology. Thus, the *phalanstères* are societies that abolish the divide between individual, family, and collective along with that between public and private spheres, even as these societies expose reification by fusing, in sometimes hilarious and sometimes hallucinatory fashion, man and machine, technology and the supernatural, and nature and second nature. Indeed, the boundaries erased by Fourier extend to the phenomenon of reification itself, for Fourier dreams of a world where the worker will once more take possession of the commodity in "attractive work," a form of labor that erases the distinction between production and consumption.

Daguerre, or the panoramas

Benjamin settled on the popular spectacle of the panorama as a locus to explore the radical transformations in art and aesthetics resulting from industrial technologies of reproduction. The panoramas were interior spaces where the viewer contemplated mechanized, painted façades representing famous cities and natural scenes from walkways running around the top. As Benjamin observes, "one sought tirelessly, through technical devices, to make panoramas the scenes of a perfect imitation of nature" ("Exposé of 1935," *Arcades*, 5). The panoramas thus capture how the pervasive industrialization and commodification characterizing high capitalism transforms nature to an effect of second nature. Benjamin finds a textual equivalent to the panorama in what he calls panoramic literature, a genre of non-fictional, descriptive writing invented in the mid-nineteenth century that offered a totalizing overview of contemporary society by classifying its inhabitants into social types. Such classification harkened back to the naturalist classifying project of the century before – only this time social groups were naturalized as the denizens of a new world of second nature. But with his remarkable ability to grasp the ambivalence of modernity's ideologemes, Benjamin suggested that such naturalization not only sought to make class domination as inevitable as the sun's course across the sky, it also indicated yearning for classless society from the primal past that could be the model of a society to come. Benjamin also hints at a second potentially redemptive possibility inhering in the transformation of nature into second nature that is the basis of all Marxist praxis: the fact that what is made by humans can be transformed by them. Specifically, he mentions photography liberated from the demand to reproduce nature as able to enter into the project to change history, alluding to the use of montage "for political agitation" ("Exposé 1935," *Arcades*, 6). But Benjamin's account of the dialectical reversal enabling Daguerre, inventor of photography, to demystify the panoramas is much less worked out than his discussion of Fourier as satirist of his age. The confrontations of photography with modernity are most thoroughly explored not in the Convolutes but rather in Benjamin's "Little History of Photography" and his "Work of Art in the Age of its Technological Reproducibility."

Grandville, or the world exhibitions

The World Exhibitions were another phantasmagoria, where viewers came on what Benjamin called a pilgrimage to worship the marvels of industry. From the first World Exhibition, the Crystal Palace show of 1851, the preferred architectural form for housing this glittering display were structures built from the same glass and iron as the arcades. In showcasing the technology enabling industrial production, the World Exhibitions might seem to draw attention to processes of production but, in turning technology into entertainment, they glorified "the exchange value" of the commodity, pushing its use value "into the background" ("Exposé of 1935," *Arcades*, 7). In multiple excerpts on the World Exhibitions in the folders, Benjamin also hints at their interest in showcasing the imperializing dimension to high capitalism, but this content is not well worked out in his analysis. Benjamin placed the World Exhibitions at the dawn of mass culture, and was interested in the responses they elicited. Benjamin writes of "the enthronement of the commodity with its luster of distraction," and "distraction" is the state he posits as distinctive to post-auratic art in the "Work of Art," essay, endowed with both corrosive and liberating potential ("Exposé of 1935," *Arcades*, 7).

Benjamin uses the caricaturist Grandville to undo the enchantments of the World Exhibitions because Grandville's drawings erase precisely the boundaries elided in its phantasmagoria, but do so in a fashion exposing rather than perpetuating their power. In his witty monsters derived from the fashions of the moment that Benjamin calls both "utopian and cynical," Grandville creates new species and denizens of society which humorously couple inorganic and organic as well as nature and second nature and thereby reveal the processes producing commodity fetishism which yokes "the living body to the inorganic world" ("Exposé of 1935," *Arcades*, 8). Grandville, however, "ends in madness," as Benjamin cautions that the critic exposing the underwriting ideologies of modernity does so at his or her peril ("Exposé of 1935," *Arcades*, 8). Benjamin will reiterate this point when he stresses that historiographical rescue occurs under the sign of danger in his "On the Concept of History."

Louis Philippe, or the interior

The notion that the individual can heroically take on collective forces itself, of course, derives from modernity's hypostatization of the individual that is one more manifestation of reification's subject/object divide. It is thus fitting that Benjamin's section devoted to this foundational bourgeois ideologeme uses a historical figure not as the agent of dialectical reversal, but rather as the emblem of all its mystifications. This figure is Louis Philippe, the bourgeois king who presides over a regime which enters with the promise of expanding the democratic basis of citizenship, but which very quickly reveals itself devoted not to the revolutionary trilogy of liberty, fraternity, and equality but rather to "the private individual managing his affairs" ("Exposé of 1935," *Arcades*, 8). As in other sections, Benjamin ties the apotheosis of bourgeois individuality once more to a site, in this case "the phantasmagorias of the interior," which create a comforting and entertaining private version of the universe walled off from the economic realities that press all too closely on the individual in the public sphere ("Exposé of 1935," *Arcades*, 9).[8]

In keeping with the aim to expose the individual as a phantasmagorical expression of social processes, Benjamin looks to collective practices for dialectical reversal. These practices are, specifically, *Jugendstil* (art nouveau) an avant-garde movement centrally concerned with the place of the ornament in the home. Fundamental to *Jugendstil*'s vision of ornamentation are the technological possibilities of new building materials to transform the interior into nature, as *Jugendstil* explicitly materializes the conflation of nature and second nature worked by high capitalism. Benjamin also finds a demystification of the interior in the quintessential bourgeois practice of collecting, which, like the World Exhibitions, releases things "from the drudgery of being useful" ("Exposé of 1935," *Arcades*, 9). In contrast to the World Exhibitions, which transform use into entertainment, however, collecting would seem to open the possibility for a radical reshuffling of the existing order, though this reshuffling is purely aesthetic. Sounding rather Brechtian, Benjamin underscores that, in the transfigurations worked by the collector, "human beings are no better provided with what they need than in the everyday world" ("Exposé of 1935," *Arcades*, 9).

Baudelaire, or the streets of Paris

In counterpoint to Louis Philippe, quintessential embodiment of bourgeois individuality, Baudelaire figures in Benjamin's account almost entirely as an agent of dialectical reversal. Torn in his poetry and prose between two states he calls *ideal* and *spleen*, Baudelaire summons up the dreams and phantasmagorias hawked on the streets of big city life the better to expose the alienation and mystification on which they are based. Crucial both to the allure of the modern and to its Baudelairean demystification are a distinctive temporality that permeates modernity's products and experiences, its historiography and its psychic states. This is the temporality of what Baudelaire called "the New" in his final poem of *Les Fleurs de Mal*, and that Benjamin reads as an effect of capitalistic economic processes whose credo is the production of surplus value.

Whether Baudelaire is delineating the flaneur's desire for a fleeting woman who can never be possessed in *A une passante*, or the pursuit of travel that ultimately leads, in a diabolical cycle of ever-increasing thrills, to death, he relentless underscores all that is false in modernity's taste for novelty. Far from renewing the world, the New participates in a temporality that Baudelaire designates as infernal, in which every moment fundamentally resembles the next; succession only offers a promise of change because each moment is empty, devoid of significance in and of itself. Coupling the Baudelairean understanding of novelty with the Nietzschean notion of the eternal return, Benjamin declares: "This semblance of the new is reflected, like one mirror in another, in the semblance of the ever recurrent. The product of this reflection is the phantasmagoria of 'cultural history,' in which the bourgeoisie enjoys its false consciousness to the full" ("Exposé of 1935," *Arcades*, 11). But even Baudelaire, lucid demystifier of progress, succumbs to it in his snobbism; the snob "is to art what the dandy is to fashion," Benjamin memorably declares ("Exposé of 1935," *Arcades*, 11). At the same time, the aestheticism that is the currency of Baudelaire's snobbism does have a critical significance; for Benjamin reads it as Baudelaire's reaction against his own status as a member of an intellectual class in the process of being proletarianized. This class finds its quintessential expression in the distinctively nineteenth-century notion of *la bohème*, arising in the interstices of the lumpenproletariat and the bourgeoisie.

Haussmann, or the barricades

In Marxist theory, the bourgeoisie is both an insurgent and a counter-revolutionary class. Benjamin is fascinated with Prefect Haussmann because his Second Empire rebuilding of Paris is at once the summit and the destruction of the dreams and phantasmagorias of nineteenth-century bourgeois ideology. With his grand boulevards that celebrate the spectacle of modern life, Haussmann extends into the street the celebration of the commodity fetish found in the arcades and World Exhibitions. At the same time, Haussmann's boulevards facilitate the circulation of merchandise and commerce essential to capitalist economy by destroying working-class quarters; and, to underscore the class antagonism of capitalist production, this destruction is specifically a way to secure bourgeois hegemony, for it responds to the threat to order posed by a large working-class population in central Paris, and, moreover, facilitates the flow of troops and munitions around the city, should workers ever repeat their insurrection. Definitively dismantling the phantasmagoria of equality between worker and bourgeois which had underwritten the Revolutions of 1789 and 1830 as well as the first days of 1848, Haussmann's reconstructions that contemporaries termed "strategic embellishments" spectacularly expose the true state of class relations in nineteenth-century Paris ("Exposé of 1935," *Arcades*, 12). Haussmann's reconstruction/destruction was an all the more eloquent demystification of the liberal phantasmagoria of equality because it provided the opportunity for financiers, Haussmann among them, to make enormous fortunes from dispossessing the working classes of their homes, and then selling this newly purchased real estate at a premium to the government building its boulevards. Benjamin pointed out, however, the dialectical consequences of revealing bourgeois domination in all its rapacity, which was to mobilize and politicize the working classes. "The barricade is resurrected during the Commune. It is stronger and better secured than ever" ("Exposé of 1935," *Arcades*, 12).

In "Reification and the Consciousness of the Proletariat" (1923), Lukács had proposed that the goal of revolutionary activity was to transform the working-classes from the object to the subject of history. Benjamin is in continuity with this ambition when he ends both the 1935 and 1939 exposés with the working-class uprising of the Commune. By choosing this moment from the history of nineteenth-century worker struggle, however, Benjamin, underscores his distance from any simple progressive notion of politics. The Commune is a utopian and apocalyptic moment of social upheaval in keeping with Benjamin's darkly redemptive political Messianism. When Benjamin concludes the exposés' comments on Haussmann, he declares, "The burning of Paris is the worthy conclusion to Haussmann's work of destruction" ("Exposé of 1935," *Arcades*, 13).

Though I have stressed the coherence of the *Arcades Project* as Benjamin himself summarized it, the Convolutes contain notes on all kinds of "fascinating" (in the Benjaminian sense of the word) material that he might have used to elaborate further phantasmagorias of modernity. Thus, we can imagine Benjamin developing the notes in Convolute C, "Ancient Paris, Catacombs, Demolitions, Decline of Paris," concerning Paris as a city whose history is written in stone to theorize more explicitly the place of architecture in modernity. Here, architecture would be coupled with the historical figure of Hugo, who theorized architecture as a foundational expression of culture in the context of demystifying the phantasmagorias of bourgeois historiography throughout his work, and who also prophecied that architecture would be superceded by mass print culture in "This will kill that," a chapter from *Notre-Dame de Paris* that can be considered the first draft of "The Work of Art in the Age of its Technological Reproducibility." Similarly, Benjamin might have developed his numerous notes on Marx to make good on his interest in "how the milieu in which Marx's doctrines arose affects these doctrines through its expressive character (which is to say, not only through causal connections)," as well as to "show in what respects Marxism, too, shares the expressive character of the material products contemporary with it" (*Arcades*, 460; N1a, 7). The upshot of this analysis would be an archeology that could free Marxism from mystifications it shared with the time and place in which it was first conceived.

Benjamin's Convolutes also contain ample material for some more extended discussion of the figurative and technological power of light in the modern city. The theoretical implication of this discussion would be to provide a historical ground for the notion of "profane illumination." In this context, one may imagine Benjamin theorizing the profound links between modernity's zones of light and its zones of darkness, shadow, and sleaze that he also documents extensively in his numerous fragments on gambling, prostitution, drugs, and *la vie bohème*, along with what he called dream houses, the narcotic sites where a collective goes to dream. The importance of transportation in the modern social formation, too, is a theme that recurs throughout the Convolutes, but that is not completely worked out. Here, perhaps the dialectical reversal might be offered by Saint-Simon and his sect, who were both master builders schooled by the Ecole Polytechnique and utopian socialists searching for a "Woman Messiah," and who went on a crusade in the Middle East to find her, though they got derailed by trying to convince the ruler of Egypt to instigate the construction of a Suez canal. I could continue, but to do so is only to enumerate the many directions in which critics have taken the challenges raised by Benjamin's "Parisian production cycle" in the past twenty years. Though we may yearn for the *Arcades Project* in finished form, this work's simultaneous brilliance and frustratingly unfinished openness have encouraged its extraordinary resonance.

Photos exist of Benjamin in one of the greatest phantasmagorias that the nineteenth century bequeathed to us, which is the archive as the repository of a culture's historical memory. Hugo wrote of the library: "Arch where dawn arises / Unfathomable ABC of the ideal where progress / Eternal reader, leans on its elbow and dreams" (*Arcades*, 482; N15a, 2). Thus Benjamin: "These notes devoted to the Paris arcades were begun under the open sky of cloudless blue that arched above the foliage; and yet – among the millions of leaves that were visited by the fresh breeze of diligence, the stertorous breath of the researcher, the storms of youthful zeal, and the idle wind of curiosity – they have been covered with the dust of centuries. For the painted sky of summer that looks down from the arcades in the reading room of the Bibliothèque Nationale in Paris has spread over them its dreamy, unlit ceiling" (*Arcades*, 457–58; N1, 5). Benjamin here refers to the tree branches that decorate the ceiling of the Bibliothèque Nationale's *salle de travail*, a room designed by the prominent nineteenth-century architect Henri Labrouste, who was himself a great reader of Hugo, dedicated to a vision of architecture where function and engineering took primacy over art.

Labrouste supported the *salle de travail*'s soaring ceilings with slender columns made of the same iron that enabled the arcades. In the *Arcades Project* exposé, Benjamin writes: "Iron is avoided in home construction but used in arcades, exhibition halls, train stations – buildings that serve transitory purposes" ("Exposé of 1935," *Arcades*, 16). At the turn of the millennium, it is the notion of the archive itself that is in transition with the transformation of mechanical into virtual technologies of reproduction. Nowhere has this transition been more famously spatialized than in the new Bibliothèque de France, which replaced the painted foliage of the *salle de travail* with the vertiginous spectacle of real trees turned to an allegory of nature exiled from the library's underground reading rooms. What Benjamin would have made of the restructuring of cultural memory in an age of virtualization is open to speculation. In any case, one hopes he would have savored the irony by which the infernal dialectics of high capitalism have superseded modernity itself, making the *Arcades Project*, in all its unfinished and broken splendor, now our paramount cultural monument to modernity's ambitions and its power.

NOTES

1. Benjamin described himself as involved in a "Parisian production cycle" in a letter to Gershom Scholem, Berlin, 30 January 1928, (C, 322; trans. modified). This chapter builds on ideas I have developed in more detail in *Profane Illumination: Walter Benjamin and the Paris of Surrealist Revolution* (Berkeley: University of California Press, 1993).
2. What has been called a "return to the archive" in literary studies of the past twenty years owes much to Benjamin as well as to Foucault. Both Benjamin and Foucault's fascination with the archive, moreover, share a common pre-history in the Nietzschean notion of genealogy, and both take from Victor Hugo the fact that this archive is not only the material housed in libraries, but a culture's material practices like its forms of architecture and technology.
3. Benjamin uses this term when he declares that "what I propose is to show how Baudelaire lies embedded in the nineteenth century" (*Arcades*, 321; J51a, 5).
4. André Breton, *First Surrealist Manifesto*, in *Manifestoes of Surrealism*, trans. Richard Seaver and Helen R. Lane (Ann Arbor: University of Michigan Press, 1986), 37.
5. Walter Benjamin, "Materials for the Exposé of 1935," in *Arcades*, 911. Here, I have modified the translation which renders *Anschaulichkeit* in this fragment as "perceptibility." Instead, I substitute the word "graphicness," that Eiland and McLaughlin use for *Anschaulichkeit* in their translation of *Arcades* fragment N, 2, 6, for both fragments, composed around the same time, belong to a single conceptual matrix.
6. See the Benjamin–Adorno exchanges in *Aesthetics and Politics*, ed. Ernst Bloch (London: NLB, 1977). On Benjamin's simultaneous interest in disenchantment and reenchantment, see, notably, Susan Buck-Morss's *Dialectics of Seeing* (Cambridge, MA: MIT Press, 1989), and Michael Taussig's use of Benjamin to understand spirit possession in *Shamanism, Colonialism, and the Wild Man* (University of Chicago Press, 1987).

7. Benjamin cites at more length from the Guide's expressive description of the arcades in the first fragment of the first Convolute (*Arcades*, 31; A1, 1).

8. As feminist critics have pointed out, Benjamin's blind spot to gender emerges vividly in his analysis of bourgeois intimacy, for Benjamin neglects to observe that the bourgeois individual has a very different relation to the interior depending on his or her sex.

I I

GERHARD RICHTER

Acts of self-portraiture: Benjamin's confessional and literary writings

> To find words for what is before one's eyes – how difficult that can be. But when they do come, they pound with little hammers against the real until they drive the image out of it as though from a copper plate.
>
> Walter Benjamin, "San Gimignano"

Languages of self-portraiture

There is nothing self-evident about the notion that we should have confessional and literary writings by Walter Benjamin.[1] After all, the abstractness and rigor that readers associate with his texts do not, on the surface, appear to conform to the sinewy and personal cadences characteristic of autobiographical reflection, from St. Augustine via Rousseau and Goethe to Nietzsche and the modernists, or to the aesthetic demands of literary discourse. From this perspective, to think of Benjamin as having written autobiographical and literary texts is, to borrow a phrase from one of his readers, "at first blush as implausible as an anthology of fairy tales by Hegel, a child's garden of deconstruction by Derrida."[2] Yet, both his confessional and literary texts belong in essential ways to the ever-shifting contours of his variegated acts of self-portraiture. Benjamin's autobiographical and literary texts stage his theory of the writerly self as one whose identity is defined by the condition of not being himself, that is, as one who negotiates the construction and dispersal of selfhood in language. As one critic, Fredric Jameson, reminds us, Benjamin poses a challenge not least of all because he "seems to dissolve into multiple readings fully as much as he turns into a unique 'self' that remains to be defined."[3] The multiple readings into which his self dissolves constitute an innovative mode of self-portraiture that functions as something other than the mere reflection or duplication of a preexisting self. Rather, Benjamin's texts reveal a self that can come into its own only in, and as, another, an alterity. For him, it is writing – the act, the object, and the concept – that names this alterity. As instances of otherness, Benjamin's literary acts of self-portraiture fulfill the logic that "transforms being into writing" ("Kafka," *SW* II, 815). Conforming to the unstable and variegated movements of writing, his self is most itself when it is becoming something else.

To understand this notion of a constantly shifting self, we need to appreciate that, in Benjamin's language, an engagement with one domain can be expressed figuratively in terms of another. Indeed, the condition of possibility for the truth of something, including the self, to emerge resides in its transformation into something else. As he tells us, "Nothing is more miserable than a truth expressed as it was thought. Committed to writing in such a case, it is not even a bad photograph. And the truth refuses (like a child or a woman who does not love us), facing the lens of writing while we crouch under the black cloth, to keep still and look amiable." If any truth ever emerges in writing, it is the truth that says something else. "Truth," Benjamin continues, "wants to be startled abruptly . . . Who could count the alarm signals with which the . . . true writer is equipped? And to 'write' is nothing other than to set them into motion" ("One Way Street," *SW* I, 480). In other words, in the movement of his rhetoric, words and concepts may at any time enter into a new relationship with what they present. The task of reading his confessional and literary writings, then, involves tracing the complex ways in which words and concepts change their meanings in order to become something else. The "truth" of our reading would then be measured not in terms of how Benjamin's language remains identical to itself, linear, and referential, but rather in its constant movement toward what it is not yet. We could say that this truth can be approached precisely by following the multiple traces that define the distance between the word's or concept's previous positions, and the position that they assume in any new, specific act of reading, here and now. These traces bring disparate words and concepts into grammatical relation. Put another way, one must read allegorically rather than symbolically. If, as Benjamin maintains throughout *The Origin of the German Tragic Drama*, we are called upon to read with an eye to what cannot be contained within figurative presentation, then our predicament can be summed up in the realization that "any person, any object, any relationship can mean absolutely anything else" (*Origin*, 175). This is not to say, however, that the movement by which this "anything else" is touched cannot be traced or that its internal logic cannot be ascertained. On the contrary, the burden of following the intricate design of Benjamin's tropes rests squarely upon us. The figurative mode of reading that he requires is both a predicament and an opportunity. It is a predicament because it forecloses the idea of a transparent, fully readable world; it is an opportunity because it invites the challenge of reading the enigmatic and complex texture of the postlapserian world of modernity. Indeed, the opportunity for productive modes of figurative reading is only called into being by the absence of what is self-evident or immediately comprehensible. There can be no birth of responsible reading without the death of transparency. It is in this space that questions of ethics, responsibility, and politics may begin to be articulated. Our hope, then, and the hope that attaches to Benjamin's contingent self, is not just to illuminate the opacity of the figurative and thus to undo it; it also *is* this opacity.

But, with regard to the written self, to confront the death of transparency in Benjamin's text is to confront a dilemma. After all, he explicitly denounces the traditional writerly stance in which the self turns into an allegedly stable narrative "I." On the one hand, Benjamin tells us that "if I write a better German than most writers of my generation, I owe it in good part to my twenty-year long observation of a single little rule: never use the word 'I' except in letters" ("Berlin Chronicle," *SW* II, 603). On the other hand, he accords his explicitly autobiographical texts a privileged place in his corpus. As Benjamin assures his friend Gershom Scholem in July 1933, his confessional texts "contain the most precise portrait that I shall ever be able to give of myself" (*C*, 424). Indeed, these writings constitute the fulfillment and radicalization of his plan, expressed one year earlier, of mapping the self as a text: "For a long time, years really, I have toyed with the idea of structuring the space of my life – *bios* – graphically on a map . . . I have devised a sign system, and on the ground of such a map there would be a real hustle and bustle" ("Berlin Chronicle," *SW* II, 596). But how do we respond responsibly to this performative contradiction? How do we face these conflicting impulses without giving in to our own resistance to contradiction? And how do we continue to read when we encounter blind spots in a text in which the construction of the self can no longer be separated fully from its destruction, its illumination from its eclipse?

The answer may well lie in the development of a manner of responsible reading that wishes not to work through – and thus undo – these contradictions and opacities, but to work *with* them, that is, to acknowledge them as an integral and forever unassimilable aspect of a singular act of reading. We could even say that any attempt to understand the significance of Benjamin's autobiographical and literary writings must not seek to resolve but rather to invite and even be *lodged in* the tension delimited by these two poles – the attempt to construct the self in writing and the simultaneous narrative renunciation of such a project. It is thus useful to think of his literary and autobiographical reflections in terms of a double gesture of constructing and undoing, along the lines of Jacques Derrida's reading of two hands in Freud – one writing, the other erasing. For Benjamin, "'construction' presupposes 'destruction'" (*Arcades*, 470; N7, 6) and his autobiographical writings enact both the aberration and the promise of this double gesture.

To acknowledge this double gesture is also to acknowledge that Benjamin's innovative art of literary self-portraiture cannot be separated from his more general critique of the modern subject. Indeed, his obsession with articulating a theory of the modern subject is one of the principal tropes of his entire corpus. For Benjamin, the fragmented, constantly revised subject eludes completion and closure, even as it strives toward them. The subject's textual figures trace the contours of this perpetual deferral. In contrast to Hegel, whose definition of the subject, as Jean-Luc Nancy reminds us, as the one that is "capable of maintaining within itself its own contradiction" has remained the dominant understanding of the metaphysical subject,[4] Benjamin rejects the notion of a continuous and self-identical subject that could account for its own multiplications and reconfigurations in the scene of writing. As he tells us in an autobiographical fragment, the "seemingly *whole* (unified) individual does not matter" ("Death," *GS* VI, 71). Benjamin's deep suspicion of the notion of a transparent "self" prompts him, already in a letter to Ernst Schoen from September 1919, to question the idea that a human subject could fully emerge through its texts and contexts. Instead, Benjamin prefers to speak of a textual event "whose relation to a subject is as meaningless as the relation of any pragmatic–historical testimony (inscription) to its author" (*C*, 149). He makes a similar point a decade later, when, in the essay "Surrealism," which is often considered the transitional point between his so-called metaphysical and Marxist phases, he again privileges language over the self: "It [language] is primary. Not only to meaning. Also to one's self. In the configuration of the world, the dream loosens individuality like a hollow tooth" (*SW* II, 208). For Benjamin, language tends to exceed both stable meaning and the self. This excess, though, need not be considered merely destructive or nihilistic. It also opens up the very possibility of thinking through the subject along innovative paths, traces that become visible only when the ideology of the transparent subject is destroyed; and, as his friend Theodor W. Adorno reminds us, "In all his phases, Benjamin thought the demise of the subject and the salvation of humanity as one thing."[5]

The scene of autobiography

From this perspective, Benjamin's often overlooked acts of literary self-portraiture are especially resonant in his corpus not only because they contain theoretical and aesthetic reformulations of the modern autobiographical act, but also because they enact, on a literary level, the historico-political concerns of his more overtly speculative texts. As hybrid texts imbricating personal confessions and cultural critique, they break with the conventional genre of autobiography in order to come to terms with the fragmentary and textual nature of thoughts that underpin memory. Their narrative gestures self-consciously assume the echo of a distant or absent voice that can only accompany the textual self as it follows the paths of intertwined traces. If Benjamin problematizes the moment of representation in which memories are to figure as texts, it is because for him representation always threatens to run awry and to subvert what the subject that set it into motion intended to say.

Indeed, the bulk of his corpus can hardly be understood in isolation from his autobiographical texts. As Werner Hamacher puts it in his stunning reading of the word "Wolke" (cloud) in Benjamin's *Berlin Childhood*, "it cannot be doubted that Benjamin's memoirs represent the impetus as well as the explication, extrapolation and fulfillment of the program that his theoretical writings formulate. But the memoirs are, for this very reason, also its radicalization."[6] This radicalization occurs in a variety of often neglected autobiographical notes, drafts, and fragments that were collected and made available by Benjamin's German editors in 1985 in the penultimate volume of his collected writings, the *Gesammelte Schriften*. These fragments of varying length address, typically in an autobiographical register, a variety of critical issues, including the relationship between the writing self and the body, the philosophy of language, anthropology, aesthetics, and history.

But his autobiographical production is not limited to short fragments and notes. Between 1926 and 1938, at significant points in the trajectory of his development, Benjamin wrote three major autobiographical texts: the *Moscow Diary* (1926–27), the *Berlin Chronicle* (1932), and the *Berlin Childhood around 1900* (1932–38).[7] The fragmentary *Moscow Diary* was written during his visit to the Soviet Union in the winter of 1926–27 and represents Benjamin's longest surviving autobiographical document. In its narrative gesture of free indirect discourse and the rhetoric of the quotidian, it holds a unique place among the texts of his autobiographical corpus. As a loose series of chronologically dated entries that examine Benjamin's shifting relation to Soviet politics and to his lover Asja Lacis, it appears more paratactical and tentative than the *Berlin Chronicle*, the text that he wrote in the spring of 1932 while on vacation in Ibiza. The *Berlin Chronicle* was Benjamin's attempt to make the strategy of literary montage – enacted in his Weimar book of aphorisms *One-Way Street* a few years earlier – productive for the language of autobiography. In it, he writes a series of fragments that interweave general confessional recollections with theoretically charged material to form a kind of montage of self-portraiture. The *Berlin Chronicle* is located somewhere in between the laconic, quotidian language of the *Moscow Diary* and the ornate prose snapshots of the *Berlin Childhood*, and contains, in a number of self-reflexive passages, some of his most sustained statements on the very possibility of autobiographical discourse. Like his allegorical miniatures of the *Berlin Childhood*, by far the most stylized and polished among his autobiographies, the *Berlin Chronicle* stages Benjamin's idiosyncratic relationship to various Berlin quarters, specific streets, and places such as Tiergarten and Peacock Island, and to his family and relatives. The images of the subject that emerge from these autobiographical reflections inform Benjamin's entire corpus. His confessional texts, which also can be read as symptoms of an ailing Weimar culture that buries itself somewhere along the one-way street between one historical catastrophe and another, perform an innovative historical materialism that intertwines general and political questions with highly personal reflections. As literary enactments of his aesthetic theories, Benjamin's autobiographical texts, perpetually in confrontation with their own irresolvable difficulties, are traversed by the melancholia of absence and finitude. Together, they offer an experience of radical singularity and transgression in which the history of the self is inseparable from the history of its culture.

All of Benjamin's texts provide their readers with the conceptual tools with which to read them, and his autobiographical texts are no exception. Indeed, in the *Berlin Chronicle* he offers us a remarkable passage that teaches us both how to read his self-portraitures and how they were conceived:

> Language has unmistakably signified that memory [*Gedächtnis*] is not an instrument for the exploration of the past but rather its scene [*Schauplatz*]. Memory is the medium of what has been experienced the way the earthen realm is the medium in which dead cities lie buried. He who wishes to approach his own buried past must act like a man who digs. This determines the tone, the stance of real memories. They must not be afraid to return again and again to the same fact of the matter, to strew it the way one strews soil, to churn it the way one churns the earthen realm. Because facts of the matter are only deposits, layers which deliver only to the most meticulous examination what constitutes the true assets hidden within the inner earth: the images which, torn from all former contexts, stand – like ruins or torsos in the collector's gallery – as the treasures in the sober chambers of our belated insights. And, in order to dig successfully, a plan is certainly required. Yet just as indispensable is the spade's careful, probing penetration of the dark earthen realm; and he who only keeps the inventory of his finds, but not also this dark bliss of the finding itself, cheats himself of the best part. The unsuccessful search belongs to it just

as fully as the fortunate search. This is why memory must not proceed by way of narrative, much less by way of reports, but must, rather, assay its spade, epically and rhapsodically in the most rigorous sense, in ever new places and, in the old ones, to delve into ever deeper layers.

("Berlin Chronicle," *SW* II, 611)

For Benjamin, the condition of possibility of the autobiographical act, memory itself, is not an instrument to be employed in order to gain access to a system of reference external to it, but rather a scene, space, or site, a spectacle or stage (*Schauplatz*). Memory is not a hermeneutic tool which assures the conjuring up of what is no longer the case. Rather, it is itself the scene in which what it cites takes place. Only in the scene of memory itself, he suggests, can what is called forth be narrativized in the virtual drama performed on its stage. This performance is inseparable from language, and Benjamin proposes a textual model of memory and writing. We could say that he proposes a logic of autobiography as "archaeological montage," insisting on both its irreducibly linguistic nature and, echoing Freud's trope of the psyche as an archaeological site, its psychoanalytic dimension.

If Benjamin wishes to situate his archaeological discussion of the self primarily in the art of self-portraiture, it is because he knows that, while the problem of the subject is inherent to a certain degree in all moments of representation, it is most acute in autobiographical discourse. The subject of an autobiography is traditionally located in the difficult attempt to project a unified, autonomous self in its pellucid historical and social context. The key figure of what Benjamin once termed his apprenticeship in German literature, Goethe, already recognized in his own confessional writing the difficulty of this autobiographical demand, what he calls "something nearly impossible to achieve," that is, "that the individual know himself and his century – himself, as a constant entity in the midst of all the circumstances."[8] This is a theoretically arduous task because autobiographical texts are more and less than the attempt to render a written account of a life story. In their self-reflexivity, these texts problematize the interrelation of the self (*autos*), life (*bios*), and the act of writing (*graphe*). Autobiographical language projects the image of a self that strives to come to grips with itself by manipulating the inscription of this or that temporality. The constructability, "the subjectivity-effect," is only guaranteed – "underwritten" – by the writer's proper name and signature. The reader is asked to enter what Philippe Lejeune has termed an "autobiographical pact," to submit to a fiction which is then legalized, countersigned by the signature of an other, a reader. This temporary legalization permits the examination of a subjective consciousness that turns itself into an object, thematizing – in the question of just what constitutes the self and differentiates it from an other (if the citation of the subject always involves such an ironic objectification) – its own conditions of possibility.

Yet, despite the promise of such an autobiographical pact, it remains difficult to treat autobiography as a genre, and Benjamin, in the *Berlin Chronicle*, registers the instability of his own text as autobiography: "Memories, even when they go into great breadth, do not always represent an autobiography. And this is certainly not one, not even for the Berlin years which, after all, are my only concern here" (*SW* II, 612). If he problematizes the moment of presentation in which memories are to figure as texts, it is because for him presentation always threatens to break down in an aporia. Benjamin's statement also suggests that his *Berlin Chronicle* is a text that wrestles with the possibility of its own presentation. The *Berlin Chronicle* announces itself, then, as a text of distinctly philosophical concerns and proportions. It intertwines questions of the "bios" with questions of presentation. Benjamin continues his thought when he writes: "For autobiography is concerned with time, with sequence and what constitutes the continuous flow of life. Here, however, I am talking of a space, of moments and discontinuities. For even though months and years appear here, it is in the figure they have in the moment of remembrance. This strange figure – one may call it fleeting or eternal: in no case is the material from which it is made that of life . . . The air of the city that is conjured here allots them [the people] only a brief, shadowy existence" (*SW* II, 612). While the traditional understanding of autobiography expects a chronological, hierarchical unfolding of the narrative of a life, Benjamin's text unfolds not in a linear fashion as the word "Chronicle" would suggest but as a montage of experiences and textual miniatures. His self-portraits reside, Benjamin tells us, not so much in time but in a space, a topography or constellation that the writing subject endows with certain meanings. While the space of these constellations can never be outside of temporality, time is here a trope that names not a linear unfolding of a vital trajectory (of the *bios*, *des Lebens*) but rather a "strange figure," that is, as a rhetorical form through which time is constructed in the moment of remembrance. This strange figure of time is thus not the product of some natural life, the mimetic double of lived experience, but rather what emerges as the figural image of temporality in the scene of writing an autobiography. Benjamin's strange figure of time thus encodes both temporality (it is written, thought, or remembered in time) *and* its suspension (it is, we are told, radically divorced from the natural material of life). This is precisely why, in the moment of the autobiographical act, the strange figure of time is both ephemeral and eternal. The scene of autobiography opens up precisely in the distance between what he terms the ephemeral and the eternal, between the struggle to capture the presence of meaning and the prospect of its absence. This scene is populated, to use Nietzsche's famous image, by a moveable army of metaphors, by dialectical images and haunting figures that conspire to call into question the certainty of reading and making sense even while enabling these activities in the first place.

The "strangeness" of autobiography that Benjamin addresses here has not escaped students of this mode of writing. Symptomatically, the noted historian of autobiography James Olney laments, "if autobiography is the least complicated of writing performances, it is also the most elusive of literary documents. One never knows where or how to take hold of autobiography."[9] And, according to Paul de Man, it is problematic to treat autobiographical texts as a distinct genre. This is so because they retreat from referentiality and because they are determined by the specificity of their linguistic medium, by "the illusion of reference."[10] Instead, de Man suggests that the concept of *prosopopoeia*, a rhetorical term signifying the impersonation or mask of an absent, distant, or dead speaker or voice, may be employed in the examination of autobiographical writing. To speak of autobiographically constructed selves is therefore to speak of their construction of a specific mask or voice that is designed to give the impression of presence. An analysis of such an autobiographical construction would hence scrutinize textual tropes less in an effort to assemble an essential presence, an "authentic" identity, but rather to examine the montage and subsequent employment of one possible mask among many competing ones, what Benjamin in the *Berlin Childhood* calls his "arsenal of masks" (*SW* III, 375). These masks are designed to produce rhetorically the most plausible "subjectivity effect," that is, the mechanisms by which, in the Nietzschean sense, the subject becomes what it is through representing itself to itself.

There are certain crucial relays between de Man's figure of prosopopoeia and Benjamin's reading of the scene of autobiography. Both prefer to think of autobiography not as the mimetic reflection of an empirical subject's life ("in no case is the material from which it is made that of life"), but as the staging of a mask (de Man) or figure (Benjamin) of an absent or deceased voice. De Man stages autobiography as the "giving and taking away of faces," while Benjamin speaks of the "brief, shadowy existence" of the faces and voices featured in his autobiographies. Like de Man's ghostly voices from beyond the grave, the selves of Benjamin's autobiography appear as ghosts, specters, and detached names, they "appear ghost-like in their windows only in order to disappear again, they sniff along thresholds like a *genius loci*, and even if they fill entire quarters of the city with their names, it is only in the way a dead man's fills the headstone on his grave." Readers of his autobiographical writing encounter a Benjaminian prosopopeia "in places and moments when it [the city] bears witness to the dead, shows itself full of the dead." The mask or voice that Benjamin's autobiographies assume is as much connected to life and presence as to death and absence. Thus, the life emplotted in the *Berlin Chronicle* "approaches the realm of the dead, where it protrudes into the realm of the living, in the same preciously attached manner ... as it approaches life itself" (*SW* II, 613).

The aspect of Benjamin's self-portraiture that pertains to the writing of death can be called "thanatographical." This aspect traverses not only his written corpus but also his empirical one, his entire intellectual being. In Adorno's terms, neither corpus corresponds to the idea of a self-present subject: "Just as Benjamin's thinking forms the antithesis to the existentialist concept of the person, empirically he seems, despite extreme individuation, hardly the person but rather the scene of the movement of the subject matter that pushed through him toward language."[11] This de-subjectified scene of the movement of thought takes place as though from beyond the grave. According to Adorno, it "was as if he [Benjamin] had paid a horrible price for the metaphysical power of what he saw and what he attempted to express in infallible words; as if he spoke as a dead man in return for his ability to recognize, with sobriety and calm, things which the living are not normally capable of recognizing."[12] Benjamin's autobiographical texts act as a kind of metonymy for this general thanatographical scene. They name the subject's finitude. It is as if his voice were always already a prosopopeia, coming from beyond the grave – even before death.

We could say that the *Berlin Childhood around 1900* responds to this engagement of the writerly voice with the thinking of finitude. This text, which Benjamin began in 1932 – by drastically reworking parts of the *Berlin Chronicle* – and continued to revise until shortly before his death, is not only his most refined and polished surviving autobiographical document, its constellation of enigmatic literary miniatures also contains what Benjamin thought would be "a kind of self-portrait" (*C*, 427). The importance of this text in his corpus cannot be overstated. It was written in close temporal and theoretical conjunction with the critical and philosophical questions that preoccupied Benjamin in the 1930s, such as memory and reproduction, politics and language, film and photography, and modernity and materialist historiography. Even though the text was not published until 1950 under the editorship of Adorno, its place and status in his œuvre is next to the *Arcades Project*. Indeed, the *Berlin Childhood* should be read as a kind of autobiographical *Arcades Project*.[13] As an extensive collection of quotations and observations concerning early industrial culture and technological mediation, the *Arcades Project* was meant to account for the historical, cultural, and ideological specificity of modernity from a bird's-eye perspective, while the literary *Berlin Childhood* was to ground these reflections figuratively in the subjective experiences of a childhood. In a series of fragmentary and intricately wrought narrative images, paratactically arranged, Benjamin surveys the various quarters and neighborhoods of Berlin, its courtyards and markets, its train stations and streets, its zoo and its ice-skating rink, its monuments and amusements. The reader confronts in each textual fragment a new sign system whose mastery remains out of reach. If the allegorical tableaux of the *Berlin Childhood* belong, as Peter Szondi remarks, "to the most beautiful prose poetry of our time,"[14] their beauty is always touched by the rigorous language of an otherness that prevents the self it depicts from coming into its own.

In the *Berlin Childhood*, the language of this otherness is one of *harte Fügung* – or "severe conjunction" – as Hermann Schweppenhäuser has observed, rhetorical images and poetic constructions that perpetually interrupt the flow of reading and compel the reader to linger with each sentence to ponder its manifold meanings.[15] As figures of a *harte Fügung*, the sentences of the *Berlin Childhood* are scissions or caesuras that suspend the textual self in the act of reading. Benjamin's "sentences," as Susan Sontag once put it, "do not seem to be generated in the usual way; they do not entail. Each sentence is written as if it were the first, or the last."[16] In the same way that Benjamin's sentences do not entail, they can never project the image of a coherent writerly self.

This dispersal of the writerly self is, for Benjamin, also an eminently political act. In contrast to the Fascist machine of stable concepts and fixed meanings, his writings enact the retreat of transparent sense, performing a resistance to the threat of being appropriated by the politics of this or that form of compulsive instrumental reason and the singularity of meaning. Indeed, written during the most difficult years of his exile and persecution, there is no page of the *Berlin Childhood* that is not touched by the images and threats of fascism. In a letter to Scholem from 3 March 1934 concerning the difficulties of finding a publisher for the book, Benjamin registers the political preoccupations that traverse his work on the text and that reveal themselves only during nightly visions – in the form of photographic negatives, as it were – to be the intensive engagements with the politics of fascism that they are: "In these times, when my imagination is preoccupied with the most unworthy problems between sunrise and sunset, I experience at night, more and more often, its emancipation in dreams, which nearly always have a political subject. I would really like to be in a position to tell you about them someday. They represent a pictorial atlas of the secret history of National Socialism."[17] In his afterword to the *Berlin Childhood's* posthumous publication, Adorno takes up the secret preoccupation with the political that traverses the text of Benjamin's life when he suggests that the "historical archetypes that [Benjamin] wished to develop in [the *Arcades Project*] out of their pragmatico-social and philosophical origin were, in the Berlin book, to flash up abruptly out of the immediacy of memory – with the force of pain felt for the irretrievable which, once it is lost, coagulates into an allegory of one's own demise." As Adorno continues, "For the images that the book conjures up to estranging proximity are neither idyllic nor contemplative. The shadow of Hitler's Reich lies cast upon them . . . The air surrounding the sites that are about to awake in Benjamin's presentation [*Darstellung*] is deadly. Upon them falls the gaze of the condemned one, and he perceives them as condemned."[18] If the *Berlin Childhood*'s topography of representation is linked to something deadly, then the shifting movements of its language stage a consistent confrontation with this deadly threat. In a constellation of figurative tableaux that bear titles such as "The Moon," "Winter Morning," "Butterfly Hunt," "The Stocking," "A Ghost," "Colors," "Society," "Two Puzzling Images," or "Victory Pillar," Benjamin's corporeal self disappears into language itself, a movement it shares with the shifting self of Proust's *A la Recherche du Temps Perdu*, the great inspiration of, and intertext to, the *Berlin Childhood*.

The space of literature

The writerly self that, as an alterity, is always already in retreat, is not only enacted in Benjamin's explicitly autobiographical texts, but it is also staged in his belletristic production. Next to his numerous satires, polemics, and glosses, his fictional and literary output can, like his autobiographical texts, best be described as *Denkbilder*, or thought-images. Thought-images are brief, aphoristic snapshots in prose in which literary, philosophical, aesthetic, and political impulses intersect, and Benjamin was influenced by the textual performances of such masters of the thought-image as Nietzsche and Karl Kraus. His 1928 avant-garde collection of thought-images and philosophico-cultural aphorisms, *One-Way Street*, stages the ways in which the city and its life become a semiotically charged text to be read by the self. As such, *One-Way Street* exerted an important influence on the projects of modern cultural criticism, such as Roland Barthes's *Mythologies*. With a brilliant dust-jacket pastiche by Benjamin's friend, the Weimar photographer Sascha Stone, *One-Way Street* belongs to the most refined of his belletristic writings. Its montage principle brings together through narrative images – each under a suggestive title such as "Imperial Panorama," "First Aid," or "Construction Site," – a variety of reflections on the relation between a writerly voice and early twentieth-century industrial culture. In its self-reflexively apodictic manner, the text gathers some of Benjamin's most provocative thoughts: "The work is the death mask of intention"; "When will we be ready to write books like catalogs?"; "What, in the end, makes advertisement so superior to criticism? Not what the moving red neon sign says – but the fiery pool reflecting it in the asphalt."[19]

We could say that *One-Way Street* includes something like Benjamin's poetics of a literary montage of history. Suspicious of any form of totality, the gaze of his literary self is always directed at the marginal and forgotten, and he is fascinated in the realm of writing with the hidden illuminating power of seemingly insignificant cultural objects such as children's books (of which he was an avid collector) and kitsch objects (his analyses of kitsch, literary and otherwise, continue to be the standard studies in postmodern approaches). Indeed, children's snow globes, as Adorno tells us, were Benjamin's favorite items. This looking, mediated by the language of literary presentation, for the strange or insignificant is an eminently political gesture not because it enacts any preconceived program of what deserves to be collected and studied and what does not, but because it refuses to accept the state of insignificance as something natural, unmasking it instead as a cultural, political, and *textual* construction that relies on problematic unspoken assumptions. In the segment "Construction Site," for instance, he describes the joy that children experience in rummaging through the debris of a construction site and the delight that they take in putting together seemingly disparate objects to build new forms. This image should be read figuratively because it is also that of Benjamin's historical materialist, the ragpicker and garbage collector of history. He looks awry, seeking his material and inspiration not in the officially sanctioned sites of a cultural text but in the refuse and debris that has been overlooked, repressed, or marginalized. Through a strategic montage, in which the neglected debris of history is put into a new grammatical constellation, a true revolutionary image emerges. This image, lodged in the language of its literary performance, is, for Benjamin, that of history itself.

What we could call the literary voice's non-mimetic relation to what is external to it – its irreducible alterity–is also enacted in Benjamin's other belletristic texts. Next to *One-Way Street*, among the most significant thought-images are his meditations on drugs from the late 1920s and 1930s – such as "Myslovitz – Braunschweig – Marseille," "Hashish in Marseille," and various specific drug protocols – as well as the transcripts of his radio broadcasts for children, pedagogico-philosophical pieces read by Benjamin on German radio, on such topics as Berlin toys, American bootleggers, the earthquake of Lisbon, stamp fraud, Caspar Hauser, and "true dog stories." Further, his thought-images include meditations on such topics as dreams, short shadows, eating, Paris, the beauty of horror, writing well, and the Easter Bunny revealed. Here, Benjamin focuses his gaze on a variety of seemingly marginal and occasional issues that, upon closer inspection, reveal themselves as central venues for meditations on memory, history, collecting, politics, and the relation among subjectivity, aesthetics, and the politics of culture. His literary thought-images enact and radicalize the stance that allows Benjamin, according to the *Arcades Project*, "to discover in the analysis of the small individual moment the crystal of the total event," in an effort "to break with vulgar historical naturalism" and to "grasp the construction of history as such" (*Arcades*, 461; N2, 6).

While these movements of construction and destruction of history in the orbit of the literary self have attracted a variety of commentary, Benjamin's formulations of these themes in his overtly lyrical attempts have received very little attention. Among the most significant aspects of his lyric poetry are over seventy sonnets, written between 1915 and 1925. Until their first publication in 1986, only a few people who were personally close to Benjamin were aware of the existence of these poems.[20] They were discovered in 1981 by Benjamin's Italian editor, the theorist Giorgio Agamben, in the Parisian Bibliothèque Nationale, in whose stacks Benjamin's friend, the French philosopher George Bataille – at the time a librarian there – had hidden his manuscripts when the Nazis invaded Paris. Benjamin conceived of the better part of his corpus of sonnets as an epitaph for his beloved friend Fritz Heinle and Heinle's girlfriend Rika Seligson, who committed a double suicide to protest the outbreak of The First World War. Like his autobiographical acts, which are always also thanatographical performances, these sonnets – which often resonate with the pathos and stylized elevation of a Hölderlin – encrypt a mourning that is depicted as having no common measure with what came before. As acts of singular commemoration, they depict what Benjamin understands as a fundamental subscript of his writings, that is, the relationship between the writing self and the notion of loss, between language and absence. As such, his poems not only stage the process of mourning in language, they also offer a meditation on the condition of possibility of writing. It is only because the other a text addresses is absent or dead that one writes in the first place. Were the other present, one would not write but employ spoken language. Writing, then, is always already a gesture of mourning an absence. There is no writing without an absent other, and Benjamin's poems will not cease to show themselves responsible to the ethical and political demands of this condition.

Ultimately, in the thought-images of both his fictional and his confessional writings, to read the self is to be thrown back upon the emptiness that is its textual form. Like the *Berlin Childhood*'s thought-image of "The Stocking," a stocking that, once unrolled, presents us only with the void at its core, the self consists not in some essential or metaphysical realm but only in its linguistic movements. To unravel their *textum* – the Latin word both for text and woven textile – is to unweave the self. For Benjamin's rolled-up stocking does not simply contain the gift that it brings, it also is this gift: "Now I decided to roll 'the gift' out of its woolen bag. I pulled it toward me ever more closely until something consternating occurred: I had unpacked 'the gift' but the 'bag' in which it had been was no longer there." Benjamin continues: "I could not repeat this process often enough. It taught me that form and content, cover and the covered are the same thing. It instructed me to pull truth to the fore out of literature the way that my child's hand pulled the stocking out of its 'bag'"(*SW* III, 374). Benjamin's confessional and literary texts show us how what emerges from a text, what becomes legible or understandable, including perhaps the confessional self, also cancels the text. This double movement literalizes the figure of unraveling: to understand but also to undo, in a comprehension that is, at the same time, a destruction.

Benjamin once wrote that "all great works of literature found a genre or dissolve one – they are, in other words, special cases." His autobiographical and literary writings can be considered such special cases, because they, like Proust's text of which he speaks here, are "unfathomable" in the ways in which they are "at once fiction, autobiography, and commentary, to the syntax of boundless sentences" ("Proust," *SW* II, 237). Further, they are special cases not only because of their enigmatic beauty and sustained theoretical interest but also because they mark something peculiar in Benjamin's œuvre. They stage a language in which the writing self remains suspended between construction and dispersal. In these texts, the self acts the way he tells us the self of Goethe's protagonists behaves in *Elective Affinities* – it "disappears under the arch of a . . . rhetorical question, in the perspective, so to speak, of infinite distance" ("Goethe," *SW* I, 333). Within this infinite distance, the language of the vicissitudinous self is, in turn, inscribed in a figure that, in its perpetual turnovers and slippages, refuses itself to any kind of politics of presence and transparency. If, in Benjamin's innovative art of self-portraiture, the self is always in retreat – that is, both disappearing and being treated one more time – then it belongs to those concepts that elude ideologemes of self-identity and the powerful myth of stable meanings. The self that his autobiographical and fictional texts present not only retreats but also signifies *that* it retreats, delivering a commentary on the movement of its own withdrawal. We could therefore say that his corpus dwells in the abyss that is its allegorical meaning. As Benjamin tells us in the *Arcades*

Project, the "'abyssal' sense ['*abgründige*' *Sinn*] is to be defined as 'meaning' ['*Bedeutung*']. It is always allegorical" (*Arcades*, 271; J24, 1). The quotation marks that he places around the words abyssal and meaning suggest their allegorical function. Like the written self, we can access meaning, and even its abyss, only in the conditional mode, as something figurative, something that remains in quotation marks. To the extent that this written self remains in quotation marks, the narratives in which it is staged unfold on the far side of transparent meaning, straightforward expression, and even explanation itself. As Benjamin writes in his literary thought-image, "The Art of Storytelling": "Every morning instructs us with news from around the globe. And yet, we are impoverished when it comes to noteworthy stories. Why is that? It is because no event reaches us that is not shot through with explanations. In other words, almost nothing that happens benefits the story, while almost everything benefits information. It is, after all, half the art of story-telling to keep a story, when it is rendered, free of explanations."[21] That Benjamin, in his acts of self-portraiture, keeps his confessional and literary texts free of explanations is his *gift* – in both the English and German senses of the word (that is, as present and poison) – to us, as we attempt to come to terms with the forms of alterity that these writings mobilize. After all, when the textual affirmation of a self can no longer be differentiated reliably from its erasure, any explanation will always only have begun.

NOTES

1. Some of the reflections and formulations that follow include or condense ideas from my book-length study of Benjamin's confessional writings, *Walter Benjamin and the Corpus of Autobiography* (Detroit: Wayne State University Press, 2000), as well as from my general essay on Benjamin, "Walter Benjamin, 1892–1940," in *Twentieth-Century European Cultural Theorists*, ed. Paul Hansom (Detroit: Gale Group, 2001). Vol. 242 of *Dictionary of Literary Biography*, 59–82.
2. Jeffrey Mehlman, *Walter Benjamin for Children: An Essay on His Radio Years* (University of Chicago Press, 1993), 2.
3. "Benjamin's Readings," *Diacritics* 22: 3–4 (1992), 19–34.
4. "Introduction," in *Who Comes After the Subject?* ed. Eduardo Cadava, Peter Connor, and Jean-Luc Nancy (New York: Routledge, 1991), 6.
5. "A Portrait of Walter Benjamin," *Prisms*, trans. Samuel Weber and Shierry Weber (Cambridge, MA: MIT Press, 1981), 231. For considerations of how the subject's demise of which Adorno speaks causes a series of ghostly returns in Benjamin's entire work, see the essays collected in Gerhard Richter (ed.), *Benjamin's Ghosts: Interventions in Contemporary Literary and Cultural Theory* (Stanford University Press, 2002).
6. "The Word 'Wolke' – If It Is One," trans. Peter Fenves, in *Benjamin's Ground: New Readings of Walter Benjamin*, ed. Rainer Nägele (Detroit: Wayne State University Press, 1988), 166.

7. The first two texts are available in English translation: *Moscow Diary*, ed. Gary Smith, trans. Richard Sieburth (Cambridge, MA: Harvard University Press, 1986); "Berlin Chronicle," in *SW* II, 595–637; *Berlin Childhood around 1900* in *SW* III, 344–413. Reliable and handy German editions of the texts are *Berliner Kindheit um neunzehnhundert: Fassung letzter Hand und Fragmente aus früheren Fassungen* (Frankfurt am Main: Suhrkamp, 1987) and, in a new alternate version, the recent bibliophile edition *Berliner Kindheit um neunzehnhundert: Gießener Fassung* (Frankfurt am Main: Suhrkamp, 2000).

8. *From My Life: Poetry and Truth*, trans. Robert Heitner (New York: Suhrkamp, 1987), 17.

9. "Autobiography and the Cultural Moment: A Thematic, Historical, and Bibliographical Introduction," in *Autobiography: Essays Theoretical and Critical*, ed. James Olney (Princeton University Press, 1980), 3.

10. "Autobiography as De-Facement," *The Rhetoric of Romanticism* (New York: Columbia University Press, 1984), 69.

11. Adorno, "Benjamin the Letter Writer," in *C*, xvii.

12. "Erinnerungen," *Über Walter Benjamin* (Frankfurt am Main: Suhrkamp, 1990), 2nd rev. ed., 82.

13. Adorno was the first reader to comment on the *Berlin Childhood* as a "subjective" counterpart to the *Arcades Project*. See "Nachwort zur 'Berliner Kindheit um neunzehnhundert,'" in *Über Walter Benjamin*, 74. That Benjamin himself thought of the *Berlin Childhood* as an autobiographical pendant to the *Arcades Project* is suggested by Sigrid Weigel, *Enstellte Ähnlichkeit: Walter Benjamins theoretische Schreibweise* (Frankfurt am Main: Suhrkamp, 1997), 31.

14. "Hoffnung im Vergangenen: Über Walter Benjamin," *Schriften*, vol. 2 (Frankfurt am Main: Suhrkamp, 1978), 276.

15. "Physiognomie eines Physiognomikers," *Zur Aktualität Walter Benjamins*, ed. Siegfried Unseld (Frankfurt am Main: Suhrkamp, 1972), 149.

16. "Under the Sign of Saturn," in *Under the Sign of Saturn* (New York: Farrar, Straus, Giroux, 1980), 129.

17. *The Correspondence of Walter Benjamin and Gershom Scholem: 1932–1940*, ed. Gershom Scholem, trans. Gary Smith and Andre Lefevere (New York: Schocken, 1989), 100.

18. "Nachwort," 74f.

19. See *One-Way Street*, *SW* I, 444–88.

20. While they still await their translation into English, Benjamin's sonnets are readily available in German, in addition to the *Gesammelte Schriften*, in *Sonette* (Frankfurt am Main: Suhrkamp, 1986).

21. "Kunst zu erzählen," *Denkbilder* (Frankfurt am Main: Suhrkamp, 1994), 136f.

GUIDE TO FURTHER READING

Editions

German

Gesammelte Schriften. 7 vols. Ed. Rolf Tiedemann and Hermann Schweppenhäuser. Frankfurt am Main: Suhrkamp: 1972–89.
Gesammelte Briefe. 6 vols. Ed. Christoph Gödde and Henri Lonitz. Frankfurt am Main: Suhrkamp, 1995–2000.

English

Arcades Project, The Trans. Howard Eiland and Kevin McLaughlin. Cambridge, MA: Belknap Press of Harvard University Press, 1999.
Charles Baudelaire: A Lyric Poet in the Era of High Capitalism. Trans. Harry Zohn. London: NLB, 1973.
Illuminations. Trans. Harry Zohn. Ed. Hannah Arendt. New York: Harcourt Brace, 1968.
Moscow Diary. Ed. Gary Smith. Trans. Richard Sieburth. Cambridge: Harvard University Press. 1986.
One-Way Street and Other Writings. Trans. Edmund Jephcott and Kingsley Shorter. London: NLB, 1979.
Reflections: Essays, Aphorisms, Autobiographical Writings. Trans. Edmund Jephcott. Ed. Peter Demetz. New York: Harcourt Brace Jovanovich, 1978.
Selected Writings. 4 vols. Ed. Michael Jennings, et al., Cambridge, MA: Harvard University Press, 1996–2003.
The Origin of the German Tragic Drama. Trans. Peter Osborne. London: NLB, 1977.
Understanding Brecht. Trans. Anna Bostock. London: NLB 1973.

Biographical writings

Adorno, Theodor W. "A Portrait of Walter Benjamin." In Adorno, *Prisms*, trans. Samuel Weber and Shierry Weber. Cambridge, MA: MIT Press, 1981, 227–41.
Bloch, Ernst. "Recollections of Walter Benjamin." Trans. Michael Jennings. In *On Walter Benjamin: Critical Essays and Reflections.* Ed. Gary Smith. Cambridge, MA: MIT Press, 1988, 338–45.

Broderson, Momme. *Walter Benjamin: A Biography*. Trans. Malcolm R. Green and Ingrida Ligers. Ed. Martina Derviş. London: Verso, 1996.

Eiland, Howard and Michael Jennings. See the Chronology published at the end of each volume of the *Selected Writings*.

Richter, Gerhard. "Walter Benjamin, 1892–1940." In *Twentieth-Century European Cultural Theorists*. Ed. Paul Hansom. Detroit: Gale Group, 2001. Vol. 242 of *Dictionary of Literary Biography*, 59–82.

Scheurmann, Ingrid and Scheurmann Konrad. Eds. *For Walter Benjamin*. Bonn: AsKI, 1993.

Scholem, Gershom. *Walter Benjamin: The Story of a Friendship*. Trans. Harry Zohn. Philadelphia: Jewish Publication Society of America, 1981.

Witte, Bernd. *Walter Benjamin: An Intellectual Biography*. Trans. James Rolleston. Detroit: Wayne State University Press, 1991.

Critical studies

The works listed here comprise by no means an exhaustive or comprehensive list of the wealth of material now available on Walter Benjamin. The list of critical writings is defined by its complementary relation to the issues presented by the essays in this volume. It has been compiled from the suggestions of the contributors and the editor.

Collections of essays

Andersson, Dag. T. and Reinton, Ragnhild. E. Eds. *Walter Benjamin: Language, Literature, History*. Oslo: Solum Forlag, 2000.

Benjamin, Andrew. Ed. *The Problems of Modernity: Adorno and Benjamin*. London: Routledge, 1989.

Benjamin, Andrew and Hanssen, Beatrice. Eds. *Walter Benjamin and Romanticism. Walter Benjamin Studies*. London: Continuum, 2002.

Benjamin, Andrew and Osborne, Peter. Eds. *Walter Benjamin's Philosophy: Destruction and Experience*. London: Routledge, 1994.

Ferris, David S. Ed. *Walter Benjamin: Theoretical Questions*. Stanford University Press, 1996.

Walter Benjamin on Romanticism. Special Issue. *Studies in Romanticism*, 31:4 (Winter 1992).

Fischer, Gerhard. Ed. *"With the Sharpened Axe of Reason": Approaches to Walter Benjamin*. Oxford: Berg, 1996.

Marcus, Laura and Nead, Lynda. Eds. *The Actuality of Walter Benjamin*. London: Lawrence & Wishart, 1998.

Nägele, Rainer. Ed. *Benjamin's Ground: New Readings of Walter Benjamin*. Detroit: Wayne State University Press, 1988.

Patt, Lise. Ed. *Benjamin's Blind Spot: Walter Benjamin and the Premature Death of Aura*. Santa Monica, CA: Institute of Cultural Inquiry, 2001.

Richter, Gerhard. Ed. *Benjamin's Ghosts: Interventions in Contemporary Literary and Cultural Theory*. Stanford University Press, 2002.

Smith, Gary. Ed. *On Walter Benjamin: Critical Essays and Recollections*. Cambridge: MIT Press, 1988.

Benjamin: Philosophy, Aesthetics, History. University of Chicago Press, 1989.

Steinberg, Michael P. Ed. *Walter Benjamin and the Demands of History*. Ithaca: Cornell University Press, 1996.

Books and articles

Bahti, Timothy. "History as Rhetorical Enactment: Walter Benjamin's Theses 'On the concept of History.'" *Diacritics* 10 (Fall 1979): 2–17.

Benjamin, Andrew. *Art Mimesis and the Avant-Garde*. London: Routledge, 1991.

Buck-Morss, Susan. *The Dialectics of Seeing: Walter Benjamin and the Arcades Project*. Cambridge, MA: MIT Press, 1989.

Bullock, Marcus. *Romanticism and Marxism: The Philosophical Development of Literary Theory and Literary History in Walter Benjamin and Friedrich Schlegel*. New York: P. Lang, 1987.

Cadava, Eduardo. *Words of Light: Theses on the Photography of History* (Princeton University Press, 1997).

Caygill, Howard. *Walter Benjamin: The Colour of Experience*. London: Routledge, 1998.

Cohen, Margaret. *Profane Illumination: Walter Benjamin and the Paris of Surrealist Revolution*. Berkeley: University of California Press, 1993.

De Man, Paul. "Conclusions: Walter Benjamin's 'The Task of the Translator.'" In *The Resistance to Theory*. Minneapolis: University of Minnesota Press, 1986.

Derrida, Jacques. "Des Tours de Babel." Trans. Joseph Graham. *Difference in Translation*. Ed. Joseph Graham. Ithaca: Cornell University Press, 1985.

Eagleton, Terry. *Walter Benjamin, or, Towards a Revolutionary Criticism*. London: Verso Editions and New Left Books, 1981.

Gasché, Rodolphe. "On Critique, Hypercriticism, and Deconstruction: The Case of Benjamin." *Cardozo Law Review* 13:4 (1991): 1115–32.

"Saturnine Vision and the Question of Difference: Reflections on Walter Benjamin's Theory of Language." *Studies in Twentieth-Century Literature* 11:1 (Fall 1986): 69–90. Reprinted in *Benjamin's Ground: New Readings of Walter Benjamin*. Ed. Rainer Nägele. Detroit: Wayne State University Press, 1988.

Gilloch, Graeme. *Walter Benjamin, Critical Constellations*. Oxford: Polity Press, 2002.

Hamacher, Hamacher. "The Word 'Wolke' – If It Is One." Trans. Peter Fenves. In *Benjamin's Ground: New Readings of Walter Benjamin*. Ed. Rainer Nägele. Detroit: Wayne State University Press, 1988, 147–76.

Hansen, Miriam Bratu. "Benjamin and Cinema: Not a One-Way Street." *Critical Inquiry* 25 (Winter 1999): 306–43.

Hanssen, Beatrice. *Walter Benjamin's Other History: Of Stones, Animals, Human Beings, and Angels*. Berkeley: University of California Press, 1998.

Jacobs Carol. *In the Language of Walter Benjamin*. Baltimore: Johns Hopkins University Press, 1999.

Jay, Martin. "'The Aesthetic Ideology' as Ideology; or, What Does it Mean to Aestheticize Politics?" *Cultural Critique* (1992): 41–61.

Jennings, Michael. *Dialectical Images: Walter Benjamin's Theory of Literary Criticism*. Ithaca: Cornell University Press, 1987.

Koepnick, Lutz. *Walter Benjamin and the Aesthetics of Power*. Lincoln: University of Nebraska, 1999.

Kracauer, Siegfried. "On the Writings of Walter Benjamin." In *The Mass Ornament.* Ed. and trans.Thomas Y. Levin. Cambridge, MA: Harvard University Press, 1995, 259–64.

Leslie, Esther. *Walter Benjamin: Overpowering Conformism.* London: Pluto Press, 2000.

Levin, Tom. "Walter Benjamin and the Theory of Art History: An Introduction to 'Rigorous Study of Art,'" *October* 47 (1988): 76–83.

McCole, John. *Walter Benjamin and the Antinomies of Tradition.* Ithaca: Cornell University Press, 1993.

"Benjamin's Passagen-Werk: A Guide to the Labyrinth." *Theory and* Society 14 (1985): 497–509.

Mertins, Detlef. "Walter Benjamin and the Tectonic Unconscious: Using Architecture as an Optical Instrument." In *The Optic of Walter Benjamin, de-, dis-, ex-.* Vol. 3. Ed. Alex Coles. Black Dog Publishing Limited, May 1999, 196–225.

Mehlman, Jeffrey. *Walter Benjamin for Children: an Essay on his Radio Years.* University of Chicago Press, 1993.

Missac, Pierre. *Walter Benjamin's Passages.* Trans. Shierry Weber Nicholsen. Cambridge, MA: MIT Press, 1995.

Nägele, Rainer. *Theater, Theory, Speculation: Walter Benjamin and the Scenes of Modernity.* Baltimore: Johns Hopkins University Press, 1991.

Pensky, Max. *Melancholy Dialectics: Walter Benjamin and the Play of Mourning.* Amherst: University of Massachusetts Press, 1993.

Preziosi, Donald. "The Crystalline Veil and the Phallomorphic Imaginary: Walter Benjamin's Pantographic Riegl." In *The Optic of Walter Benjamin, de-, dis-, ex-.* Vol. 3. Ed. Alex Coles. Black Dog Publishing Limited, May 1999, 120–36.

Rampley, Matthew. *The Remembrance of Things Past: On Aby Warburg and Walter Benjamin.* Wiesbaden: Harrassowitz, 2000.

Richter, Gerhard. *Walter Benjamin and the Corpus of Autobiography.* Detroit: Wayne State University Press, 2000.

Roberts, Julian. *Walter Benjamin.* Atlantic Highlands, NJ: Humanities Press, 1983.

Rochlitz, Rainer. *The Disenchantment of Art: The Philosophy of Walter Benjamin.* Trans. Jane Marie Todd. New York: Guilford Press, 1996.

Weber, Samuel. *Mass Mediauras: Form, Technics, Media.* Ed. Alan Cholodenko. Stanford University Press, 1996.

"Taking Exception to Decision: Walter Benjamin and Carl Schmitt." In *Enlightenments: Encounters between Critical Theory and Contemporary French Thought.* Ed. Harry Kunneman and Hent de Vries. Kampen, The Netherlands: Kok Pharos, 1993.

"Criticism Underway: Walter Benjamin's *Romantic Concept of Criticism.*" In *Romantic Revolutions.* Ed. Kenneth Johnston et al. Bloomington: Indiana University Press, 1990. 302–19.

Weigel, Sigrid. *Body- and Image-Space: Re-Reading Walter Benjamin.* New York: Routledge, 1996.

Wolin, Richard. *Walter Benjamin, an Aesthetic of Redemption.* Berkeley: University of California Press, 1994.

Absolute 9–11, 12–13, 14, 15, 45, 52, 57, 98, 101, 102, 104–5, 106–7, 110–11, 112–13, 136, 138, 140, 144, 147, 148
Adorno, Theodor Wiesengrund 41–42, 52, 68, 72, 115, 130–131, 153, 154, 156, 157, 160, 161, 162–64, 166, 167, 171, 173, 174, 182, 207, 224, 230, 232, 237
aesthetics 42–44, 56, 60, 80, 144, 179
    and politics 36, 38
Agamben, Giorgio 174
allegory 45–47, 51, 60, 69, 87–88, 89, 98, 149, 158, 159, 189, 209, 236
    and symbol 98
ambiguity 138, 141
ambivalence 136, 139
antinomy 138, 139
aphorism 24–25, 54
appearance 35, 103–4, 105, 110, 112, 179
Aragon, Louis 171, 204
architecture 217
Aristotle 66
art 35–42, 44–52
    and authenticity 39–40, 41, 51
    and politics 41
    and technology 38, 50–51
art history 35, 36–37, 75, 76, 77, 78–79, 91, 186
Artaud, Antonin 165, 175
aura 39, 40–41, 52, 55, 61, 69, 71, 139, 144
authenticity, see art and authenticity
autobiography 221, 228–230
    see also self-portraiture
autonomy 149
avant-garde 21, 23, 33, 35, 55, 186

Balzac, Honoré de 196
barbarism 73, 89, 92, 94, 96

Baudelaire, Charles 69, 118, 131, 173, 188, 191, 215–16, 219
beautiful 103, 105–6, 110
Benjamin, Walter
    "Agesilaus Santander" 61, 72
    "Antitheses Concerning Word and Name" 67, 68, 69
    Arcades Project 14, 15–16, 32, 48–51, 54, 64–65, 69, 72, 89, 94–95, 96, 98, 109, 110, 111–13, 121, 127, 131, 144, 148, 155, 157, 158, 162–63, 170, 177–78, 180–188, 190–191, 193, 196, 197, 198, 199–201, 202–6, 210, 212, 217–218, 223, 230, 234, 236
    "Astrology" 67
    Berlin Chronicle 13, 223, 225–30
    "Books by the Mentally Ill" 119, 120
    "Books that Remain Alive" 80
    Concept of Criticism in Early German Romanticism 9–10, 11–12, 35, 44–45, 56, 57, 71, 98, 99, 101, 106, 134, 137, 138, 139, 140–43, 144, 145, 146, 147, 148
    "Death" 224
    "Doctrine of the Similar" 56, 65, 66, 68, 70, 71, 72, 125
    "Eduard Fuchs, Collector and Historian" 73, 79, 89–94, 131, 199
    "Experience" 69, 70
    "Experience and Poverty" 20, 55, 70
    "Franz Kafka" 20, 165–66, 222
    "From the Brecht Commentary" 164
    "Goethe's Elective Affinities" 47–48, 71, 98–105, 106, 123, 235
    "Graphology Old and New" 72
    "Ibizan Sequence" 34
    "In the Sun" 34

"Karl Krauss" 20, 62, 67, 72, 118, 148
"Language and Logic" 71
"Life of the Students" 18, 191–92
"Little History of Photography" 52, 129, 199, 213
Moscow Diary 33, 225
"On the Image of Proust" 68, 235
"On Language as Such and on the Language of Man" 56, 58–60, 69, 70, 71, 88, 143, 171
"On Some Motifs in Baudelaire" 55, 70, 106, 116, 117–18, 200
"On the Concept of History" 13, 28, 73, 105, 108–9, 110, 139, 145, 146, 149, 178, 193–95, 200, 201, 202, 210
"On the Mimetic Faculty" 56, 64, 65, 68, 71, 126, 149
"On the Present Situation of Russian Film" 33
"On the Present Social Situation of the French Writer" 162
"On the Program of the Coming Philosophy" 70
One-Way Street 23–33, 222, 232–33
Origin of the German Tragic Drama 3–9, 45–47, 60, 66, 67
"Paris, Capital of the 19th Century. Exposé of 1935" 48, 184, 197, 204, 205, 208–9, 211, 213, 214–17, 219
"Paris of the Second Empire in Baudelaire" 199
"Reflections on Humboldt" 70
"Reply to Oscar A. H. Schmitz" 33
"San Gimignano" 221
"Short Shadows" 34
"Sonnets" 234
"Surrealism. The Last Snapshot of the European Intelligentsia" 167–73, 199, 224
"The Author as Producer" 20
"The Political Groupings of Russian Writers" 33
"The Return of the Flâneur" 70
"The Rigorous Study of Art" 78, 82
"The Storyteller" 70, 120, 199
"The Task of the Translator" 57, 60, 62–64, 67, 71, 132, 143, 148
"The Work of Art in the Age of its Technological Reproducibility" 38–42, 49, 95, 105–6, 129, 130, 145, 149, 199, 211, 213

"Thought Figures" 34, 68, 158–59
"Toys and Play" 127
Bibliothèque Nationale 218
Blanqui, Louis Auguste 191, 209
Bloch, Ernst 154, 201
Boehme, Jacob 58, 59
Brecht, Bertolt 54, 65, 72, 153, 154, 157, 162, 164–66, 167, 169, 172, 173–74, 176
Breton, André 170, 204
Breuer, Josef 115
Buber, Martin 11, 57, 159
Buck-Morss, Susan 71, 178, 197, 219
Burckhardt, Jacob 74–77, 82, 83, 84
Büchner, Georg 161, 173

caesura 36, 57, 71, 98–100, 101–2, 110, 111–12, 136, 153, 156, 162, 169
  and symbol, 98
capitalism 180, 182, 183, 185, 187, 188, 193, 200, 201–2, 205, 216
Cassirer, Ernst 65
Caygill, Howard 113
citation 132, 144, 148, 150
Cohen, Hermann 134
Cohen, Margaret 196
commodity 26–27, 180, 183–84, 187–88, 193, 196, 201, 208, 214, 216
commodity fetishism 26, 183–84, 201, 207–8
communism 160, 172
Communist Party 157
constellation 31, 75, 90–91, 116, 117, 125, 156, 168, 177, 186–87
constructivism 29–30
continuity 97, 108–9, 110
criticism 10–13, 18, 48, 62, 98, 100–1, 102, 103–5, 106, 107–8, 140–45, 146, 148, 150, 165, 181, 182, 188, 195, 202, 210
  and absolute 111
  and interruption 108
  and knowledge 106
  cultural 182, 183, 195
criticizability 101, 107, 108, 148
cult value 40, 41
Culture 73, 183

Dadaism 22, 30–31
Daguerre, Jacques 213
Damaye, Henri 130
De Man, Paul 145, 229

Denkbild, see thought figure
Derrida, Jacques 223
Descartes, René 136
destruction 99, 110
dialectic 158, 177, 179, 188, 193, 195
   dialectical 65, 128, 162 *see also* materiality
Dialectics at a standstill 156, 193, 195
digression 3
Dilthey, Wilhelm 55
distraction 30, 41
dream 32, 51, 115, 127, 168, 188, 191, 205,
   206, 208
Dürer, Albrecht 86–88

Eisenstein, Sergei 129
emblem 158
Engels, Friedrich 90, 91, 92
Enlightenment 113, 141
esoteric 12, 17, 65, 146
experience 55, 68, 69, 70–71, 93, 94, 138
   and history 90
expressionless 36, 47, 51, 57, 99–100, 102,
   107

fascism 50, 51, 123, 174
Ferris, David 151
fetish 26, 183–84, 201
   see also commodity fetishism
Fichte, Johann Gottlieb 135–39, 144, 145,
   151
film 22, 30, 32, 35, 38, 39, 41, 49, 149, 169
   and psychoanalysis 129
form 3, 5, 6, 7, 8, 9, 14, 15, 16, 20, 23, 24,
   29–31, 32, 33, 42, 44, 45, 78, 99
   presentational 44, 45
Foucault, Michel 219
Fourier, Charles 212
Fragment 5–6, 8, 30, 57, 62, 64, 88, 95, 99,
   133, 138, 141, 147–48, 180, 186–87
Frankfurt School 128, 130, 154, 160, 161,
   162–63, 173, 174
Freud, Sigmund 65, 115–20, 121, 122, 124,
   125–28, 129–33, 138, 155, 157, 161,
   163, 204, 205, 206–7
   and trauma 117, 121, 129
Fromm, Erich 161
Fuchs, Eduard 74, 79, 91
futurism 50

Gasché, Rodolphe 9–10, 52
Genesis 58, 59
George, Stefan 123

gesture 165–66
G-Group 21–23
   see also avant-garde
Goethe, Johann Wolfgang von 141, 158,
   159, 227
Grandville, Jean Ignace Isidore Gérard 214
graphology 124–26

Hamacher, Werner 225
Hamann, Johann Georg 54, 56, 60, 61, 63,
   70
Hansen, Miriam Bratu 129
Haussmann, Georges-Eugène, Baron 216–17
Hegel, Georg Wilhelm Friedrich 48, 49,
   73–75, 76, 95, 109, 135, 142, 145,
   146–47, 151, 156–57, 172, 179, 180,
   185, 188–191, 195, 196, 197, 198, 202,
   224
hermeneutics 181
hieroglyph 67, 121, 124, 125
historicism 51, 90, 92, 97, 107, 108–9, 111,
   145, 179, 194
historicity 37
history 2–3, 13–15, 28, 37, 73, 76, 91, 95,
   97–98, 105, 107, 110, 112, 134, 139,
   146, 149, 160, 177, 179, 180–81, 185,
   186–87, 188, 190, 191–93, 197, 200,
   202, 206, and time 97, 98, 104, 188,
   190, 191
   cultural 73–95
   origin of 74
   dialectical 73, 74, 80, 85, 90, 91, 92,
   93–94, 179, 187–88
Hofmannsthal, Hugo von 71
Horkheimer, Max 72, 94, 96, 131, 160, 163,
   174
Hölderlin, Friedrich 36, 56, 57, 60, 63, 71,
   98, 100, 101–2, 121, 153, 156, 169
Hugo, Victor 219
Humboldt, Wilhelm von 70

iconoclasm 48
idealism, German 60, 135, 136
identity 137, 156
ideology 135, 145, 160, 203, 205
   aesthetic 144
illumination, profane 169, 218
image 172, 179, 180, 186, 187, 188–89,
   192–93, 204
   dialectical 16, 35, 83, 111, 113, 124, 132,
   156, 167, 178, 180, 181, 185, 188, 189,
   190–91, 193–95, 197, 206, 208, 210

Index

Imago 120
individuality 215
inexpressible 11
infinite 135–36, 137, 138, 145
Institute for Social Research, *see* Frankfurt
    School
interruption 3, 97–98, 101–2, 105, 107,
    109–13, 114, 179, 180, 184, 191
    and caesura 98
    and expressionless 100
intertextuality 116, 123, 132–33
irony, Romantic 138, 151

Jacobs, Carol 113
Jameson, Frederic 221
Jugendstil 50, 215
Jung, Carl Gustav 55, 115, 124, 128, 130

kabbalah 54, 56, 57, 65
Kafka, Franz 62, 142, 157
Kant, Immanuel 42, 43, 48, 52, 55, 60, 77,
    109, 113, 134, 135, 136, 138, 140, 143,
    145, 156, 201
Karplus, Gretel 154, 166–67
Kierkegaard, Søren 55, 174
Klages, Ludwig 55, 72, 124–125, 128, 130,
    131
Kristeva, Julia 123, 132
Kunstwollen ("artistic will") *see* Riegl

Labrouste, Henri 218
Lacis, Asja 20, 33, 128, 154–55, 201
Lacoue-Labarthe, Philippe 151
Landau, Luise von 153
language 54–70, 88, 100, 111, 127, 143,
    148, 156, 160, 161, 171, 224, 226–27
    and graphology 67, 72
    and magic 54, 56–57, 58, 59, 65,
    68, 70
    and materiality 68
    and onomatopoeia 67, 72
    pure language 55, 58, 60, 62, 64
Leibnitz, Gottfried Wilhelm 146, 152
Lessing, Gotthold Ephraim 141
literalness (*Wörtlichkeit*) 63–64, 68, 101
Lukàcs, Georg 20–21, 25, 154, 155, 180,
    201, 212, 217

magic 67
    see also language and magic
Mallarmé, Stéphane 54, 70
Marcuse, Herbert 161, 174, 189

Marx, Karl 25, 26, 34, 42, 161, 180, 182–85,
    187, 200, 201–2, 203, 205, 207–8,
    217
Marxism 20–21, 23, 73, 89, 154–55, 156,
    160, 162, 163, 174, 202, 206, 209
mass 41–42, 149
mass culture 41, 69, 214
materialism 65, 79–80, 139, 158, 170,
    172–73, 179, 180, 187, 204, 209
    anthropological 161, 172–73
    historical 23, 37, 38, 73, 80, 89, 90, 92,
    93, 94, 110, 111, 149, 156, 170, 185,
    193, 194, 195, 202
materiality 40
mediation, 156, 171
melancholy 86–89, 118, 120
memory 117, 118, 189
Mendelssohn, Georg 126, 128
Menninghaus, Winfried 71
Messianic 63, 64, 135, 139, 145–46, 149,
    151, 193–95, 210, 217
method 20, 31, 110, 178, 179, 181–82, 185,
    187, 194
Mette, Alexander 120–23
mimesis 46, 56, 64–70
modernism 3, 33, 116, 155, 186
modernity 2, 64, 97–98, 113, 136, 155, 183,
    185, 188, 200–1, 202, 204, 206, 208,
    211, 213, 214, 215, 217, 219
    and Enlightenment 97
    and interruption 97
    capitalist 187
montage 30–31, 33, 90, 186, 187, 200, 210,
    213, 225, 227, 228, 232–33
mosaic 5–6
mourning 88–89
    see also, Benjamin, *Origin of the German
    Tragic Drama*
mysticism 56, 64, 146
myth 57, 112

naming 61
Nancy, Jean-Luc 151, 224
National Socialism 72, 231
Nägele, Reiner 116, 120
Nietzsche, Friedrich 54, 60, 87, 151, 155,
    173, 191, 207
nonsensuous-similarity 67, 69, 149
Novalis (Friedrich von Hardenburg) 44, 71,
    134, 135, 137, 139, 140, 141, 142, 144
"Now of recognizability" 180, 191, 193,
    195

Index

Osborne, Peter 113

painting 52
Panofsky, Erwin 77, 78, 82, 83, 87
panorama 190, 197, 213
Paris 200–1
Pavlov, Ivan 128
phantasmagorical 184, 187, 190, 207–9,
    210, 213, 215–16
phenomenology 179
Philippe, Louis 214
photography 38, 49–50, 213
Plato 66, 68
politics 36, 38, 39, 57, 109, 112, 156, 157,
    168, 171–73, 194, 213, 223, 231–32
    and history 37
    and theory 156
postmodern 186
praxis 162, 165
present 39, 40, 64, 66, 76, 90, 93, 109, 110,
    177, 180–81, 188, 193
    see also "now of recognizability"
presentation 103, 106, 142, 172, 228
profane 168
progress 55, 74, 92, 95, 134, 135, 145, 180,
    187, 191, 200
prosaic 101
Proust, Marcel 68–69, 71, 117, 132, 200,
    203
pyschoanalysis 115–33, 204, 206

Ranke 74, 105
reflection 135–36, 138–40, 141, 145
reification 26, 155
religion 169
reproducibility 39–40, 149
revolution 168, 169, 173, 184, 191
Richter, Hans 22
Riegl, Alois 74, 77, 79, 80–83, 84, 95
    and Kunstwollen 80–82
Rimbaud, Arthur 173, 204
Romanticism, German 9–13, 18, 36, 44–45,
    54, 56–57, 62, 68, 71, 97–98, 105, 113,
    134–36, 138–50, 151
Rühle, Otto 207

Schelling, Friedrich Wilhelm Joseph
    74, 76
Schiller, Friedrich 9, 43–44
Schlegel, August Wilhelm 71, 144
Schlegel, Friedrich 9, 44–45, 56, 71, 100,
    134, 135, 137, 140, 141, 142, 143, 146,
    147–48, 149, 151

Schmitt, Carl 152, 175
Scholem, Gershom 57, 64–65, 72, 118–19,
    127, 142, 153, 154, 162, 164, 166, 167
Schreber, Daniel Paul 119, 127
Schweppenhäuser, Hermann 231
secularization 161
self-portraiture 221–36
    see also autobiography
shock 30, 56, 117–18, 132, 149, 179, 181,
    186, 187, 188, 192, 193
similarity 71
Social Democrats 92
Sontag, Susan 231
sovereignity 152
Soviet Union 19, 128
Sprachmagie, see language and magic
sublime 48
Surrealism 22, 31–32, 36, 127, 128, 168,
    169, 171, 185–86, 196, 203–5
symbol 45, 52, 56–57, 62, 69, 87,
    98–100
    and allegory 98
Szondi, Peter 145, 231

technology 50–51, 129, 149, 183
telepathy 126–27
temporality 102, 107, 177, 215
theater 155–56, 159, 165, 169, 172, 173
theological 156, 160, 163, 169, 170, 178,
    181, 184, 193, 209
theory 156–57, 159–60, 161–62, 165, 180,
    181–82
    and politics 156
thought figure (Denkbild) 24, 26–27, 68,
    158, 162, 232
"Thought Figures" 34, 68, 158–59
Tiedemann, Rolf 178
time 107, 112, 113, 114, 145, 149, 179, 188,
    191, 193, 228
    and history 97–98, 105, 188
time differential 190, 192–93
torso 99
tradition 140, 142, 181
translation 58, 59–64, 148
truth 181
    and appearence 112
    content 103
    historical 180, 181, 183, 194

unconscious 119, 120, 124, 133
unconsciousness 32

violence 48, 132

Warburg, Aby 74, 77, 82, 83–89, 96
Weber, Samuel 41
Weigel, Sigrid 116, 118, 237
Weimar Republic 25, 33, 226
work of art 35, 37, 142, 186
World Exhibition 213–14, 215

Worringer, Wilhelm 81
Wölfflin, Heinrich 74, 77–80, 82, 83, 84, 91
writing 6–7, 57, 67

youth movement, German 134, 135, 145, 191

Zohar 57, 58, 63, 65

CAMBRIDGE COMPANIONS TO LITERATURE

The Cambridge Companion to Greek Tragedy
edited by P. E. Easterling

The Cambridge Companion to Old English Literature
edited by Malcolm Godden and Michael Lapidge

The Cambridge Companion to Medieval Romance
edited by Roberta L. Kreuger

The Cambridge Companion to Medieval English Theatre
edited by Richard Beadle

The Cambridge Companion to English Renaissance Drama,
2 edn
edited by A. R. Braunmuller and Michael Hattaway

The Cambridge Companion to Renaissance Humanism
edited by Jill Kraye

The Cambridge Companion to English Poetry, Donne to Marvell
edited by Thomas N. Corns

The Cambridge Companion to English Literature, 1500–1600
edited by Arthur F. Kinney

The Cambridge Companion to English Literature, 1650–1740
edited by Steven N. Zwicker

The Cambridge Companion to Writing of the English Revolution
edited by N. H. Keeble

The Cambridge Companion to English Restoration Theatre
edited by Deborah C. Payne Fisk

The Cambridge Companion to British Romanticism
edited by Stuart Curran

The Cambridge Companion to Eighteenth-Century Poetry
edited by John Sitter

The Cambridge Companion to the Eighteenth-Century Novel
edited by John Richetti

The Cambridge Companion to the Gothic Novel
edited by Jerrold E. Hogle

The Cambridge Companion to Victorian Poetry
edited by Joseph Bristow

The Cambridge Companion to the Victorian Novel
edited by Deirdre David

The Cambridge Companion to Crime Fiction
edited by Martin Priestman

The Cambridge Companion to Travel Writing
edited by Peter Hulme and Tim Youngs

The Cambridge Companion to American Realism and Naturalism
edited by Donald Pizer

The Cambridge Companion to Nineteenth-Century American Women's Writing
edited by Dale M. Bauer and Philip Gould

The Cambridge Companion to the Classic Russian Novel
edited by Malcolm V. Jones and Robin Feuer Miller

The Cambridge Companion to the French Novel: from 1800 to the Present
edited by Timothy Unwin

The Cambridge Companion to the Spanish Novel: from 1600 to the Present
edited by Harriet Turner and Adelaida López de Martínez

The Cambridge Companion to Jewish American Literature
edited by Hana Wirth-Nesher and Michael P. Kramer

The Cambridge Companion to the African American Novel
edited by Maryemma Graham

The Cambridge Companion to Modernism
edited by Michael Levenson

The Cambridge Companion to Australian Literature
edited by Elizabeth Webby

The Cambridge Companion to American Women Playwrights
edited by Brenda Murphy

The Cambridge Companion to Modern British Women Playwrights
edited by Elaine Aston and Janelle Reinelt

The Cambridge Companion to Virgil
edited by Charles Martindale

The Cambridge Companion to Ovid
edited by Philip Hardie

The Cambridge Companion to Dante
edited by Rachel Jacoff

The Cambridge Companion to Cervantes
edited by Anthony J. Cascardi

The Cambridge Companion to Goethe
edited by Lesley Sharpe

The Cambridge Companion to Dostoevskii
edited by W. J. Leatherbarrow

The Cambridge Companion to Tolstoy
edited by Donna Tussing Orwin

The Cambridge Companion to Proust
edited by Richard Bales

The Cambridge Companion to Thomas Mann
edited by Ritchie Robertson

The Cambridge Companion to Lacan
edited by Jean-Michel Rabaté

The Cambridge Companion to Chekhov
edited by Vera Gottlieb and Paul Allain

The Cambridge Companion to Ibsen
edited by James McFarlane

The Cambridge Companion to Brecht
edited by Peter Thomson and Glendyr Sacks

The Cambridge Companion to Chaucer, second edition
edited by Piero Boitani and Jill Mann

The Cambridge Companion to Shakespeare
edited by Margareta de Grazia and Stanley Wells

The Cambridge Companion to Shakespeare on Film
edited by Russell Jackson

The Cambridge Companion to Shakespearean Comedy
edited by Alexander Leggatt

The Cambridge Companion to Shakespeare on Stage
edited by Stanley Wells and Sarah Stanton

The Cambridge Companion to Shakespeare's History Plays
edited by Michael Hattaway

The Cambridge Companion to Shakespearean Tragedy
edited by Claire McEachern

The Cambridge Companion to Spenser
edited by Andrew Hadfield

The Cambridge Companion to Ben Jonson
edited by Richard Harp and Stanley Stewart

The Cambridge Companion to Milton, second edition
edited by Dennis Danielson

The Cambridge Companion to Samuel Johnson
edited by Greg Clingham

The Cambridge Companion to Jonathan Swift
edited by Christopher Fox

The Cambridge Companion to Mary Wollstonecraft
edited by Claudia L. Johnson

The Cambridge Companion to William Blake
edited by Morris Eaves

The Cambridge Companion to Wordsworth
edited by Stephen Gill

The Cambridge Companion to Coleridge
edited by Lucy Newlyn

The Cambridge Companion to Keats
edited by Susan J. Wolfson

The Cambridge Companion to Mary Shelley
edited by Esther Schor

The Cambridge Companion to Jane Austen
edited by Edward Copeland and Juliet McMaster

The Cambridge Companion to the Brontës
edited by Heather Glen

The Cambridge Companion to Charles Dickens
edited by John O. Jordan

The Cambridge Companion to George Eliot
edited by George Levine

The Cambridge Companion to Thomas Hardy
edited by Dale Kramer

The Cambridge Companion to Oscar Wilde
edited by Peter Raby

The Cambridge Companion to George Bernard Shaw
edited by Christopher Innes

The Cambridge Companion to Joseph Conrad
edited by J. H. Stape

The Cambridge Companion to D. H.
Lawrence
edited by Anne Fernihough

The Cambridge Companion to Virginia
Woolf
edited by Sue Roe and Susan Sellers

The Cambridge Companion to James Joyce
edited by Derek Attridge

The Cambridge Companion to T. S. Eliot
edited by A. David Moody

The Cambridge Companion to Ezra Pound
edited by Ira B. Nadel

The Cambridge Companion to Beckett
edited by John Pilling

The Cambridge Companion to Harold Pinter
edited by Peter Raby

The Cambridge Companion to Tom Stoppard
edited by Katherine E. Kelly

The Cambridge Companion to Herman
Melville
edited by Robert S. Levine

The Cambridge Companion to Edith
Wharton
edited by Millicent Bell

The Cambridge Companion to Henry James
edited by Jonathan Freedman

The Cambridge Companion to Walt
Whitman
edited by Ezra Greenspan

The Cambridge Companion to Henry David
Thoreau
edited by Joel Myerson

The Cambridge Companion to Mark
Twain
edited by Forrest G. Robinson

The Cambridge Companion to Edgar
Allan Poe
edited by Kevin J. Hayes

The Cambridge Companion to Emily
Dickinson
edited by Wendy Martin

The Cambridge Companion to William
Faulkner
edited by Philip M. Weinstein

The Cambridge Companion to Ernest
Hemingway
edited by Scott Donaldson

The Cambridge Companion to F. Scott
Fitzgerald
edited by Ruth Prigozy

The Cambridge Companion to Robert
Frost
edited by Robert Faggen

The Cambridge Companion to Eugene
O'Neill
edited by Michael Manheim

The Cambridge Companion to Tennessee
Williams
edited by Matthew C. Roudané

The Cambridge Companion to Arthur
Miller
edited by Christopher Bigsby

The Cambridge Companion to Sam
Shepard
edited by Matthew C. Roudané

CAMBRIDGE COMPANIONS TO CULTURE

The Cambridge Companion to Modern
German Culture
edited by Eva Kolinsky and Wilfried
van der Will

The Cambridge Companion to Modern
Russian Culture
edited by Nicholas Rzhevsky

The Cambridge Companion to Modern
Spanish Culture
edited by David T. Gies

The Cambridge Companion to Modern
Italian Culture
edited by Zygmunt G. Baranski and Rebecca
J. West

The Cambridge Companion to Modern Latin
American Literature
edited by John King